Learning/Work

Turning work and lifelong learning inside out

Edited by Linda Cooper
and Shirley Walters

HSRC
PRESS

Published by HSRC Press
Private Bag X9182, Cape Town, 8000, South Africa
www.hsrcpress.ac.za

ISBN (soft cover) 978-0-7969-2283-0
ISBN (pdf) 978-0-7969-2284-7
ISBN (e-pub) 978-0-7969-2302-8

Copyedited by Lisa Compton
Typeset by Baseline Publishing Services
Cover by Farm Design
Printed by Logo Print, Cape Town, South Africa

Distributed in Africa by Blue Weaver
Tel: +27 (0) 21 701 4477; Fax: +27 (0) 21 701 7302
www.oneworldbooks.com

Distributed in Europe and the United Kingdom by Eurospan Distribution Services (EDS)
Tel: +44 (0) 20 7240 0856; Fax: +44 (0) 20 7379 0609
www.eurospanbookstore.com

Distributed in North America by Independent Publishers Group (IPG)
Call toll-free: (800) 888 4741; Fax: +1 (312) 337 5985
www.ipgbook.com

Contents

Acknowledgements

The editors wish to thank:

Mary Ryan for her invaluable editorial assistance;

The Services Sector Education and Training Authority, the South African Qualifications Authority, the University of the Western Cape, and the University of Cape Town, for their support in the publication of the book;

Shahrzad Mojab for the inspiration leading to the sub-title of the book;

Malika Ndlovu for permission to use her poem, *Singing at the Centre, Dancing at the Periphery*, commissioned for the 5th International Conference on Researching Work and Learning hosted by the University of the Western Cape and the University of Cape Town, 3 December 2007 in Stellenbosch, South Africa;

The external reviewers of the manuscript for their helpful comments.

Acronyms

ANC	African National Congress
CEO	Chief Executive Officer
CHE	Council on Higher Education
COSATU	Congress of South African Trade Unions
DoE	Department of Education (South Africa)
DoL	Department of Labour (South Africa)
ETQA	Education and Training Qualification Assurance body
HSRC	Human Sciences Research Council
ILO	International Labour Organization
NAFTA	North American Free Trade Agreement
NEPI	National Education Policy Investigation/Initiative
NGO	Non-Governmental Organisation
NQF	National Qualifications Framework
NSB	National Standards Body
NSFAS	National Student Financial Aid Scheme
OBE	Outcomes-Based Education
RPL	Recognition of Prior Learning
SAQA	South African Qualifications Authority
SETA	Sector Education and Training Authority
UK	United Kingdom
ULR	Union Learning Representative
UN	United Nations
UNESCO	United Nations Educational, Scientific and Cultural Organization
US	United States
UWC	University of the Western Cape
Wits	University of the Witwatersrand

Singing at the Centre, Dancing at the Periphery

Malika Ndlovu

Even from the centre
Where a song of 360° can be sung
Where for half the planet a dawn is beckoning
Precisely at the moment
The other surrenders to a setting sun

Even here
At an axis from which much can be seen and shown
There co-exists a different song, a slower dance
Perhaps even in reverse
Holding the secret to myriad perspectives
From which we have yet to converse

And if our song lengthens
If we deepen our dance
There's a chance
We can penetrate the surface of assumptions
Scatter the shadows of doubt and cynicism
Hanging in our skies
Expanding our viewpoints
Our definitions
Liberating a vertical and horizontal mind's eye

Is your centre aware of mine?
Who drew these polarities, these lines?
If I am your periphery
Are we not both at the mercy of gravity?
We do not seek confusion
We are the seekers of knowledge and clarity
Merely releasing illusions
Of authority
Of superiority
Of certainty

Opening ourselves to the endless fields of possibility
Planting the seeds of questioning
Into the fertile soil of this gathering
Seeking the meeting of visions
Listening deeply for the resonance
The hidden harmonies

Dance with me
I bring my mountain to your shore
Together we manifest more and more
Listen to my story
Buried in this song
There is a place for each of us in it
A space for all voices
To belong

Introduction

Linda Cooper and Shirley Walters

Every 12 years UNESCO hosts a world conference on adult education known as CONFINTEA. A key message for the 2009 conference is that we know what policies and actions are needed for adult learning to make an impact on growing poverty and inequality worldwide. What is required now is action, with the necessary political and community will. The scholarship presented in this book feeds into these global debates and discussions by challenging dominant perspectives and providing illustrations of action located in a range of contexts in the South, North, East and West.

Background to the genesis of the book

This book has its genesis in the Fifth International Conference on Researching Work and Learning (RWL5), which was held in Cape Town, South Africa, in December 2007. The conference, which was co-hosted by University of Western Cape (UWC), the University of Cape Town (UCT), the South African Qualifications Authority (SAQA) and the Human Sciences Research Council (HSRC), attracted 330 scholars from 30 countries and provided the space for rethinking 'work', 'knowledge' and 'learning' within a context in which the global economy increasingly challenges the accepted dichotomies between home life and work life, between employment and unemployment, and between paid work and unpaid work.

The conference took place against a background where globally and locally, in both the North and South, the social and economic impacts of globalisation have been uneven and contradictory, drawing new lines of inequality between core and periphery, between insiders and outsiders – those at the centre and those at the margins of contemporary society. As Bauman (1998) has noted, despite the new freedom of mobility at the centre of globalisation, this freedom to move is a scarce and unequally distributed commodity: '[b]eing on the move' has a radically different sense for, respectively, those at the top and those at the bottom of the new hierarchy (1998: 4). Since the conference, the financial turmoil in the world has exacerbated these levels of poverty and insecurity.

There is also a new diversity of work, with growing flexibilisation, virtualisation and rationalisation; blurring of boundaries between work and non-work; and an increasing spread of non-standard forms of work. Some developments, which at first glance might seem remote from the labour market (such as ecological changes), will be of great significance for the future of work (Beck 2000).

The conference posed the question, What theoretical perspectives and evidence from empirical research might allow us to think more inclusively about work, knowledge and learning, and in ways that are able to capture the diversity of experiences that constitute work and learning internationally?

South(ern) African context

The context within which the conference took place inevitably infused the shape and content of the conference, and this book. South Africa is the dominant economic power in southern Africa, a region consisting of 14 countries with a wide spread of developmental needs and great polarities between rich and poor. The countries of southern Africa are peripheral capitalist economies and their development has been shaped very directly by this fact, by colonialism, by the macro policies of international development agencies and by their socio-economic, environmental and cultural realities.

Most of the countries of the region have experienced major political and economic upheavals in the last 50 years. During this time all of them have been through more or less traumatic processes of decolonisation. The last five countries to gain independence or liberation were Mozambique (1975), Angola (1975), Zimbabwe (1980), Namibia (1990) and South Africa (1994). All five have experienced extended liberation struggles and subsequent processes of reconstruction and development towards building new nations. The approaches adopted by the different countries were shaped strongly by dominant development theories of the time which reflect particular ideologies and material interests (see, for example, Youngman 2000), and since then the political and economic upheavals have continued to varying degrees, with ongoing contestations by citizens in response to the failures of governments to deliver 'a better life' for the majority.

That 10 of the chapters in this book centre on South or southern Africa reflects the fact that the conference was held in that region. In addition, the contexts of the region provide a very useful lens to refract global phenomena, as migration of workers or employers is widespread in the area, and the economic North and South are intertwined in complex ways. The conference, and now the book, poses questions on the most useful understandings and approaches to work and lifelong learning in the interests of the majority of people who are engaging, most often at great personal and collective cost, in a wide spectrum of economic and social activities to sustain themselves and the environment. The collection of chapters challenges any simplistic understandings and argues that multiple viewpoints must be taken into account to understand learning/work, both locally and globally. However, this does not imply that a political and moral stand on the side of the majority of girls, boys, women and men throughout the world should not be taken. Implicit within many of the chapters is an argument for the promotion of what Prozesky (2007) refers to as 'citizens of conscience' who are concerned with 'greater, sustainable well-being for all'.

In several of the chapters, the attempts by South Africans to democratise and rebuild their economic and social lives after the devastating effects of years of legalised racial oppression (apartheid) and patriarchy are revealed in their diverse and textured ways. While the South African context is very specific, in many ways it also mirrors dominant global/local relationships, and many chapters based in a range of countries of the world illustrate similar concerns.

Organisation of the book

The book consists of 25 chapters contributed by 34 authors from 10 different countries. While many of the chapters report on empirical research, others are sustained reflections on research and theorising of work, knowledge, learning and power. The chapters have been grouped into three main thematic sections, two of which are divided into sub-themes, in order to help readers navigate the text. However, the chapters could easily have been ordered differently, as many of them address a range of themes, and there is much overlap in terms of thematic focus.

We support strongly the notion that learning/work can be envisaged as a continuous spiral of pedagogy, politics and organisation – viewed most accurately as concentric circles rather than discrete activities. The use of the spiral as a metaphor for the organisation of this book not only signals the iterative relationship between pedagogy, politics and organisation, but also echoes popular education approaches: starting with the known, then moving to systematic investigation – adding new information and theory – then strategising and planning for action, returning once more to interrogate what has been done, and so deepen possibilities for creating positive change.

With the popular education learning spiral in mind, the first section, or whorl of the spiral, is titled 'Challenging perspectives'. The first five chapters make up the subsection titled 'Challenging dominant discourses', with the following six chapters comprising the subsection headed 'Critiquing structural inequalities'. All the chapters in the first section suggest the need to challenge dominant, hegemonic frameworks for locating and analysing learning/work. The second whorl of the spiral, 'Recognising knowledges', contains chapters that question what and whose knowledge counts. It broadens understandings and deepens critiques of accepted assumptions of whose worldviews matter. The third whorl of the spiral is titled 'Exploring possibilities, creating change' and focuses on thoughtful action. Here there are two subsections: the first is a clutch of chapters on the sub-theme 'Workers organising/learning', and the second subsection highlights 'Pedagogical innovations in higher education'. All of the chapters are infused in various ways with imaginings of alternative futures that prioritise social justice and sustainability for the majority of the world's people.

Critical contributions of the book

This book aims to make a contribution to the critical literature on lifelong learning and work. Fenwick (2005), in a review of research on learning and work between 1999 and 2004, notes that although the field of work and learning has 'expanded in an unprecedented volume of publication and diverse perspectives' (2005: 1), nevertheless '[a]n overall impression is that power and politics is not a topic that is receiving much attention in research on workplace learning'. If it is taken into consideration, 'power can best be likened to a backpack that sits outside the study and never really becomes an intricate part of it' (2005: 7).

This book departs from some of the mainstream literature on work and learning reviewed by Fenwick. First, power relations are central to the key issues and themes of the book. Many of the chapters draw on the perspectives of the radical adult education tradition, which foregrounds critiques of social relations and practice rather than 'how to do workplace learning better'. Second, instead of interrogating learning/work processes per se, the book critically explores how the global political economy and policy contexts have shaped social relations and impacted on learning processes, knowledge hierarchies, and educational policies and practices. The critical roles of women at work in the factories, fields, streets and homes foreground the importance of a feminist framing both to understand learning/work and to explore possibilities for creating positive change.

Shahrzad Mojab of the University of Toronto, and one of the conference keynote speakers, invited the research community to 'turn work and lifelong learning inside out'. There are two key dimensions to this notion of turning work and lifelong learning inside out. The first is that we cannot understand the significance of current conceptions of knowledge and learning, or current practices of work-related education and training, unless we are able to uncover and critically analyse the social relations that underpin these conceptions and practices. Sometimes this is possible only by turning current conceptions of learning on their head. For example, it is widely accepted that the current era of globalisation has hastened the process of commodification of learning – that is, transforming learning into a possession, something to be traded for gain in the marketplace; occurring simultaneously – although less visible – is the parallel process of 'learning as dispossession', where people are stripped not only of their individuality, but also of their very understanding of their own exploitation.

There is another dimension to the notion of turning work and learning inside out, one which was richly illustrated in the address by a second keynote speaker at the conference, Anannya Bhattacharjee, International Organiser for Jobs with Justice. She argued that in order to transform 'workplaces of dislocation', workplace struggles have to be 'fought from the inside out': those at the heart of the system of exploitation but on the periphery of the international labour market in terms of social power – migrant workers, contract workers, women workers – have to lead in forging new ways of organising towards a more just and fair system of work. Thus it is not enough to research work and learning to support work as it is, but rather there is a need to research ways in which we can learn to work and learn differently.

Authors in this book share a common starting point: they are critical of (in the sense of questioning as well as criticising) globalisation's impact on education and training, learning and knowledge. Implicitly or explicitly, they set themselves apart from those who argue that globalisation has been beneficial in a number of ways: for example, that globalisation has upset old hierarchies of knowledge (Gibbons et al. 1994) and created new status for forms of knowledge associated with the workplace (Barnett 2000); that it has multiplied and diversified sites of, and opportunities for, learning (Marsick & Watkins 1999; Mathews & Candy 1999; Fenwick 2001); and that it has created the necessity for education providers to be much more responsive to market and social needs (Gibbons 2005).

The arguments in this book are premised on the critiques of the new shape of the labour markets and new forms of work associated with globalisation, put forward by sociologists such as Castells (2001) and Beck (2000). Castells (2001) shows how the last two decades have seen increasing polarisation between the new economy and survival activities, with the labour market becoming unevenly divided into a globalised, high-skilled labour market on the one hand, and local, 'generic labour' in the service sector, and informal and survival sectors on the other. Beck (2000) writes of the new diversity of work – jobs that are increasingly flexible, virtual, individualised and temporary, and without social obligations. He points to the blurring of boundaries between work and non-work, and notes that unemployment too 'is becoming invisible, as it seeps away in the no-man's land between employment and non-employment' (2000: 78).

The chapters in the book make a specific contribution to these debates, as summarised below.

Building a more inclusive definition of work

The polarisation between the 'new economy', on the one hand, and 'generic' or 'low-skills' labour, and work in the informal or survival economies, on the other, means that large areas of work are devalued and rendered invisible. One of the key objectives of a number of chapters is to make these forms of majority work visible, and to point to their essential role in the reproduction of society. For example, Von Kotze argues for a shift in our views of work as pure commodity production, to seeing work as the 'production of life'; with more than 50 per cent of working people not employed in the formal economy, the informal sector needs to be taken seriously as a site of research into work and learning. Grossman turns our attention to the numerous roles played by domestic workers in South Africa, whose work sits at the intersection of multiple forms of oppression based on gender, race and class. Sawchuk and Kempf, in their study of guest workers in Canada, argue that these 'peripheral transnational labour markets' are increasingly central to the labour and learning of the twenty-first century, while Hays's chapter proposes that the traditional subsistence practices of San communities in southern Africa need also to be viewed as forms of 'knowledge work'.

Illuminating enduring social inequalities

New labour market divisions and new forms of work are associated with more intense forms of social inequality. Bauman (1998) argues that globalisation 'divides as much as it unites', while Castells (2001: 15) refers to the 'double logic on inclusion and exclusion', where 'the global economy is at the same time extraordinarily creative and productive and extraordinarily exclusionary'.

What implications do these developments have for education and training? From the outset of the Researching Work and Learning conferences in 1999, participants have raised critical questions about who benefits educationally in the global economy. Since 1999, numerous publications have also addressed this question in a critical vein (for example, Jackson & Jordan 2000; Mojab 2001; Cruikshank 2002; Mojab & Gorman 2003; Bierema 2006; Maitra & Shan 2007).

In this book, chapters explore how the essential fault lines of global capitalism are reflected in shifting but enduring inequalities. Letseka shows how the historical legacy of apartheid in South Africa continues to impact on university students' chances of completing their studies as well as finding employment. Boughton examines how 300 years of colonialism and 30 years of oppression under Indonesian rule have left Timor-Leste the poorest country in Asia, and poses the question of what work skills people need to find their way out of poverty. Sommerlad focuses on the structural and cultural barriers to entry to the legal profession in Britain, particularly for the growing number of students in the 'new universities' who are generally from ethnic minorities and/or lower socio-economic groups. Boughton's chapter, as well as the chapters by Von Kotze, Walters and Daniels, and Spencer, critique education and training policies which, rather than addressing enduring structural inequalities linked to race, class, gender and ethnicity, may well act to reinforce the historical exclusion of large numbers of people from access to quality education and training opportunities. Walters and Daniels illustrate how the discourse of 'short courses' naturalises the commodification or 'take-away' notion of education and training,

The issue of citizenship is an implicit thread running through several of the chapters. In his seminal work, Mamdani (1996) provides a rich analysis of the complexity of how 'citizen' and 'subject' have been constructed in post-colonial states in Africa. While this book does not deal directly with post-colonial states in Africa, chapters such as those by Barter, Hays, Härnsten and Rosén, and Boughton echo the themes of the bifurcated state which reproduces the unequal and highly gendered power relations between urban and rural, between modern and customary, and between North and South.

Ong (1999, 2006) extends the discussions of differentiated notions of citizenship by arguing that citizenship is a social process. She develops the concept of 'flexible citizenship' to explain how individuals as well as governments develop flexible notions of belonging, citizenship and sovereignty as strategies to accumulate capital and power:

> [Flexible citizenship] refers to the cultural logic of capitalist accumulation, travel, and displacement that induce subjects to respond fluidly and opportunistically to changing political-economic conditions. (Ong 1999: 6)

The chapters by Sawchuk and Kempf, Marshall, Grossman, Mojab, Härnsten and Rosén, and Bhattacharjee illustrate these differentiated notions by showing how citizenship is exclusionary through migration of different kinds, between and within countries.

Gaventa (2007) points to the fact that there is a growing crisis of legitimacy in the relationship between citizens and the institutions that affect their lives. In countries both in the North and the South, citizens speak of mounting disillusionment with governments, based on concerns about corruption, lack of responsiveness to the needs of the poor and the absence of a sense of connection with elected representatives and bureaucrats. The rights and responsibilities of transnational corporations and other global actors are being challenged as global inequalities persist and deepen. Organisations such as trade unions and social movements, within and across national borders, are rethinking their responses within these contexts, which are complex and often contradictory. Several of the chapters that focus specifically on trade union organising, including those by Marshall, Brown, Cooper, and Forrester and Li, contribute to debates on these issues.

Recognising and challenging continuing hierarchies of knowledge

Contrary to claims that the reorganisation of work under globalisation has led to significant new demands for skills and knowledge, Livingstone and Sawchuk (2004) point to the opposite conclusion. They show that in the US and Canada over the past few generations, there has been only a very gradual net upgrading of the actual skill requirements of jobs (2004), and that working people are far more likely to be underemployed in their jobs than to be under-qualified for them (2004). Elsewhere, Livingstone (2003) concludes that we will find

> [the] highest levels of underutilisation of working knowledge in the jobs
> held by those in lower occupational class positions, as well as among
> those job holders whose general subordination in society has put them
> at a disadvantage in negotiations over working conditions, especially
> women, younger people, ethnic and racial minorities, recent immigrants
> and those labelled as 'disabled'. (2003: 6)

These findings – specific to Canada but, Livingstone and Sawchuk argue, confirmed by studies elsewhere – are echoed and expanded upon in a number of chapters in this book. For example, Mojab argues that when we present accounts of knowledge that is excluded and/or denigrated, we need to take into account that 'the waste of the skilled labour force is endemic to the dynamics of the capitalist society'; for example, 'immigrant women's lives are not abnormalities produced by inadequate policies; rather, these policies are adopted in order to reproduce conditions in which capital can thrive at the expense of labour'.

Other chapters highlight the underutilisation of many people's knowledge, due to the continuing hierarchies of knowledge linked to class, urban–rural divides, gender and cultural inequalities, and the way these subjugated knowledges challenge hegemonic conceptions of knowledge. Grossman points to domestic workers as a rich source of intellectual life that remains unrecognised and under-researched. Breier's chapter focuses on the difficulty encountered in an RPL (recognition of prior learning) process, in making visible the ethical knowledge that underlies the pastoral role of teachers, a particularly important role in the current South African context. Härnsten and Rosén critically examine how the domestic knowledge of women gained through 'daily life issues' has been marginalised in the Swedish welfare state because of the gendered nature of social citizenship. Jubas and Butterwick draw on feminist epistemology to challenge knowledge and social binaries that tend to leave unacknowledged women's informal learning pathways in the information technology (IT) field. Hays argues for the value of indigenous knowledge systems (IKS) to humanity, and holds that bringing such knowledge into the formal education system will undermine its existence and reproduction. Barter's research shows that rural teachers feel that their knowledge, and rural knowledge generally, is undervalued compared to 'urban' knowledge, and that there is a need for 'rural as a concept rather than rural as an urban problem'.

In their study of 'hidden knowledge', Livingstone and Sawchuk (2004) argue that rather than workers being reluctant to learn, there has been significant growth in all spheres of learning over time, but particularly in *informal* learning. They suggest that 'adult learning is like an iceberg, with most of it submerged informal learning' (2004: 11). The chapters in this volume not only play an important role in making 'subjugated knowledges' visible, but also show that in the absence of teaching, learning still happens – even for those in the 'hidden economy' and in 'hidden work', who are excluded from the mainstream of education and training. In pointing to these 'subjugated knowledges' and to the rich 'curriculum of experience' (see the chapters by Grossman, Sawchuk and Kempf, and Tarc and Smaller), and in putting forward alternative epistemologies (see the chapter by Jubas and Butterwick), authors are not asking for the 'margins' to be mainstreamed, but rather for researchers and practitioners to reposition themselves vis-à-vis the mainstream – that is, to view the margins as the mainstream.

Reconfiguration and contestation

The needs of the global capitalist economy are not totally determining, however. Agency at the local level reconfigures the impact of globalisation, and can disrupt and destabilise it. Policies that are dominant at a global level can be contested and reconfigured at the regional or local level, and we need to be alert not only to the 'symmetries', but also to the 'tugs and pulls' between the global and the local. For example, in her analysis of South Africa's adoption of a national qualifications framework (NQF), Lugg shows that however networked our society has become, it is necessary to maintain a focus on the national state in analyses of education policy: '[i]n a globalising world, the state retains power to fix meanings for education and training'. She shows how although NQFs have been implemented throughout the world, they are increasingly taking regionalised forms: 'local concerns remain significant as borrowed policies become embedded in local contexts'. Lugg's chapter is juxtaposed with that of Jubas and Butterwick, as it describes the NQF as an ambitious attempt to create a non-binary education/training ladder that merges education and training.

The global capitalist economy does not simply impose its footprint on everything, and its hegemony is never smooth and uncontested. Several authors show that the global order can be and is being challenged in a variety of ways. A significant cluster of chapters focuses on the expression of local agency through workers' education or popular education initiatives. For example, Bhattacharjee focuses on organising and learning in migrant/immigrant working-class communities in the US and India. Trade unions are engaging with workplace training, and contesting the limits and constraints of work-based learning: Spencer's chapter focuses on the role of unions in democratising education in the workplace; Forrester and Li document campaigning and critical union dimensions to national policy initiatives in work-based learning; and Cooper alerts readers to the need to keep trade unions and other popular organisations in mind when discussing the 'learning organisation'.

New ways of organising and networking – including renewing connections between the workplace and community – are being forged for the advantage of the working poor. Marshall explores workers' exchange programmes as powerful learning tools in changing workers' perspectives, and shows how the historic ideological hegemony of North over South (described in Boughton's chapter, for example) can be challenged. Borders/boundaries – or the terms and conditions of borders/boundaries – are being challenged, and new spaces for learning opened up, as Brown shows through his discussion of new global union federations, international campaigns to support global organising and bargaining, and legal efforts that include cross-border litigation.

What is the role of adult educators in these times? A cluster of chapters focusing on the learning and development of professionals in higher education shows that there is also considerable room and necessity for the exercise of pedagogic agency, and for the development of innovative approaches to learning and teaching. Bozalek and Matthews show how e-learning can be used to build trans-institutional and cross-continental collaborative learning between social work students in South Africa and the US focusing in particular on ethical practices; Bamber and O'Shea discuss the university training of community learning and development workers in partnership with employees, and argue that conditions of success depend on 'responsive academics', 'expansive workplaces' and 'active learners'; and Lotz-Sisitka continues the argument for mutual responsiveness from workplaces and the academy if sustainable development practices are to have effect in countering the negative outcomes of ever-more-obvious global climate change. Each of these pedagogic innovations is a carefully crafted illustration of how lifelong learning approaches can be oriented towards developing 'citizens of conscience'.

Capturing complexities

As noted previously, authors in this book share a common starting point that is critical of globalisation's impact on education and training, and the learning and knowledge of the majority of citizens. However, they are also mindful to avoid oversimplification, and concerned to capture the contradictions and nuances of the real world.

Recent literature has emphasised the specificity of knowledge to context. As Farrell (2005: 3) has suggested, 'Time and space still matter, now, perhaps, more than ever…a single, uniform global context doesn't really exist.' Just as there are differential relationships of people to the global circuits of capital, so the literature points to the increasingly differential nature of learning and knowledge and its specificity to context – hence the value of case studies as a means of research. This is the dominant methodological approach in this book. However, Grossman raises a question about the robustness of our own methodologies of research – their potential and their limitations in terms of being able to capture the rich and varied forms of intellectual life found among ordinary people.

Several chapters try to capture the intricate and often contradictory dimensions of knowledge. For example, Mojab points to the 'dual characteristic' of learning: while learning produces skill and knowledge, at the same time it perpetuates capitalist social relations. Field and Malcolm examine some of the particularities of emotional work, and argue that while it is subject to management control, scripting and surveillance, it can also express worker agency and identity.

A number of chapters also address dimensions of social relations in different contexts: power relations do not simply exist between 'oppressors' and 'oppressed', but also pervade relations between different groupings among the oppressed. For example, as Marshall notes of the labour-exchange programmes that are the focus of her chapter: 'Working the global dynamics is not easy. Each union is embedded in a particular social context, and the North–South power relations do not cease to be operative simply because all those involved are trade unionists.'

Furthermore, there are always elements of both accommodation and resistance in the strategies adopted, as shown by Spencer's study of unions' responses to management's work-based learning initiatives; but valuable understandings and knowledge can be found precisely in the acts of 'collaboration' in which they participate. As Sawchuk and Kempf argue, '[W]orkers understand the game, and…their willingness to play should not be confused with an endorsement of the rules.'

Limitations and caveats

This book in no way attempts to be comprehensive and we recognise a number of glaring omissions and limitations. Firstly, the logic of the argument that context matters implies that insights from the range of examples with very different socio-economic backdrops cannot simply be transferred. However, they can shed light. Secondly, various critical areas of concern have not been covered. Some examples of these are the lack of debate about learning/work for children who are workers (see Qvarsell 2007); the lack of any systematic discussion of the impact of different aspects of people's lives, such as violence, sexuality and spirituality, on learning/work; and the lack of deeper discussions on identity and community and how these understandings shape learning/work.

Words about words

A number of terms used are contentious. We have not tried to standardise their use across chapters but have left authors to speak from their own contexts. For the sake of clarity we have avoided using inverted commas around certain terms. In some contexts it is the convention to refer to race in this way to signal that the term is understood as not natural but as a socially constructed category. While we share this understanding, we have not used the convention. However, given the legacy of apartheid in South Africa, racial groupings remain significant, and we use 'African', 'coloured', 'white' and 'Indian' to refer to these. Unless otherwise stated, the term 'black' refers collectively to all three formerly disenfranchised groups. We also use the terms 'North', 'South', 'East', 'West' and 'Third World' with some reservation, because of the way such terms can homogenise those regions and implicate all the inhabitants in the politics of imperialism, obscuring class, racial or ethnic differentiation. We understand these terms as designating constructs referring to degrees of relative poverty or affluence rather than to geographic regions. We also support Jubas and Butterwick's argument in this volume that binary conceptualisations are both persistent and tenuous, and we move from an either/or to a both/and understanding of them. In the title of the book we have tried to capture this by linking learning/work in order to encourage a different way of talking about how these processes are observed and experienced.

Building capacity for researching learning/work in South(ern) Africa

In South Africa, after 15 years of implementing bold new education and training strategies to enhance learning at work and realise a more equitable and just society, there is growing realisation that it is time to pause and investigate systematically what works, what does not work, and why. It is time to turn work and lifelong learning inside out, in order to re-examine understandings of work, knowledge and learning. The chapters in this book help to do this.

Never before in the history of the country have so many resources been made available to enhance workplace learning, but on a daily basis there are still discussions in the popular media on 'the skills crisis' or 'skills shortages'. As we see from the chapters in this book, these are not peculiar to South Africa but must be understood within the global capitalist economy. Therefore, we are required to challenge perspectives; to recognise multiple knowledges across social class, gender, race, geography, ability and age; and to explore transformative possibilities for environmental and human sustainability. As Lotz-Sisitka states in her chapter:

> Sustainable development issues…impact on households at every level of the social strata, and on all sectors of society. Small and large production systems are implicated and affected, as are service providers and the social sectors including the health care sector…Change-oriented workplace learning processes across the sectors…are necessary for sustainable development…

In summary, the authors in this book argue that power relations are key to understanding learning/work processes, and that the global political economy and policy contexts have shaped social relations and impacted on learning processes, knowledge hierarchies, and educational policies and practices. Therefore work and lifelong learning need to be turned inside out in order to uncover and critically analyse the social relations that underpin the conceptions and the practices.

In order to move from where we are to where we aspire to be, researching learning and work 'as it is' is not enough; we need also to be researching how to learn to learn/work differently. Part of this is to develop scholarship differently, through encouraging intellectuals within civil society, workplaces, government and the academy to work together across institutional boundaries to co-create new understandings and knowledge. The participants in the RWL5 Conference, who are academics, trade unionists, employers and activist/scholars, have made a significant contribution to this undertaking, for which we are very appreciative.

References

Barnett R (2000) Working knowledge. In J Garrick and C Rhodes (eds) *Research and knowledge at work: Perspectives, case-studies and innovative strategies*. London and New York: Routledge

Bauman Z (1998) *Globalisation: The human consequences*. Oxford: Blackwell Publishers

Beck U (2000) *The brave new world of work*. Oxford: Blackwell Publishers

Bierema LL (2006) Women's learning and development in the workplace. In SB Merriam, BC Courtenay & RM Cervero (eds) *Global issues and adult education: Perspectives from Latin America, Southern Africa and the United States*. San Francisco: Jossey-Bass

Castells M (2001) The new global economy. In J Muller, N Cloete & S Badat (eds) *Challenges of globalisation: South African debates with Manuel Castells*. Cape Town: Maskew Miller Longman

Cruikshank J (2002) Lifelong learning or re-training for life: Scapegoating the worker. *Studies in the Education of Adults* 34(2): 140–156

Farrell L (2005) The problem with 'common knowledge' at work. *Proceedings of the 4th International Conference on Researching Work and Learning*, University of Technology, Sydney, Australia (12–14 December)

Fenwick T (2001) Tides of change: New themes and questions in workplace learning. *New Directions in Adult and Continuing Education* 92: 3–17

Fenwick T (2005) Taking stock: A review of research on learning in work, 1999–2004. *Proceedings of the 4th International Conference on Researching Work and Learning*, University of Technology, Sydney, Australia (12–14 December)

Gaventa J (2007) Foreword. In A Cornwall & VS Coelho (eds) *Spaces for change? The politics of citizen participation in new democratic arenas*. London: Zed Books

Gibbons M (2005) Engagement with the community: The emergence of a new social contract between society and science. Paper presented at the Griffith University Community Engagement Workshop, South Bank campus, Queensland, Australia (4 March)

Gibbons M, Limoges C, Nowotny H, Schwartzmann S, Scott P & Trow M (1994) Introduction. In *The new production of knowledge: The dynamics of science and research in contemporary society*. London: Sage Publications

Jackson N & Jordan S (2000) Learning for work: Contested terrain. *Studies in Continuing Education* 32: 2

Livingstone DW (2003) Hidden dimensions of work and learning: The significance of unpaid work and informal learning in global capitalism. Keynote address, 3rd International Conference on Researching Work and Learning, Tampere, Finland (25–27 July)

Livingstone D & Sawchuk P (2004) *Hidden knowledge: Organised labour in the information age*. Aurora, ON: Garamond Press

Maitra S & Shan H (2007) Transgressive vs conformative: Immigrant women learning at contingent work. *Journal of Workplace Learning* 19(5): 286–295

Mamdani M (1996) *Citizen and subject: Contemporary Africa and the legacy of late colonialism*. Princeton, NJ: Princeton University Press

Marsick V & Watkins K (1999) Envisioning new organisations for learning. In D Boud & J Garrick (eds) *Understanding learning at work*. London and New York: Routledge

Mathews P & Candy P (1999) New dimensions in the dynamics of learning and knowledge. In D Boud & J Garrick (eds) *Understanding learning at work*. London and New York: Routledge

Mojab S (2001) The power of economic globalisation: Deskilling immigrant women through training. In RM Cervero, AL Wilson & Associates (eds) *Power in practice: Adult education and the struggle for knowledge and power in society*. San Francisco: Jossey-Bass

Mojab S & Gorman R (2003) Women and consciousness in the 'learning organisation': Emancipation or exploitation? *Adult Education Quarterly* 53(4): 228–241

Ong A (1999) *Flexible citizenship*. Durham, NC, and London: Duke University Press

Ong A (2006) *Neoliberalism as exception*. Durham, NC, and London: Duke University Press

Prozesky M (2007) *Conscience: Ethical intelligence for global well-being*. Pietermaritzburg: University of KwaZulu-Natal Press

Qvarsell B (2007) Children's rights and perspectives as global educational challenges. *Paideia: Revista de Educación* 42: 213–238. Universidad de Concepción, Chile

Youngman F (2000) *The political economy of adult education and development*. London and New York: NIACE/Zed Books

Challenging perspectives

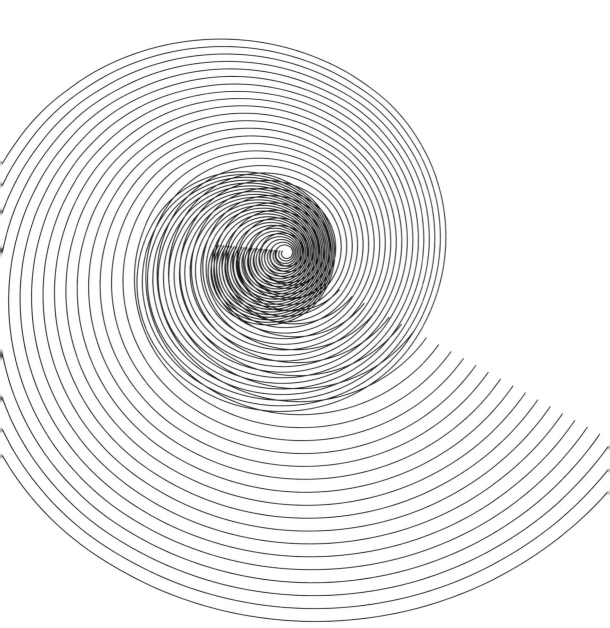

Challenging dominant discourses

1 Turning work and lifelong learning inside out: A Marxist-feminist attempt

Shahrzad Mojab

Introduction

Thinking through the two concepts of 'work' and 'lifelong learning' and the modes and methods through which they intersect, contradict or collude is not an easy task. It is even more daunting to attempt a Marxist-feminist approach, which has a special interest in both work and learning. There are at least two obstacles. First is the proliferation of literature on work and lifelong learning, which is theoretically and methodologically diverse, with much borrowing from disciplinary-based knowledges such as sociology and psychology, and from more interdisciplinary-based knowledges such as women's studies and adult education. It is not possible to cover critically this vast body of knowledge in this chapter; rather, I will limit the scope by engaging in arguments that claim 'critical' as a theoretical positioning. The second barrier is the fierce intellectual animosity towards Marxist analysis, in particular Marxist-feminism, and the declaration of it as an irrelevant and outdated mode of analysis. The two situations are closely intertwined in the sense that the exclusion of radical, critical and revolutionary perspectives is disguised in the diversity of disciplinary and area-studies approaches to work and learning. It is in this complex context that I embark on a journey of self-inquiry on my own intellectual relationship with this topic, which has been uneasy and inconsistent, and even at times ambivalent and unsettling.[1]

In this chapter I ground the analysis of the relations between work and lifelong learning in a historical and materialist understanding of the current world order. From this perspective, capitalism, unevenly developed throughout the world, is the material logic of social life and shapes the ways in which people live, learn, work, relate and think. Labour and capital, major building blocks of the current world order, co-exist in unity and conflict. However, it is the contradictions between the two that have shaped political and ideological struggles in adult education.

It is not difficult to see in daily news reports that the ongoing structural transformations in capitalism – for instance, the current round of globalisation – have exacerbated rather than changed the nature of contradictions between labour and capital. This observation challenges the claim that with the emergence of communication technologies, or mobile, flexible, service-oriented labour, capitalist production practices and relations have fundamentally changed and radically transformed. However, the particularity of the current moment of capitalism – that is, globalisation-as-imperialism – cannot be ignored. In its advanced imperialist stage, capitalism today, as in the past, combines the need to cross national borders (for purposes of 'free trade') with the urge to maintain spheres of influence and even new forms of colonisation through war and occupation. While the borders may be loosened for the flow of commodities, they are tightened in order to exclude unwanted immigrant labour and refugees. Borders within the European Union have indeed fallen down in unprecedented ways, but the continent has emerged as 'Fortress Europe', closing its doors to 'economic migrants' and refugees from African and Asian countries. Similarly, Australia, Canada, the US and other Western states have tightened their borders. At the same time, surveillance of citizens, enhanced by new technologies, has taken unprecedented dimensions. Capitalist states identifying themselves as 'liberal democracies' have turned into 'national security' states. The gap between the rich and the poor has been growing worldwide, and new forms of slavery have emerged in Asia, Africa and Latin America (Bales 2005). The trafficking of women and children, war, poverty, ecocide and global warming pose real threats to the welfare of human beings and all other species. In the midst of an apparent disorder in the world system, the US, as the largest economic power, is able to mount wars (in Afghanistan and Iraq) and shape policy in major international organs such as the G8, the World Bank, the International Monetary Fund, and UNESCO and other UN agencies. While the US may be seen as an imperialist power in decline, as Britain and France were by World War II, its hegemony may also be challenged by emerging imperialist rivals such as India, China and Russia.

My goal in this chapter is to engage with a wide range of debates on work and lifelong learning in this specific historical moment. The location of this knowledge is within what is known as 'Western democracies' although similar critical thinking is available throughout the world. In order to organise my thoughts, I present 'three observations' and then propose 'three theses' as a way to push our thinking forward. I hope that through this process of Marxist-feminist self-inquiry and interrogation I will be able to initiate renewed radical/critical thinking on the connections/disconnections or resonances/dissonances between work and lifelong learning.

Three observations

Observation 1: Lifelong learning is a contested concept. In my reading of the existing literature, lifelong learning has been deployed in two ways. First, it is a central concept in the hegemonic claim that lack of skill causes unemployment; it supposes that constant retraining prepares workers to be ultimately adaptable and always ready to acquire new skills as the needs of capital dictate. Second, lifelong learning has been marshalled as an ideological concept in two ways: one, which is intrinsically related to the previous point, is that the concept has become an ideological distraction that shifts the burden of increasing adaptability to the worker, and the other is at the same time a ray of hope for a more democratic and engaged citizenry. It is the responsibility of individuals to make themselves better citizens by participating fully in democracy. This ideological conception of lifelong learning is at the core of the neo-liberal articulation of the relations between education/learning/training/skilling and the project of liberal democracy.

Despite the knowledge explosion on lifelong learning,[2] I still find the most comprehensive critique of the concept in Frank Coffield's important article 'Breaking the consensus: Lifelong learning as social control' (Coffield 1999). Coffield notes that despite all the debates, there is a consensus that has developed over the last 30 years to the effect that lifelong learning, on its own, will solve a wide range of educational, social and political ills. He states that this consensus is naive, limited, deficient, dangerous and diversionary. Coffield asks: 'If the thesis is so poor why is it so popular?' (1999: 479). He provides an answer by arguing: 'It legitimates increased expenditure on education'; 'It provides politicians with the pretext for action'; 'It deflects attention from the need for economic and social reform'; and 'It offers the comforting illusion that for every complex problem there is one simple solution' (1999: 486). He calls this policy response to market demands 'compulsory emancipation' through lifelong learning (1999: 489). Nonetheless, Coffield's alternative proposal is framed in notions of liberal democracy which avoid a deeper analysis of capitalist relations of power. It is important to note that a similar critique was provided by Ivar Berg two decades earlier (Berg 1970).

The presence of contestation, as I have observed it, does not make 'lifelong learning', as a policy and practice, irrelevant. It is the circularity of the argument and the illusive nature of the concept that is not being sufficiently articulated in the literature; hence my second observation.

Observation 2: The literature provides a 'critique', without being 'critical', of the policy and practice of lifelong learning and its implications for work, training and adult education. I am borrowing from Teresa Ebert (1996) the distinction between 'critique' as a descriptive process and 'critical' as an analysis for change. There is a sizeable body of literature in lifelong learning that provides a 'critique' of capitalism. While this body of literature is important in understanding relationships between adult education and capitalist social relations, it does not provide the 'critical' tools to engage in a rigorous analysis of the ideological link between lifelong learning and the capitalist mode of labour exploitation. Adult educators have been interrogating the process of knowledge production and the conception of knowledge as an object with the same propositions used in the explanation of commodity. This engagement is best manifested in the critique of human capital theory. The main argument of human capital theory revolves around the positive and direct relations between knowledge and skill attainment and social status and mobility. The theory assumes that people with more years of schooling and training inevitably end up with higher-status jobs and higher wages; therefore, an expanding market economy needs not only the availability of economic capital but also human capital in the form of an educated, well-trained, flexible and skilled workforce. In human capital theory knowledge is an unchanging, unproblematic object or thing, unrelated to human beings, possessed by some and imparted to others.

The 'critique' of human capital theory directs us to the oppositional discourse of adult education and learning, but this theoretical position obscures the relationship between capital and labour. Ebert argues that this type of analysis will make visible the *effects* of social phenomena (training/learning) and will 'hollow out the materialist sense of class as relations of property and exploitation' (Ebert & Zavarzadeh 2008: xiv). The diverse perspectives one finds in human capital theory all converge in their insistence on working *within* the system of capitalism to reform it.

The reformist approach calls for the reorganisation of adult education into a training and skilling enterprise fully responsive to the requirements of the market. Although visions about the goals and directions of adult education are diverse and difficult to synthesise, I will focus here on a significant divide among adult educators. This division appears to be over the relationship between education and economy or work and learning, but in essence the theoretical and practical struggle is about the position of human beings in this rapidly shifting and changing economy. Simply put, it is about class position and struggle. In this economy, the workforce is expected to be adaptable, flexible and able to respond quickly to skill demands of the market under conditions of the unceasing movement of capital in search of more profitable opportunities. The workforce – that is, the majority of people, particularly in the South – is rendered disposable. It is not difficult to realise that capital always finds the cheap labour that it requires, and it is only where capital requires particular labour skills, and particular levels of education, that it might be interested in investing in upgrading, skilling and retraining of workers.

Observation 3: One outcome of the conceptual and theoretical messiness in researching work and lifelong learning has been the normalisation of capitalism. I have argued so far that the descriptive 'critique' of lifelong learning and work renders capitalist relations invisible in lifelong learning and work. Lifelong learning in a 'critical' analysis will be interpreted as the logic of capital. In other words, it is the capitalist exploitation of labour that produces the need for lifelong learning. The policy attention to a skilled labour force and the need for training/retraining is a capitalist response to its own logic. Turning workers into 'learning subjects' or 'learning citizens' is consistent with the politics of citizenship in liberal democracies.

In Canada, there is an important site of scholarship on lifelong learning with a focus on immigrant women. I will use this work to illustrate the notion of 'normalisation' of capitalist relations in the literature on lifelong learning and work. Research on immigrant women and work has produced a credible body of knowledge crossing disciplinary boundaries and encompassing contending theoretical and methodological perspectives. This body of literature is consolidated around the following themes: access/accommodation, training/skilling and work ghettoisation – that is, the prevalence of immigrant women in service work, contingent work and home-based work. My argument is that we have exhausted this topic within the spectrum of divergent theoretical perspectives. I also claim that studying different work settings, diverse immigrant communities or a different region of the world will not significantly add to our knowledge in understanding what constitutes the fundamental contradictions in exclusion, discrimination or marginalisation of immigrant women in the market economy. The dominant discourse has been no more than a liberal-capitalist mystification of what is known in Marxist theory as exploitation of labour. Indeed, concepts such as 'access', 'accommodation', 'marginalisation', 'discrimination' or 'exclusion' only reframe exploitation into legal, administrative, managerial, moral or cultural preferences, and limit our understanding of the dynamics of exploitation within the capitalist social and economic formation. What about racialised, gendered, national divisions of labour that enhance the exploitability of sectors of the vulnerable labour force? Are these mere mystifications, or the modalities through which exploitation is achieved?

In the context of Canada, the last two decades have been pivotal in creating a body of credible knowledge that crosses disciplinary boundaries in explaining, analysing, and proposing change in order to improve access, accommodation, inclusion, work conditions and work status of women of colour and immigrant women in workplaces and the labour market. Immigrant women's work has been the focus of this flourishing knowledge production. In the past decade in my institution (the University of Toronto) alone, roughly 50 MA theses and PhD dissertations have taken immigrant women as their object of study. We have analysed how and why immigrant women come to Canada, how they get jobs and what are the processes that determine which ones they get. We have examined the prior experience and learning competency of these women, as well as assessed what kind of skills they acquire. We have also examined the cultural processes that keep them in certain sectors of the labour market, and studied the learning needs imposed upon them by their social placement.

The literature has also developed a set of terms that enables us to identify various trends, structures and social relations. For instance, marginalisation, access/accommodation, discrimination and exclusion, racism and sexism allow us to critically examine the conditions under which labour of a certain kind *remains* labour of a certain kind. Some of the scholarship has used a framework that assesses immigrant women in marginalised sectors against an ideal type of immigrant women, the professionals, and determines the former's needs by proposing how we can make them more like the latter group. I argue that issues of 'professionalisation' and 'accreditation', more than any other issues arising from this literature, have captured the imagination of policy-makers, politicians and those who advocate for and represent immigrant constituencies. The response has been the funding of organisations, sometimes ethnic-specific, or profession-focused service-oriented agencies.

Tracing my own intellectual and epistemological trajectory in understanding this social phenomenon, I have noticed that so far I have been able, at best, to provide a partial explanation and reveal the appearance of a complex social phenomenon but not its essence. In recent decades, with the acceleration of the global neo-liberal agenda, comprising war, militarisation, displacement, increasing population movements and new immigration policies, a series of important changes has taken place in the labour force. One such change is further hierarchisation of the labour force. This complex process is happening, first, through the creation of a highly specialised workforce to serve the demands of the 'knowledge economy'; and second, through structuring a workforce that is contingent, flexible, expendable, disposable and replaceable, in order to engage in shifting and more precarious, scattered, mobile forms of production relations made possible by technological advances and the rapidity of electronic capital flows. To explain where immigrant women are located in this hierarchy, I contributed to the debate on 'skilling', 'deskilling' and 'reskilling' of immigrant women, where I have also noted that lifelong 'learning', as far as women of colour are concerned, becomes lifelong 'training' in its policy and practice formulation (Mojab 2000). I concluded, based on fieldwork among more than 80 immigrant women, that the waste of the skilled labour force is endemic to the dynamics of the capitalist economy.

To sum up, the literature on lifelong learning and work often normalises the capitalist mode of production and reproduction and therefore fails to analyse capital/labour contradictions, especially exploitation based on race and gender, as the source or cause of capitalism rather than its effect. Based on these observations, I would like to propose the following three theses.

Three theses

Thesis 1: Any adequate theory of work, learning and lifelong learning should give equal attention to the complex relations of production under capitalism. Our understanding of work, especially women's work, continues to be obscured by conceptual and theoretical frameworks that present the capitalist organisation of society as a natural order that can be perfected but never replaced. As argued above, the rather vast literature on the topic is filled with concepts that seem to provide radical insights into the dynamics of work. For instance, concepts such as marginalisation, discrimination or exclusion give a critical direction to our understanding. However, these concepts veil rather than unveil one crucial social relationship between capital and labour – that is, 'exploitation'. Concepts such as 'access', 'accommodation' and 'inclusion' provide a panacea to the more dehumanising aspects of the relationship but fail to envision a systemic alternative to it.

Social theory, especially since the proclamation of the 'end of history', shies away from system-changing concepts and ideas. For instance, it is now appropriate to conceptualise the relationship between labour and capital in any imaginable way except in terms of exploitation, alienation or conceptual frameworks that direct our thinking to the domain of alternatives to capitalism. We are led to believe that capitalist prosperity is created independent of labour. Dorothy Smith lays out a foundation for thinking through these complexities which is important to repeat at length here:

> It is important to preserve a sense of capitalism as an essentially dynamic process continually transforming the 'ground' on which we stand so that we are always continually experiencing changing historical process. It is one of the problems of the strategy of the intellectual world that our categories and concepts fix an actuality into seemingly unchanging forms and then we do our work in trying to find out how to present society in that way. This we must avoid. We must try to find out how to see our society as continually moving and to avoid introducing an artificial fixity

into what we make of it. The society as we find it at any one moment is the product of an historical process. It is a process which is not 'complete' at any one time. The various 'impulses' generated by the essentially dynamic process of capitalism do not come to rest in their own completion or in the working out to the point of equilibrium of systematic interactions. The process of change is itself unceasing and at any moment we catch only an atemporal slice of a moving process. Hence to understand the properties, movement, 'structure' of the present, we must be able to disentwine the strands of development which determine the character and relations of the present in Western capitalism. (Smith 1985: 7–8)

This is a guideline for the analytical frame that I identify as Marxist-feminist. A framework that is feminist, historical-materialist, dialectical and critical leads us to ask these four central questions: Why does the concept of lifelong learning arise at this particular moment? How does work and learning relate to the capitalist mode of production? What are the contradictions within the concept of lifelong learning? How can we uncover the social relations of work and learning that are not visible on the surface? In other words, what, specifically, is it about the current relations of production that fosters a preoccupation with training and lifelong learning?

Thesis 2: A Marxist-feminist dialectical conception of work and lifelong learning is the most productive mode of analysis for analysing immigrant women's work. Employing Marxist-feminist dialectical conceptions of work and lifelong learning, we can see that it is not simply women of colour's class, race, sexuality or gender that is determined by the economic system, but also their whole subjectivity. Immigrant women are 'marginalised' by capital, and we can now see that their 'marginalisation' is not a product of contingent structures such as call centres, but is constitutive and necessary to the capitalist relation. We study women and come to know what particular groups of marginalised women of colour experience or lack training, and we may even develop methods and programmes that facilitate the movement of particular women from peripheral work into professional work, but we cannot ameliorate or improve the precarious nature of their work.

The current literature on immigrant women and work has described their position in the labour market in much detail. This body of research is incredibly useful in describing barriers that lock them into marginalised or contingent work, such as language problems, lack of recognised accreditation and a lack of access to professional jobs. Furthermore this literature, where it has been critical, deals with issues in globalisation, including offshore production, free-trade-zone processing and cheap labour, and has described how present immigration policies result from labour planning rooted in settler-colonialist ideologies. We can assert that the literature has developed a sufficiently deep understanding of the way in which race and gender construct the positions of these subjects and the labour market as a whole.

What has been lacking, however, is an attempt to integrate an analysis of race, gender and class in a Marxist dialectical sense with lifelong learning, work and adult learning. Where the literature has invoked a critique of capitalist relations, it has done so superficially, by treating these relations as a *thing* that can be separately analysed, rather than as the context that produces not only the barriers and policies under examination, but also the subjects themselves, and our study of them. By leaving aside capitalist relations, or at best by treating them as a force among others, this literature has done little besides explaining the appearance of a problem, rather than explaining the essential characteristics of the social formation that produces this appearance. By treating only the appearance of this force, we have oversimplified the problematic so that research presents a picture in which the amelioration of immigrant women's positions requires no more than the changing of labour, learning and work policies and funding allocations. However, immigrant women's lives are not abnormalities produced by inadequate policies; rather, these policies are adopted in order to reproduce conditions in which capital can thrive at the expense of labour.

It is not surprising, therefore, that the body of academic literature in adult education has produced no perceptible changes either in state or corporate policy, or in the situations of immigrant women themselves. Instead, what we have created is a series of structures, organisations and policies that have revolved around the issue of 'access' to jobs, to education or to training, all of which not only act as an additional layer of bureaucratic control, but also allow further exploitation of immigrant women by charging fees and demanding their time, all the while producing no discernible results. With the kind of analysis I am proposing, one that centres itself on the concept of gender and race exploitation, we can see that these structures are no more coincidental than the forces whose effects they were developed to combat. Now, immigrant women are not only estranged from the products of their labour and their own knowledge, but are also alienated from the possibility ('access') provided by commodified, exchangeable labour power.

Thesis 3: If we relocate and reread the literature on work and lifelong learning in the context of war, occupation, militarism, poverty and patriarchy, new sets of contradictory relations will emerge between lifelong learning and work. I began by stating the obvious: lifelong learning is a highly contested concept. Now I am proposing to muddy these already murky waters by dislocating its pedagogical, theoretical and policy frames to sites of war, occupation, displacement and dispossession. By doing so, we can see that the connecting thread here is the discovery of a universal 'life in transition' as a mode of being and learning. Women whose experience of the actualities of violence falls outside the boundaries of lifelong learning policy, pedagogy, practice and theorisation are women who are or who have been historically excluded as adult learners. But, in addition, learning is happening regardless of this exclusion. Helen Colley, drawing extensively on the results of my research and analysis on Kurdish women's lives and struggles, concludes that '[o]ne lesson we have to learn from studies like that of the Kurdish women is that we may need to devote further attention to learning associated with collective consciousness, resistance and struggle and to the life-course transition associated with that learning, if those power relations are to be challenged or overturned' (Colley 2007: 440).

The discussion here has so far largely avoided the classification of learning according to concepts derived from the institutional practice and study of lifelong learning. As I have noted elsewhere:

> What is lacking…is an attempt to integrate an analysis of race, gender, class, and learning in a Marxist dialectical sense. An inquiry into 'learning', not in terms of its forms – that is formal, non-formal, and informal – but learning as class consciousness will require a merging of Marxist methodology and anti-oppression frameworks. While class consciousness can be thought of in terms of the distance between subjective and objective interests, this does not mean that the goal is to move a group toward a static set of objective interests. (Mojab 2006: 167)

Where to go from here?

In trying to understand what I have been doing so far, I raise two simple questions. First, what is lifelong learning for? Second, how do we understand and explain the relationship between work and lifelong learning? The more likely or more sincere response to both questions would be, 'Lifelong learning is for the purpose of training skilled labour and delivering it to the capitalist market', a response that reduces lifelong learning to an appendage of the market. I realise that most of us do not aim at reducing lifelong learning to the requirements of the market. Indeed, we have for a long time pursued lofty ideals in relation to what we are doing. In 1997, participants in CONFINTEA V in Hamburg reaffirmed 'that only human-centred development and a participatory society based on the full respect of human rights will lead to sustainable and equitable development'. Even more, the participants insisted that

> [a]dult education thus becomes more than a right; it is a key to the twenty-first century. It is both a consequence of active citizenship and a condition for full participation in society. It is a powerful concept for fostering ecologically sustainable development, for promoting democracy, justice, gender equity, and scientific, social and economic development, and for building a world in which violent conflict is replaced by dialogue and a culture of peace based on justice. Adult learning can shape identity and give meaning to life. Learning throughout life implies a rethinking of content to reflect such factors as age, gender equality, disability, language, culture and economic disparities.[3]

Twelve years after CONFINTEA V, I believe that even if we have taken one step forwards, we have taken many steps backwards. The very idea of citizenship and democracy is under attack. In many parts of the world, adult education is not a right; in fact, illiteracy is still a major obstacle to development. About one-fifth of the adult population of the world is illiterate, and 100 million children do not attend primary school.[4] By the mid 1990s there were about 100 million street children.[5] The trafficking of women and children has taken unprecedented dimensions (Anti-slavery International 2001; US State Dept 2008).

Is there any trace of 'human-centred development or a participatory society', which the Hamburg Declaration calls for? The neo-liberal regime that emerged in North America and Europe in the last two decades and has been imposed on the rest of the world is based on the supremacy of the market. The market is the arbitrator of relations not only among human beings but also among nations, cultures and countries. Under this economic order, poverty is on the rise while tiny groups get richer and richer.

Capitalism, both liberal and neo-liberal, is the most productive system in history. It produces much more than the population of a country can consume. Yet it does so in part by generating poverty. Furthermore, in order to reproduce itself, it has to expand. This expansion happens both within the borders of a given nation and on a world scale – unceasing globalisation. Capital cannot survive without colonial domination. War is inevitably tied to this economy. Capitalism has created a military-industrial complex that calls for wars even when the need for them cannot be justified; annual military spending is now more than a trillion dollars. Since the 1990s, 44 countries, or 25 per cent of the world's states, have been at war, generating enormous human and ecological devastation. The capitalist ability to produce is at the same time the ability to destroy. It is now argued that neo-liberal capitalism thrives on disaster (Klein 2007). We may take a step further and suggest that capitalism itself has turned into disaster. If early commercial capitalism had thrived on slavery and colonialism, the globalised neo-liberal regime of late capitalism is also reviving slavery. There is slavery of the old style in parts of Asia, Africa and Latin America. Today, Western capitalism prospers on the cheap labour of two billion people in China and India, where workers and peasants are subjected to new forms of serfdom and slavery.

Many of us in adult education have indeed been aware of this evolving disaster. Feminist theory helped us in understanding the ways in which women's labour contributes to the reproduction of both capitalism and patriarchy. Advances in the study of race and colonialism allowed us to understand the racial component of learning, education, work and capitalism. Today, we have rather advanced theorisations of learning. For example, Allman (1999, 2001 and 2007), Colley (2004) and Rikowski (1999, 2001 and 2002) treat capital and labour not as things but as social relations. They see labour and capital as unity and conflict of opposites forming the capitalist socio-economic formation. However, even when we see labour/capital as social relations constitutive of the capitalist system, we do not think about its negation. We critique and often succeed in our critique of capitalism but we do not take the next step. We do not envision the future. And our failure is part of the success of capitalism in reproducing itself.

To envision alternatives to capitalism is a process of understanding it. In other words, looking at capitalist social relations philosophically, it requires a process of understanding necessity and how to negate it. The capitalist world order, as it exists, is given to us by past and present societies. Philosophically, this is the realm of necessity and we are subject to its rules, although it is possible to be free from its constraints if we are conscious of it and if we envision its negation as a condition of freedom. I am confirming here that *freedom* exists in unity and conflict with *necessity* (existing conditions, the status quo).

Freedom consists in *understanding* and *transforming* necessity. And this is a process of conscious intervention in class interest, religious or ethnic belonging, and gender and racial hierarchy. As a final point, let me suggest a framework for understanding the dialectics of necessity and freedom as it applies to the relationship between work and lifelong learning. To do this I will draw on David Harvey's conception of 'accumulation by dispossession' (Harvey 2003) and name this process 'learning by dispossession', by which I mean that in the process of learning and work something other than 'learning' (which can be measured, evaluated or assessed on the basis of categorisation of 'formal', 'informal' and 'non-formal', or 'paid' and 'unpaid') is happening. Much like primitive capital accumulation, learning, too, has a dual characteristic – that is, it produces learning as well as something 'outside of itself' that is deeply entrenching self/mind/ consciousness into a perpetual mode of capitalist social relations; to put it differently, learning produces new skills and knowledge as well as alienation and fragmentation of self/community, and confuses 'worker' with the idea of 'capitalism'. Harvey proposes that we take the dialectic of 'inside-outside' relations of capitalism seriously and that in fact 'this helps us better understand what the capitalistic form of imperialism is about' (2003: 142). I also would like to propose that we expand our theoretical and methodological analysis of the relationship between work and lifelong learning to a qualitatively more sophisticated analysis of the materiality of capitalist social relations, one in which these relations are gendered, racialised and sexualised.

Notes

1   An earlier version of this chapter was first presented as my keynote address at the Fifth International Conference on Researching Work and Learning at the University of Cape Town, Cape Town, South Africa, in December 2007. I am grateful to Shirley Walters for inviting me. Her envisioning of different approaches to this topic was the impetus for my own rethinking. I am indebted to Linzi Manicom for her usual intellectual care in reading and commenting on an earlier draft of this chapter. Paula Allman's sharp critique is a source of reverence and inspiration; I remain obliged.

2   In preparing this chapter I have drawn extensively from my previously published work, including the following: 'Adult education without borders', in T Fenwick, T Nesbit and B Spencer (eds) *Contexts of adult education: Canadian perspectives* (Toronto: Thompson Educational Publishing, 2006); 'Race and class', in T Nesbit (ed.) *Class concerns: Adult education and social class: New directions in adult and continuing education, no. 106* (San Francisco: Jossey-Bass, 2005); 'From the "Wall of Shame" to September 11: Wither adult education?', in P Kell, M Singh and S Shore (eds) *Adult Education @ 21st Century* (New York: Peter Lang, 2004); and, with Rachel Gorman, 'Women and consciousness in the learning organisation: Emancipation or exploitation?', *Adult Education Quarterly* 53 no. 4 (2003): 228–241.

3   Hamburg Declaration on Adult Learning. Accessed 13 August 2001, http://www.unesco.org/education/uie/confintea/declaeng.htm.

4   Illiteracy 'hinders world's poor'. BBC News, 9 November 2005. Accessed 25 November 2007, http://news.bbc.co.uk/2/hi/uk_news/education/4420772.stm.

5   Exploitation of children – a worldwide outrage. Casa Alianza, September 2000. Accessed 25 November 2007, http://www.hiltonfoundation.org/press/16-pdf3.pdf.

References

Allman P (1999) *Revolutionary social transformation: Democratic hopes, political possibilities and critical education.* Westport, CT, and London: Bergin and Garvey

Allman P (2001) *Critical education against global capitalism: Karl Marx and revolutionary critical education.* Westport, CT, and London: Bergin and Garvey

Allman P (2007) *On Marx: An introduction to the revolutionary intellect of Karl Marx.* Rotterdam: Sense Publishers

Anti-slavery International (2001) Slave labour on the increase in China. Accessed 25 November 2007, http://www.antislavery.org/homepage/news/china130801.htm

Bales K (2005) *New slavery: A reference handbook* (2nd edition). Santa Barbara, CA: ABC–CLIO

Berg I (1970) *Education and jobs: The great training robbery.* New York: Praeger Publishers, Center for Urban Education

Coffield F (1999) Breaking the consensus: Lifelong learning as social control. *British Educational Research Journal* 25(4): 479–499

Colley H (2004) Learning experiences of adults mentoring socially excluded young people: Issues of power and gender. In D Clover (ed.) *Adult education for democracy, social justice, and a culture of peace.* Proceedings of the Joint International Conference of the Adult Education Research Conference and the Canadian Association for the Study of Adult Education, Victoria, BC, Canada (28–30 May)

Colley H (2007) Understanding time in learning transitions through the lifecourse. *International Studies in Sociology of Education* 17(4): 427–443

Ebert T (1996) *Ludic feminism and after: Postmodernism, desire, and labour in late capitalism.* Ann Arbor: University of Michigan Press

Ebert T & Zavarzadeh M (2008) *Class in culture.* Boulder, CO: Paradigm Publishers

Harvey D (2003) *The new imperialism.* Oxford: Oxford University Press

Klein N (2007) *The shock doctrine: The rise of disaster capitalism.* New York: Henry Holt and Company

Mojab S (2000) The power of economic globalisation: Deskilling immigrant women through training. In RM Cervero, AL Wilson & Associates (eds) *Power in practice: Adult education and the struggle for knowledge and power in society.* San Francisco: Jossey-Bass

Mojab S (2006) War and diaspora as lifelong learning contexts for immigrant women. In C Leathwood & B Francis (eds) *Gender and lifelong learning: Critical feminist engagements.* London: Routledge

Rikowski G (1999) Nietzsche, Marx and mastery: The learning unto death. In P Ainley & H Rainbird (eds) *Apprenticeship: Towards a new paradigm of learning.* London: Kogan Page

Rikowski G (2001) Education for industry: A complex technicism. *Journal of Education and Work* 14(1): 29–49

Rikowski G (2002) Fuel for the living fire: Labour-power! In AC Dinerstein & M Neary (eds) *The labour debate: An investigation into the theory and reality of capitalist work.* Surrey: Ashgate Publishing

Smith D (1985) Women, class, and family. In V Burstyn & D Smith (eds) *Women, class, family and the state.* Toronto: Garamond Press

US State Dept (2008) Trafficking in persons report. *Human trafficking and modern-day slavery.* Accessed 25 November 2007, http://www.gvnet.com/humantrafficking/China.htm

2 But what will we eat? Research questions and priorities for work and learning

Astrid von Kotze

Introduction

Let me begin by introducing three people. Firstly, Sipho, a young boy in torn, dirty clothes standing at a traffic intersection with one hand clutching an old plastic juice bottle filled with cobbler's glue and the other stretched out in a gesture of begging.[1] He is one of a group of street children working the first shift of the day. Secondly, Thembisa, a woman sitting under an umbrella with a baby on her lap and a toddler next to her. On the ground in front of them are small piles of vegetables for sale. Thirdly, Khumalo, who is pushing a home-made trolley heaped high with scrap metal collected over time and being delivered to a weighing station where he will sell it for a few rand.

These three people could be just about anywhere in the global South. Street children are a growing phenomenon of poor countries and socially and economically deeply stratified societies. For women who have been excluded from formal education and who have no start-up capital to create an enterprise, selling basic goods is often their only option for generating an income while at the same time taking care of children and grandchildren. The modern 'hunter-gatherer' attempts to make cash from found objects, from junk and discards, from the scraps tossed out by those who have. With the spread of untreated HIV/AIDS, the impact of major disasters that create widespread homelessness and displacement, and the growing hunger of resource-poor households especially in urban areas, encounters with people such as these three have become normal, raising little more than an eyebrow.

Sipho, Thembisa and Khumalo are part of the more than 50 per cent of the world's people not employed in the formal economy. They and others like them work hard trying to make a living, yet remain largely invisible in formal deliberations about learning, education and training. The report on the 1997 CONFINTEA V deliberations (UNESCO Committee 1998: 99–100) included some excellent conclusions and recommendations about education for and in the informal economy, such as the need to design interventions in a participatory way, building on existing capacities and skills within specific sectors both in terms of content and methodology; the importance of constructing bridges between non-formal and formal education; cooperation with existing networks and organisations; promoting practices of economic solidarity; and the need to consider households as economic unities.

Yet, later documents seem to have ignored the studies and recommendations of the committee rather than building on their insights in order to identify appropriate research priorities (Von Kotze 2008). While recent UNESCO-UNEVOC documents (2003, 2006) emphasise the importance of work in the informal economy, planning largely excludes the radically changed structures and processes of workplaces in an increasingly neo-liberal world. This is not surprising given the diminishing role of the state in education and training interventions, the increasing commodification of learning, and the impossibility of designing one-size-fits-all curricula for radically different conditions. However, their omission is very worrying, particularly in the context of rising food prices, food shortages as crops are turned into biofuels, and looming deadlines for meeting Millennium Development Goals (MDGs).

In this chapter I want to do two things: firstly, critique the persistent development thinking that informs education and work agendas, and suggest instead the 'livelihoods perspective' as an alternative way of approaching work, learning and education particularly with regard to the majority world; and secondly, outline research questions and priorities that derive from such a reorientation.

Accounting mentality

There is an incredible preoccupation in development thinking with what is measurable and quantifiable: the amount produced, the cash in the pocket, the number of people employed, etc. Along with the accounting mentality goes the production of models and systems that make it easier to reckon, calculate and tally 'outcomes'. Tick lists allow for easy stocktaking and hence appraisal of hours worked, barrels moved, containers filled, people trained. Assessment is based on the growth, increase and accumulation of whatever is being counted. Somehow, people like Sipho, Thembisa and Khumalo and their resourceful attempts to make a decent living and lead dignified lives disappear behind the statistics, inventories and measurables.

In-depth studies of learning, education and training in the informal economy are hard to come by. Statistics indicate that the informal economy is growing, and in developing countries informal employment represents one-half to three-quarters of non-agricultural employment.[2] The contribution of income from informal work to national income amounts to between 30 and 60 per cent in different countries (Chen et al. 2005, Shier 2006).[3] Contrary to popular perceptions, the informal economy contributes between 7 and 12 per cent of gross domestic product (GDP) (Shier 2006). Yet the norm for what constitutes work remains employment in the formal economy, and the priority for education and training is human resource development or 'capacity building', accessible mainly to those who are already 'in the know' and in the system. Market conditions favour the provision of learning programmes that target individuals who want to 'invest' in themselves, hoping that in return for enrolling in life-skills and vocational training courses they will find employment. The belief that investment in personal development will generate quantifiable returns is so persistent that donors are not deterred even by a lack of reliable (or credible) figures on how the names on enrolment forms tally with 'bums on seats' and with newly employed or self-employed people.

Capacity building or personal development

Even in UNESCO-UNEVOC documents work is still predominantly defined as formal employment. By implication, the majority of people in the global South (including the three introduced at the beginning of the chapter) don't work. Not surprisingly, therefore, if you were to ask Khumalo about his work he would probably respond with 'I am not working'. Gathering and selling scraps, trading small quantities of products, housekeeping and care work – and indeed, the whole care economy – are not 'work'.[4] While the care work undertaken by grandmothers, young unemployed women or community members may support and reproduce life and living, it is not valued and it is considered unproductive. The skills and knowledge of those engaged in such work are not formally recognised and accredited – and as 'unskilled workers' they become the target of training programmes.

The argument most commonly advanced is that people are unemployed because they lack (a) skills and (b) self-esteem and self-confidence. Hence, they are offered 'life skills' to alter their behaviour, and skills training to make them more employable. The resource pack produced by UNEVOC on behalf of UNESCO in 2006 is one example of this – except here the 'bottom line' seems to be that locals are unmotivated (and, by implication, lazy). Titled 'Learning and Working: Motivating for Skills Development', the pack is well presented: it comprises bright and colourful booklets with pictures and CDs and it offers exactly what everyone says we need – skills-training activities designed with youth in mind. The publishers explain what the pack is about:

> The Campaign Package 'Learning and Working: Motivating for Skills
> Development' is a resource kit that provides information and tools for the
> preparation and implementation of awareness and motivation campaigns
> for marginalised groups in least developed countries. The package is
> relevant to all who are involved in the provision of capacity building
> and skills development for disadvantaged populations at the local level.
> The idea behind this is to encourage people living in adverse economic
> conditions to enhance their social and economic perspectives by enrolling
> in technical and vocational education and training (TVET) to improve
> their occupational skills and/or by taking up self-employment activities.[5]

This introductory note reveals a number of assumptions: firstly, that 'marginalised groups' are excluded because they lack awareness and motivation; secondly, that 'disadvantaged populations' need capacity building and skills development; and thirdly, that 'people living in adverse economic conditions' will enhance their social and economic perspectives by improving their occupational skills through enrolling in TVET. 'Marginalised groups', 'disadvantaged populations', 'people living in adverse economic conditions' need to be brought into the (formal/dominant) economy. Training in personal and leadership development that leads to 'empowerment' is the way to do that – not, of course, effecting a shift in conditions or a change in economic policies that caused the exclusion in the first place.

There is no doubt that positive mental attitudes, vision, goal setting and development of self-confidence are important attributes towards participation and assumption of leadership roles. However, motivational teaching packs often reinforce the perception that the failure to participate in decision-making is the result of personal deficiencies rather than structural constraints, and that powerful participation and leadership require individual transformation rather than broader social change, particularly with regard to patriarchal relations rooted in customs and traditional beliefs. Unless instructional strategies go hand in hand with, or supplement, structural ones, the outcome of training will be people who are more confident but still just as oppressed.

In 2000, Singh published the results of a study that had revealed many of the essential qualities and competencies that people demonstrate as necessary for functioning in the informal economy: dispositions, personality traits and orientations such as being able to compromise, to be patient, to tolerate contradictions; and a range of social communicative abilities based on the history within a community or location. None of these are likely outcomes of training courses, even though personal development-type programmes claim to 'teach' these competencies, which are packaged as 'communication skills', 'cooperation and team-building' or 'negotiation skills'. As Singh showed:

> A small producer depends largely on his or her informal relationship with customers; advertising takes place through recommendations of friends and acquaintances; information regarding new machinery is transmitted through personal contacts. (2000: 601)

Thus, much of the ability to conduct business as a street vendor such as Thembisa, for example, is premised on connections and personality: who you know and how you can use that knowledge, and how to engage people in conversation, establish relations of trust, and call on or grant favours based on common friends or acquaintances.

Singh's study (2000) showed that in order to improve people's economic position, individualising them as targets of personal development was not as effective as linking them to networks in which they could learn about new technologies and new markets, enlarge their client base, pool knowledge and know-how, and improve their social security by establishing and strengthening social ties.

The UNESCO document *Orienting Technical and Vocational Education and Training for Sustainable Development* (UNESCO-UNEVOC 2006: 5) acknowledged that there cannot be a single development objective for the global South; instead, 'appropriate strategies must be developed for both rich and poor nations'. Critical of 'the global market economy' in terms of its exploitation of the environment and exclusion of 'roughly half of the world's people' (2006: 8), the document charged future TVET graduates with the task of 'working at the interface between nature, technology, economy and society' and thus having to learn about 'sustainable concepts, practices and examples' (2006: 9). Consistent with this, sustainable development was defined as

> a culturally-directed search for a dynamic balance in the relationship
> between social, economic and natural systems, a balance that seeks to
> promote equity between the present and the future, and equity between
> the countries, races, social classes and genders. (2006: 5)

Achieving a 'balance' suggests a number of radical shifts, the first of which would have to be the way we consider work, especially with regard to learning and education.

A livelihood approach to work and learning

Maria Mies (1986) reminds us that '[t]he aim of all our work and human endeavour is not a never-ending expansion of wealth and commodities, but *human happiness* (as the early socialists had seen it), or the *production of life itself* (1986: 212; italics in original). Similarly, Andre Gorz (1999) pointed out that work has come to be understood only as a paid activity undertaken on behalf of a third party, to achieve goals set by someone other than ourselves and according to procedures and schedules laid down by the employer. If work is regarded as 'livelihood activities', it is taken out of pure commodity production and refocused to include the production of life. In its simplest sense a livelihood is a means to gaining a living (Chambers & Conway 1991). A livelihood perspective takes into account the social, economic, political, historical, geographic and demographic contexts that influence the options that people within those contexts have with regard to making a living. It considers available resources and assets and the access different people have to these, and the institutions that support the efforts of people. It also considers particular risk factors and the strategies employed by people to cope with and overcome these.

Thus, a livelihood perspective takes seriously not just all those actions undertaken in order to make a living, but also includes those labours and responsibilities associated with reproducing life (Mies 1986; Mies & Bennholdt-Thomsen 1999), and in this way provides the foundation for other kinds of work. This includes housework and childcare, home gardening and fuel collection, as much as community organising and the often small acts of reciprocity and solidarity that establish and contribute to social protection.

Going beyond work as employment in the formal economy towards work as livelihood activities should not simply mean replacing one word with another. Rather, it means thinking more holistically about the actions people employ in order to do more than just survive physically, but to live a dignified, decent life. More holistic thinking is required if we want to consider sustainability, and especially establish less exploitative relationships to the environment and natural resources, and to people as our partners in systems of conviviality. If actions are to impact positively on the context of differential poverty and wealth, 'livelihood studies' rather than 'workplace learning' studies will generate better understanding of how the complex daily struggles for food and the necessities of life are intertwined with care-giving, child rearing and community building, and about the kind of education and training strategies that would best support those struggles.

Taking on a sustainable livelihoods perspective compels us to consider people's lives and life chances in terms of high-risk environments. The impact of hazards such as diseases/epidemics and weather phenomena on already vulnerable conditions and people renders them unable to cope. As informal workers they face additional threats: firstly, in terms of the conditions under which they live and work; and secondly, because they have low levels of income they are less likely to be able to save for emergencies or special occasions (Chen et al. 2005; Lund & Nicholson 2003). As a result, these workers are far more exposed to common contingencies such as illness, property loss, and death, without having access to the means to address these. Furthermore, as they face exclusion from the state, political institutions, and markets – that is, all those people and institutions who make the decisions that affect them most directly – they have fewer rights or knowledge of their rights, and less access to information, infrastructure and services.

To cope and to make their livelihoods sustainable requires the creation and maintenance of systems of support and a power base for wielding influence in order to effect policy changes. As the state assumes less and less responsibility for social security, people have to make their own arrangements for social protection. In the world of the rich and comfortable, this translates into insurance policies and the like; in the majority world, it means all those actions that people undertake in order to expand their capacities to cope and create safety nets for emergencies, rather than simply waiting for the delivery of commodities and services (Lund & Nicholson 2003). Primarily, this involves establishing relationships of mutuality, solidarity and collective action. In rural areas – whether in subsistence production oriented towards food security, or cash-crop raising – there is mutual assistance out of the recognition that economic activity is not an individualistic action but one that involves others. Workers in the informal economy organise themselves in a variety of forms, depending on issues of geography, culture, the nature and spatial/time conditions of their work, and the different types of work performed.

A livelihood perspective would steer our focus towards the informal economy (and the interdependence of the formal and informal economies), making the invisible visible, and exposing poor working and living conditions and the absence of (formal) social protection. It would mean creating access to productive assets and other resources, to land, credit, marketing and technological assistance – and, hopefully, once those conditions have been created, access to and provision of education and training would follow.

Therefore, a livelihood perspective as the starting point for thinking about work, learning and education would mean a new, more inclusive definition of work – one that includes care work and all the unpaid, 'free' labour provided mainly by women. It would mean an orientation towards supporting and sustaining life rather than the accumulation of commodities in the vain hope that 'more' and 'bigger' would also translate into 'better'; an understanding of the diversification of livelihood activities, as opposed to 'one job', within a highly differentiated risk environment; a focus on the informal economy as the main employer of poorer people; and, finally, a debunking of the claimed 'inertia' and passivity of people who require 'motivation'.

Research priorities

What kind of research questions and priorities would arise from a livelihood approach? In the following sections I outline five of these.

Participatory curriculum design

Despite extensive research that has shown the need for participatory local curriculum construction, learning, education and training interventions are consistently designed by experts outside the target group of learners. As Gouthro (2000) put it:

> A key question to be addressed in determining the future possibilities of civil society in the globalised world is who defines the educational agenda? Right now, it is determined by business and corporations, and profit thinking and investment into individual consumers rather than the future of all. (2000: 70)

Eleven years ago Karcher (1998) suggested that, with the growth of the informal economy all over the world, the North could learn lessons from the South and that

> [t]he concepts of teaching and learning that have relevance for the informal sector must be subjected to closer scrutiny if adult education is to take account of the altered working processes and the people involved in them. It must ask itself how a dignified life can be made possible outside formal conditions of employment and which educational strategies both informal and formal are conducive to this aim. (What, why and how is learning to take place?) (1998: 88)

Further, he argued that

> [a]n appropriate teaching and learning concept can only be achieved through active involvement of the concerned group, i.e. through extensive participation. For those groups are themselves best placed to formulate their needs and to define the limits of their possibilities. Appropriate approaches therefore have to be designed differently according to the situation and for each specific group – particularly for women. (1998: 89)

Similarly, Singh (2000) has suggested that provision of education and training needs to

> take into account the traditions and values of the system of vocational learning in working life, cater to the requirements of local development and be based on an understanding of the kinds of competencies people in the informal economy want, need and utilise, the socio-economic and cultural contexts within which they work, and how they cope and sustain their livelihood strategies. (2000: 599)

The first research priority, therefore, is to learn more systematically from those we wish to support. We need to better understand what would make a difference rather than rush in with prescriptions and offerings based on assumptions. What specific knowledge and know-how is required by particular sectors and groups, and how best are such knowledges acquired? Answering such questions also requires innovative research methodologies. For example, experiences in participatory rural appraisal processes illustrate how it is useful to live with, for example, poor traders in order to learn together about the particular political economies of their specific sectors and the place, time and conditional factors that would allow for concentrated learning activities. Listening, observing and working together may generate the kind of questions that need to be asked in order to ascertain what education and training might make a real difference to their livelihood security.

Local and specific

Generic training modules are rarely helpful, as Chen et al. (2005) observe:

> What is needed is a context-specific mix of interventions, developed in consultation with working-poor women and men and informed by an understanding of their significance in the labour force and their contribution to the economy. (2005: 89)

Therefore, recognising the importance of a small-scale, local and specific orientation must be the starting point. This pertains not only to potential syllabi but also to processes and methodologies. Once the subject matter of programmes has been designed, the skills and knowledge development must take into consideration the local capabilities and traditions and dynamics of social relations with regard to their transmission or production. 'Without a thorough analysis of local circumstances and adaptation as necessary and appropriate, the super-imposition of foreign training methods and curricula is likely to be counter-productive as well as costly', warned Singh (1998: 98). Moreover,

> developing education for the informal sector can only be successful to the extent that it reflects innovations, initiatives and approaches emerging from the informal sector itself. This is a sector the epitomises self-help, civil society participation, transformative, on the job, autodidactic and intergenerational learning as well as learning out of school contexts – such as learning through participation in social movements. (Singh 2005: 5)

This also suggests that, in particular, two important factors must be included in deliberations about learning and education: the (unpaid) care work performed by people, particularly women; and the networking and organisation building that are time- and energy-consuming but crucial for survival and success.

Another challenge is the question of how to build bridges between formal and informal learning and how to valorise informal and non-formal learning and education, and yet avoid the 'credentialism' so typical of the neo-liberal world. Gorz (1999) has reminded us that

> nothing is more impoverishing for a culture than to see the most
> spontaneous effective bonds between people – sympathy, empathy,
> compassion, attention, communication, etc. – 'objectified in training and
> qualifications', and used to satisfy an employer or gain a client, used to
> 'knowing how to sell oneself' to the former, or how to sell things to the
> latter. (1999: 70)

Effective bonds between people cannot be taught or enshrined in qualifications.
What they require is more than simply a delivery of information. How can generic
outcomes-based provision be avoided in favour of negotiated ways of assessing and
evaluating practice-based/site-specific learning equivalents?

The second research priority, therefore, is learning about and using specific, local
and traditional forms of apprenticeship, and socialisation into particular work
and teaching processes and contexts. Learning that is isolated from the particular
dynamics and realities of everyday livelihood activities is seldom sustained and
transfer from the 'classroom' to the field rarely happens.

Focus on women

Much has been said about the dramatic changes in the labour force, in working
conditions and in rising insecurity for poor people – and in particular women – due
to globalisation, the increasing feminisation of both the labour force and poverty,
and ongoing gender discrimination (Kabeer 2007; Bush 2007). The United Nations
Economic and Social Council (ECOSOC) report of 2006 spells out the condition of
women with regard to poverty and employment:

> Of roughly 520 million working people living in extreme poverty (earning
> less than $1 a day), an estimated 60 per cent are women. Women find
> it more difficult than men to break out of poverty, owing to gender
> inequalities in the share of household responsibilities, access to education,
> training and employment, as well as in economic and political decision-
> making. Women are less likely than men to hold paid and regular jobs
> and more often work in the informal economy; fewer women than men
> own businesses; and worldwide, over 60 per cent of unpaid workers in
> family enterprises are women. Women provide important contributions
> to the economy through both remunerated and unremunerated work
> in the labour market, at home and in the community. However, gender
> stereotypes, and horizontal and vertical sex segregation in the labour
> market contribute to gender inequality in employment worldwide.
> (ECOSOC 2006)

Kabeer (2007) has shown how the casualisation, flexibilisation and informalisation
of women's labour has been justified with the old ideology of men as the 'main
breadwinners', thus warranting low pay for women as 'secondary earners'. However,
with the increasing insecurity of men's paid labour many women have been forced

to take up paid work – sometimes involving migration – to survive or meet the rising expectations of households. Given unequal formal educational opportunities, land ownership and access to land use, demands on care work and other activities previously carried out within the formal economy, women have less choice about where to work and what to do (Alsop & Healey 2008).

While it is known that women spend more time in work overall but less time in paid work, and generally have less discretionary time than men, detailed accounts of how increasing pressures on their time and energy impact on available time for dedicated learning are lacking. If poverty is to be addressed effectively, there is therefore an urgent research priority aimed at better understanding women's changed position in terms of work. Furthermore, the migrancy of poor women in search of employment in the service economy in wealthier countries and how this affects their potential to 'learn their way out' of exploitative relations is yet to be investigated.

Part of a specific research focus on women should be explorations of the ongoing and changing gender division of labour in terms of time, place and particularly value. The increase in women's breadwinning roles has already been highlighted; the refusal of men to do a fairer share of the unpaid household and care work, however, requires further insight, particularly as this has contributed to 'an increase in the demand for paid female labour in services hitherto provided through the unpaid relations of marriage and family' (Kabeer 2007: 49), or social services provided and paid for by the state. Exemption from unpaid domestic chores appears to be one of the privileges most strongly defended by men, and contribution to such work is often glossed over in order to preserve the masculine image. What needs to happen so that we overcome the old myth that 'women's work' can only be done by women? How will care work come to be recognised as morally desirable and economically important? Answering such questions may constitute the first step towards men coming to embrace home-based work as legitimate and productive work. It also raises educational challenges.

Addressing risk

In the hurry to provide training to improve economic access and performance, the everyday realities and conditions under which poor women and men work are overlooked and, by implication, rendered unimportant. Livelihood studies assist in identifying the risks and uncertainties associated with poor people's work 'as well as the common contingencies of property loss, illness, disability and death' (Chen et al. 2005: 90). For Sipho, Thembisa and Khumalo, deciding whether or not to participate in organised learning involves a complex process of weighing up costs and benefits, risks and advantages, rather than a lack of motivation. Poor households spend proportionately more resources on meeting food costs than do richer households, and the cost of forfeiting a daily income in part or wholly due to attending learning sessions is high. Similarly, the energy and cash expenditure for transport to learning sessions often exceeds a person's capacity or puts meeting food or health necessities at risk.

Detailed work studies may assist in identifying and appreciating the exact nature of hazards and their impact on multiple vulnerabilities. For example, threats associated with the informal work of street vendors include exposure to weather (extreme temperatures), poor sanitation and access to clean water, lead poisoning and respiratory problems from vehicle fumes, and harassment from members of the public or municipal officials. Traders exposed to these pressures do not need to learn (from outsiders) about risk any more than they require lessons on poverty; however, different ways of organising and mobilising to address access to water and shelter, to forge agreements and information on by-laws about the use of public spaces and so on may well be the subject matter of teaching and learning sessions. Such lessons can only be learned collectively and therefore space and time issues must be negotiated.

Another example of relevant lessons may be a focus on 'natural' disasters, showing how it is often people, not nature, who create crisis situations and emergencies. For example, blaming famines on persistent drought removes the spotlight from politicians who fail to read and respond to advance warning systems in order to create mechanisms for averting or reducing loss of life and destruction (Von Kotze & Holloway 1996). Suggestions that hunger is caused by economic policies remedied through 'improved governance', 'increased investments' and 'spending cuts on social services' are neo-liberal solutions that obfuscate the cause of hunger in global capitalism. As Bush (2007: 152) points out, 'The dominant characterisation of food crisis has deterred explanations that involve any attack on the structures of power that create and perpetuate food insecurity.'

The importance of food

Research into local perceptions of poverty demonstrates that words and metaphors for poverty are most often related to hunger.[6] This is because from experience people know about 'a cat sleeping in the fireplace', 'eating wild food with sticks' or 'eating so little that it would fill a bird's stomach'. The biggest crisis currently confronting the world is food – and this becomes especially visible when there is an emergency triggered by hazards such as earthquakes, tsunamis, cyclones and floods and affecting huge numbers of people. Conditions of nutritional insufficiency related to social and economic isolation and exclusion, poor health status and political oppression render poor communities vulnerable to further shocks. Yet most of the deliberations on work and learning remain silent on these issues. How would our thinking about learning and education have to change if we were to rearrange our concerns and put accessible and sufficient nutrition for all at the top of our priority list? While food has come to be seen as a commodity and a lifestyle choice for some, for others it remains a basic necessity over which they often have no control.

Increasingly, there are figures about the current rise in food prices and its impact. For example, the Economic Commission for Latin America and the Caribbean (ECLAC) states in its 2007 poverty projections for Latin America countries that

> a 15 per cent increase in the food prices raises poverty incidence by almost three percentage points, from 12,7 per cent to 15,9 per cent.

This means that the price increase will force 15,7 million of Latin Americans into indigence. Regarding poverty levels, price increases will have similar effects because an equivalent number of residents will become poor. (Cited in Ballara 2007)

The remedy suggested is the implementation of strategies to incorporate the global South into the world economy, including export-led growth, increased cash-crop production and the creation of 'efficient' markets. A common education and training response is to 'build local capacity' through the creation of paraprofessional extension workers in agriculture, nutrition and health. While extension-worker training and financial inputs for hardware may be useful, they often go hand in hand with agricultural systems that seek to replace the old (subsistence-based) ones. How local people make sense of the replacement of one knowledge system and set of technologies with another would be the subject of further research investigations.[7]

The main producers of food remain women, not just in terms of preparation for consumption, but also in terms of growing, storing and preserving crops and trading produce. Women most often are the preservers and teachers of knowledge about food and so they remain core to healthy living and survival. Yet social and economic policies and practices often undermine women's ability to reproduce and implement their knowledge and skills, as capitalism does not place value on food production for self-provisioning but only on cash crops for sale. What are we going to eat in the future if women leave the land as migrant labourers and youth leave the countryside in search of other lifestyles? Surely there are also research and education challenges here!

Conclusion: Adult educators in neo-liberal times

Education is hailed as the panacea to all social injustices, yet the challenge for critical educators is to join the call for, and support, practical interventions that pave the way for education: social grants, loans without collaterals (as in Bangladesh through Grameen Banks), the cancellation of debts, and childcare provision pave the way for people engaging and participating in education as a preparation to shape the world in a more just and equal way. Then, as Gouthro (2000) suggests,

> as adult educators, we have to assess whether it is our role simply to sustain and support educational trends that are mandated by government and the corporate sector, or whether we have a critical role to play in assessing the ongoing purpose of adult education. (2000: 60)

Clearly, I am suggesting that in the context of globalising capitalism, educators with a social purpose have a crucial role to play in asking the important questions, pushing the counter-hegemonic research agendas, and taking a stand on the side of those who are excluded from social justice, including the promotion of education and training. By the mere fact of being co-humans and fellow world citizens, adult educators are deeply implicated in the life and living of Sipho, Thembisa and Khumalo. There is much to learn from them, and research into work and learning should begin with listening and observation, asking questions and entering into productive dialogue. Such listening must be infused with respect and compassion, or what Gorz (1999) called 'love'. He demanded that the act of teaching be an act of loving, where the teacher/educator is a reference person who makes the learner '*feel* deserving of *unconditional* love, and *confident* of their capacity to learn, act, undertake projects' (1999: 68; italics in original). Education, learning and work relationships must be more than mere instrumental relations and processes. Let's take a stand for learning and working in the framework of livelihood security.

Notes

1   It must be noted that the outfits of begging street children are often carefully chosen work clothes. As they argue, no one would give them anything if they looked 'decent'.

2   In South Africa, the October Household Survey (1997–99) and the Labour Force Survey (2000–05) show that employment in the informal economy increased from 965 000 persons in October 1997 to just over 2.3 million in September 2005 (cited in Devey et al. 2006).

3   See also Women in Informal Employment: Globalising and Organising (WIEGO). Accessed 15 January, http://www.wiego.org.

4   A livelihood study of street children in Durban has generated insight into younger boys' begging activities being perceived as work and, indeed, constituting the main income-generating activity they engage in (Trent & Von Kotze 2008, forthcoming).

5   Reference to 'disadvantage' rather than injustice suggests arguments of 'exclusion' of the 1980s and 1990s.

6   This is ongoing research conducted by me among different groups across nations.

7   A current research project by Janice Busangye (University of KwaZulu-Natal) looks at the tensions between different agricultural knowledge systems and technologies among small-crop farmers in Uganda in order to ascertain whether new imported systems put the food security of farmers at risk, and what strategies they employ to avert crises.

References

Alsop R & Healey P (2008) Gender equality and economic growth – for poverty reduction. *Poverty in Focus* 13(January): 14–15. Accessed 9 February 2008, http://www.undp-povertycentre.org

Ballara M (2007) Gender and rural employment: A view from Latin America. *Convergence* 40(3–4): 239–245.

Bush R (2007) *Poverty and neoliberalism: Persistence and reproduction in the global South.* London and Ann Arbor, MI: Pluto Press

Chambers R & Conway GR (1991) *Sustainable rural livelihoods: Practical concepts for the 21st century.* IDS Discussion Paper 296. Brighton, UK: Institute of Development Studies

Chen M, Vanek J, Lund F, Heintz J, Jhabvala R & Bonner C (2005) *Progress of the world's women 2005: Women, work and poverty.* New York: UNDFW/UNIFEM

Devey R, Skinner C & Valodia I (2006) Definitions, data and the informal economy in South Africa: A critical analysis. In V Padayachee (ed.) *The development decade? Economic and social change in South Africa, 1994–2004.* Cape Town: HSRC Press

ECOSOC (United Nations Economic and Social Council) (2006) *Innovation at work: National strategies to achieve gender equality in employment.* Accessed 12 February 2008, http://www. un.org/ecosoc

Gorz A (1999) *Reclaiming work: Beyond the wage-based society.* Cambridge: Polity Press

Gouthro P (2000) Globalisation, civil society and the homeplace. *Convergence* 33(1/2): 57–77

Kabeer N (2007) *Marriage, motherhood and masculinity in the global economy: Reconfigurations of personal and economic life.* IDS Working Paper 290. Brighton, UK: Institute of Development Studies

Karcher W (1998) Vocational competencies in the informal sector. In M Singh (ed.) *Adult learning and the changing world of work.* Hamburg: UNESCO Institute for Education

Lund F & Nicholson J (2003) *Chains of production, ladders of protection: Social protection for workers in the informal economy.* Durban: School of Development Studies, University of KwaZulu-Natal

Mies M (1986) *Patriarchy and accumulation on a world scale: Women in the international division of labour.* London: Zed Books

Mies M & Bennholdt-Thomsen V (1999) *The subsistence perspective: Beyond the globalised economy.* London/New York and Australia: Zed Books and Spinifex Press

Shier J (2006) *The state of the informal economy.* Policy brief. University of KwaZulu-Natal (Durban), School of Development Studies. Accessed 4 November 2007, http://www.Sanpad.org.za

Singh M (1998) Adult learning in the context of self-help organisations. In M Singh (ed.) *Adult learning and the changing world of work.* Hamburg: UNESCO Institute for Education

Singh M (2000) Combining work and learning in the informal economy: Implications for education, training and skills development. *International Review of Education* 46(6): 599–620

Singh M (2005) Meeting basic needs in the informal sector. *UNESCO-UNEVOC Bulletin* 11(December): 4–6

UNESCO Committee on Educational Research in Co-operation with Third World Countries within the German Educational Research Association (1998) Adult learning and vocational training in the informal sector in developing countries. In M Singh (ed.) *Adult learning and the changing world of work.* Hamburg: UNESCO Institute for Education

UNESCO-UNEVOC International Centre for Technical and Vocational Education and Training (2003) *UNESCO-UNEVOC in brief.* Bonn: UNESCO

UNESCO-UNEVOC International Centre for Technical and Vocational Education and Training (2006) *Orienting technical and vocational education and training for sustainable development.* Bonn: UNESCO

Von Kotze A (2008) Negotiating TVET for sustainable livelihoods. *Journal of Workplace Learning* 20(7/8): 480–491

Von Kotze A & Holloway A (1996) *Reducing risk: Participatory learning activities for disaster mitigation in southern Africa.* Durban: IFRC and Oxfam

3 Hard/soft, formal/informal, learning/work: Tenuous/persistent binaries in the knowledge-based society

Kaela Jubas and Shauna Butterwick

Introduction

This chapter[1] explores insights from a study of women's learning pathways to jobs in the information technology (IT) field. Between 2003 and 2006, the study team interviewed 75 women in the urban centres of Vancouver, Victoria and Toronto, Canada, who were working, or seeking or preparing for work, in the IT field. In contrast to the mainstream instrumentally oriented discourse about skills development and formal credentials, we aimed to map varied alternative, informal learning pathways. We noted participants' work settings and jobs, and the contributions they make to a field that is characterised, paradoxically, as highly masculine *and* filled with opportunities for all workers, including women. At issue is how and whether alternative educational and career pathways are acknowledged by employers, colleagues and the participants themselves.

We bring a feminist standpoint epistemology to this project, one that calls for knowledge generated from the situated experiences of women whose lives are significantly shaped by the gendered, raced and classed division of labour. Our analysis also challenges assumptions about educating a so-called global workforce and learning pathways within the IT field. It helps to re-theorise dominant conceptions of learning by interrogating epistemological and social binaries. We establish that binary conceptualisations such as female/male, formal/informal, learning/work, hard/soft are both persistent and tenuous. Binaries remain strong cultural constructions with material impacts, even as they are disputed. In moving from an either/or to a both/and understanding of them, we offer a different way of talking about how they can be observed and experienced.

We begin with a review of the literature exploring gender, technology, work and learning. In this review, we include information from Canada, as well as from the US, the UK and other countries. Like other scholarship in the area of globalisation – to which technology is centrally linked – this literature illustrates the importance of local discourses and material conditions, and trends that might be visible worldwide.

Gender and technology: Literature review

International labour force research indicates that women are less likely than men to work in the IT field (Habtu 2003; Miller & Jagger 2001). Statistics also indicate that women who do work in the IT field are most likely to work in certain niches. Despite these two common observations, different occupational categories determine how statistics are analysed and discussed from study to study. Moreover, some studies are limited to an examination of what is classified as the IT 'sector' – those workplaces focused on development, production, sale and service of IT – while other studies have examined IT work in a broader context.

In Canada, women in the IT sector have most often worked as database analysts and data administrators, systems testing technicians, or web designers and developers; they are less commonly found working as systems analysts or computer programmers (Habtu 2003). A multinational study of IT, electronics and communications jobs found it most likely for women to work as computer analysts or programmers and computer systems managers (Miller & Jagger 2001). This latter report is both more extensive in that it considers work in fields related to but not part of the IT field (e.g. telecommunications and electronics), and narrower in its consideration of jobs within those fields. As Krista Scott-Dixon (2004) notes, statistics are difficult to interpret

> since IT work cuts across many industrial and occupational categories. Some IT workers are hidden at home, doing contract, freelance, part-time or other forms of precarious work. Some IT workers do technical tasks as part of their daily routine, but their official job title is not considered a technical one…What I call hybrid jobs – jobs that combine various backgrounds, disciplines and types of tasks – have emerged. IT work, then, is a category of convenience rather than precision, which suggests a loose grouping of work types that can vary by actual tasks performed, by work practices and by the relationship between employer and employee. (2004: 15)

What ultimately emerges is a picture of a field that is most likely to attract or accommodate male workers. One way that this is evident is through income. Research indicates that women tend to work in niches with lower-paying jobs and that, regardless of the niche or the job, women tend to earn less than their male colleagues (Habtu 2003; Woodfield 2000). They are also more likely to leave the IT field before retirement (Adam et al. 2006; Woodfield 2000), a phenomenon that, within Europe, seems especially pronounced in Britain (Platman & Taylor 2004, cited in Adam et al. 2006: 369).

For the most part, research exploring women's IT learning has focused on educational programmes and jobs most centrally associated with IT (such as computer programming and software engineering). US scholars Sherry Turkle and Seymour Papert (1990) characterise the learning and problem-solving style of female participants in their study of computer science students as 'bricolage'. Bricoleurs apply knowledge across contexts as needs arise, rather than relying on abstract, formulaic solutions. Also in the US, Jane Margolis and Allan Fisher (2002) outline women's ' "counternarrative" to the stereotype of computer scientists who are narrowly focused on their machines…Instead, these women tell us about their multiple interests and their desire to link computer science to social concerns and caring for people' (2002: 54). For both women and men, '[l]ove of puzzles, creating something from nothing, the art of thinking, interaction, communication: all are facets of the computing endeavour but not always part of the traditional lexicon' (2002: 58); however, men seem more interested in getting the programme to work for the sake of the programme alone, whether or not it has any practical application. Although both men and women might engage in social, intuitive learning, such approaches are gendered as feminine and were more openly adopted by female participants.

Based in a British IT firm, Ruth Woodfield's (2000) ethnographic study found similar gender differences, despite the presence of a high proportion of women with science degrees in that workplace. Female participants tended to describe technology as one of several interests, while men described an almost obsessive interest in computers. Colleagues and supervisors tended to describe women as workers who see 'the broader picture' and offer the corporate ideal of a 'hybrid worker' who combines technical, interpersonal and organisational skills. Male workers were seen as narrowly focused on 'software solutions which grew out of specific technical detail' (Woodfield 2000: 98). Still, men were promoted more frequently and quickly, while women were saddled with administrative responsibilities such as coordinating meetings – tasks which took time and energy but brought no corporate rewards. Finally, Woodfield (2000) found that women often thought about their technical skills and work as 'somehow always provisional' (2000: 94), and often talked about leaving their jobs and the IT field entirely.

Alison Adam et al. (2006) note 'the strong link between [the] notion of skill, in particular technical skill, and the ways in which something becomes defined as a technical skill, and therefore a masculine attribute' (2006: 372). Niki Panteli et al. characterise the IT field as a 'masculine culture' (2001: 11). As they explain:

> What emerges from this literature is that computing may be particularly
> vulnerable to the stereotyping of female and male roles through the
> ideologies of respective styles and competencies, whether these are
> accurate or not. If they are descriptors of real differences, then they are
> accompanied by a devaluation and marginalisation of feminine skills and
> styles; if they are misplaced, they still brand and help to herd women into
> ghettoised tasks and positions. (2001: 12)

As Ursula Huws (2000) notes, the basis of gendered divisions in IT learning and work is related primarily to social constructions of gender, as well as class and race, rather than the inherent qualities of IT. The extent to which the IT field is gendered so that men are more likely to reap 'perks' and benefits reflects gender divisions present throughout society. Employers in the 'just-in-time' IT field might not intend to encourage men and discourage women; however, expectations of long, unpredictable work hours are more likely to conflict with women's home- and family-based responsibilities and priorities. As Scott-Dixon (2004) writes, 'Providing opportunities for women in IT that don't address the substantive barriers to their involvement and career development is like providing access to a person in a wheelchair by installing a staircase' (2004: 183).

Some recent scholarship focuses on how working with IT affects women's gender, as well as professional, identity. Adam et al. (2006) assert that women in the IT field must construct strategies to deal with challenges, not only to their technical expertise and capabilities, but also to their gender identity. They posit that female IT workers cope in this field by diminishing their femininity, becoming 'it' rather than 'he' or 'she'. We return to our analysis of these binary divisions following an overview of our study.

Purpose and methodology

Our study was one of 12 case studies in the Canada-wide Work and Lifelong Learning (WALL) network.[2] Case study teams brought together academic researchers with community-based experts to investigate different settings of work-related learning. We were based at the University of British Columbia, and our partner was a Toronto-based umbrella organisation of non-profit training providers called A Commitment to Training and Employment for Women (ACTEW). Working from a feminist perspective, we conducted 75 life-history interviews with mostly white and middle-class women working in various IT occupations in Vancouver, Victoria and Toronto.

Borrowing from feminist standpoint theory, we wanted to invite women, whose voices and experiences are overlooked in mainstream accounts of the IT field, to articulate a 'counternarrative' (Margolis & Fisher 2002). This is not to imply that we see women as a uniform group. As Nancy Hartsock (1997) clarifies, what is at issue is 'a complex interplay of "individuals" and larger-scale social forces...Moreover, the constitution of the "collective subject" posited by standpoint theories requires an always contingent and fragile (re)construction/transformation of these complex subject positions' (1997: 372).

Our participants were between 24 and 60 years old. One noteworthy point is that most of them did not have children. Many were fairly young and might still have children; on the other hand, we wonder if the relative lack of parenting responsibilities among participants reflects the image of this field as highly demanding of workers' time.

Participants worked in diverse areas, including project management, database development, website design, help-desk support, technical writing and secretarial work. We also talked to a few computer programmers, software engineers and network administrators — jobs typically seen as IT work. We purposefully sought women who did not have a computing science or engineering degree, the credentials at the centre of the IT field. Most participants had completed some form of post-secondary education, mainly in the social sciences or the arts, and had worked in other jobs before coming to IT. Except for the few women who had completed IT-related programmes immediately after high school, entry into the IT field was usually serendipitous.

Once they entered the IT field, participants engaged in a complex mix of on- and off-the-job learning, much of which was self-directed. They described learning informally by playing with their computers, observing and listening to others, asking questions and using intuition. In terms of technical resources, participants relied on manuals, help functions, listservs or chat rooms and, to a lesser extent, books and periodicals. Many participants also recognised the importance of emotional support, and cited mentors, supervisors, and networks of colleagues, peers and ex-classmates as crucial in their learning. Finally, some participants described 'lunch-and-learns' or other organised learning opportunities in their workplaces. These were appreciated as a way to share information and build positive relations with colleagues.

Regardless of their educational backgrounds, work settings and jobs, almost all the participants had completed an IT-related course or short programme. Some had earned a diploma or gained a professional credential, while others had taken workshops or seminars. We turn now to our analysis of several binaries that we found to be both problematic and persistent ways that framed our participants' lived experience in the IT field.

Female/male

Although 'there is no single version of "masculinity" or "femininity", and people's gender ideologies can be fluid and diverse' (Selwyn 2007: 534), many spheres of activity are characterised as masculine or feminine. We concur with Huws (2000) that gender discrepancies in IT are largely explained by the complex interplay between skill development, occupation and gender, all of which operate in the context of patriarchy and capitalism. As women working in a man's field, female IT workers embody both sides of the male/female binary. During their interviews, many participants suggested some of the implications of this for their identity construction. For some, IT moved into the background of their identities, as other, more stereotypically feminine qualities moved into the foreground. In her comments, Marion,[3] a credentialed network administrator in a non-profit community agency, recalled the provisional attachment that women often have to IT skills and work (Woodfield 2000):

> Kaela: ...And so would you describe yourself as an IT worker?
>
> Marion: I have trouble saying that, because I don't think I'm quite there yet. I don't feel confident or have the experience yet.
>
> Kaela: So it's an expertise issue. Okay, so how do you describe yourself to other people?
>
> Marion: Oh, I work with the computers in this place or whatever...
>
> Kaela: Is that an important part of your job, [working in this place]?...
>
> Marion: Definitely. This is a really important place socially and politically. I mean, I'm so glad that I have the chance to work in an organisation like this because with my other background I wouldn't be doing anything in a place like this. So it is very important, yeah.

Another response to this binary surfaced in interviews during which participants eagerly adopted their identity as an IT worker. It was their identity as a woman that became more provisional. This recalls Adam et al.'s (2006) point that women in IT downplay their femininity. While many participants acknowledged having to temper their inclination to be sensitive and open, and learn how to be 'thick-skinned', we identified three participants who discussed their preference for working in a masculine environment. They appreciated the blunt style of communication that was permissible, and welcomed a work setting where they did not feel pressured to compete with peers around fashion and appearance. Claire, a self-educated computer programmer/architect, offered this comment:

> I think to succeed you have to be masculine. Guys are a different animal, and I think part of the problem is like, I'll yell at [my colleague], I don't mean anything by it, I'm not mad at [him]. I'm just mad and I'm like, just do it! And to do that to a woman, like in general, you have to be careful because they're like, 'Well, what do you mean by that?' We have to talk about it. No, there's no feelings, there's no emotion, it's just, I need you to do it and I said it too loud.

One participant saw gender as an issue in her workplace in still another way. Recently promoted to a management position, she thought that her employer was sensitive to the optics of a male-dominated workplace. In her mind, this political correctness helped balance her chances with those of generally favoured male colleagues.

Some participants also described a form of 'ageism' in the very youthful IT field that was noted by both older and young participants. Older participants thought that their skills and knowledge were often overlooked and questioned, especially if they had tried to enter the field after their early thirties. Even in this youthful field, however, some participants wondered how their own youth was perceived. They sensed that supervisors and colleagues thought that they lacked professional experience and technical knowledge. While generally valued in IT workers, youth became one more reason to doubt the competence of women.

Formal/informal learning

Although they all relied heavily on informal learning in the course of everyday work and social interaction, most of the participants had completed some sort of organised IT-related education or training. In their interviews, participants discussed their alternating use of formal and informal learning. Although some scholars further refine the classification of learning, using terms such as 'incidental' or 'non-formal' (see Colley et al. 2002), in this chapter we simply refer to formal learning, which is based in the classroom, and informal learning, which occurs outside an intentionally educational setting.

Rather than trying to refine further the distinction between forms of learning, some scholars dispute the possibility of distinguishing forms of learning on the basis of their (in)formality. Concentrating on workplace learning, Stephen Billett (2006) argues that to characterise learning in educational programmes as formal and learning in the workplace as informal is not only misleading, it also reinforces social structures and inequities. As he explains, 'Workplace learning experiences are shaped by structural factors associated with work practices. These regulate and are reproduced by the division of labour and by the distribution of opportunities for participation in work, and learning about it' (2006: 32). What is commonly thought of as informal work-based learning is, according to this logic, formalised according to the politics of gender, class and race, which are never absent. Returning to a formal learning setting, Tisdale (1998) clarifies that gender, race and class are also manifest in the classroom. As they participate in and observe the goings-on of their classes, students can also learn about social relations and the politics of education.

Helen Colley et al. (2002) suggest that, rather than seeing formal and informal learning as dichotomies, 'our research suggests that it is high time to step outside the frames of this contest between formal and informal learning, in which each set of protagonists exaggerates the weaknesses of the opposite case' (2002: 9). Discussing several case studies, they relate informal learning to formalised curriculum. Informal learning is seen as helping students develop stronger skills and knowledge. Within the classroom, students are continually exposed to and participate in learning beyond the intended curriculum.

This more nuanced understanding of formal and informal learning was clearly articulated in one of our interviews. In this excerpt, Fiona explained how the line between formal and informal learning was blurred as students first developed impromptu processes outside the formal classroom, and then structured them:

> Fiona: I was quite disappointed with the programme. Because they just throw you the book and say learn it. When you put your hand up and...ask for help, well, I don't know. The teacher's not here, and I say, well, hello. We don't get the chance to take apart the computer and put it together...
>
> Shauna: So you were just basically book learning and no hands-on?
>
> Fiona: No hands-on. My hands-on, I actually had...students, like my classmates, we came here [to my home], we set up four stations, we all take a computer apart and put it together and some know more than the others and some don't know nothing. Hey, what's going on here, why is it not working? And then they learn, let's figure that out.
>
> Shauna: They didn't set that up at all at the school?
>
> Fiona: No...they didn't. They have a tech room but they don't use it and the tech teacher is never there. Hello? And we were supposed to acquire 300 tech hours. We never had them, we never had them.

Through a process that was both formal and informal, Fiona learned a hard lesson about a central function of formal education in the context of corporate globalisation. Increasingly framed as a starting point for career development, formal credentials often replace learning as the notable, desired outcome. This recalls Philip Brown's (2003) point that 'if one does not play the game, there is little chance of winning.

This is the *opportunity trap* as few can afford to opt out of the competition for a livelihood' (2003: 142; italics in original).

Learning/work

> I remember when I first started I said to the guy who now is our VP of product development,…I don't understand what's going on. Can you just direct me to a book or something that I can read and get up to speed on? He looked at me and said, 'We're the only ones doing this'. You're going to have to sit in on more meetings and you're going to have to learn more of it. It's all about being here and being part of what's going on… And I'm a good researcher. I mean, I've had to have been over my years at school, right. So the research skills are very, very handy. I use…the internet…all the time for researching. I talk to our guys about what they're doing and how they're doing it and try to get information that way. If I ever come across books I grab them. (Connie, operations manager at a high-tech firm)

As Connie pointed out, the IT field demands continual learning. While participants appreciated this, they also found it stressful given the rapid and constant changes in technology and the demand to 'keep up', as well as the financial costs involved in purchasing hardware and software, and the need to budget money and time for training. While some employers provided or financed IT training, most participants drew on their own resources at least some of the time. Not surprisingly, workers in unionised workplaces typically had greater employer support for formal learning. Technical IT training emphasising formulaic learning, although common, did not transfer easily to participants' work settings. Recalling research discussed above (Margolis & Fisher 2002; Turkle & Papert 1990), participants preferred education grounded in real-life, team-based problem solving. For some, such as Connie, the only way to develop essential knowledge was to be on the job. Moreover, even participants with IT-related credentials agreed that they could not rely on a programme to teach them everything they needed to know. As Marion explained, 'I would say I learn something every time I try to solve a problem. I mean it's not every time now because I keep running into the same problems but…I would say informal learning is part of the job.' Regardless of the job, work is a site of learning.

Some participants found that the time for informal learning during work hours was limited; for them, learning 'ate into' their home lives. Because it is impossible to be an expert in all areas, specialisation is an increasingly recognised necessity in the IT field. This can create a sense of having to predict where things are headed, and a realisation that making a mistaken prediction can have high long-term costs. Technical learning, whether it happened at the workplace or on participants' own time, and whether or not it was supported and recognised by employers, was a steady part of the work that participants did to maintain and advance their IT careers. Learning is a demanding – if also rewarding – form of work.

Hard skills/soft skills

Skills are often described as 'hard' or 'soft', discursive clues about the role of gender in this arena. In general, hard skills refer to those that are technical; in the IT field, these are generally assumed to be developed through relevant education and work in the central niches of the IT field. Because both these educational programmes and occupational niches are highly masculinised, 'hard skills' becomes code for masculine. In contrast, 'soft skills' refers to the interpersonal, communication and organisational skills that are seen as feminine qualities. The use of the words *hard* and *soft* is insidious, however, as the former term implies skills that are solidly entrenched and evident, while the latter implies a lack of definition and reliability.

Employers generally valued participants' communication, teamwork and problem-solving skills, understanding them as crucial to the development, provision and marketing of IT products and services. Like the women in Woodfield's (2000) study, many of our participants also encountered discrimination, as their IT skills were tested or questioned while men's IT knowledge was assumed. For example, Sally discussed how her skills and knowledge were doubted simply because she was a woman:

> One thing that I have noticed working here is that it's a bit of a fight because people perceive me as the assistant, as the secretary. People tell my co-worker all the time, 'You've got a great secretary'. It's kind of the old boys' network, right? So they see me as a secretary. What do you do?

The presence of one set of skills, embodied in female workers, seemed to convey the automatic absence of another set of skills. This was exacerbated in workplaces and settings where jargon was a marker of knowledge and status. Linda, whose job included technical writing at a high-tech firm, said this in her interview:

> Linda: [W]e used to do these lunch-and-learns and they kind of make you sit down and understand everything. And if I had to turn around and tell it back to them, I couldn't do it. I don't know if it's because I don't have that background knowledge so I don't have the sort of jargon…to explain back what's just been told to me. And I'm trying so hard to understand it when they're telling me that I probably don't take the time to remember the words they're using, like I'm just visualising what they're saying to me, so I'm not actually taking it in as…as words…All I can see is this picture in my head…What do they call those little Russian dolls, you know, I mean the information just keeps getting tucked inside another doll and then it gets sent out and…which is pretty much what happens but they would just be horrified if that's how I explained it to them.
>
> Kaela: Why would they be horrified?…
>
> Linda: I don't…actually, now that you've asked…I don't really think they would be horrified. They'd probably think it was cute, oh, isn't that cute!

Although Linda's metaphor of nested dolls could be understood as a creative, sophisticated, alternative representation of technology, she knew that it would be demeaned in her workplace. IT jargon reinstates the hard skills/soft skills binary division, justifying the association between soft communication skills and a lack of technical know-how.

Centre/periphery

So far we have talked about learning that helps people *do* their jobs better in the context of workplace standards, as well as learning that helps them *understand* their jobs and workplaces better in the context of a broader political economy. Still another way of talking about learning is as the manifestation of *relating* to others through shared practice. This is the conception of learning developed by Jean Lave and Etienne Wenger (1991). Their paradigm sees practice in communities, such as workplaces, as a learning process and outlines an inclination for novices to move from the periphery of the community of practice towards its centre, as they gain relevant experience and expertise and build relationships.

Lave and Wenger (1991) insist that what they call 'legitimate peripheral participation' is understandable only as a singular concept, rather than in terms of an amalgam of three distinct conceptual binaries: legitimate versus illegitimate, peripheral versus central, and participation versus non-participation. As they explain:

> Given the complex, differentiated nature of communities, it seems important not to reduce the end point of centripetal participation in a community of practice to a uniform or univocal 'centre,' or to a linear notion of skill acquisition…The partial participation of newcomers is by no means 'disconnected' from the practice of interest. Furthermore, it is also a dynamic concept. In this sense, peripherality, when it is enabled, suggests an opening, a way of gaining access to sources for understanding through growing involvement. (1991: 36–37)

Although we agree with Lave and Wenger (1991) and others (see Colley et al. 2002) that adult learning is relational, situational and experiential, we disagree with the insistence that legitimate peripheral participation cannot and, more importantly, *should* not be split into its constitutive elements. It makes sense to talk about a periphery only if there is a centre. Like periphery, centrality is relational and fluid; however, as we have already explained above, social relations are structured so that cultural status and material success tend to be distributed in particular ways within a community or society. Although Lave and Wenger (1991) acknowledge that identity and status are politically contested, other scholars note that they do not deal satisfactorily with this reality (see Fuller et al. 2005). We surmise that newcomers – such as women in the IT field – both confirm and disrupt discourses and practices of legitimate peripheral participation and communities of practice.

In thinking about IT workplaces as communities of practice, we were interested in how participants traced their learning about and practice of gender politics. Melanie, a project manager/technical trainer, articulated what became a typical refrain:

I mean, it's still such an old boys' network, the domain of software. I mean, you go into a software company and the programming department is likely to be 80 per cent men. What do they joke about? They joke about, you know, they make offensive sexual comments. And, as a woman, you are, you end up being uncomfortable. But what can you say? You are completely in an environment where you...there isn't a space to say, 'You know what,...I don't really like that'.

We were struck by repeated references to the IT field as a 'boys' club'. Even participants who did not use that term agreed that it was an appropriate descriptor. Part of their informal learning was developing a deeper understanding of the social structures noted by Tisdale (1998), and of how to be women within structures that privilege men. This is similar to the considerations outlined in another WALL study about disabled individuals employed in the banking sector. Like their 'regular' (Church et al. 2006: 4) colleagues, disabled workers have to learn how to do their job tasks; additionally, they learn about the importance of 'keeping up', 'waiting', 'making claims' and 'keeping it light'. Learning how to relate to a masculine centre as women on the periphery is a complicated, often unspoken, part of participants' work and learning in their communities of practice.

Despite the range of responses to the meaning of gender in the IT field reviewed above, the most common message among participants was one of concern and discomfort. In our conversations with participants who had worked in central IT settings such as software programming companies or jobs, several women, including Melanie, described their attempts or desires to move out of the centre of the IT field to more peripheral, feminised niches such as website design, project management or technical writing. This suggests that Lave and Wenger's (1991) assumption about the inclination to move towards the centre is not always indicated. Sometimes, peripheral participation can be legitimate even for experienced community members.

Conclusion

We have reviewed several binary categorisations that are evident in our exploration of women's learning and work in Canada's IT field. Our analysis challenges the efficacy of an either/or distinction between categories such as formal and informal learning, learning and work, and hard and soft skills, even as it reinstates these categories in terms of a both/and understanding of them. Our concluding discussion of communities of practice and the division between centre and periphery similarly reinterprets these categories, offering a comment on the limitations of Lave and Wenger's (1991) model. We dispute the notion that the centre of a community of practice is always the ideal destination for community members, illustrating that individuals can develop critiques of the centre and construct, through their learning-in-practice, legitimate and well-reasoned identities based in peripheral locations.

Notes

1   This chapter first appeared in the *Journal of Workplace Learning* 20(7/8): 514–525 (2008), © Emerald Group Publishing Limited, all rights reserved. It is reproduced here with permission.

2   WALL was funded by the Social Sciences and Humanities Research Council of Canada's Initiatives of the New Economy programme, and coordinated by David Livingstone at the Ontario Institute for Studies in Education, University of Toronto.

3   Pseudonyms are used in place of interviewees' names.

References

Adam A, Griffiths M, Keogh C, Moore K, Richardson H & Tattersall A (2006) Being an 'it' in IT: Gendered identities in IT work. *European Journal of Information Systems* 15(4): 368–378

Billett S (2006) Constituting the workplace curriculum. *Journal of Curriculum Studies* 38(1): 31–48

Brown P (2003) The opportunity trap: Education and employment in a global economy. *European Education Research Journal* 2(1): 141–179

Church K, Panitch M, Frazee C & Luciani T (2006) Recognising the invisible work of doing corporate disability. Paper presented at Rethinking Work and Learning: Research Findings and Policy Challenges Workshop, Toronto, Canada (4–5 June)

Colley H, Hodkinson P & Malcolm J (2002) *Non-formal learning: Mapping the conceptual terrain. A consultation report.* Leeds: University of Leeds Lifelong Learning Institute. Accessed 12 March 2009, http://www.infed.org/archives/e-texts/colley_informal_learning.htm

Fuller A, Hodkinson H, Hodkinson P & Unwin L (2005) Learning as peripheral participation in communities of practice: A reassessment of key concepts in workplace learning. *British Educational Research Journal* 31(1): 49–68

Habtu R (2003) Information technology workers. *Perspectives on Labour and Income* (Statistics Canada, Catalogue 75-001-XIE) (July): 5–11

Hartsock NCM (1997) Comment on Hekman's 'Truth and method: Feminist standpoint theory revisited': Truth or justice? *Signs: Journal of Culture and Society* 22(21): 367–374

Huws U (2000) The changing gender division of labour in the transition to the knowledge society. In K Rubenson & HG Schuetze (eds) *Transition to the knowledge society: Policies and strategies for individual participation and learning.* Vancouver: Institute for European Studies, University of British Columbia

Lave J & Wenger E (1991) *Situated learning: Legitimate peripheral participation.* Cambridge: Cambridge University Press

Margolis J & Fisher A (2002) *Unlocking the clubhouse: Women in computing.* Cambridge, MA, and London: MIT Press

Miller J & Jagger N (2001) *Women in ITEC courses and careers. Final report.* Department for Education and Skills, Government of the United Kingdom. Accessed 7 January 2004, http://www.dfes.gov.uk/research/data/uploadfiles/ACFE89.pdf

Panteli N, Stack J & Ramsay H (2001) Gendered patterns in computing work in the late 1990s. *New Technology, Work and Employment* 16(1): 3–17

Scott-Dixon K (2004) *Doing IT: Women working in information technology.* Toronto: Sumach Press

Selwyn N (2007) Hi-tech = guy-tech? An exploration of undergraduate students' gendered perceptions of information and communication technologies. *Sex Roles* 56: 525–536

Tisdale EJ (1998) Poststructural feminist pedagogies: The possibilities and limitations of feminist emancipatory adult learning theory and practice. *Adult Education Quarterly* 48(3): 139–157

Turkle S & Papert S (1990) Epistemological pluralism: Styles and voices within the computer culture. *Signs: Journal of Women in Culture and Society* 16(1): 128–157

Woodfield R (2000) *Women, work and computing.* Cambridge: Cambridge University Press

4 Making different equal? Rifts and rupture in state and policy: The National Qualifications Framework in South Africa

Rosemary Lugg

Introduction

The first piece of education legislation passed by South Africa's first democratically elected government provided for the development of a National Qualifications Framework (NQF).[1] By integrating education and training through a coherent approach to qualifications, the framework was intended to build new forms of equality across apartheid's differences, not only between education and training but across other divisions they buttressed. Yet by 2001, only six years after the idea of an NQF had enjoyed extraordinary consensus in Parliament, the minister of education was so concerned about its implementation that he commissioned a review of progress (DoE/DoL 2002). The review revealed widespread dissatisfaction with practices associated with the NQF, and a deep rift between the fields of education and training that threatened integration. It seemed that instead of weakening differences, the NQF had strengthened them.

This chapter[2] explains the development of the NQF[3] and its failure to bring the worlds of education and training closer together through an examination of its discursive construction. By engaging Laclau and Mouffe's (1985) discourse theory, struggles over education policy in the post-apartheid era in South Africa are discussed and located within the broader, complex power struggles between state and institutions of civil society, including struggles over the nature of the state.[4] Formed through social practices, discourses join objects within relational systems of meaning, but in excluding possibilities give rise to frontiers or 'antagonisms' (Laclau & Mouffe 1985). At frontiers, meanings are contested and power enacted through two political logics: equivalence and difference. Through a 'logic of equivalence', differences within a discourse are weakened by a shared opposition to an external, excluded force and simultaneously equivalences between internal differences are strengthened. In contrast, practices involving a 'logic of difference' attempt to weaken antagonism by breaking down chains that structure the opposing discourse, and assimilating elements of it into its own order (Howarth & Stavrakakis 2000).

In examining the making of the South African NQF, this chapter explores how antagonisms were constructed through varying forms of equivalence and difference, shaping education and training policy discourses across the changing political conditions. However, the process of forming NQF policy and the subsequent crisis cannot be understood in isolation from a second set of discursive practices with which it is interwoven throughout the period under review, a discourse I call the 'single system' of education and training. The chapter shows how practices building these two discourses constructed the frontier with the apartheid state differently during the transition, were articulated with contradictory globalised discursive practices and were associated with differing forms of the post-apartheid state.

The sections that follow trace the development of the NQF through seven historical periods, each characterised by different hegemonic political discourses with shifts between hegemonic regimes marked by key political moments.

1. Equivalent struggles against apartheid

Roots of the NQF as a policy for post-apartheid South Africa can be traced to struggles against apartheid's fragmented and racially divided education system. The idea of an 'integrated system' of education and training emerged through practices within organised labour (McGrath 1996; Spreen 2001; Lugg 2007). Built in opposition to apartheid, these practices were characterised by strong, democratic structures (Cooper et al. 2002; Kraak 1993) that articulated workers' demands for wages and equitable participation in the workplace (Kraak 1993).

The demand for a 'single system' of education and training emerged through struggles against the iniquitous practices of apartheid's education for black children. An education alliance, the National Education Crisis Committee, united students, parents and teachers in opposition to apartheid education through the construction of a single education campaign called 'People's Education' (Kruss 1987; Motala & Vally 2002). People's Education articulated demands for a non-racial education and developed new education practices within captured spaces in schools and universities (National Education Crisis Committee 1985).

Differences between struggles in the workplace and in education were weakened within the discourse of liberation through shared antagonism to apartheid, and initially the two discursive streams developed in support of each other. However, the apartheid state's response to each differed. Expanding hegemonic control in industrial relations through a logic of difference, government reforms assimilated elements of the opposition into some sites (for example, black trade unions were invited to join the Industrial Council system) but excluded them from others (for example, black trade unions were excluded from the tripartite National Training Board [NTB]) (Marais 1998; Kraak 1993). In contrast, in the field of education the regime's antagonism to liberation remained resolute. The apartheid government refused to negotiate with the education alliance, banned the discussion of People's Education on school premises and detained several National Education Crisis Committee leaders (Kruss 1987; Levin 1991). Constructing the frontier through a logic of equivalence, a strong boundary between the state and the opposition movement for education was maintained.

2. 'Stakeholders' prepare to negotiate

On 2 February 1990, then President FW de Klerk announced the unbanning of political parties, including the African National Congress (ANC), and the unconditional release of political prisoners. The unbanning weakened antagonism between the discourses of apartheid and liberation but did not dissolve it. Instead, it heralded a new form of engagement: 'stakeholder negotiation'. Within new social relations, the apartheid state continued to construct the frontier with the liberation movement differently in education and industrial relations. Links between political negotiation and re-entry into a global economy made discussions about economic development meaningful, and in 1991 the state agreed to the participation of the black trade union federation, the Congress of South African Trade Unions (COSATU), in the NTB, opening up dialogue on training. In contrast, determined to protect institutionalised privilege, the apartheid state remained impervious to negotiation on education and made it clear that it retained control over decisions on education until a new Constitution came into force (Metcalfe et al. 1992). Even so, now positioned as 'stakeholders', organisations built through the practices of liberation became key sites for the formulation of new education and training policy options.

A COSATU affiliate, the National Union of Metalworkers of South Africa (NUMSA), built on the strengths of organised labour to generate policies that would deliver on workers' demands for wages and democratic participation in the economy. In changing political conditions the frontier with apartheid began to be redrawn as groups within organised labour began to view *global* markets and international competition as the new threat to workers' survival. Drawing on international discussions about social democratic alternatives to state socialism (McGrath & Badroodien 2006) and on strategies that had benefited organised labour in Australia and Canada, NUMSA's leaders argued that South African workers' interests would be best protected through a new corporatist pact between the state, labour and business and a shared focus on a high-skill labour market strategy to drive economic growth (Kraak 1992; McGrath 1996). South African workers' demands for wages and participation became rearticulated into new chains linking negotiated consensus, economic development, job security, skills and training. Recognising that high-skills policies would exclude millions of workers denied access to education under apartheid, NUMSA's training policies became partly constituted in terms of expansion of education. The idea of an 'integrated system' of training and education emerged, with equivalence between learning pathways constructed through qualifications.

Discursive practices concerned with a 'single system' of education and training strengthened through a policy process established by the education alliance of the National Education Coordinating (formerly Crisis) Committee, known as the National Education Policy Initiative (NEPI). Here, the antagonism to apartheid education was maintained. Constructing the frontier through a logic of equivalence and strengthening chains set up by People's Education, the new education system would be everything that apartheid education was not: a unitary system founded on non-sexism, non-racism, redress and democracy (National Education Coordinating

Committee 1993). NEPI set up research groups on sectors that would make up a 'single system' of non-racial education and training, establishing new sites of difference.

The NEPI research group set up to develop policy proposals for the human resources development (HRD) sector became the site where discursive practices associated with organised labour's proposals for an 'integrated system' came into conflict with practices building a 'single system'. Constructing the frontier between them through a logic of equivalence, the 'single system' excluded elements structuring the 'integrated system' – namely, negotiated institutional reform, a corporatist state, and integration of education and training through a framework of qualifications. Drawing on different international discussions, in particular on experiences of late industrialising economies, practices building a 'single system' articulated a strong interventionist post-apartheid state that would focus on the delivery of education and training and would prioritise resources to the most marginalised (Wolpe 1992; Bennell 1992; Swainson 1992). A rupture began to develop within the mass democratic movement with one frontier crystallising in opposition to discursive chains helping to forge new equivalences within negotiations on training. The NEPI leadership attempted to suture the rupture within the movement by refusing to make policy choices within its framework report, and by articulating the idea of a framework for qualifications into its recommendations. Supporting the system of difference underpinning the 'single system', it proposed that curriculum councils and qualification boards be established in each education and training sector (National Education Coordinating Committee 1993).

3. Sufficient consensus

In response to levels of violence, negotiation practices changed at the end of 1992 and the transition came to be characterised by a more direct engagement between the ANC and the National Party (Atkinson 1994). In a drive to secure a political settlement the practice of trading away policies to reach 'sufficient consensus' became hegemonic. Two individuals seeking the terms of a settlement on behalf of their constituencies was not uncommon (Guelke 1999; Shaw 1994). The discourse of sufficient consensus put the government under pressure to establish a negotiation forum on education, and the National Education and Training Forum was set up (Chisholm & Kgobe 1993; Badat 1995). However, education remained a key site of conflict between the apartheid government and the ANC, and continued to be strongly linked to the negotiations for an Interim Constitution (Nzimande 2001). In the NTB, however, practices of 'sufficient consensus' shaped the nature of the settlement on training policy, and the government's refusal to negotiate on education aided its hegemonic expansion.

Through practices of sufficient consensus, organised labour's proposals for an 'integrated system' of education and training became rearticulated as a recommendation for an NQF. The settlement was aided in part by different training board constituencies looking to similar international experiences of education and training reform in Commonwealth countries (Jansen 2001; McGrath & Badroodien 2006). However, the construction of a new alliance also emerged in the context of new frontiers. Resistance from white craft unions to black workers' proposals for a framework of training qualifications gave rise to antagonism between those supportive of a settlement on training and those against reform, strengthening equivalences being forged through negotiations across frontiers of state, business and labour. A second frontier emerged through business and COSATU's shared antagonism to apartheid's education and training institutions (NTB 1994). While excluding education institutions through differing discursive practices, coherent displacement of apartheid's education providers enabled agreement on a new system of meaning: a framework of new standards in education and training that all providers would be required to meet. If 'sufficient consensus' on labour's demands for an 'integrated system' was achieved through a settlement on an NQF, it represented the *limits* to that agreement. An NQF was acceptable to those resistant to fundamental institutional change because it represented 'the least intrusive option… for an integrated approach to education and training' (NTB 1993: Appendix 2, section 2.2). The NQF presented practices to reform education and training in ways that need not necessarily bring about profound change.

Distanced from substantive negotiations on education, policies for the 'single system' of education and training were strengthened within the ANC's Centre for Education Policy Development (CEPD). Here, the system of difference established by the education alliance in NEPI was maintained by research groups on discrete sectors of education and training. Suturing the rupture within the mass democratic movement exposed within NEPI, and building equivalence with negotiation processes taking place in the NTB, an additional working group on the NQF was added to the education policy chain. In contrast to the NTB, where the NQF sought to weaken differences between education and training, in the education policy process the NQF was positioned as a discrete site of difference, equivalent to other areas of education and training. Informed by practices concerned with building sufficient consensus, the NQF group extended membership beyond the mass democratic movement and included members of the NTB alliance. Structures to implement the NQF proposed by the NTB – namely a South African Qualifications Authority (SAQA) and standard-setting bodies – were also advocated by formal ANC policy statements emerging from the CEPD. However here, as in NEPI, they worked to support equivalences structuring the 'single system' (ANC 1994).

Different institutional arrangements were subsequently proposed, however, in the implementation plan produced by the CEPD's NQF research group. This proposed that SAQA would be a stakeholder body and would establish two types of institution that would cut across all sectors of education and training: National Standards Bodies (NSBs) to register standards on the NQF, and Education and Training Qualification Authorities to accredit providers and assessors (CEPD 1994). Constructed as agents for change, these new structures were argued to be necessary given 'vested interests operating in education at the time'.[5] Yet, in so doing, practices holding the NQF to the post-apartheid state and constructing equivalences within the 'single system' were weakened once again. Institutions articulated within each of the differing discourses would become sites of future contestation, revealing antagonisms and rifts within the post-apartheid state.

4. National unity

On 27 April 1994 South Africa's first democratic elections brought an ANC government to power. Although President Mandela's inauguration signalled the beginning of post-apartheid South Africa, the establishment of a Government of National Unity effectively extended the transition for a further five years. Practices building national unity continued to weaken difference between the outgoing regime and the incoming ANC government (Nzimande 2001), as earlier imperatives to secure 'sufficient consensus' were replaced by a commitment to reconstruction, development and reconciliation. Power continued to be practised within stakeholder structures, although the main sites now shifted to structures associated with government. The discourse of national unity supported the expansion of both education and training projects immanent within the mass democratic movement. However, building on logics established during the transition, the two projects continued to be structured in contradictory ways, and came to be driven from different parts of the post-apartheid state. Responsibility for the NQF became lodged within a new statutory body called the South African Qualifications Authority (SAQA). The Department of Education (DoE) began the challenging task of forming a 'single system' of non-racial education and training out of apartheid's multiple, fragmented, racially-based systems.

In keeping with discursive practices for national unity, the newly appointed ANC ministers of education and labour set up a stakeholder structure, the Inter-Ministerial Working Group, to develop consensus on an appropriate way forward on the NQF. The group was asked to draft legislation that would establish SAQA and the NQF, and also to provide advice about whether, as a strategy for integration, the training responsibilities of the Department of Labour (DoL) should be transferred to the DoE (McGrath 1996). The government's commitment to the NQF as part of an integrated approach to education and training was stated clearly in its first White Paper on education and training in March 1995 (DoE 1995a). Here, integration was expressed as 'a view of learning which rejects a rigid division between "academic" and "applied", "theory" and "practice", "knowledge" and "skills", "head" and "hand" ' (DoE 1995a: 7). This construction of the NQF, as 'a universal structure or institution, covering the entire national learning system…which did not exclude…downgrade… or] privilege'[6] resonated with the 'single system's' concern with equity.

During the process of public consultation on the draft Act, this coherence enabled progressive interest groups within the Higher Education (HE) sector to support participation in the NQF. Framed by the discourse of national unity, associations between the NQF and inclusion *also* mirrored the aspirations of the 'rainbow nation'.

Articulated for a moment within a nexus bringing together equity, inclusion and integration, the NQF became overdetermined as a powerful signifier of new social relations. Yet the draft legislation said almost nothing about how the NQF would be developed. In leaving so much unsaid, the NQF took on the role of 'empty signifier', linking different elements into a precarious unity, representing unattainable ideals of closure and fullness by signifying what was absent (Laclau 1996: 53). With the NQF symbolising the ideal of a complete world of equitable learning for all South Africans, the bill 'evoked an extraordinary consensus' in Parliament.[7]

No sooner had the SAQA Act been passed than a frontier between education and training resurfaced. This time practices constructing a new skills development discourse maintained the frontier, and as a result the transfer of the NTB to the DoE did not happen (McGrath 1996). With support from international agencies including the GTZ and the World Bank (McGrath & Badroodien 2006), newly appointed officials within the DoL were moving ahead with the development of active labour market policies. These linked corporatist governance by state, employers and labour with the transformation of the training boards, new strategies for skills development and a compulsory training levy – chains that would have been ruptured by the removal of the NTB from the DoL. Policy-makers chose to protect chains structuring an increasingly powerful skills development discourse, and maintained responsibility for training.

Lodged within the new state, practices building skills development were constructed in antagonism to education. In contrast to earlier concerns with integration, a Green Paper released in 1997 identified the skills development sector as the 'specific and separate' concern of the DoL (DoL 1997: 5). In contrast to the DoE's responsibility with 'supply side' provision (i.e. public providers), the DoL's policies were concerned with meeting 'demand' for skills and employment. Twenty-five new intermediary institutions called Sector Education and Training Authorities (SETAs) were established in every sector of the economy. In addition to driving skills development in areas of demand, the new SETAs were required to assure the quality of workplace training and in turn be accredited by SAQA for this purpose, articulating SETAs within practices building the NQF and as a site within its system of differences (DoL 1997).

At the same time as the Inter-Ministerial Working Group was driving the development of the SAQA Act and the DoL was constructing skills development, stakeholder processes in every sector of education laid the foundations for the 'single system' of education and training. Practices transforming the HE sector emerged from the National Commission on Higher Education (NCHE). The commission consulted widely within the sector, and drew extensively on research from international higher education policy organisations, and on research undertaken by the Union of Democratic University Staff Associations (Sehoole 2005). The commission proposed that the post-apartheid state would steer the transformation of the sector towards greater access for larger numbers of students from a greater diversity of backgrounds, improved relevance and higher quality (Kraak 2001). This would be achieved by strengthening the capacity of the national department, and establishing the Council on Higher Education (CHE) to advise on policy and to assure quality provision (NCHE 1996). The central role of quality assurance was made clear. National quality-assurance practices linked to incentives would be used to steer institutions towards national goals and 'tackling differences in quality' (NCHE 1996: section 1.4.1).

Within these chains, an interventionist state acting in the interests of development and equity began to emerge in higher education. Similar chains structuring a new Further Education and Training (FET) sector emerged through a fragile stakeholder process, the National Committee on Further Education, and a subsequent Green Paper. These linked the state and its priorities for training and vocational education programmes to the transformation of schools and colleges through a new funding framework (DoE 1998), a stakeholder advisory body on FET and a quality-assurance body responsible for accrediting further education programmes (DoE 1997). Practices building a post-apartheid FET sector also articulated a steering role for the state. The establishment of a quality-assurance body in each sector of education reflected the logics of the 'single system' and sustained proposals that had emerged within earlier education policy processes about how a framework of qualifications might be implemented.

In the schooling sector, separate stakeholder processes were established to develop new policies on school governance and on curriculum. The split resulted from a settlement on the Interim Constitution just before the elections; a single national Ministry of Education would be responsible for setting norms and standards but provincial ministries of education were responsible for delivery (ANC 1994). Responsibility for work on national standards was initially delegated to the education stakeholder body, the National Education and Training Forum, but when it deadlocked, education activists pressed for a more representative stakeholder process and the DoE set up the Consultative Forum on Curriculum (DoE 1995b). In the schooling sector, discursive chains shaping national standards remained linked to the state within corporatist structures, but connections between standards and institutional governance were weakened through the coming together of practices associated with national unity and those of decentralisation.

5. Implementation as hegemonic expansion

As the formal end of the period of the Government of National Unity came into view, ministers placed the bureaucracy under increasing pressure to make visible progress with implementation before the elections in 1999. Lodged within the post-apartheid state, two education and training discourses had become three. Discursive practices building the NQF, skills development and the 'single system' of education and training competed for hegemonic expansion, contributing to a developing rupture in state policy. Intense conflict emerged over two elements articulated by each: standards and quality assurance.

Practices building the NQF were strengthened with the establishment of SAQA in 1996. The first board's decisions reflected hegemonic ideas for the NQF: it would be an eight-level framework with three bands, implemented by two types of structure – National Standards Bodies (NSBs) and Education and Training Quality Assurance bodies (ETQAs) (SAQA 1997). While SAQA drove the establishment of NSBs in 12 areas of learning, what could be described as a laissez-faire approach was advocated for ETQAs. In 2001, quality-assurance agencies were invited to apply for accreditation as an ETQA in one of three categories: social sector, economic sector or education and training subsystem (a category that became known as the 'Band ETQAs') (SAQA 2000). This typology weakened differences between skills and education, making provision for SETAs to apply for registration as 'economic ETQAs' and for the quality-assurance bodies being established in education sectors to apply to become 'Band ETQAs'. Within a year, close to 40 ETQAs had applied to be registered, most of them operating in the HE sector, and many, including all SETAs, operating in the FET sector (DoE/DoL 2002).

Hegemonic expansion of practices building the NQF was most successful in sectors where discursive chains linking standards and provider institutions had been weakened by practices set up by the transition. Although NSBs were established to register standards generated across *all* areas of education and training, only standards generated within the skills development and Adult Basic Education and Training (ABET) sectors came to be associated with them. In the skills sector this was made possible by the coherent positioning of SAQA and the SETA/ETQAs within chains structuring both the discursive practices of the NQF and those building skills development. Indeed, claims that accredited workplace skills were portable across economic sectors *depended* on equivalences set up by the NQF. Articulation of ABET standards benefited from the emphasis placed on standards within earlier COSATU and ANC policies, the work that had been done for some years in this area by the Independent Examinations Board and by the stakeholder forum for ABET. Yet registration of standards stood in stark contrast to provision. Marginalised from practices building a developmental state, public provision in this sector withered (Baatjes & Mathe 2004).

The school curriculum carries a trace of its articulation by discursive practices building the NQF: it is outcomes based. This meaning for school standards was conferred within the Consultative Forum on Curriculum after senior managers in the DoE asked members of the forum to ensure that the school curriculum was consistent with the government's emerging policy on the NQF. The forum's first discussion document asserted that because of requirements laid down by the SAQA Act, the school curriculum had to be outcomes based (DoE 1995b). This was the first time that an outcomes-based approach was advocated for the school curriculum in education policy statements.

In sectors in which programmes remained closely tied to public providers – the FET and HE sectors – standards and qualifications were less easily articulated by practices emanating from SAQA. These sectors presented robust frontiers to the hegemonic expansion of the NQF. Limits to expansion were most starkly revealed in fierce contests over the second moment articulated by each discourse – quality assurance. The existence of multiple ETQAs operating within sectors, and thus within individual provider institutions, gave rise to intense conflict between 'Band ETQAs' (the education quality-assurance bodies) and SETA/ETQAs (the skills development quality-assurance bodies) over meanings and practices of quality assurance. Seeking to weaken antagonism, the 'Band ETQA' in the HE sector, the CHE[8] attempted to coordinate all ETQAs operating in the sector through Memoranda of Understanding (MoU). However, in seeking to assure the quality of programmes provided by institutions of higher education, SETAs not only contested meanings and practices for 'quality assurance'; their presence disrupted and destabilised chains building the 'single system' and linking the sector to an interventionist state. SETAs in higher education threatened the identity of the CHE as *the* quality-assurance agency for higher education, and with this the role of the state in driving institutional change.

Conflict over quality assurance was constructed differently by the 'Band ETQA' operating in the FET sector, known as Umalusi. Deploying a logic of equivalence in constructing the frontier with the NQF, Umalusi refused to engage with SAQA. As a strategy to safeguard the constitutional requirement that provinces deliver education,[9] the Act which established Umalusi stipulated that the Council 'must be regarded as having been accredited' by SAQA.[10] Thus, SAQA could not de-accredit Umalusi, and Umalusi was free to pursue quality-assurance practices as it pleased. Constructing equivalence between SAQA and the SETAs, Umalusi refused to sign MoU with SETAs and to accredit the provision of education unit standards offered by private providers. The limits to the practices of the NQF were starkly revealed by Umalusi's refusal to engage with them.

6. Rupture revealed

At the second democratic elections in June 1999, the ANC was returned to power and Thabo Mbeki inaugurated as president. Mbeki's first term of office was associated with a shift from practices concerned with building national unity that characterised the Mandela era towards new practices that would position South Africa as a leading African nation. The government's neo-liberal Growth, Employment and Redistribution (GEAR) strategy became a long-term adjustment to global realities (Marais 2002; Ryklief 2002). Yet the state was simultaneously constructed as an agent for redistribution, responsible for engineering trade-offs between policies that benefit capital and those that reallocate resources to the poor (Tripartite Alliance 1997; Marais 2002). Within Mbeki's government, the different, contradictory but now equivalent roles of the state were reflected in committee clusters within the Cabinet. The Ministry of Education belonged to social services, a cluster concerned with poverty alleviation and practices building a developmental state. The Ministry of Labour was part of the economics cluster, aligned with practices building a corporatist state.

Held accountable to Cabinet clusters, new practices of policy review emerged within the state. In response to concerns expressed about the NQF, the ministers of education and labour commissioned a study on the implementation of the NQF in 2001 (DoE/ DoL 2002). Bringing antagonism between the 'single system' and 'integration' into the public gaze, the study revealed deepening rifts between the DoE and the DoL, each of which had 'mirror-image perceptions' of threats to education and training from the institutional arrangements of the NQF (DoE/DoL 2002: ii). The DoE held SAQA responsible for problems in implementing the NQF. It experienced SAQA as subverting public education through the proliferation of standards in specific job-related competencies and lack of progress on qualifications for general formative education (DoE/DoL 2002). Constructing equivalence between the NQF and skills, the DoE also contested the 'vigorous marketing by SETAs of unit standards-based qualifications in higher education institutions' (2002: 23), and a lack of regard among SETAs for the ministry's transformation agenda in higher education. Agents of the market acting against the political practices of the developmental state, SETAs subverted transformation. Recommendations from the DoE reflected the logics of the 'single system': SAQA should be brought under the department's direct control, the SETAs kept out of the HE sector and their quality-assurance responsibilities limited to the FET sector (DoE/DoL 2002).

A similar frontier emerged at the limits of practices building skills development. The review revealed that the DoL held the HE sector responsible for problems in implementing the NQF, particularly the CHE. The CHE was experienced as subverting the NQF through its refusal to accept SETAs as part of the institutional landscape within the HE sector. Furthermore, in refusing to accept the SETAs, the CHE was also the enemy of skills development. Excluding the SETAs' skills development programmes (known as learnerships) from the HE sector was viewed as equivalent to excluding the majority of school leavers from opportunities for 'further learning and economically valuable employment' (DoE/DoL 2002: 33), *and* as a rejection of the value of skills. The DoL recommended that a strong SAQA reporting to both ministers should continue to suture the divide between education and skills.

The study team attempted a compromise and recommended that SAQA remain accountable to both departments, and that the SETAs comply with the accreditation practices of Band ETQAs. But the departments did not agree. An interdepartmental task team of senior officials negotiated a new compromise and in 2003 proposals for a new equivalence were made public (DoE/DoL 2003). The departments' new 'interdependent approach' was based on a smaller SAQA with three new Qualifications Councils responsible for standards and quality assurance in three different learning pathways; one for education, one for career-focused education and one for workplace learning (DoE/DoL 2003). It was, in essence, a strategy to construct a new equivalence between the SETA ETQAs and education Band ETQAs, in order to enable engagement on qualifications with a career focus offered by public providers. A period of consultation and debate followed, but for four years the departments failed to make an announcement on the future of the NQF. Mirroring the fracture within the post-apartheid state, the implementation of the NQF was stalled at a frontier between two different constructions of the state at work in different sites within it. SAQA could no longer suture the rift between education and skills development because the discursive practices of each were constructed in antagonism with the other, and because SAQA itself was constructed in conflicting ways by each of the departments. Hegemonic practices forming the state reinforced, rather than weakened, the rupture.

7. Renewed unity?

Following the government's review of its first 10 years of democracy, a new development policy suggested a shift towards a greater emphasis on the leadership of the state in halving unemployment and poverty by 2014 (McGrath & Akoojee 2007), a shift seemingly in keeping with hegemonic expansion of the developmental state. In July 2005, then President Mbeki launched the Accelerated and Shared Growth Initiative for South Africa (ASGISA), which placed skills and education at the core of the state's development strategy. Links to skills development were strengthened through a new committee, the Joint Initiative for Priority Skills Acquisition (JIPSA), and although JIPSA was established to accelerate processes to address priority skills, many of its key strategies are driven by education institutions, for example FET colleges and universities (McGrath & Akoojee 2007; Ministers of Education & Labour 2007).

Arguments that the success of the new development policy depended on skills development provided new impetus for a resolution on the NQF. In September 2007 the ministers of education and labour finally agreed on a joint policy statement on new institutional arrangements (Ministers of Education & Labour 2007). It announced the establishment of three structures, Qualifications and Quality Assurance Councils (QCs), two of which would be based in the existing councils (namely Umalusi and the CHE), and a new body to oversee workplace learning, (to be called the Quality Council for Trades and Occupations [QCTO]). SAQA would be accountable to the minister of education, but the QCTO would be accountable to the minister of labour (Ministers of Education & Labour 2007). Equivalence would now be built across *three* sites of difference through shared involvement in the NQF, and collaboration on quality assurance and qualification design. Whether these new institutional arrangements construct new forms of equivalence between skills and education, whether they mark the articulation of skills by the developmental state in support of equity and poverty reduction, or whether they herald the hegemonic expansion of market forces within the state and its education institutions, only the nature of future conflicts over qualifications and practices to assure their quality will tell.

Conclusion

By considering the discursive construction of the NQF over an extended historical period and across all sectors of the national education and training system, this chapter has documented the significance of bringing 'the state' back into our analysis of education policy. It has shown that in a globalising world, the state retains power to fix meanings for education and training. Practices constructing the state were necessary to the emergence of the NQF in South Africa; its rise was allied with the apartheid state's concern to fix market-friendly practices within the new state *and* its refusal to negotiate on the future of education institutions. The policy's recent crisis has been associated with antagonisms generated within the post-apartheid state, between two constructions of the state – and of the NQF – at work in different sites within it. Each sought to address the state's legitimation and accumulation roles but did so in different ways, through different practices, and by building dissimilar chains of equivalence between the state, its providers and organisations in civil society. Quality-assurance practices and meanings for qualifications linking practices of the corporatist state to labour market opportunities and education service providers differed from those connecting the developmental state with its education institutions.

Although NQFs are being implemented throughout the world (Keevy 2006) and increasingly are taking regionalised forms (Chisholm 2007), the South African experience reveals that local concerns remain significant as borrowed policies become embedded in local contexts (Ozga & Jones 2006; Chisholm 2007; Chisholm & Leyendecker 2008). Local struggles over the NQF have been simultaneously struggles over the nature of the state, the economy, education institutions and the relationships between them – struggles articulating with differing and often contradictory globalised discourses but played out within local histories and political contexts. Articulated within both national policy discourses and globalised discursive practices, NQFs link the national and the global, weakening boundaries between them, and offering points at which global pressures may be brought to bear in the restructuring of nation states, but at which they are also contested.

Fractures built into the South African NQF point to complex and contradictory challenges that states 'at the margins' face when simultaneously articulating with globalised discursive practices and also seeking to establish equitable national education systems. These connections suggest that the future of the NQF in South Africa cannot be separated from ongoing struggles over the nature of the post-apartheid state, and the forms that ethical leadership might take in the face of demands for a globalised economy on the one hand and rampant local poverty and inequality on the other. Through mapping the changing ways in which frontiers were drawn and differences were constructed as equivalent within education policy-making, the chapter has reaffirmed the political and contingent nature of what it means to be equal. A more radical politics of policy-making is called for, one that avoids totalising moves for consensus and recognises difference, that seeks to build new hegemonic formations based on shared commitments to democracy and equality, working to strengthen a developmental post-apartheid state and build new social conditions.[11]

Notes

1 The South African Qualifications Authority Act (Act No. 58 of 1995).

2 This chapter is a revised version of the article 'Making different equal? Fractured state and ruptured policy: The National Qualifications Framework in South Africa', originally published in 2008 in the *International Journal of Educational Development*, copyright Elsevier 2009 (DOI: 10.1016/j.ijedudev.2008.06.001).

3 Much research has examined the South African NQF. Three broad perspectives emerge. For some, the NQF is linked to a radical project transforming relations between the state and market and bringing about social justice through access to education and training for all (Isaacs 2001; Kraak 1998). For others, the policy is inimical to social justice, associated instead with globalised neo-liberal socio-economic policies and a regulatory state (Allais 2007; Chisholm & Fuller 1996; Cooper 1998; Samson & Vally 1996). A third view argues that the nature of the NQF in South Africa is less easily determined, emphasising its association with negotiations and superficial consensus. As a result, the NQF is mired by internal contradictions (Allais 2003; Ensor 2003; Jansen 2001; McGrath 1996; Unterhalter & Young 1994).

4 Discourse analysis has been useful in explaining why progressive change is difficult to achieve (Bacchi 2000). Foucauldian perspectives (e.g. Ball 1993) have been particularly influential in understanding constraints operating in and through discourse. However, these approaches have also been contested for decentring the state (Dale 1992; Hatcher & Troyna 1994). This paper seeks to 're-centre' the state within an examination of policy-making, using Laclau and Mouffe's (1985) theory of discourse. This rejects Foucault's distinction between 'discursive' and 'non-discursive' structures, and argues for a view of the social world as made up of essentially incomplete, articulated sets of discourses (Laclau & Mouffe 1985). Within this ontology, the state can be understood as 'sedimented discourses' (Howarth 2000). The emergence, hegemonic expansion and crisis in implementation of the NQF are explained in terms of conflict and complexity in remaking the South African state.

5 Interview with member of CEPD NQF Research Group (June 2006).

6 Interview with member of Inter-Ministerial Working Group (October 2001).

7 Interview with member of Inter-Ministerial Working Group (October 2001).

8 Specifically the Higher Education Quality Committee within the Council of Higher Education.

9 This refers to the consequences of SAQA not accrediting or de-accrediting a province.

10 General and Further Education and Training Quality Assurance Act (Act. No. 58 of 2001): 6 para 30 pt 5(1).

11 Thanks to Professor Elaine Unterhalter, my PhD supervisor, and to all the policy-makers interviewed in the course of this research.

References

Allais SM (2003) The National Qualifications Framework in South Africa: A democratic project trapped in a neo-liberal paradigm? *Journal of Education and Work* 16(3): 305–324

Allais SM (2007) The rise and fall of the NQF: A critical analysis of the South African National Qualifications Framework. PhD thesis, University of the Witwatersrand, Johannesburg

ANC (African National Congress) (1994) *A policy framework for education and training.* Johannesburg: ANC

Atkinson D (1994) Brokering a miracle? The multiparty negotiating forum. In S Friedman & D Atkinson (eds) *South African review 7. The small miracle: South Africa's negotiated settlement.* Johannesburg: Ravan Press

Baatjes I & Mathe K (2004) Adult basic education and social change in South Africa, 1994–2003. In L Chisholm (ed.) *Changing class: Education and social change in post-apartheid South Africa.* Cape Town: HSRC Press

Bacchi C (2000) Policy as discourse: What does it mean? Where does it get us? *Discourse* 21(1): 45–57

Badat S (1995) Education politics in the transition period. *Comparative Education* 31(2): 141–159

Ball SJ (1993) What is policy? Texts, trajectories and toolboxes. *Discourse* 12(2): 10–17

Bennell P (1992) *Industrial training in the New South Africa: Some lessons from the LICs and MICs.* Paper presented at the NEPI Conference on Human Resources Policy for a New South Africa, Durban, South Africa (10 May)

CEPD (Centre for Education Policy Development) (1994) *A National Qualifications Framework (NQF): Implementation plan including the establishment of the South African Qualifications Authority (SAQA).* Johannesburg: CEPD

Chisholm L (2007) Diffusion of the National Qualifications Framework and outcomes-based education in southern and eastern Africa. *Comparative Education* 43(2): 295–309

Chisholm L & Fuller B (1996) Remember People's Education? Shifting alliances, state-building and South Africa's narrowing policy agenda. *Journal of Education Policy* 11(6): 693–716

Chisholm L & Kgobe P (1993) Gearing up for an integrated system: Policy and conflict in South African education and training. *EPU Quarterly Review of Education and Training in South Africa* (September). Johannesburg: University of the Witwatersrand

Chisholm L & Leyendecker R (2008) Curriculum reform in post-1990s sub-Saharan Africa. *International Journal of Educational Development* 28: 195–205

Cooper L (1998) From 'rolling mass action' to RPL: The changing discourse of experience and learning in the South African labour movement. *Studies in Continuing Education* 20(2): 143–157

Cooper L, Andrew S, Grossman J & Vally S (2002) 'Schools of labour' and 'labour's schools': Worker education under apartheid. In P Kallaway (ed.) *The history of education under apartheid, 1948–1994.* Cape Town: Pearson Education South Africa

Dale R (1992) Whither the state and education policy? Recent work in Australia and New Zealand. *British Journal of Sociology of Education* 13(3): 387–395

DoE (Department of Education, South Africa) (1995a) *White Paper on education and training.* Pretoria: DoE

DoE (1995b) *Curriculum framework for general and further education and training.* Discussion document developed by the Consultative Forum on Curriculum. Pretoria: DoE

DoE (1997) *Report of the National Committee on Further Education: A framework for the transformation of further education and training in South Africa.* Pretoria: DoE

DoE (1998) *Green Paper on further education and training: Preparing for the twenty-first century through education, training and work.* Pretoria: DoE

DoE/DoL (Department of Education/Department of Labour, South Africa) (2002) *Report of the study team on the implementation of the National Qualifications Framework.* Pretoria: DoE and DoL

DoE/DoL (2003) *An interdependent National Qualifications Framework system. Consultative document.* Pretoria: DoE and DoL

DoL (Department of Labour, South Africa) (1997) *Green Paper: Skills development strategy for economic and employment growth in South Africa.* Pretoria: DoL

Ensor P (2003) The National Qualifications Framework and higher education in South Africa: Some epistemological issues. *Journal of Education and Work* 16(3): 325–346

Guelke A (1999) *South Africa in transition: The misunderstood miracle.* London: IB Tauris

Hatcher R & Troyna B (1994) The 'policy cycle': A ball by ball account. *Journal of Education Policy* 9(2): 155–170

Howarth D (2000) *Discourse.* Buckingham: Open University Press

Howarth D & Stavrakakis Y (2000) Introducing discourse theory and political analysis. In D Howarth, AJ Norval & Y Stavrakakis (eds) *Discourse theory and political analysis: Identities, hegemonies and social change.* Manchester: Manchester University Press

Isaacs S (2001) Making the NQF road by walking reflectively, accountably and boldly. In Y Sayed & J Jansen (eds) *Implementing education policies: The South African experience.* Cape Town: UCT Press

Jansen JD (2001) The race for education policy after apartheid. In Y Sayed & J Jansen (eds) *Implementing education policies: The South African experience.* Cape Town: UCT Press

Keevy J (2006) A Foucauldian critique of the development and implementation of the South African National Qualifications Framework. PhD thesis, University of Pretoria, Pretoria, South Africa

Kraak A (1992) *Re-interpreting the equity–development debate and its relevance for higher education in South Africa.* NEPI Working Paper. *Accessed at Resource Centre, Centre for Education Policy Development (CEPD), Braamfontein, South Africa*

Kraak A (1998) *Competing education and training policies: A 'systemic' versus 'unit standards' approach.* Pretoria: HSRC

Kraak A (2001) Policy ambiguity and slippage: Higher education under the new state, 1994–2001. In A Kraak & M Young (eds) *Education in retrospect: Policy and implementation since 1990.* Pretoria/London: HSRC/IoE

Kraak G (1993) *Breaking the chains: Labour in South Africa in the 1970s and 1980s.* London: Pluto Press

Kruss G (1987) *People's Education in South Africa: An examination of the concept.* Cape Town: Centre for Adult and Continuing Education, University of the Western Cape

Laclau E (1996) *Emancipation(s).* London: Verso

Laclau E & Mouffe C (1985) *Hegemony and socialist strategy: Towards a radical democratic politics.* London: Verso

Levin R (1991) People's Education and the politics of negotiations in South Africa. *Perspectives in Education* 12(2): 1–18

Lugg R (2007) Making different equal? Social practices of policy making and the National Qualifications Framework in South Africa between 1985 and 2003. PhD thesis, London University

Marais H (1998) *South Africa – limits to change: The political economy of transformation.* Cape Town: UCT Press/Zed Books

Marais H (2002) The logic of expediency: Post-apartheid shifts in macroeconomic policy. In S Jacobs & R Calland (eds) *Thabo Mbeki's world: The politics and ideology of the South African president.* Pietermaritzburg: University of KwaZulu-Natal Press

McGrath S (1996) Learning to work? Changing discourses on education and training in South Africa, 1976–96. PhD thesis, University of Edinburgh

McGrath S & Akoojee S (2007) Education and skills for development in South Africa: Reflections on the Accelerated and Shared Growth Initiative for South Africa. *International Journal of Education Development* 27: 421–434

McGrath S & Badroodien A (2006) International influences on the evolution of skills development in South Africa. *International Journal of Educational Development* 26: 483–494

Metcalfe M, Vadi I & Nkomo M (1992) From the Mandela Education Delegation to the National Education Conference: Setting the stage for negotiations. *Perspectives in Education* 13(2): 107–122

Ministers of Education & Labour (South Africa) (2007) *Enhancing the efficacy and efficiency of the National Qualifications Framework.* Joint policy statement by the Ministers of Education and Labour. Pretoria: Ministry of Education and Ministry of Labour

Motala S & Vally S (2002) People's Education: From people's power to Tirisano. In P Kallaway (ed.) *The history of education under apartheid, 1948–1994.* Cape Town: Pearson Education South Africa

NCHE (National Commission on Higher Education) (1996) *An overview of a new policy framework for higher education transformation.* Pretoria: NCHE

National Education Crisis Committee (1985) *Resolutions of the National Consultative Conference on the Crisis in Education.* Johannesburg: National Education Crisis Committee

National Education Coordinating Committee (1993) *National education policy investigation: The framework report and final report summaries.* Cape Town: Oxford/National Education Coordinating Committee

NTB (National Training Board) (1993) *NTB Task Team: National training strategy initiative. Working group 2: Draft report.* Pretoria: NTB

NTB (1994) *A discussion document on a national training strategy initiative. Preliminary report by the National Training Board.* Pretoria: NTB

Nzimande B (2001) Inside Parliament: Making laws and contesting policy in South African education. In Y Sayed & J Jansen (eds) *Implementing education policies: The South African experience*. Cape Town: UCT Press

Ozga J & Jones R (2006) Travelling and embedded policy: The case of knowledge transfer. *Journal of Education Policy* 21(1): 1–17

Ryklief S (2002) Does the emperor really have no clothes? Thabo Mbeki and ideology. In S Jacobs & R Calland (eds) *Thabo Mbeki's world: The politics and ideology of the South African president*. Pietermaritzburg: University of KwaZulu-Natal Press

Samson M & Vally S (1996) Snakes and ladders: Promises and potential pitfalls of the NQF. *South African Labour Bulletin* 20(4): 7–14

SAQA (South African Qualifications Authority) (1997) *South African Qualifications Authority Bulletin 1*. Pretoria: SAQA

SAQA (2000) *The National Qualifications Framework and quality assurance*. Pretoria: SAQA

Sehoole M (2005) *Democratising higher education policy: Constraints of reform in post-apartheid South Africa*. London: Routledge

Shaw M (1994) The bloody backdrop: Negotiating violence. In S Friedman and D Atkinson (eds) *South African review 7. The small miracle: South Africa's negotiated settlement*. Johannesburg: Ravan Press

Spreen CA (2001) Globalisation and educational policy borrowing: Mapping outcomes-based education in South Africa. PhD thesis, Columbia University, New York

Swainson N (1992) Training in the informal sector: What has been learned? Paper presented at the NEPI Conference on Human Resources Policy for a New South Africa, Durban (7–10 May)

Tripartite Alliance (1997) Alliance Summit discussion documents. The role of the state. *African Communist* 148(Fourth Quarter): 13–33

Unterhalter E & Young M (1994) Integrating education and training in South Africa: Radical utopia or practical necessity? Paper presented at the Journal of Southern African Studies 20th Anniversary Conference, University of York, York, UK (9–11 September)

Wolpe H (1992) *Towards a short-term negotiating policy on education and training*. NEPI Discussion Document. *Accessed at Resource Centre, Centre for Education Policy Development (CEPD), Braamfontein, South Africa*

5 'Where can I find a conference on short courses?'

Shirley Walters and Freda Daniels

Introduction

Recently a newly appointed colleague at a South African university asked us if we could guide her to 'conferences on short courses', either nationally or internationally. She had been appointed to coordinate the delivery of short courses at her institution. We responded that to the best of our knowledge there were none and that if she was interested in connecting with a community of practitioners and scholars who are engaged in researching, organising, designing or facilitating 'short courses', we suggested she look for conferences relating to continuing education, adult non-formal education or lifelong learning. The question that our colleague posed increased our disquiet as to the possible negative impact of the dominant discourse and practice of 'short-course provision', which has come to describe the offering of accredited or non-accredited courses, programmes, training workshops or seminars that are of limited duration, both in South Africa and elsewhere.

In this chapter we argue that the shift from a discourse of 'continuing education' to one of 'short-course provision' reflects tendencies towards the marketisation and commodification of learning within the contemporary neo-liberal economy. Through a case study of changes in the policy framework and provision of short courses in South Africa since the transition to democracy, we analyse these trends and their impact on practice. To frame our study, we begin with a discussion of assumptions about knowledge and learning and then go on to describe the educational policy underpinning the National Qualifications Framework (NQF) in South Africa that gave rise to the changes we now see. We explore what this shift means in terms of its impact on the pedagogical or organisational practices of continuing education or non-formal adult education and conclude that the discourse of 'short-course provision' is contributing, intentionally or unintentionally, to the maintenance of the status quo rather than enabling the majority of people to challenge prevailing hierarchies of power and privilege.

Assumptions underlying theories of knowledge and learning

It is widely accepted that the current era of globalisation has hastened the process of the commodification of learning, or what Mamdani (2007) calls the 'commercialisation of knowledge': that is, transforming learning into a possession, something to be traded for gain in the marketplace. Happening at the same time – less visibly but nonetheless significantly – is the parallel process of 'learning as dispossession', by which people are stripped not only of their individuality, but also of their very understanding of their own exploitation (Spencer 2007). Trowler (2001) describes how standardised units of learning are based on a marketplace rationality in which knowledge is commodified and treated like money: it can be exchanged, transferred, 'cashed in' and assumed to be of equitable value irrespective of where and how it was 'earned'.

Different conceptions of knowledge (different epistemologies) generate different conceptions of learning. Morrow (2007: 18) summarises succinctly when he says we have inherited two main rival epistemological traditions:

> Much learning psychology during the previous century was behaviourist and based on an atomistic conception of knowledge as a collection of independent bits of information and skills. Learning is conceived of as additive…Despite the fact that it is easy to see the flaws in this way of understanding learning, it lives on in the widespread views about the purpose of 'short courses'. One indication of the vitality of this legacy is the common idea that links 'short courses' to 'plugging gaps'.

In contrast, he continues:

> The Piagetian developmental psychology tradition – which was the start of the rival tradition of cognitive psychology – was founded on a different epistemology, one which conceives of knowledge as structured. And if we think about 'short courses' on this basis, it yields a different conception of learning…A 'short course' would need to fit into an already established knowledge structure. However, both these stances conceive of learning as essentially individualistic; neither can take account of the extent to which shared practices are the basis of all human learning and the way in which this changes our understanding of learning.

In setting up the NQF, South Africa embarked on a radical transformation of the education and training system, in line with the broader transformation goals of the country. (This is well described by Lugg in Chapter 4 of this volume.) The adoption of an outcomes-based education and training (OBET) approach, framed within the broad constructivist tradition, was intended as a move away from behaviourism. Moll (2003: 17) describes constructivism as 'the building of networks of knowledge that have both a crucial individual developmental dimension and a necessary location in patterns of interaction between people involved in solving problems and carrying out practical tasks'. By engaging in such practical activities and discussions that challenge them to make meaning of their social and physical environment, learners are actively using these networks of knowledge in building progressively more complex understandings of their subject. But despite the ways in which cognitive psychology has challenged behaviourist learning theory, the latter continues to influence educational practices today through an operational approach of prescriptive outcomes embedded in a behaviourist approach that often fails to achieve quality education (Jansen 1999; Morrow 2007; Moll 2008).

Shahrzad Mojab argues in Chapter 1 of this volume that we cannot understand the significance of current conceptions of knowledge and learning, or current practices of work-related education and training, unless we are able to uncover and critically analyse the social relations that underpin these conceptions and practices. Sometimes this is possible only by turning current conceptions of learning on their head. Understanding knowledge and learning therefore requires an understanding of the political economy that prevails at a given time and place.

We move now to the South African case study, focusing in particular on the ways that the discourse and provision of short courses have developed within the contemporary political and economic moment.

South African case study

This study situates the contemporary genesis of the discourse of 'short courses' within the socio-political and economic developments of South Africa.[1] We do this through studying relevant national and international texts, and interviewing key people who were involved in varying roles as policy developers and regulators, directors and providers of continuing education and 'short courses'. We analyse the South African Qualifications Authority (SAQA) database of short-course provisioning, in order to obtain a sense of the scale and scope of short courses in South Africa at one point in time across most sectors. We also draw on our own experiences of setting up and managing continuing education policies and practices at our workplace, the University of the Western Cape, as well as the discussions and debates that were generated when we presented drafts of the working paper in various forums.

Policy framework for the provision of short courses

South Africa has a rich tradition of continuing education, non-formal adult education and short courses, which have been delivered by public higher education institutions, private sector educational providers, civil society organisations and workplaces. Some of the courses are geared to the development of particular skills, knowledge or attitudes for workers in the formal or informal economy; to citizen education for sustainable livelihoods, such as that relating to health, literacy, environment or housing; and to cultural, personal or political education. The courses have largely been outside of any regulatory framework.

The imperatives for the new democratic government of 1994 were linked closely to the development of both economic and democratic citizenship, as stated in the *Education White Paper 3: A Programme for the Transformation of Higher Education*:

> (T)he South African economy is confronted with the formidable challenge of integrating itself into the competitive arena of international production and finance…*Simultaneously*, the nation is confronted with the challenge of reconstructing domestic social and economic relations to eradicate

and redress the inequitable patterns of ownership, wealth and social and economic practices that were shaped by segregation and apartheid. (DoE 1997: 5; italics added)

The new government inherited an economy that was isolated, inefficient and probably bankrupt. South Africa had to learn quickly how to operate in the new global economy, which Castells (2001) describes as being dominated by the changing nature and scale of the financial markets, the internationalisation of trade and production, the rapid growth and integration of new information and communications technologies, and the fact that it is organised in and through networks with powerful inclusive and exclusive capabilities across corporate, national and international boundaries. The evidence he produces is of a divided, unequal and increasingly unstable global society, in which those who don't have access to knowledge, skills and resources to function in this new economy are increasingly relegated to functions within the informal sector, the criminal economy or survivalist sectors of the economy. Lifelong learning was adopted as a key philosophical and political framework in 1994, with concern for economic development, redress, equity and social justice for the women and men who had been systematically disadvantaged through apartheid. This approach emphasised both political and economic citizenship, and the new government set about developing a wide range of new education and training policies and institutions for its implementation (Walters 2006).

There was agreement from all sectors of society to develop an NQF, which was to be a key lever in bringing all the fragmented education and training bodies into one structure. The South African Qualifications Authority (SAQA) was established through legislation (SAQA Act of 1995) to oversee its development. SAQA set about constructing the most comprehensive NQF anywhere in the world, with higher education, schooling at all levels, and workplace vocational training linked into one system. The ambitious objectives of the SAQA Act highlighted the principles of integration, relevance, credibility, coherence, flexibility, legitimacy and access (King 2007). The NQF was based on an outcomes-based model, including unit standards and whole qualifications, which had the potential to encourage transparency, access and popular participation in the education and training systems that were widely acknowledged as elitist and opaque.

Fourteen years on, there is vibrant debate about what has been achieved through the NQF[2] (Allais 2007; Parker 2007; Mukora 2007; Parker & Walters 2008; see also Chapter 4 in this volume), and there have also been changes to the legislation. Parker and Walters (2008) describe two major changes to South Africa's NQF since its inception: a movement away from 'standardisation' to 'differentiation'; and a shift from an upfront, design-down and prescriptive approach to standards setting to a practice-based, design-up and descriptive approach. There has also been a shift from an 8-level to a 10-level NQF to accommodate greater differentiation in higher education. The standards-setting and quality-assurance functions previously carried out by SAQA will now shift to three Quality Councils: the Higher Education

Quality Council (NQF levels 5 to 10); the Quality Council for General and Further Education (Umalusi) (NQF levels 1 to 4 – the schooling system and technical colleges); and the Quality Council for Trades and Occupations (NQF levels 1 to 10 – occupational qualifications). This will allow for the emergence of different sub-frameworks shaped to the needs of each distinct knowledge field and its associated forms of learning within a unitary NQF.

Other complementary legislation introduced was the Skills Development Act of 1998, which established the Sector Education and Training Authorities (SETAs) and the Skills Development Levy Act of 1999. In February 2001 the minister of labour launched the National Skills Development Strategy (NSDS) and SETAs have been established to implement the NSDS and to increase the skills of the people in their sector. Sectors are made up of economic activities that are linked and related (for example, the banking, manufacturing and information technology sectors). Employers, who contribute monthly, fund the skills development strategy; the skills levy is currently 1 per cent of a company's payroll. Twenty per cent of this money is allocated to the National Skills Fund and 80 per cent to the relevant SETA. Employers who have their own learnerships or other registered training programmes can claim back a portion of their contribution. While there is some dissatisfaction with the rate of delivery of the SETAs, a major achievement of the legislation has been the fact that for the first time there is some compulsion for employers to train staff rather than perpetuate the previous practices of importing mainly 'white' labour as and when required.

Relevant changes also occurred in the area of continuing professional development (CPD) through professional associations. For the first time continuing education is a requirement for re-registration of certain professionals, as with the Health Professions Council of South Africa. The professional medical councils, for example, introduced compulsory CPD for all medical practitioners in 2000.[3] Professionals working in allied medical fields, such as pharmacists as well as doctors, are now required to attend a range of courses each year in order to retain their licence. The scale of take-up of CPD is not known, but there seems to be a proliferation of private and public institutions that are offering continuing education of various sorts.

In 2001/02 the framework for a national quality-assurance system was established with the accreditation of 31 Education and Training Quality Assurance bodies (ETQAs). This accreditation process included the Council for Higher Education (CHE) as well as 25 SETAs. There was an imperative for organisations, including higher education institutions, to begin to assure the quality of their short courses or continuing education (HEQC 2005).

Short-course provisioning in South Africa

According to a SAQA report released in 2002, the total number of short courses uploaded on the national database system at the time amounted to 6 144 courses

(SAQA 2002).[4] These courses were submitted by 12 National Standards Bodies (NSBs). The NSB with the most sub-field courses and the most providers was Business, Commerce and Management Studies (NSB 03). The sub-fields Generic Management and Human Resource Management and Practices recorded the highest number of courses and providers. There was a significant difference between NSB 03 (total of 2 077 courses and 206 providers) and the second highest NSB – Education, Training and Development (NSB 05) – with 626 courses and 179 providers. Interestingly, within NSB 05, the sub-field Adult Basic Education and Training (ABET) submitted the highest number of courses (189). The number of short courses submitted by providers to NSB 05 is indicated in Table 5.1.

A relatively small number of education and training organisations – increasingly known as 'providers'– submitted their short courses for recording; these providers ranged from consultancies run by one person to large institutions such as universities and technikons (SAQA 2004). A further analysis of the number of providers recorded on the SAQA database is given in Tables 5.2 and 5.3.

Table 5.1 *NSB 05 short courses*

NSB 05 (Education, Training and Development)	
Sub-field courses	Number
ABET	189
Higher Education and Training	176
Occupationally directed Education, Training and Development Courses	97
Early Childhood Development	54
Educators: Schooling	42
Environmental	19
Assessor Standards	11
Development	9
HIV/AIDS	1
Courses not assigned to any SGB	28
Total	626

Table 5.2 *NSB 03 short-course providers*

NSB 03 (Business, Commerce and Management Studies)	
Private providers	106
Private companies and in-house training institute providers	33
Private college/institute providers	20
Higher education institute providers	17
Further Education and Training colleges	7
Unidentified providers	23
Total	206

Table 5.3 *NSB 05 short-course providers*

NSB 05 (Education, Training and Development)	
Private providers	75
Private companies and in-house training institutes	30
Civil society organisations	27
Public higher education institutes	15
Further Education and Training colleges	5
Unidentified providers	27
Total	179

In an attempt to categorise the organisations, we sent out a number of emails and made telephone calls to trace them. It is interesting that most of the emails were returned as 'failed' and 13 telephone numbers were no longer in existence, suggesting that the organisations may have closed down.

The SAQA recording process of the short courses was intended to point out gaps in the system, which could be used together with registered qualifications and unit standards to help bring some order and quality to a fragmented system. However, the recording process revealed the enormity and complexity of the task and it was not taken forward at that time. While the database is far from comprehensive, for the purpose of this study it provides useful information about the number and range of courses and organisations. It is interesting to observe that the field of business, management and commerce has by far the most courses, for which private companies represent the majority of providers. This could indicate that the employers within the private sector are most invested in 'short courses' and/or were most willing and able to provide the data as requested by SAQA.

Terminology

It is important to note the way the language and terminology in relation to short courses and continuing education has changed since the transition to democracy. For example, in the National Education Policy Investigation's *Framework Report* of 1993, which reflects the views of progressive educators who were aligned to the democratic movement, the language of 'continuing education' is used:

> [Continuing education encompasses] planned formal and non-formal education programmes for adults who wish to continue their education beyond the point reached through the system of formal initial education during their youth. It preserves the strength of both non-formal and formal education, including certification; resists the weakness of becoming a poor substitute for formal education; addresses a functional need in the adult population in developmental terms that are both personal and social; and provides scope for the targeting of areas and groups where continuing education is seen to have maximum developmental impact. (NEPI 1993: 86)

However, this is no longer the case in the post-apartheid policy documents. For example, the key SAQA document published in 2004 which defines terminology speaks of 'short courses', and 'skills programmes' within 'short learning programmes' (SAQA 2004: 14).

During interviews with people who were associated with the development of this document, it was stated that the current terminology reflected the dominant views of those participating in the processes. Such terminology was strongly influenced by workplace concerns of the Skills Development Act, and 'it was SAQA's role to reflect the dominant discourses'. However, it was made clear during the interviews that while the terminology was broadly supported, it was not uncontested. One of the respondents felt strongly that the discourse of 'short courses' has had negative impacts:

> The terminology has hampered lifelong learning and the developmental goals of what we want to achieve. So the more we speak of continuing education [CE], the more people would become aware of the role of CE and adult development. 'Short courses' does not provide a sustainable solution to the problems we have. Workers are exploited by offering all kinds of short courses without any pedagogical base or without considering the learning needs of the worker, that is in the workplace as well as by private providers, because it's all about making money.
> We are limiting ourselves and South Africa cannot afford to waste any more money.

Another respondent, who had an educational rather than a marketing background, made the observation that '"[s]hort courses" is a strategy while "continuing education" is a philosophy'. From the majority of interviews there was an overriding sense that the language of 'short courses' reflected what people wanted, that it was a 'brand' that the public could relate to. While there are instances where the discourse of adult and continuing education is used, it seems that the language of 'short courses' has become the catch-all terminology. This same language of 'short courses' used in South Africa is also used by several other institutions in places such as Australia and the UK. Isaacs (2007), the executive officer of SAQA, believes that further debate around the terminology is needed as the tensions between formal and non-formal education remain systemically unresolved and this is clearly reflected in the terminology in the SAQA documents. He suggests that there may be merit in reintroducing the language of 'continuing education'.

Impact on quality teaching and learning: The case of assessor training

One of the interviewees, a leading educationalist, made telling remarks about quality, and cited 'assessor training' as a clear example of what had gone wrong. She said:

> Millions of people have gone through two- to five-day assessor training courses and people believe that you can do this. Without a teaching base it has no meaning…Assessment is part of education, training and development practices. There is a flaw in the assessor bubble because

> there is no real understanding and a tick-box approach is applied. The idea of professional competence was not that it was a compliance exercise. It has become all about moneymaking. People think they know everything about assessment after three days…It only created the mushrooming of assessor trainers and some of them have never been inside a classroom, with delivery of courses at high prices…This illustrates the flaw in our thinking around short courses. We allowed short courses to take root with limited pedagogical value.

This quote points to the limitations of presenting 'short courses' within an atomistic view of knowledge and learning, and it prompted us to explore in more depth the merits of 'assessor training' as an example of 'short-course provision' within contemporary South Africa.

In 2001, a regulatory framework was established for assuring quality of assessment and moderation practices, which required institutions (or 'providers') to use only 'qualified assessors'. This was to ensure that all facilitators involved in assessment of learners across all fields, economic sectors and NQF levels met a consistent set of criteria to ensure consistent practice (SAQA 2001). However, rather than assuring quality, it seems that OBET assessment as is widely used is inclined to entrench behaviourist principles and encourage reductionist, mechanistic and atomistic understandings of knowledge and learning, often adopting a tick-box approach. Several of the training courses for assessors are of three to five days' duration without requiring any prior education, training expertise or experience. Moll (2008: 13) describes this approach to assessment as a 'drive away from a constructivist understanding of outcome statements as rigorous descriptions of the criteria, structure and depth of knowledge required at various levels of the curriculum'. Mackrory (2008) clearly identifies the challenges related to assessment practices, and points out that assessment training often fails to encourage a deeper understanding of the difficulties of assessment. Moll (2008) argues that knowledge developed during the 'assessor training' is fundamentally dependent on the existence of prior knowledge, conceptual processes, theories, beliefs and understandings. Without a shared practice or expertise in a relevant field of practice, an assessor would find it difficult to make valid and reliable assessment judgements about evidence of learner progress. The judgement of expert communities plays a vital role in assessing knowledge and skill among learners, and therefore encourages the development of 'assessment communities of practice'.

There are a number of good assessor training courses, as exemplified by that for lecturers at the Academic Development Centre of Rhodes University. This course utilises well-developed approaches to adult learning based on the premise that the primary impetus for adults to become involved in formal learning is when the experience is linked to problems, challenges or needs arising from their social or vocational roles (Grant 2005; Sayigh 2006). The community of assessment practitioners at Rhodes University have developed a conception of knowledge and practice that is firmly rooted in the social constructivist tradition and, as an assessment community, have built up their expertise over a period of time. However, despite this example of good practice, we believe that assessor training and its development in South Africa in many instances reflects epistemological understandings that are inclined towards a short-term, atomistic approach of 'plugging gaps', rather than towards sustained, long-term human development.

Towards a conclusion

The language of 'short courses' as used by 'providers' of education and training – as opposed to, for example, the language of adult or continuing education – does not refer to the educational purposes or fields of knowledge or communities of practice. Instead it emphasises the length of a course, signalling that this has more significance than other educational, philosophical or pedagogical dimensions. It also has limited meaning (shorter than what?). In many instances, organisers of 'short courses' and assessors of education and training do not see themselves primarily as educators, but rather as marketers of learning products to consumers – and this, we believe, is a problem. As Parker and Harley elaborate:

> Within a strong community of practice there is a strong sense of shared values and beliefs: a consciousness of, and commitment to, an overall holistic purpose that shapes the activities for the community; and agreement on the set of practices that constitute 'competent practice'…The existence of educational communities of practice is a necessary condition for learning to take place. (Parker & Harley 2007: 22)

'Providers' of 'short courses' are often on short-term contracts to deliver cost-effective products to organisations to which they have no long-term affiliation. The short course is a type of commodity that is sold in the marketplace, with little relationship to the social practices where it is delivered. This situation applies not only to private providers but also to cases in, for example, public higher education. This is well illustrated through the Ugandan case study of Makerere University, where Mamdani (2007) outlines the shift to 'money-generating activities', with academic staff members teaching courses outside their areas of specialisation. He shows how these short courses often ignore the study of methods, disciplinary traditions and the critical role of research.

Our research suggests that many 'short courses' are driven primarily by business interests. There is a sense that the branding of education and training as 'short courses' appeals to the notion of the 'instant society' and that the impact of this could have added to the erosion among learners of the need to 'do your time'. The 'consumers' of education and training and their employers often want immediate gratification, 'just in time'. The language of 'short courses' reflects the hegemonic global economic paradigm where education and training is a commodity in the 'free market'.

In a context where post-1994 education and training within a lifelong learning framework was to contribute to redress of the past 'gutter education' and to greater equity and social justice for the black majority, the idea that 'consumers' can do a three- to five-day 'short course' to become, for example, an assessor has in all likelihood contributed to the diminishing of quality in teaching and learning. As one of the respondents in our study said, 'If you are a well-educated person, you can learn certain things quickly, as you are starting from a good base.' However, the intentions of the national education and training policies were to support the majority of black people who have limited education and are poor. From the very low base of apartheid education, it is not possible to imagine poor and working-class people being able to take less time through 'short courses' to attain reasonable levels of skills, knowledge and understanding to improve their social and economic positions. Therefore, we suggest that the language of 'short-course provision' contributes, intentionally or unintentionally, to the maintenance of the status quo rather than enabling the majority of people to challenge prevailing hierarchies of power and privilege.

Notes

1   We appreciate very much the time given to us by the interviewees, and by our colleagues within the Division for Lifelong Learning (DLL) for feedback to working drafts; the open access given to us by SAQA; and the discussions we have had at the Researching Work and Learning Conference in December 2007 and at the SAQA Chairperson's Colloquium on Continuing Education in November 2007.

2   By May 2007, 11 062 unit standards and approximately 818 outcomes-based qualifications had been developed and registered on the eight levels of the NQF (Allais 2007).

3   Information accessed from a website for pharmacy interns in KwaZulu-Natal province. Accessed 7 May 2002, http://www.kznhealth.gov.za/interns2.pdf.

4   We appreciate very much the assistance given to us by SAQA staff who made their databases and reports available to us.

References

Allais SM (2007) What's wrong with the NQF? Paper presented at Wits/Umalusi seminar, 29 August

Castells M (2001) Universities as dynamic systems of contradictory functions. In J Muller, N Cloete & S Badat (eds) *Challenges of globalisation: South African debates with Manuel Castells.* Cape Town: Maskew Miller Longman

DoE (Department of Education, South Africa) (1997) *Education White Paper 3: A Programme for the Transformation of Higher Education.* Pretoria: DoE

Grant R (2005) A phenomenological investigation into lecturers' understanding of themselves as assessors at Rhodes University. PhD thesis, Rhodes University, Grahamstown, South Africa

HEQC (Higher Education Quality Committee) (2005) A good practice guide to the provision of continuing education courses for South African higher education institutions. Draft document, May. Document available from the authors

Isaacs S (2007) Towards a more empowering discourse of continuing education. Pretoria: SAQA. Accessed 30 March, http://www.saqa.org.za/show.asp?include=docs/conference/lecture/towards.html

Jansen J (1999) Why outcomes-based education will fail: An elaboration. In P Christie & J Jansen (eds) *Changing curriculum.* Cape Town: Juta

King M (2007) Going beyond the buzz into the real business: A response to the second NQF colloquium. *SAQA Bulletin* 10(2): 56–62

Mackrory P (2008) Progress report for scoping meeting on assessment unit standards. Report made available to the authors

Mamdani M (2007) *Scholars in the marketplace: The dilemmas of neo-liberal reform at Makerere University, 1989–2005,* Dakar: CODESRIA

Moll I (2003) *'What is a learning-centred learning centre?' Key questions for distance education.* Johannesburg: SAIDE

Moll I (2008) Understanding learning, assessment and the quality of judgements. Paper made available to the authors

Morrow W (2007) Plugging the gap: 'Short courses' and continuing education. Pretoria: SAQA. Accessed 30 March, http://www.saqa.org.za/show.asp?include=docs/conference/lecture/plugging.html

Mukora J (2007) Response to Dr Matseleng Allais. Presented at Wits/Umalusi seminar, 29 August

NEPI (National Education Policy Investigation) (1993) *Framework report.* Cape Town: Oxford University Press/NECC

Parker B (2007) Notes for response to Dr Matseleng Allais's paper: 'What's wrong with the NQF?' Presented at Wits/Umalusi seminar, 29 August

Parker B & Harley K (2007) The NQF as a socially inclusive and cohesive system: Communities of practice and trust. *SAQA Bulletin* 10(2): 17–37

Parker B & Walters S (2008) Competency-based training and national qualifications frameworks: Insights from South Africa. *Asia Pacific Education Review* 9(1): 70–79

SAQA (South African Qualifications Authority) (2001) *Criteria and guidelines for the registration of assessors: Policy document.* Pretoria: SAQA

SAQA (2002) *Report to ETQA and NSB Sub-Committee.* 19 February. Pretoria: SAQA

SAQA (2004) *Criteria and guidelines for short courses and skills programmes: Guideline document.* Pretoria: SAQA

Sayigh EA (2006) Refining lecturers' assessment practices through formal professional development at Rhodes University. *South African Journal for Higher Education* 20(1): 159–171

Spencer B (2007) The primordial link: HRM and workplace learning. *Proceedings of the 5th International Conference on Researching Work and Learning*, Cape Town, South Africa (2–5 December)

Trowler P (2001) Captured by the discourse? The socially constitutive power of new higher education discourse in the UK. *Organization* 8(2): 183–201

Walters S (2006) Adult learning within lifelong learning: A different lens, a different light. *Journal of Education* 39: 7–26

Critiquing structural inequalities

6 Challenging donor agendas in adult and workplace education in Timor-Leste

Bob Boughton

Introduction

Timor-Leste (often called East Timor in the English-speaking world) is one of the world's newest and smallest nations. Its one million people occupy the eastern half of a small island at the eastern end of the Indonesian archipelago, a few hundred kilometres from Australia's northern coastline. Timor-Leste is at present the poorest country in Asia and one of the poorest in the world, despite having rich offshore oil and gas fields in the sea that separates it from Australia. Timor-Leste achieved its independence only in 2002, after a long and brutal occupation by the Indonesian military dictatorship of General Suharto, who invaded East Timor in 1975. Suharto aimed at preventing the island from achieving independence following the collapse of the previous occupying power, the fascist regime of Portugal, which had ruled East Timor for nearly 500 years. The current abject poverty in which 44 per cent of Timorese now live (UNDP 2006) is a direct result of those two colonial occupations, which plundered the natural and human resources of the country and maintained the Timorese in a state of total economic and political dependency (Dunn 1996).

To overcome the poverty of its people, Timor-Leste must build an independent economy able to provide basic food security for the population, 80 per cent of whom work in subsistence agriculture. It must also generate sufficient cash income to pay for the essential requirements for modern economic development, which can be obtained only through the international market. Each of these tasks requires a rapid development of state institutions, the people to staff them, and the capacity of the mass of people to participate and interact effectively with them via the new democratic Constitution. Workplace learning research has tended not to focus on the needs of such 'undeveloped' or 'peripheral' economies;[1] yet here lie some of the biggest challenges for the twenty-first century. What 'work skills', we need to ask, are needed by populations such as that of Timor-Leste to find a pathway out of poverty, and how can they acquire them? What knowledge and skills are needed to transform traditional village-based subsistence economies, which have barely maintained themselves in the presence of predatory colonial capitalist exploitation, into economies that deliver the benefits to be gained from becoming part of the global system of production? Just as importantly, what skills are needed to ensure that these benefits are delivered equitably and fairly to all their people, rather than to only a small post-colonial elite? And how do new nations develop a leadership at the different levels of society that is able to understand and deal strongly with the exploitative agendas of world capitalism, and avoid replacing direct colonial dependency with new forms of neo-colonial exploitation?

Such questions require a much broader international research effort, which goes well beyond some of the more conventional questions of workplace learning research. This chapter begins such a process, by mapping and analysing critically the efforts of the international aid and development agencies that currently are assisting Timor-Leste to build its workforce. I begin by describing the overall research project of which the work reported here is a part. I then identify some of the major national and international actors who are currently involved in the economic reconstruction of the country, before focusing in on the agencies that have assumed responsibility for workforce development, with a case study of the International Labour Organization. I argue that a workforce development strategy whose principal focus is a national qualifications framework and competency-based training supports a wider ideological agenda aimed at ensuring that newly independent peripheral capitalist countries do not stray too far from the orthodox economic path set down by neo-liberalism. I conclude by defining a core problem that the research has identified – namely, the lack of fit or connection between, on the one hand, the revolutionary nationalist tradition of political and economic struggle that has formed the leadership of the first independent government and its cadre force, and, on the other, the technocratic language of poverty reduction and human resource development in which policy debates about adult education and training are conducted within the international agencies.

The research project

Intellectuals do not stand above the societies they study, and there is no research that does not align itself, either explicitly or implicitly, with other social actors engaged in 'the struggle for knowledge and power' (Cervero et al. 2001). My research project began as an act of solidarity with the political leadership of the newly independent Timor-Leste, the FRETILIN government of Prime Minister Mari Alkatiri that took office in May 2002, when the United Nations Transitional Authority formally handed over power to the first elected Timorese parliament. FRETILIN (*Frente Revolucionária Do Timor-Leste Independente*; in English, the Revolutionary Front for the Independence of Timor-Leste) formed in 1974 and was the leading political force in the 27-year struggle for independence (1974–2002) (Hill 2002). My relationship with FRETILIN dates from 1975, when, as a young university student in Australia, I became involved with solidarity work organised by the Communist Party. The work of the Australian solidarity movement, which became quite broad over time, continued throughout the 1980s and 1990s, led mainly by Timorese refugees, most of them FRETILIN members living in exile in Australia. When the opportunity arose in 2004 to visit Timor-Leste, I initiated a long-term project with colleagues at the University of New England, the focus of which was to identify ways we could support the new FRETILIN government to develop an appropriate adult education system for their new country (Durnan 2005; Boughton & Durnan 2007). In 2006, we obtained a three-year Australian Research Council grant to conduct a study titled 'An Investigation into the Contribution of the National Adult Education System to the Post-Conflict Reconstruction and Development of East Timor', and the findings reported here are part of that larger study. They are based on the analysis of documents produced by the FRETILIN government and by international agencies and donors; on interviews and meetings with representatives of the government, non-government organisations (NGOs) and the international agencies and donors; and on observations and reflections recorded in field journals during time spent in Timor-Leste since April 2004, but particularly in the last two years.

I make no pretence of neutrality. From the start, I intended that my work should aim to support the Timorese people's right of self-determination, the right, as the United Nations Charter has it, 'to freely determine their economic, political and social future', a right they had won only after a long and bitter struggle. Within this broad framework, our project has sought to assist the Timorese, chiefly through their leaders within FRETILIN,[2] to enjoy the rights to which they are entitled under the new Constitution. This Constitution, like the South African one that served as a model, is one of the most progressive modern constitutions to be found in the world today. Our work was also informed by FRETILIN's analysis of the history of the last 30 years, in which those basic human rights were denied – in fact trampled on – by the international community, even by many of the countries, Australia included, that now seek to play a major role through their aid and development programmes in the country's reconstruction.

This chapter explores the following research questions:
- Who are the major international 'actors' currently intervening in workforce development in Timor-Leste, and what are their perspectives and proposals?
- How do these proposals sit within the wider context of the education and training needs of Timor-Leste's adult population as determined by their specific historical experiences and struggle?
- To what extent is it necessary to develop a more critical view of these proposals in order for Timor-Leste to gain the kind of adult education and training system it needs to achieve its own independent development aspirations?

Who are the main international actors?

The United Nations (UN) and its agencies have played a major role in Timor-Leste since the referendum of August 1999, when over 80 per cent of the population rejected an Indonesian proposal to remain an autonomous province within the Republic of Indonesia. Since then, the UN has maintained an active presence, including, from September 1999 until May 2002, being the sovereign authority over the territory. The UN agencies most involved in education and workforce development have been the United Nations Development Programme (UNDP), the International Labour Organization (ILO) and UNICEF. UNESCO has also played a role, but its resources have been limited and its attention focused more on community education, in particular the promotion of community learning centres. The other most significant international agency has been the World Bank.

These international agencies source their funds from a range of different donor countries. For example, advisers employed by the UNDP in the Ministry of Education and Culture are actually funded by New Zealand, under its aid programme; while UNICEF recently submitted a major proposal for funding to the Swedish development agency SIDA. However, individual donor countries can also contribute funds and programmes directly, either independently or in partnership with the international agencies. These 'bilateral' donors in Timor-Leste include Australia, Portugal, the US, Brazil, Japan, China and Cuba. Both Portugal and Brazil, for example, each fund their own vocational training centres in different parts of the capital, Dili. Sometimes, bilateral agencies combine, as is common, for example, with USAID and AUSAID, the development agencies of the United States and Australia respectively. Sometimes, bilateral donors partner on specific projects with international agencies, and on occasion the government of Timor-Leste also contributes some of its own funds. This is currently occurring in a large-scale five-year education project that includes $6 million from the World Bank's International Development Agency, $6 million from AUSAID and $3 million from the government's own budget.

In addition to the above-mentioned international agencies, there are also a large number of international NGOs, including, for example, Oxfam/Community Aid Abroad, Care International and Caritas, all of which have projects that directly impact on workforce development, both in terms of the employment and training of their own national staff, and through projects that deliver training in one or more areas of work to project recipients. Each of these NGOs also develops its own relationships with both the international agencies described above and the bilateral donors, creating a complex web of interrelationships, alliances and conflicts in the process. For example, in the lead-up to the June 2007 elections, the UNDP received funds from USAID to employ a US NGO, the International Republican Institute (IRI), an offshoot of George Bush's Republican Party, to deliver training for members of local political parties.

Note that none of these international actors is directly accountable to the people of Timor-Leste, or to its democratically elected government. The conventional wisdom is that agencies operate as guests in the country, and that they deliver programmes in partnership with local people and organisations, programmes that are consistent with the wishes and needs of the host country. But it remains an empirical question whether this in fact is the case, and how the sovereign government would even know if it was not, let alone how they might seek to intervene if they found their interests were not being served. Unlike international business operators, for example, there is as yet no system for the registration and accreditation of international development agencies. It is highly unlikely that international agencies would *not* have their own agendas and objectives developed through their own processes, many of which occur in centres far from the reality of Timor-Leste. What is clear is that a nation's right of self-determination is not absolute, and that it depends very much on its ability to monitor and control the activities of non-nationals within its borders. Most urgently needed, in the first instance, is a systematic concrete analysis of who is doing what, with whom, and with what effect or impact.

The most effective means for a country such as Timor-Leste to assert its sovereignty in respect of the development of its system of adult education and training, and of that part of the system responsible for workforce development, is through having its own policies, planning mechanisms and legislative and administrative systems for the implementation of its own goals. This, however, presents a classic 'chicken–egg' problem. How can a country develop policies and administrative legal systems for their implementation in the absence of a workforce of its own with the expertise and skills to undertake such system-level work? The solution, in Timor-Leste as in many other countries, is to employ outside expertise, in the form of advisers and consultants from countries that have an excess of such professionals. These people are usually recruited, selected and funded with help from the same international agencies whose activities one is trying to monitor and control. As a consequence, lines of accountability remain confused, contradictory and blurred.

Agencies engaged in workforce development

The above discussion conveys little of the complexity of what the international actors are actually doing in Timor-Leste. Below is a brief and incomplete list of the kinds of programmes and projects in the area of workforce development that are delivered utilising international funds and personnel:

- health worker, nurse and medical doctor training;
- a national adult literacy campaign;
- agricultural extension services;
- construction industry training;
- agricultural colleges;
- non-formal primary and secondary school 'equivalence' courses;
- a workforce development agency to set competency standards and register training providers;
- small-business training;
- youth life-skills programmes;
- public sector capacity building;
- policy development in education and training;
- tourism and hospitality industry training;
- trade union training;
- market gardening;
- training in contract preparation and tendering;
- cooperative development services;
- micro-financing of small income-generating projects;
- establishment and support of community learning centres;
- university-level courses in priority areas;
- a 'polytechnic' college;
- vocational education and training in schools;

- teacher training;
- political party training.

At this stage, we are still developing an analytic or classificatory system able to make sense of the similarities and differences among all these different projects and programmes. In an attempt to map the role of such agencies more systematically, we have drawn on the work of Youngman (2000) by asking what local and international interests are served by specific programmes and by the total aid effort. What is clear already is that there is a massive international effort under way to 'form' the Timorese adult working-age population, to change it from its current configuration. What is not clear is whether this effort, in its individual elements or in aggregate, will actually give Timor-Leste the workforce and citizenry it needs to survive and prosper as an independent country in the twenty-first century.

A case study: The ILO

One way to clarify things is to examine a specific agency. The International Labour Organization (ILO), a UN agency, had previously operated in Timor-Leste during the Indonesian occupation, and its current programmes in Timor-Leste continue to be managed from its Jakarta office. Like most international agencies, it actually 'brokers' funds from other sources. One of its main initiatives in Timor-Leste has been to provide a small team of technical advisers who work inside the Ministry of Labour and Community Re-insertion (the MTRC – formerly the Secretariat of State for Labour and Solidarity).[3] This unit assists the ministry in managing funds obtained via the ILO, sourced in turn from the European Union, for a project known by the acronym STAGE (Skills Training for Gainful Employment). Its stated aims are to

- reduce poverty and promote economic growth;
- build national capacity;
- deliver demand-driven enterprise and skills training;
- contribute to the establishment and development of income-generating activities within communities (ILO 2006).

However, one of the difficulties faced by analysts of the work of international development agencies is that 'projects' and their component parts can appear under different names and with slightly different aims in reports intended for different donors. So it is that the STAGE programme included several components that also appear in 'projects' funded by other donors. For example, a component exists for the development of a 'Labour Force Development Institute' (LFDI), also sometimes called a 'Workforce Development Authority', a 'project' that has also been funded independently from other sources, including the Technical and Further Education (TAFE) sections of two Australian state governments, New South Wales and Victoria; the World Bank; and, most recently, as part of a massive infrastructure project, known as the Program for Accelerated National Development, originally prepared by consultants from a US government-owned corporation called the Millennium Challenge Corporation.

In its various guises, the LFDI bears a strong resemblance to national authorities in other countries that oversee vocational and workplace training through the establishment of an NQF, the registration of providers according to national standards, the establishment of competency standards for specific priority occupations, and the promotion and support of standard curriculum and training 'packages'. Other elements of the workforce and employment development 'system' that is emerging within Timor-Leste under the ILO's guidance include:

- an employment and vocational training fund, on which providers and communities can draw to undertake training and job creation projects in priority areas;
- a micro-finance agency, which provides credit for small income-generating projects;
- enterprise training centres, where potential small-business operators and contractors learn some basic business and marketing skills;
- skills training centres, running short training courses in skills for which it is considered there is a potential demand;
- a programme to assist contractors to develop skills in tendering for work;
- several different 'cash for work' projects, providing short-term work paid for by government and donors, an attempt to reduce unemployment in and around the major cities following the political crisis of 2006;[4]
- the development of a national employment strategy.

One of the major strengths of the ILO programme is that its relatively small team of international technical advisers work inside the MTRC and are engaged in a deliberate programme of skills transfer and training with the Timorese counterparts. As a result, over time staff within the ministry's Employment Development Division are gradually acquiring the skills and knowledge needed to manage and develop the system that the ILO has helped to design.[5]

However, there is no 'independent' source of advice. As an institution with decades of history and its own stakeholders, the ILO has developed its own clear views about the needs of developing countries in relation to workforce development. Its staff are professionals who have studied these topics and participated in international conferences. Moreover, there is a politics to all this, and while the advice may appear to come from neutral, well-qualified 'experts', it also reflects the dominant thinking in many countries about the connection between training and employment, including the highly contestable view that training in itself leads to lower unemployment. This should come as no surprise. In order to access funds from donor countries, in order to obtain the needed support from private companies, especially ones from overseas, in order to survive and succeed as an international development agency, ILO staff must stay within a certain set of boundaries as to what does and does not constitute effective workforce development. For example, USAID, which is a major donor in this field, holds very strong views about the central role of the private sector in economic growth. One of the most dramatic examples of the international hegemony is the acceptance by the ILO and virtually every other donor of the view that Timor-Leste urgently needs an NQF, a set of industry-endorsed competency standards and the delivery of training by largely non-government providers within the paradigm of competency-based education.

A 'literacy first' approach

A major challenge in Timor-Leste over the next two years is to develop an integrated policy framework and strategy for adult education and training. At present, vocational education and training needs are being addressed in the context of skills development for the workforce in nominated key sectors. This work is led by the MTRC with some involvement of the Ministry of Education and Culture (MEC) via its technical schools and skills training centres. This is occurring independently of the overwhelming need for adult literacy and adult basic education 'equivalence' courses for the majority of adults, which are the responsibility of the MEC's Centre for Non-Formal Education. Both the MTRC and the MEC in turn develop their work in relative isolation from adult education and training programmes designed to support democratic citizenship, participation and community development, which tend to be led by other ministries and NGOs. At the same time, there has been a tendency to import adult and vocational education and training models and policies from other countries, including ones that have much higher levels of adult literacy and basic education, and developed labour markets that are more integrated into the global economy (for example, Australia, Brazil, Malaysia and Singapore).

The reality of Timor-Leste may well require a very different approach. It is a very small country in which nearly 50 per cent of the adult population are illiterate, where 88 per cent of the labour force work in subsistence agriculture and have little or no primary schooling, where there has been no culture of democratic participation, and where women in particular lack education and access to economic opportunity. In these circumstances, there is a risk that too great a focus within the adult education and training system on workforce development for the new labour markets intended to drive economic growth will exclude a substantial proportion of the population. This could lead to more rather than less social inequality in the medium to long term, thereby exacerbating existing social divisions and instability, and ultimately derailing the overall economic growth strategy of the national development plan. Experiences in other countries and regions of the global South show that the introduction of NQFs with competency-based training (CBT) can have negative as well as positive consequences (Allais 2007), and this is actually acknowledged in one of the ILO's own publications (Young 2005). NQFs have tended not to value the skills and knowledge of the traditional subsistence economy and society and to exclude the majority of people who are illiterate in what is known as the 'deficit' model of training. CBT-based NQFs have also failed to encompass and recognise the non-vocational skills, knowledge, understandings and attitudes that individuals and communities need to transform their country from a society divided by colonisation and violent conflict to one characterised by peace, democracy and the rule of law (Boughton 1998). The work of women as community builders and peace builders is one example of work not easily encompassed in CBT-based NQFs, and there are many others.

There is therefore an urgent need to engage the two responsible ministries, the MEC and the MTRC, along with other stakeholders, in a policy and institutional development process aimed at designing an integrated and coordinated adult education system in which the needs of all sectors of the population are addressed equitably. International experiences should be drawn on in this policy development work, through the services of experts in adult education and training in post-colonial and post-conflict societies of the global South. The proposed LFDI should be a key stakeholder in this process, as it will be the main driver of the vocational education and training system. But equally, there is a need to involve the MEC's Non-Formal Education Centre, and the national commission established in January 2007 to lead the national literacy campaign, which is being supported by a small team of literacy advisers from Cuba. The ministries of health, of agriculture and of state administration are also key stakeholders, because each of these ministries has functions and responsibilities that depend for their success on improving adult literacy levels and developing a more educated adult population. A national council for adult learning such as those that already exist in some developing countries is potentially one institutional framework for achieving greater coordination and equity in the adult and vocational education and training system.

The geopolitics of decolonisation and development: A tale of two discourses

Paulo Freire taught us to think about illiteracy as an integral feature of the societies in which it appears, rather than a 'residual' problem to be 'mopped up' in remedial programmes:

> [Illiterates]…are not marginal to the structure, but oppressed men [sic] within it. Alienated men, they cannot overcome their dependency by 'incorporation' into the very structure responsible for their dependency. (Freire 1972: 27–28)

The same can be said of whole countries, like Timor-Leste, where illiteracy is a major impediment to development. Illiteracy in Timor-Leste is a product of a specific history, one in which nearly one million people were forced to live for over three decades under a brutal, exploitative colonial regime. The overthrow of that regime required a political struggle, one that drew not only on the resources of the people themselves, but also on the resources of an international movement that has been more than 200 years in the making. For the UN and its agencies and the bilateral donors, many of whom actually supported that brutal occupation, now to 'take charge' of the process of poverty reduction and workforce development, as if this were a relatively simple 'technical' problem well within the boundaries of their expertise, is simply to reimpose, in a new form, the old relations of dominance and subordination, and could be argued to be a 'recolonisation' rather than a 'decolonisation'.

Ilda Maria da Conceição was, until July 2007, FRETILIN's vice-minister of education and culture. In 1975, at the age of 18, she joined FRETILIN's mass literacy campaign, in which students went to the countryside to teach the rural poor. When the Indonesians invaded she retreated into the FRETILIN-held areas, where she continued to work as an educator, eventually joining FALANTIL, the armed resistance. After being captured by the Indonesians and released, she worked for OPMT, FRETILIN's women's organisation, the backbone of the clandestine movement that supported the armed struggle. In a recent film, she spoke of her experiences:

> At that time when we came down (from the mountains), we were told that FRETILIN was communist, that FRETILIN was against religion. We only said this, that FRETILIN's principles are these, first, we wanted to end forms of exploitation from man to man. First, what's exploitation?... This made the people start thinking...Then we clarified, during the Portuguese times, how were their lives different between the kings and the people? We made these comparisons. We opened the people's mind so that they, too, can know it for themselves...So these things made the people realise what exactly were FRETILIN's programmes. Where is the objective of FRETILIN's programmes? It is to free the people from obscurantism. When the education and illiteracy programmes were under way, they were all startled. This is what we have been waiting for [they said]... (Da Conceição 2007)

FRETILIN, the leading party in Timor's struggle for independence, maintains a commitment to a tradition of anti-colonial struggle dating back to the 1960s and 1970s. It speaks in a language growing out of that tradition, tempered nevertheless by the experiences of the last 30 years. In particular, some of its key leaders lived in exile in Mozambique, where they saw first-hand the effects of international agencies such as the Word Bank.

Since the 1970s, 'poverty reduction' has become a highly technical and sophisticated field of study and practice, employing many thousands of tertiary-educated economists and social scientists, experts in 'developing economies'. In 2005, a team of experts from the World Bank helped the new FRETILIN government produce a set of sector investment plans (SIPs) to guide its investment decisions and the investment decisions of the donor community over the next five years. Here is an extract from the overview of the SIPs:

> Relative to other low-income countries, Timor-Leste will give strong emphasis to improving the educational status of the population; it is only in this way that a small nation such as Timor-Leste can be competitive in the global economy and, with a well-informed citizenry, function effectively as a democratic society. The approach to vocational and adult education is built around two main programs: expanding capacities for vocational and technical training to improve skills for productive employment; and expanding programs of adult education aimed at improving functional literacy. The vocational and technical program focuses especially on younger people in the 15–24 year age group. There are about 6,000 students enrolled in Government and private institutions

> that provide these programs. When set against the 10,000 new entrants into the labor force each year, the current institutional capacities are inadequate...Vocational education will be built around a system that certifies skills of students, an authority to establish skill standards in partnership with industry, and a registration process for organizations offering vocational training... (DRTL 2005: 7)

In Timor-Leste, as the two quotations above show, there are two totally disparate 'traditions' or 'paradigms' attempting to talk to each other about how Timor-Leste can overcome its people's abject poverty and recover from the trauma of a brutal military occupation. While the FRETILIN leaders were willing to engage with the language of agencies such as the World Bank, it is not nearly so clear that the World Bank can make any sense of the language of anti-colonial nationalism and social democracy with which FRETILIN leaders talk to each other and to their members, militants and sympathisers.

How scientific, we have to ask, is a theory of workplace learning if it cannot understand and facilitate the learning that the vast majority of the world's people engage in when they work in subsistence and peripheral economies, including what they learn and need to learn about how to overcome their own exploitation? What theories do we need, we can also ask, to transform a colonial economy based on relations of exploitation into one where people enjoy their full citizenship rights? How can we develop a theory and a practice that does not marginalise, de-legitimise and 'rule out' from the debate the knowledge and understandings that have developed over two centuries of socialist and anti-colonial struggles, replacing it with a technocratic discourse of 'poverty reduction'? Previously, I have argued that if workplace learning theory could not recognise and account for that kind of learning, whose historical role in processes of economic change and development was undeniable, then it remained an ideological activity, rather than a genuine social science (Boughton 2006).[6]

These are not just academic questions or fine points of theory. The ideological theories of workplace education and training that dominate Western academic research and policy-making are increasingly being 'exported' to the South, through the work of international agencies and consultants who believe their experiences in restructuring training systems in the industrialised countries can usefully be transferred to the development of national training systems for the countries of the South. To the extent that such theories are ideological, they misrepresent to the people most concerned, the Timorese themselves, the real conditions of their own historical situation, and reduce their capacity to act on those conditions in ways that are genuinely self-determining.

Politics matters. Poverty is not simply a technical problem to be overcome by improved economic management. Poverty results from exploitation, and in order to overcome it people have to learn to recognise exploitation and struggle against it. Unless this kind of 'political' education is included in the workforce development agenda, the Timorese run the risk of simply being reinserted in relations of exploitation at a regional and global level – not, as previously, as expendable sources of slave labour, as they were under the Indonesians and the Portuguese, but as 'free' wage labourers in a regional labour market. The NQF may, in this case, simply give them a 'portable' qualification that enables them to be exploited, not just by their own employing class, but by international employers as well.

Conclusion

Many countries in recent years, South Africa included (Walters 1996), have had to face the challenge of improving productivity and the livelihoods of a previously 'colonised' population, while also dealing with the challenges of both 'post-conflict' development and the threat of reintegration into the world economy via a transformed but still exploitative relationship with the dominant global powers. Too many, it seems, have been willing to frame the development debate within the ideological language of human capital theory, from which the NQF and its CBT partner have sprung. Once this happens, the tasks of political, social and cultural development, which have been central to the ideology or 'discourse' of the national liberation movement and its educational practices, can too easily be sidelined, perhaps as 'civics and citizenship' training, or that ubiquitous term community 'capacity building', rather than remaining an integral part of the new independent education and training system.

It is also important to see that different donors and agencies pursue quite different interests, competing with each other for influence via specific aid programmes. For example, USAID and Cuba are each funding separate efforts at combating adult illiteracy, while Australia, the US, Brazil and Portugal are all competing for influence in the field of vocational training. Different donors in turn mobilise different local constituencies via their programmes, in the process helping to consolidate and exacerbate old social divisions and to create new ones. Until recently, the independence leadership in Timor-Leste remained largely united behind a radical social democratic nationalist ideology, which placed just as much emphasis on the political development of the people via a mass national literacy campaign as on the more technocratic model of workforce development inspired by the human capital theorists of the World Bank. Nevertheless, the underlying contradictions between these two paradigms of development were a significant factor in the political crisis that erupted in 2006, with anti-government forces drawing significant public support from political leaders in Timor-Leste and Australia who opposed FRETILIN's nationalist programme. The change of government that followed the elections of June 2007 has seen many international agencies and external donors increase their efforts to influence policy development, via a large increase in international 'technical advisers', while FRETILIN, now in opposition, continues to advocate for a more independent approach.

The challenge for radical workplace education theorists is to devise a common language in which these two paradigms can be 'reconciled', or rather the contradictions between them resolved in a new synthesis, one that reframes for a twenty-first-century audience the challenge that faced the Maoist development leadership in post-revolutionary China – namely, to develop a workforce that was both 'red' and 'expert' (Youngman 1986). Such a language, or theory, can only come from one place, from social practice. So the question becomes, what are the institutional or organisational means via which these two separate accounts of development can be brought together in a way that does not reproduce the unequal relations that currently prevail between, on the one hand, the international development agencies and, on the other, the political leadership of the national liberation movement?

Notes

1 An exception was the *International Journal of Lifelong Education* vol. 24, no. 5, which discussed the role of adult education in poverty reduction. See, for example, the article in that issue by Pieck (2005).

2 In the national elections of June 2007, held after the first draft of this chapter was written, FRETILIN won the most parliamentary seats but lost power to a coalition of smaller parties led by Xanana Gusmao, the former resistance commander and first president of Timor-Leste. The stance of the new coalition government on the issues raised in this chapter is as yet unclear, but some commentators are predicting a move towards a more neo-liberal economic development policy, more strongly influenced by the US and Australia.

3 Following the June 2007 elections, the MTRC was restructured and its workforce-development functions, along with the ILO advisers, were transferred to the Secretariat of State for Employment and Training.

4 A rebellion by a disaffected group within the defence force and police in mid 2006 created a major political and security crisis, forcing the return of an Australian-led peacekeeping force and the resignation of the then prime minister Mari Alkatiri. Local gang violence fanned by the political conflict forced thousands of Dili residents to flee their homes into hastily erected refugee camps in and around the city.

5 In August 2007, the new government transferred responsibility for workforce development to a new agency, the Secretariat of State for Employment and Training. However, on my last field visit, in September 2007, the ILO programmes continued to operate as previously.

6 These questions are not dissimilar to those I raised at the Researching Work and Learning (RWL4) Conference in Sydney (2005), in the symposium 'What does the working class learn as it works?' This symposium tried to widen the discussion of the learning that occurs at work beyond the learning that must occur for enterprises and industries to become smarter, more productive and more globally competitive, to embrace other sorts of learning that workers can and do undertake at work. Our particular focus then was on how people learn to understand, in the 'labour process', the nature of class society and the relations of exploitation it institutionalises in work practices. Some papers from the symposium were published in the *Economic and Labour Relations Review* vol. 17, no. 2 (April 2007).

References

Allais SM (2007) Education service delivery: The disastrous case of outcomes-based qualifications frameworks. *Progress in Development Studies* 7(1): 65–78

Boughton B (1998) *Alternative VET pathways to indigenous development.* Adelaide: National Centre for Vocational Education Research

Boughton B (2006) Researching workplace learning and class. *Economic and Labour Relations Review* 17(2): 157–164

Boughton B & Durnan D (2007) The political economy of adult education and development. In D Kingsbury & M Leach (eds) *East Timor: Beyond independence.* Melbourne: Monash University Press

Cervero RM, Wilson AL & Associates (eds) (2001) *Power in practice: Adult education and the struggle for knowledge and power in society.* San Francisco: Jossey-Bass

Da Conceição I (2007) Transcript from *Rise Up Maubere People!* FRETILIN election DVD (available from www.timortruth.com). Copy of transcript provided to the author by the film-makers, Timor-Leste Institute of Popular Education, Farol, Dili, Timor-Leste

DRTL (Democratic Republic of Timor-Leste) (2005) *Overview of sector investment plans. Volume 2.* Dili, Timor-Leste: Ministry of Planning and Finance

Dunn J (1996) *Timor: A people betrayed* (revised edition). Sydney: ABC Books

Durnan D (2005) *Popular education and peacebuilding in Timor-Leste.* Master's thesis, University of New England, Armidale, Australia

Freire P (1972) *Cultural action for freedom.* Harmondsworth: Penguin

Hill H (2002) *Stirrings of nationalism in East Timor: Fretilin 1974–1978: The origins, ideologies and strategies of a nationalist movement.* Sydney: Otford Press

ILO (International Labour Organization) (2006) *Bring people to work, work to people. Special edition on Timor-Leste, January 2006.* Jakarta: ILO

Pieck E (2005) Work-related adult education: Challenges and possibilities in poverty areas. *International Journal of Lifelong Education* 24(5): 419–430

UNDP (United Nations Development Programme) (2006) *Paths out of poverty: Integrated rural development. Human development report 2005 for Timor-Leste.* Dili, Timor-Leste: UNDP

Walters S (1996) Education, training and development practitioners (ETDPs) within the reconstruction and development of South Africa. *Adult Education and Development* 46: 9–22

Young M (2005) National qualifications frameworks: Their feasibility for effective implementation in developing countries. In *InFocus programme on skills, knowledge and employability. Skills Working Paper No. 22.* Geneva: International Labour Organization

Youngman F (1986) *Adult education and socialist pedagogy.* London: Croom Helm

Youngman F (2000) *The political economy of adult education and development.* London and New York: Zed Books

7 University drop-out and researching (lifelong) learning and work

Moeketsi Letseka

Introduction

South Africa suffers from one of the most enduring high rates of unemployment. In 2003 the average unemployment rate was 31.5% (Stats SA 2007). And while there has been a steady decline, to 28.4% in 2004, 26.9% in 2005, and 25.9% in 2007 (see Figure 7.1), the unemployment rate is still high. The seriousness of this scenario becomes evident when one notes that while unemployment for white South Africans has been below the average in the last seven years, unemployment for Africans has been above average.

There are a number of theories to explain this persistent high rate of unemployment. For instance, Bhorat and Oosthuizen (2005) maintain that the South African economy is not creating a sufficient number of jobs commensurate with the annual proportion of job seekers. They argue that while the South African economy created more than 2 million jobs between 1995 and 2003, unemployment levels rose exponentially. Others have suggested that South Africa suffers from a severe skills crisis: there is no critical mass of qualified people ready to take up the available jobs (DoL 2007; Kraak 2003, 2004, 2006). Some have sought a more conciliatory approach, suggesting that South Africa

Figure 7.1 *Unemployment rate by population group, March 2001 to March 2007 (%)*

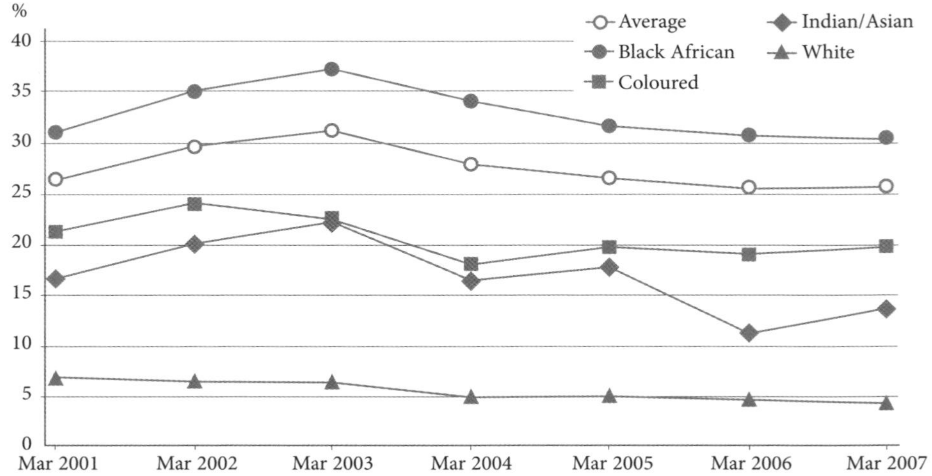

Source: Adapted from Stats SA (2007)

suffers from a skills misalignment – that there are too many people with qualifications that do not match the skills required by potential employers (Kraak 2008).[1] Others, such as Jimmy Manyi, the chairperson of the Commission for Employment Equity, have dismissed the skill crisis theory as mere 'urban legend', arguing that there is an underutilisation of skills: that is, there is an abundance of skilled people in the country who are simply ignored.[2] These views reinforce Ramphele's (2005) venomous attack on the political machinations of the country's employment practices. Ramphele argues that there are too many skilled professionals who are being denied job opportunities at various levels of government because they are outside of the party political networks that have captured civil service jobs for patronage.

If we accept the premise that a good-quality education system is sine qua non to economic growth and a vibrant labour market, we can then reasonably argue that South Africa's socio-economic maladies are far from over. In a Centre for Development Enterprise (CDE) report, Simkins et al. (2007) argue that South Africa spends proportionately more on education than many developing countries, yet its education system performs far worse than those of comparable developing countries in international tests in maths, science and literacy.[3] This suggests that the country's public education system is inefficient and makes ineffective use of resources. Similarly, a *FinWeek* lead story on South Africa's education crisis[4] notes that 'each year, quite literally thousands of school leavers – a generation of potential key players in any successful economy – either fail the grade or drop out of the education system'.[5] The article cites University of Stellenbosch economist Servaas van der Berg, who projects that ameliorating the education crisis in South Africa requires an effort lasting an entire generation (30 to 40 years) before the results of a well-educated society working its way through the labour market and economy can be realised. The CDE and *FinWeek* reports confirm previous studies on the inefficiency of the country's education system (Reddy 2006; Fiske & Ladd 2004; Fedderke et al. 2000).[6]

Against the backdrop of this dual crisis of the high unemployment rate and an inefficient education system, a situation which owes much to South Africa's apartheid legacy and its inequitable allocation of educational resources, this chapter examines student drop-out rates in selected public higher education institutions in South Africa. Based on the Human Sciences Research Council (HSRC) Student Pathways Study, which I managed over a period of four years, I interrogate factors affecting student drop-out and sketch their implications for the labour market.

The chapter is structured around five key sections. The first section provides some background on the inequitable spending on education under apartheid. In the second section I introduce the Student Pathways Study. The third section sketches the drop-out phenomenon as a matter of grave concern. The fourth section briefly presents the key findings of the Student Pathways Study. And in the final section I describe students' labour market pathways and experiences within the context of continuing inequalities in earnings by race and gender.

Racially skewed educational expenditure under apartheid

The specific context of South Africa's higher education is characterised by the challenges of student under-preparedness, lack of epistemological access, and first-generation university students, all attributes of the legacy of apartheid education policies and legislation (Nekhwevha 1999; Kallaway et al. 1997; Kallaway 1984; Rose & Tunmer 1975). This legacy left a racially differentiated education system that privileged the minority whites while excluding the majority blacks, especially Africans, from opportunities and privileges. Elsewhere I have shown that in 1993, a year before the transition from apartheid to democracy, the white minority government allocated R4 504 for the education of a white pupil, R3 625 for the education of an Indian pupil, R2 855 for the education of a coloured pupil, and a paltry R1 532 for the education of an African pupil (Letseka 1997). There is no doubt that the average white pupil benefited from educational expenditure that was nearly three times as great as that for the average African pupil (Lemon 2004).

Fiske and Ladd (2004) argue that, at the height of apartheid, per pupil spending in white schools was 10 times that in the African schools. Even after a significant increase in spending on behalf of black students during the waning years of apartheid, spending on white students remained two and a half times that of African students in urban areas, and three and a half times that of African students in most of the homelands. Ramphele (2001: 3) is unequivocal that 'South African whites were raised to become citizens while black South Africans were denied not only the rights of citizenship, but also the kind of education that would prepare them to become morally autonomous agents'. In this regard, apartheid 'gave to whites the status of full citizens while providing restricted, ethnically ascribed, second-class citizenship for blacks in separate and ostensibly independent states' (Enslin 2003: 76). The HSRC Student Pathways Study confirms that the challenges sketched here continue to beset both the provision of education in South Africa and the performance of the labour market.

The HSRC Student Pathways Study

The Student Pathways Study is a tracer of the 2000–02 cohort of leavers (drop-outs) and graduates in seven selected public higher education institutions (HEIs). The HEIs are the University of the Witwatersrand (Wits), the former Pretoria Technikon (now part of the merged Tswane University of Technology), the University of Stellenbosch (US), the former Peninsula Technikon (now part of the merged Cape Peninsula University of Technology), the University of the Western Cape (UWC), the University of Fort Hare (UFH) and the former University of the North (now part of the merged University of Limpopo). The rationale behind this institutional typology was to capture the characteristic features of South Africa's higher education sector in both rural and urban locations. On the one hand, we have the disadvantaged historically black institutions (HBIs) that were established by the apartheid system to serve particular ethnic and cultural groups and are located in areas that were demarcated for residence by specific racial groups. On the other hand, we have historically white institutions (HWIs) of either English- or Afrikaans-speaking background that are located in urban or peri-urban areas that were demarcated exclusively for white residence and were traditionally advantaged by the apartheid system.

The aim of the Student Pathways Study was to investigate factors influencing the transition of students through higher education, in particular students' perceptions of institutional retention strategies, factors affecting pass rates, failure rates, drop-out rates, graduation rates and throughput rates,[7] and to understand their labour market pathways as well as their employment experiences. The study drew on four data sets:

- the institutions' *unit record data*, obtained from the Department of Education's Higher Education Management Information System (HEMIS);
- the *survey data*,[8] which drew on responses of 34 548 respondents (20 353 leavers and 14 195 graduates);[9]
- the *qualitative data*, which were developed from structured interviews with senior members of management and senior academic staff;
- and the universities' *secondary sources*, mainly institutional reports and strategic planning documents, as well as independent sources on higher education nationally and internationally.

Collectively, these data sets were used to compile individual case study reports for each of the seven participating HEIs.

Understanding student drop-out

The problem of student drop-out is very disquieting because it is perceived to reflect inadequacies in the education system in terms of both quality and quantity (Letseka 2007; Sibanda 2004). There is also the perception that it reflects an inefficient use of resources (Simkins et al. 2007; McGaha & Fitzpatrick 2005). Daniel et al. (2006) define a drop-out as an individual who does not complete a learning programme or who takes a path that does not lead him or her to graduate successfully with the associated qualification. In the context of South Africa, with its history of apartheid education policies and legislation, university student drop-out has powerful socio-economic and political overtones. It is regarded as the perpetuation of past exclusions and inequalities and 'an unjust subversion of the historic promise of freedom and democracy' (Pandor 2007). Badad (2004) notes that in 1998 South African universities and technikons produced about 75 000 graduates and diplomates. Had there been reasonable throughput rates, they should have produced at least 100 000 graduates/diplomates. For Badad, environments need to be built in which especially historically disadvantaged learners can, through academic support, excellent teaching, mentoring and other initiatives, have every chance of succeeding and graduating with the relevant knowledge, competencies, skills and attributes that are required for any occupation and profession and for productive citizenship.

The Department of Education (DoE) acknowledges that drop-out rates are high and completion rates are low: there are 'high drop-out rates due to financial and/ or academic exclusions and students in good academic and financial standing not remaining in the public higher education system' (DoE 2001: 17). The DoE is concerned that the high drop-out rates cost the country R1.3 billion a year and divert resources from the expansion of higher education and from redressing inequalities inherited from the apartheid era (DoE 2001).[10] In 2005, the DoE determined that out of the 120 000 students who enrolled in 2000, an estimated 36 000 (or 30%) dropped out in their first year of study. In its report (summarised in Table 7.1) it stated:

> The data [Table 5 of the report] show that about 36 000 (or 30%) of the total cohort of 120 000 first-time entering undergraduates in universities and technikons dropped out at the end of their first year of studies, and that a further 24 000 dropped out after either two or three years of study. The total of the cohort that had dropped out by the 2003 academic year was therefore 60 000 (or 50%). Only 26 500 (or 22%) of the total cohort had graduated by the end of their third or fourth years of study. The remaining 33 500 were studying in 2003 but did not complete their qualifications in that year. It seems possible that this first-time entering cohort of the 2000 academic year may not achieve an overall graduation rate of even 40%. (DoE 2005: 9)

Between 2000 and 2003, the cost of drop-outs increased more than threefold to R4.5 billion in subsidies and bursaries to HEIs. All these data confirm long-held views about the country's low graduation rates (DoE 1997; Cloete & Bunting 2000).[11] There is no doubt that at 50% South Africa's drop-out rate is high and thus a matter of national concern. Although in the US the estimated drop-out rate is 46%, the drop-out rate in parts of Western Europe remains at just under 30% (House of Commons 2008; HESA 2007).[12] For instance, the drop-out rate in the UK is estimated to be 22%, while in Germany it is 27%. While UK universities are under pressure to increase participation in higher education to 50% for the under-thirties by 2010,

Table 7.1 *Higher education undergraduate drop-out rates, 2000–2003*

Progress of 2000 cohort of undergraduates	Universities	Technikons	Total
Dropped out at the end of 2000 (%)	25	34	30
Dropped out at the end of 2001 (%)	9	13	11
Dropped out at the end of 2002 (%)	7	11	9
Total dropped out 2000–02 (%)	41	58	50
Graduated in 2002 or 2003 (%)	26	19	22
Studying in 2003 but not completing (%)	33	22	28
Total in cohort	59 000	61 000	120 000

Source: DoE (2005: 9)

too many of the school leavers lack skills such as sufficient concentration to read a monograph, the ability to identify pertinent points from a lecture, or the knowledge of basic grammar and punctuation.[13] When they enrol at universities their level of under-preparedness is exacerbated by a lack of interaction with tutors. Many senior academics take little interest in teaching undergraduates primarily because most grants from the government are based on output in research and publications. It has been noted that nearly £1 billion spent by the government over the past five years on various schemes to cut student drop-out rates has had no impact.[14]

Key findings of the study

The Student Pathways Study revealed that while there was a combination of reasons why South African students drop out of higher education without obtaining a qualification, four reasons stood out prominently: lack of finance, academic failure, reasons related to institutional culture, and personal or family reasons.

Lack of finance

On average, 70% of the surveyed students came from family backgrounds of low socio-economic status (SES) (see Figure 7.2). Their parents'/guardians' levels of education ranged between 'no formal education' to 'some secondary education', and their monthly income ranged from 'no income' to between R1–R400 and R801–R1 600 per month. Altman (2007) argues that in South Africa earnings from employment and self-employment are low relative to the cost of living. Despite the projected 6% economic growth rate, 65% of working people still earn less than

Figure 7.2 *Average socio-economic status (SES) of families*

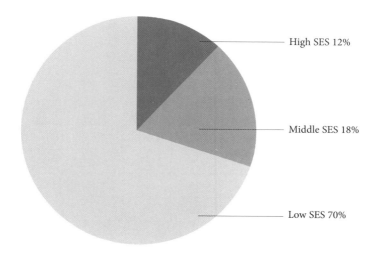

High SES 12%

Middle SES 18%

Low SES 70%

Source: Calculations by author from HSRC Student Pathways Study, 2005

R2 500 per month, the same as a decade ago. Fifty per cent of South Africans live below the poverty line of R430 per person a month. Altman argues that even

> people who earn more than R430 per month per person are still extremely poor. With current dependency ratios, R430 is just slightly more than the MDG [Millennium Development Goal] target of $2 per day which is a ghastly thought in a middle-income country cost structure. (2007: 22)

Koen (2007) points to the working-class and lower-middle-class origins of many UWC students. Similarly, Case and Deaton (1999) found that African households generally spent R13.80 a month per child in primary school and nearly twice as much, R25 per child, in secondary school, while white households spent R129 per month for a primary school child and R165 for a secondary school child. Thus white households spent roughly 9 and 7 times, respectively, what African households spent on their children's education. The small share of educational expenses in the budget of African households can be attributed to their low SES. The Student Pathways Study shows that low SES is more pronounced among HBI students' households, where it is above the 70% average for the seven HEIs included in the study. For instance, at both the University of Fort Hare and the former University of the North the percentage of low SES was 82%, while at UWC and the former Pentech it was 79% and 74%

Figure 7.3 *Distribution of socio-economic status (SES) within institutions*

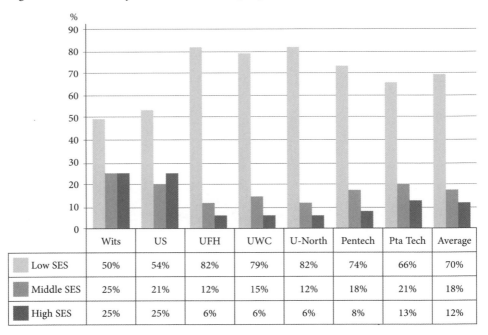

	Wits	US	UFH	UWC	U-North	Pentech	Pta Tech	Average
Low SES	50%	54%	82%	79%	82%	74%	66%	70%
Middle SES	25%	21%	12%	15%	12%	18%	21%	18%
High SES	25%	25%	6%	6%	6%	8%	13%	12%

Source: Based on data from HSRC Student Pathways Study, 2005
Note: Wits = University of Witswatersrand; US = University of Stellenbosch; UFH = University of Fort Hare; UWC = University of the Western Cape; U-North = former University of the North; Pentech = former Peninsula Technikon; Pta Tech = former Pretoria Technikon

Figure 7.4 *Number of NSFAS awards granted, 1991–2006*

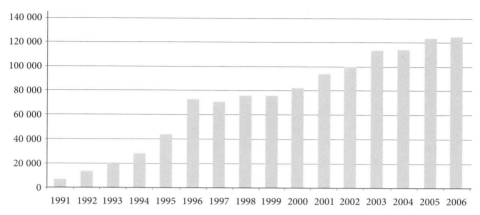

Source: Adapted from NSFAS (2007)

respectively. It should be kept in mind that the areas in which these HEIs are located are characterised by high unemployment especially among the graduates[15] and the youth,[16] abject poverty,[17] and dependence on social welfare grants and pensions.[18] While there was evidence of low SES in historically white institutions (HWIs), it was below the average of the seven participating institutions. For instance, at Wits it was 50%, while at Stellenbosch and at the former Pretoria Technikon it was 54% and 66% respectively (see Figure 7.3).

The National Student Financial Aid Scheme (NSFAS), a legal entity established by an Act of Parliament in 1999 to support talented but needy students, especially from previously disadvantaged communities, has had reasonable successes. Jackson (2002) points out that between 1993 and 1999, the NSFAS made over 400 000 awards to students, 99% of whom were black. Indeed, the number of awards granted by NSFAS to needy students almost doubled, from 72 788 in 1996 to 124 730 in 2006 (see Figure 7.4). But it remains to be seen whether NSFAS support reaches far and deep enough to ameliorate the plight of 70% of students of low SES, who are dropping out of higher education because of financial difficulties.

Academic failure and poor or no career guidance

Academic failure and poor or no career guidance were other reasons for dropping out. For instance, 80% of the surveyed drop-outs indicated that they were failing some or all of their courses and realised that they were unlikely to pass at the end of the year. There was evidence of a mismatch between the students' choices of field of study and their ability to do well in their chosen field. This can be attributed to poor career guidance or, in some cases, to no career guidance at all. At one institution students reported that they battled with the concepts and terminology in their chosen field of study; they struggled to learn all the new terminology or 'think' in their chosen field, and eventually lost interest and dropped out. At the former University of the North an estimated 59% of drop-outs reported that they did not receive any career guidance at school; 55% at the former Pentech and 66% at UWC reported likewise. The challenge of lack of career guidance at schools was cited during interviews at the University of Fort Hare, where it was indicated that the university builds career guidance into its outreach recruitment strategy. It can therefore be reasonably inferred that the choices of institution and field of study that the students made were limited by their lack of exposure to different institution types and available career options.

There was consensus among the interviewed senior academics and senior members of management that upon arrival at HEIs most young people do not know what they want to study; they are ill-prepared and emotionally immature for the complex nature of higher education teaching and learning; they lack self-esteem, have poor general knowledge and fail university entry tests. These shortcomings are consistent with research in higher education in South Africa and internationally, which suggests that most first-year university entrants lack the necessary 'epistemological access' (Boughey 2005; Morrow 1992), are under-prepared for university study (Moll 2004; Nyamapfene & Letseka 1995),[19] and in most cases are first-generation university students who have little access to social networks with reservoirs of experience of university study (Slonimsky & Shalem 2006).

Slonimsky and Shalem (2006) argue that students who have matriculated are generally expected to be highly practised in working on text-based realities and creating their own text-based realities through writing. However, a significant proportion of students currently enrolling in universities do not appear to have mastered properties of text-based realities. They tend to follow a series of pervasive patterns in their approach to texts and epistemic practices when they first engage in university study. These include verbatim reproduction or plagiarism; a tendency to focus on examples rather than on principles; a tendency to write from a highly subjective viewpoint without depersonalising; a failure to pull out arguments in text or to cast them; a tendency to include anecdotes as a justification for claims; and a tendency to be prescriptive or normative when asked to be analytic. As alluded to above, the academic problems of many black South African students are not an isolated phenomenon. Furthermore, these problems are manifestations of the impact of many years of their families' exclusion from opportunities and privileges by apartheid policies and legislation.

Institutional cultures

Jonathan Jansen, former dean of education at the University of Pretoria, contends that the notion of institutional cultures is succinctly captured in the expression 'the way we do things around here'. Jansen (2004) argues, with reference to schools and universities, that institutional culture has to do with whose portraits and paintings appear in the corridors; what collections dominate the library; who gets an honorary degree (and who does not); who dominates the school governing bodies and who gets relegated to the status of observer; whose liturgy is represented in the school assembly and whose is excluded. Institutional culture has to do with whose language dominates at public meetings or events and whose is excluded; who has access to institutional contracts and who remains marginalised; the complexion of who works in the school's secretarial pool and the complexion of those who clean the swimming pool; who sits together in the staffroom and who sits somewhere else; who gets called 'Mr' and who, irrespective of age, is simply called 'Klaas'. It has to do with the content of what appears on the emblem of the institution, the content of school songs, the metaphors for talking about others, and the ways in which schools or universities talk about the future.

Senior academics who were interviewed at some HWIs made reference to the 'deep-end dilemma', which occurred when students' failure to cope with their studies was callously dismissed as 'someone else's problem', that 'someone else' being either the student himself or herself or the institution's student academic support services. Some of the surveyed students reported that culturally they did not 'fit in'; they felt insecure on campus; they were frustrated by the way university administration dealt with 'some' students' issues, and got the sense they either had to 'sink or swim'. According to Tinto's (1975) Integration Model, lack of integration into the social system of an institution leads to low commitment and increases the probability that individuals will decide to leave the institution and pursue alternative activities. As Tinto puts it: '[A] person can conceivably be integrated into the social sphere of the college and still drop out because of insufficient integration into the academic domain of the college (e.g. through poor grade performance)' (1975: 92). Central to Tinto's Integration Model is the degree to which students' participation and involvement in internal institutional practices enhance or inhibit their perseverance in academic performance. Where the experience of the institution is negative, the individual tends to experience diminished academic and/or social integration, and may come to the conclusion that the costs (academic, social, emotional and/or financial) of persisting outweigh the benefits.

At some institutions, respondents to the HSRC survey reported that students' academic and support services, such as the foundation-year programme, the bridging programme, and guidance and counselling services, were dysfunctional, poorly coordinated and not prioritised but treated as peripheral or voluntary services. While such services are perceived to be critical for students, especially for those from previously disadvantaged communities who are regarded as 'at risk', there was a perception that they were not taken seriously by senior, more experienced academics, but were instead passed over to younger, less qualified and inexperienced junior members of staff.

Personal and family reasons

While some of the surveyed students attributed their dropping out to poor or dysfunctional provision of student and academic support services, others candidly reported on their hectic lifestyles or some aspects of their personal lives that sidetracked them from their studies and resulted in their premature withdrawal from the HEIs. For instance, 77% of the respondents reported that they were disappointed with the poor quality of student life and sought pleasure off campus. Some reported that they took permanent or odd jobs, which left them with little time to concentrate on their studies. My contention is that juggling work and study impacted negatively on the students' stress levels and sidetracked them from prioritising their studies. Other respondents reported on their state of health or on personal circumstances that did not allow them to continue with their studies. For instance, some students gave birth and dropped out to look after the baby; others dropped out to look after a sick relative; and some had to travel too far to get to the institution.

Students' labour market pathways and experiences

In this section I compare pathways of both the graduates (those who successfully completed their university qualification) and the leavers (those who left before completing). An emergent but encouraging trend from the HSRC study is that both the leavers and the graduates found work. However, there is a recognisable poor performance of leavers relative to graduates, across race, institution and field of study. What is worrying but not unexpected, given South Africa's enduring history of labour market discrimination, is the astounding incidence of earning inequalities by race and gender (see Table 7.2). There is extensive research on the discriminatory nature of South Africa's labour market (Pauw et al. 2006; Bhorat & Oosthuizen 2005; Moleke 2005, 2006; Bhorat 2004). As Moleke (2005: 2) argues, '[T]he occupational segregation and inequalities in the South African labour market are a result of two phenomena – discrimination and acquired human capital. The labour market is characterised by racial job segregation both between sectors and between occupational categories.' Moleke (2006: 4) contends that '[w]hites are still overrepresented in skilled occupations and their representation at senior-management level is also relatively high'.

As shown in Table 7.2, the data from the study confirm claims of earning inequalities by race and gender (Woolard & Woolard 2006). For instance, the estimated nominal mean monthly earning for female graduates was R7 982, compared with R15 195 for male graduates. In other words, the average salary of male graduates is almost double the estimated nominal mean monthly earning for female graduates. However, there was evident bias in earnings favourable to female leavers relative to the male leavers. The estimated nominal mean monthly earning for female leavers was R5 962,

Table 7.2 *Nominal mean monthly earnings for graduates and leavers (in rands)*

	Male		Female	
	Graduates	Leavers	Graduates	Leavers
All population groups	15 195	5 136	7 982	5 962
African	13 072	5 163	9 285	5 909
Coloured	14 949	4 182	5 905	3 886
Asian	25 597	5 726	7 091	7 924
White	16 679	5 363	7 373	7 825

Source: HSRC Student Pathways Study, 2005, H Bhorat's calculations

compared with R5 136 for male leavers. African female leavers earned an estimated R5 909, while their male counterparts earned R5 163. Similarly, Asian female leavers earned R7 924 – more than their male counterparts, who pocketed a monthly income of R5 726. The only exceptions were coloured female leavers, whose monthly earning of R3 886 was less than their male counterparts' earning of R4 182.

In some cases female leavers earned more than female graduates. For example, Asian female leavers earned R7 924, compared with Asian female graduates' monthly earning of R7 091. White female leavers earned R7 825, compared to white female graduates' monthly earning of R7 373 and white male leavers' monthly earning of R5 363. The trend seems to suggest that except for coloured females, the labour market appears to be generally favourable to female leavers with respect to monthly earnings.

That the South African labour market continues to be discriminatory is evident in the disparities in unemployment rates of African and white graduates and leavers, and of Africans from HWIs relative to Africans from HBIs (see Table 7.3). The estimated unemployment rates for African leavers and graduates at HBIs were 68% and 53% respectively, compared with the estimated unemployment rates for white leavers and graduates at HWIs, which were 13% and 27% respectively. This suggests that Africans and whites have distinctly different probabilities of finding employment. Furthermore, African graduates from Wits had an unemployment rate of 35%, while African graduates from the UFH had an unemployment rate of 56%. The Wits unemployment rate is 21 percentage points lower than that of UFH.

Total unemployment rates of Africans who studied at HWIs are lower than those of their counterparts who studied at HBIs. As noted in the *Econometrix Ecobulletin*, '[G]iven that the lion's share of business is owned by Whites, there is a tendency to

Table 7.3 *Expanded unemployment rates (%) by institution and population group**

| | Population group | | | | | | | |
| | African | | Coloured | | Asian | | White | |
Institution	L	G	L	G	L	G	L	G
University of Fort Hare	75	56	–	–	–	–	–	–
University of Stellenbosch	–	40	7	35	–	45	6	3
University of the North	68	59	49	–	–	–	–	–
University of the Western Cape	50	54	38	22		62	–	–
University of the Witwatersrand	68	35	68	–	70	41	37	17
Peninsula Technikon	58	55	50	28	–	62	–	–
Technikon Pretoria	58	55	50	28	–	–	13	16
Historically white	53	45	45	28	57	37	13	27
Historically black	58	53	38	22	–	60	–	–

Source: Adapted from H Bhorat's calculations using data from HSRC Student Pathways Study, 2005
Notes: G = graduates; L = leavers
*The expanded unemployment rate as defined by Statistics South Africa includes those people who are out of the labour market, or who are not economically active, or who are not available for work. This category includes full-time scholars and students, full-time homemakers, those who are retired, and those who are unable or unwilling to work.

Table 7.4 *Unemployment by field of study (%)*

	Institution type (apartheid classification)					
	Historically black		Historically white			
	African		African		White	
Field	G	L	G	L	G	L
Business/commerce	24	78	58	59	14	–
Education	39	39	11	19	52	17
Humanities	63	74	61	64	38	21
SET	58	70	43	62	21	29
Other	57	56	54	54	35	2

Source: Adapted from H Bhorat's calculations using data from HSRC Student Pathways Study, 2005

recruit from the former white universities than from the more rural Black [African] educational institutions.'[20] What is also evident from the study is that HBIs are poor in ensuring the success of their student clientele in the labour market. Even when race, type of institution and field of study are controlled for, African graduates are still finding it harder to secure employment than their white counterparts.

When the above data are disaggregated by field of study, unemployment rates of whites remain significantly lower than unemployment rates of Africans for all fields of study except education (see Table 7.4). In business and commerce, white graduates experienced a 14% unemployment rate, compared with 24% for African graduates from HBIs, a difference of 10 percentage points. The rates for science, engineering and technology (SET) were 21% and 58% respectively, while for humanities the rates were 38% and 63% respectively.

The unemployment rates for Africans at HWIs were lower than those of Africans from HBIs across all fields except in business and commerce. For instance, while the unemployment rate for African graduates in the field of education at HBIs was 39%, the unemployment rate for their African counterparts at HWIs was 11%. The unemployment rate of African graduates in business and commerce at HBIs was 24%, compared with the rate of their African counterparts at HWIs, which was 58%. This is surprising given persistent perceptions that HWIs offer a better quality of education than HBIs.

Conclusion

In this chapter I have situated the problem of university drop-outs against the backdrop of high levels of unemployment in South Africa. I have interrogated factors that contribute to university drop-out rates and argued that they can be attributed to South Africa's historical legacy of apartheid, which excluded the vast majority of blacks from opportunities and privileges while availing these opportunities and privileges to the minority whites. I have also demonstrated that for those students who do find jobs, glaring labour market discrimination and race and gender inequalities persist. These arguments cohere with the broad aim and key theme of this book, which is to understand and develop the relationship between 'lifelong learning' and 'work' for the majority of people who are engaged in a wide spectrum of economic and social activities to sustain themselves within the shifting but persistent lines of social inclusion and exclusion, as well as the challenges facing higher education development in 'peripheral economies' in the globalised world.

Notes

1   See also Khumalo S and Mmope N, Skills shortage is genuine threat to growth, say bosses, *Business Report,* 24 May 2007, and Quintal A, Shortage of skills in SA not chronic, *Pretoria News*, 24 May 2007.

2   See Ensor L, SA's skills shortage an urban legend, *Business Day*, 23 May 2007, and Hamlyn M and Khumalo S, Skills shortage an urban legend – Manyi, *Business Report*, 23 May 2007.

3   In their evaluation of South Africa's performance in the Trends in International Mathematic and Science Study (TIMSS) of 2003, Reddy et al. (2006) note that South Africa has one of the highest gross national incomes (GNI in US dollars) per capita of the group, yet has the lowest average mean score in mathematics and science. They argue that the implication of this is that there would be very few learners graduating from the school system with results in mathematics good enough to permit access to tertiary studies in the science or engineering fields.

4   Ray M, Educashen crysis: Wanted: 68 000 engineers/artisans, *FinWeek*, 7 February 2008.

5   In a series of research papers on the drop-out crisis in US high schools, Robert Belfanz and associates (2004, 2006, 2007) at the John Hopkins University's Center for Social Organization of Schools have coined the term 'dropout factories' to describe nearly 2 000 US high schools with low graduation rates and high drop-out rates. A critical question to ponder is, are some of South Africa's high schools 'dropout factories'?

6   See also Keating C, Too few SA graduates to close skills gap, *Cape Argus*, 31 October 2007.

7   In this study, throughput rate means the number of years taken to complete a qualification for which one is registered (see Subotzky 2003).

8   The survey covered a broad range of areas, including information on schooling; transition from school to higher education; passage through higher education; transition from higher education to the labour market; and personal information, including household characteristics such as parents'/guardians' highest level of education, parents'/guardians' employment situation, their monthly earning as well as the sector in which they are employed (i.e. families' socio-economic status).

9   The survey yielded 5 491 valid responses, or a 15.9% return rate.

10   See also Drop-outs add to SA problems, *Times Higher Education*, 22 June 2001.

11   See also Meintjies F, Higher education registers a fail mark overall, *Sunday Times*, 6 August 2000.

12   See also Garner R, £800m funding fails to slow university drop-out rates, *The Independent*, 20 February 2008; Grimston J, Student dropouts cost taxpayer £1bn, *The Sunday Times* (London), 17 February 2008; Grimston J, Nearly a quarter of students do not finish their university courses: What is going wrong? *The Sunday Times* (London), 24 February 2008.

13 Grimston J, Nearly a quarter of students do not finish their university courses: What is going wrong? *The Sunday Times* (London), 24 February 2008.

14 Grimston J, Student dropouts cost taxpayer £1bn, *The Sunday Times* (London), 17 February 2008.

15 See Pauw et al. (2006).

16 See Bernstein A, Tales of the young and the jobless, *Business Day*, 6 July 2007; and Unemployment rate amongst young South Africans as high as 88% in Polokwane, CDE media brief, 9 July 2007. Accessed 28 July 2008, http://www.cde.org.za.

17 See Gyekye & Akinboade (2003); Punt et al. (2005); Oosthuizen & Nieuwoudt (2003); DSSPA (2005).

18 See What can we expect after Mbeki and Manuel go? *Financial Mail*, 23 February 2007, and Mamburu (2004).

19 See also Grimston J, Student dropouts cost taxpayer £1bn, *The Sunday Times* (London), 17 February 2008; Grimston J, Nearly a quarter of students do not finish their university courses: What is going wrong? *The Sunday Times* (London), 24 February 2008.

20 Employment equity and skills shortage: Myths and realities, *Econometrix Ecobulletin* No. 15107/0719, 23 July 2007.

References

Altman M (2007) *Evidence-based employment scenarios: Employment scenarios to 2040.* HSRC Research Paper. Pretoria: HSRC

Badad S (2004) Transforming South African higher education 1990–2003: Goals, policy initiatives and critical challenges and issues. In N Cloete, P Pillay, S Badad & T Moja (eds) *National policy and a regional response in South African higher education.* Cape Town: David Philip

Belfanz R & Byrnes V (2006) Closing the mathematics achievement gap in high-poverty middle schools: Enablers and constraints. *Journal of Education for Students Placed at Risk* 11(2): 143–159

Belfanz R & Legters N (2004) Locating the dropout crisis: Which high schools produce the nation's dropouts? Where are they located? Who attends them? Paper prepared for the Center for Social Organization of Schools, Johns Hopkins University, Baltimore, MD, USA

Belfanz R, Legters N, West TC & Weber LM (2007) Are NCLB's measures, incentives, and improvement strategies the right ones for the nation's low-performing high schools? *American Educational Research Journal* 44(3): 559–593

Bhorat H (2004) Labour market challenges in the post-apartheid South Africa. *South African Journal of Economics* 72(5): 940–977

Bhorat H & Oosthuizen M (2005) The post-apartheid South African labour market. Working paper. Development Policy Research Unit (DPRU), University of Cape Town, South Africa

Boughey C (2005) Epistemological access to the university: An alternative perspective. *South African Journal of Higher Education* 19(3): 230–242

Case A & Deaton A (1999) School inputs and educational outcomes in South Africa. *Quarterly Journal of Economics* 114(3): 1047–1084

Cloete N & Bunting I (2000) *Higher education transformation: Assessing performance in South Africa*. Pretoria: Centre for Higher Education Transformation

Daniel SS, Walsh AK, Goldston DB, Arnold EM, Reboussin BA & Wood FB (2006) Suicidality, school drop-out, and reading problems among adolescents. *Journal of Learning Disabilities* 39(6): 507–514

DoE (Department of Education, South Africa) (1997) *Education White Paper 3: A Programme for the Transformation of Higher Education*. Pretoria: DoE

DoE (2001) *National plan for higher education*. Pretoria: DoE

DoE (2005) *Student enrolment planning in public higher education*. Pretoria: DoE

DoL (Department of Labour, South Africa) (2007) *National master scarce skills list for South Africa*. Pretoria: DoL

DSSPA (Department of Social Services and Poverty Alleviation, Western Cape province, South Africa) (2005) *The integrated poverty reduction strategy for the Western Cape province*. Cape Town: DSSPA

Enslin P (2003) Citizenship education in post-apartheid South Africa. *Cambridge Journal of Education* 33(1): 73–83

Fedderke JW, De Kadt R & Luiz JM (2000) Uneducating South Africa: The failure to address the 1910–1993 legacy. *International Review of Education* 46(3/4): 257–281

Fiske EB & Ladd HF (2004) *Elusive equity: Education reform in post-apartheid South Africa*. Washington, DC: Brookings Institution Press

Gyekye AB & Akinboade OA (2003) A profile of poverty in the Limpopo province of South Africa. *Eastern Africa Social Science Research Review* 19(2): 89–110

HESA (Higher Education Statistics Agency, UK) (2007) *University dropout rate*. Cheltenham: HESA

House of Commons (2008) *Staying the course: The retention of students in higher education courses. Tenth report of Session 2007–08*. London: HM Stationery Office

Jackson R (2002) The National Student Financial Aid Scheme of South Africa (NSFAS): How and why it works. *Welsh Journal of Education* 11(1): 82–94

Jansen J (2004) Race, education and democracy after ten years: How far have we come? Paper prepared for the Institute for Democracy in South Africa (IDASA), *Lessons from the Field: A Decade of Democracy in South Africa* (July)

Kallaway P (ed.) (1984) *Apartheid and education: The education of black South Africans*. Johannesburg: Ravan Press

Kallaway P, Kruss G, Fataar A & Donn G (eds) (1997) *Education after apartheid: South African education in transition*. Cape Town: UCT Press

Koen C (2007) *Postgraduate student retention and success: A South African case study*. Cape Town: HSRC Press

Kraak A (2003) HRD and the skills crisis. In A Kraak & H Perold (eds) *Human resources development review 2003: Education, employment and skills in South Africa*. Cape Town and East Lansing: HSRC Press and Michigan State University Press

Kraak A (2004) *An overview of South African human resources development*. Cape Town: HSRC Press

Kraak A (2006) High skills and joined-up policy: An introduction to the debate. In A Kraak, H Lauder, P Brown & D Ashton (eds) *Debating high skills and joined-up policy*. Cape Town: HSRC Press

Kraak A (2008) The education–economy relationship in South Africa, 2001–2005. In A Kraak & K Press (eds) *Human resources development review 2008: Education, employment and skills in South Africa*. Cape Town: HSRC Press

Lemon A (2004) Redressing school inequalities in the Eastern Cape, South Africa. *Journal of Southern African Studies* 30(2): 269–290

Letseka M (1997) Research and the empowerment of teachers. In J Mouton & J Muller (eds) *Knowledge, method and the public good*. Pretoria: HSRC

Letseka M (2007) Why students leave: The problem of high university drop-out rates. *HSRC Review* 5(3): 8–9

Mamburu DN (2004) Evaluation of the poverty relief programme in the Limpopo province within the context of the Reconstruction and Development Programme: A social work perspective. PhD thesis, University of Pretoria, South Africa

McGaha V & Fitzpatrick J (2005) Personal and social contributors to drop-out risk for undergraduate students. *College Student Journal* 39(2): 287–297

Moleke P (2005) Inequalities in higher education and the structure of the labour market. Cape Town: HSRC Press

Moleke P (2006) After ten years of employment equity, it's still business as usual. *HSRC Review* 4(1): 4–5

Moll I (2004) Curriculum responsiveness: The anatomy of a concept. In H Griesel (ed.) *Curriculum responsiveness: Case studies in higher education*. Pretoria: SAUVCA

Morrow W (1992) Epistemological access in university. *AD Issues* 1: 3–5

Nekhwevha F (1999) No matter how long the night, the day is sure to come: Culture and educational transformation in post-colonial Namibia and post-apartheid South Africa. *International Review of Education* 45(5/6): 491–506

NSFAS (National Student Financial Aid Scheme, South Africa) (2007) Presentation to the Portfolio Committee on Education, National Assembly, 2 November. Accessed 24 July 2008, https://www.nsfas.org.za

Nyamapfene K & Letseka M (1995) Problems of learning among first-year students in South African universities. *South African Journal of Higher Education* 9(1): 159–167

Oosthuizen MJ & Nieuwoudt L (2003) A poverty profile of the Western Cape province in South Africa. Stellenbosch Economic Working Paper No. 3, Bureau of Economic Research, University of Stellenbosch, South Africa

Pandor N (2007) Speech by Mrs Naledi Pandor, MP, Minister of Education, tabling departmental Budget vote for 2007/08 financial year, 29 May. Pretoria: DoE. Accessed 24 July 2008, http://www.education.gov.za

Pauw K, Bhorat H, Goga S, Ncube L & Van der Westhuizen C (2006) Graduate unemployment in the context of skills shortages, education and training: Findings from a firm survey. Working Paper 06/115. Development Policy Research Unit (DPRU), University of Cape Town, South Africa

Punt C, Pauw K & Van Schoor M (2005) A profile of the Limpopo province: Demographics, poverty, inequality and unemployment. Paper prepared for the Provincial Decision-Making Enabling Project (PROVIDE), Elsenburg, South Africa (August)

Ramphele M (2001) Citizenship challenges for South Africa's young democracy. *Daedalus: Journal of the American Academy of Arts and Sciences* 130(1): 1–17

Ramphele M (2005) Ten years of democracy, 1994–2004. Sixth Steve Biko Memorial Lecture, University of Cape Town, South Africa, 12 September. Transcript of lecture available from author

Reddy V (ed.) (2006) *Marking matric: Colloquium proceedings.* Cape Town: HSRC Press

Reddy V, Kanjee A, Diedericks G & Winnaar L (2006) *Mathematics and science achievement at South African schools in TIMSS 2003.* Cape Town: HSRC Press

Rose B & Tunmer R (eds) (1975) *Documents in South African education.* Johannesburg: AD Donker

Sibanda A (2004) Who drops out of school in South Africa? The influence of individual household characteristics. *African Population Studies* 19(1): 99–117

Simkins C, Rule S & Bernstein A (2007) *Doubling for growth: Addressing the maths and science challenge in South Africa's schools.* Report prepared for Centre for Development and Enterprise (CDE), Johannesburg, South Africa. Document made available to author

Slonimsky L & Shalem Y (2006) Pedagogic responsiveness for academic depth. *Journal of Education* 40: 35–58

Stats SA (Statistics South Africa) (2007) *Labour force survey, March 2007.* Pretoria: Stats SA

Subotzky G (2003) Public higher education and training. In A Kraak & H Perold (eds) *Human resources development review 2003: Education, employment and skills in South Africa.* Cape Town and East Lansing: HSRC Press and Michigan State University Press

Tinto V (1975) Dropout from higher education: A theoretical synthesis of recent research. *Review of Educational Research* 45(1): 89–125

Woolard I & Woolard C (2006) *Earning inequalities in South Africa, 1995–2003.* Cape Town: HSRC Press

8 Barriers to entry and progression in the solicitors' profession in England and Wales

Hilary Sommerlad with Jane Stapleford

Introduction

Recent years have seen a decrease in social mobility in the UK and the persistence of occupational segregation (Blanden & Machin 2007). Yet the same period has produced a policy discourse of diversity and equality and a government drive to create an education-based meritocracy by widening participation in higher education (HE) and opening up occupations to excluded groups. This chapter[1] draws on research into training for the solicitors' profession in England and Wales, conducted by the Centre for Research into Diversity in the Professions (CRDP), to reflect on some of the causes of this paradox, and on ways in which the employability of 'non-traditional' (NT)[2] law graduates might be enhanced. We begin by briefly delineating government diversity and equality policy in HE and discussing aspects of legal education and the solicitors' profession which make the occupation particularly resistant to democratisation. We then discuss the findings of a longitudinal study of student and trainee solicitors, and conclude by presenting the implications of these for legal training and the diversity agenda.

Government policy and higher education

Improving global competitiveness has provided the primary rationale for the recent proliferation of diversity and equality initiatives in the UK, and a preoccupation with supply-side deficits has focused policy on the creation of a learning society as the best means of enhancing collective and individual enterprise. This has led to the establishment of a government target that 50 per cent of 18- to 30-year-olds participate in HE by 2010.[3] The egalitarian dimension to this expansion of the university sector also features in policy discourse; thus the 2003 White Paper speaks of the 'vital role' of universities and colleges 'in expanding opportunity and social justice' (DfES 2003).[4] It is also recognised that rationalising and increasing the representativeness of occupations enhances people's *sense* of social justice, and increasing the legitimacy of social institutions is therefore proffered as another rationale for widening participation (WP) policies.[5]

However, the goal of creating an education-based meritocracy has been undermined by the failure to address the stratification of the UK HE sector. On the one hand, a policy of fiscal prudence has denied to universities the increased resources to enable them to support the learning needs of a larger and more diverse student body (DfES 2003). On the other hand, government has deployed differential funding arrangements to encourage the development of a 'tertiary tripartism' comprised of research-based, teaching-focused and locally-oriented HE institutions, described as gold, silver and bronze sectors (Ainley 2003; Boon & Duncan 1990). This stratification is matched by the social polarisation of the sector's student bodies: middle-class (especially public-school educated) students are predominantly located in the elite universities (the gold sector), while NT students are overwhelmingly concentrated in the new, 'post-1992' universities[6] (the bronze sector), producing a 'racial divide' in the HE sector (Mirza 1998). This social polarisation has contributed to the hardening of pre-existing hierarchies within HE (HEFCE 2000; Reay et al. 2002; Archer 2007), which are naturalised as the attributes of the students in the gold sector are, as Bourdieu suggests, 'misrecognised' as representing objective forms of 'merit', while the corresponding devaluation of new universities provides a meritocratic justification for elite labour markets to exclude their graduates (Brennan & McGeevor 1990; Sommerlad 2008). As a result, the assumption that the expansion of HE could open up the professions has been challenged (Walkerdine et al. 2001; Brennan & Shah 2003).

The solicitors' profession and legal education

Legal education and the solicitors' profession exemplify these tensions between the UK government's modernising, meritocratic project and the role of HE in legitimating the elite occupations' traditional exclusionary practices. Professional control over training and qualification has long been the primary occupational closure mechanism (Larson 1977), enabling law to maintain its white, male, middle-class culture (Nicolson 2005) and hence its social status (Witz 1992). The reduction in control as a result of graduate entry has had little effect since, as observed above, the elite law schools tend to draw their students from the same social strata as did the profession. The impact of the recent WP agenda on these schools has, to date, been similarly slight, both in terms of opening them up to NT students and in the area of pedagogical innovation. Instead many commentators have argued that overt closure strategies continue to operate in law schools (see, for example, Dhavan 1989; Thornton 1996),[7] which have been described as 'training for hierarchy' (Kennedy 1992). Thus law curricula generally continue to embody the classed, raced and gendered nature of the legal profession; the connections between professional status and determination of what constitutes legal knowledge have resulted in conservative pedagogies which accentuate the mystifying nature of legal doctrinalism in their predominance of black-letter law and the minimal input of socio-legal studies into the law curriculum (Rochette & Pue 2001; Thornton 1996, 1998).[8]

Beyond the academy, the profession remains its own gatekeeper, as it has retained direct control over access to, and the experience of, the training contracts that all aspiring lawyers must obtain in order to qualify. Despite rhetorical commitments to the need to increase the diversity of the profession (Braithwaite 2007), in practice 'new' university students suffer significant disadvantage in the legal labour market (Halpern 1994; Shiner 1999, 2000; Vignaendra 2001) since employers tend to give contracts on the basis of contacts or (in the case of the corporate sector) to seek graduates with an upper second-class degree from an 'old' university (Rolfe & Anderson 2003). Described as 'misguided' (Centre LGS 2005), this preference is not based on evaluative, comparative research (Tong & Pue 1999). Indeed, Quality Assessment Agency (QAA) reviews have consistently indicated broad parity between HE institutions in terms of teaching quality; and anecdotal evidence suggests that there may be an inverse relationship between the status of a university and the importance attached to teaching (Chevalier & Conlon 2003). However, the preference for universities 'marked' with class status is more than explicable if we see education as a positional good, and acknowledge the dominance of the middle class over professional education and training. It then follows that one of the primary functions of assessment and qualification is to advantage those existing class groups who have best access to prestigious institutions, 'consecrating' their social and embryonic professional identities (Bourdieu 2000). This requires wilful blindness to the contribution to academic success made by excellent primary and secondary schooling and parental support, promoting a sense that such students are entitled to enter and succeed in elite professions, thereby naturalising pre-existing hierarchies.

Moreover, employers' entry requirements also exceed simple degree and/or professional qualifications and extend to a range of attributes and practices many of which are tacit and involve insider knowledge (Sommerlad & Sanderson 2002). These attributes are likely to be so instinctive and intrinsic to professional and organisational narratives that employers themselves may not be aware of them. Their obscure and intangible character also makes them difficult for students to decode or to evidence, since they generally depend on the possession of the 'right' cultural capital or appropriate ways of 'doing' gender or class (Sommerlad 2007; Francis & Sommerlad 2008).

The profession's control over workplace training, through the training contract, is also a primary means of maintaining its social composition, since the workplace is a 'crucible of identity formation' (Hayward & Mac an Ghaill 1997). As a result, even where a law firm's intake does become more diverse, this diversity is effectively erased through professional socialisation. Studies of a range of professions reveal how a culture that is unwelcoming to outsiders (Dryburgh 1999) is produced through the taken-for-granted, micro-inequities that permeate everyday practice. For instance, Beagan's work on enculturation into the medical profession (2001) has considered how neither an institutional commitment to equality nor the implementation of anti-discrimination policies has displaced hegemonic professionalism. Drawing on Essed's concept of 'everyday racism' (1991), she notes that while bureaucratisation has reduced overt discrimination, 'micro level interactional processes' continue to convey the terms of inclusion into the dominant culture, thereby inducing assimilation.

The applicability of this work to solicitors is supported by empirical studies of entry into and progression within the profession, which reveal the pressure on practitioners to conform to professional norms, values and rituals. For instance, Goriely and Williams (1996) suggest the persistence, despite the implementation of anti-discriminatory measures, of the traditional approach to evaluating newly qualified solicitors, which relies more on measuring them against characteristics of the suitable 'chap' than on a rational, standardised approach to evaluation and appraisal (see also Sommerlad & Sanderson 1998; Sommerlad 2002; Pierce 2002). Hence, despite an 850 per cent overall increase in women solicitors over the last 25 years (Bolton & Muzio 2007), professional structures and culture have not been feminised; instead, the coincidence of mass female entry with a general expansion of the profession facilitated the redesign (Sandefur 2007; Hagan & Kay 1995) and stratification of professional work, concentrating ownership and governance in fewer hands.

A study of law students and trainee solicitors

We now reflect on the issues raised above through a discussion of the findings of an ongoing longitudinal study of students and trainee solicitors. We consider the nature of NT aspiring lawyers' encounters with the law school and the solicitors' profession, and pay particular attention to the processes of professional socialisation that those who gain entry are obliged to undergo. We conclude by discussing the implications of these findings for professional training and the diversity agenda, exploring positive strategies that might both resource such students and sensitise the professional field to the needs of diverse entrants.

Research method

The research project (which was piloted in 2003–04) was begun in September 2004 and is a longitudinal study of two cohorts of part-time and full-time postgraduate students undergoing the academic stage of their vocational training (the legal practice course [LPC]) at a 'new' university in a large provincial city. Cohort 1 comprised part-time students (2004–06) and full-time students (2004–05); cohort 2 comprised part-time students (2005–07) and full-time students (2005–06). The number of students in each cohort varied slightly in each year of the study: in 2004–05, 30 were part-time, 57 full-time; in 2005–06, 33 were part-time, 63 full-time. The research with the students was designed to track developments in career aspirations, perceptions of the legal professional field, levels of attainment during and after the vocational training stage and into qualification, and experiences of professional socialisation.

A mixture of methods was deployed: two questionnaires were administered to the student cohorts (both full- and part-time) at different stages in the LPC, the first during the students' first week and the second towards the end of their course. The data from the questionnaires were quality-checked and, where appropriate, coded before being input into an analytical statistical package (SPSS). Findings from the analysis in part determined the scope and nature of the in-depth qualitative follow-up work.

The first questionnaire was followed by focus groups. Approximately one-third of the student body participated in four groups of between 4 and 9 students, which were selected to comprise various combinations: for instance, one group was all female, one all 'non-white', one mixed both in terms of gender and ethnicity. Each group was led by a different member of the research team. The groups explored views on law as a discipline and on ideal jobs, and drew timelines charting and exploring their first awareness of a desire to do law through to where they saw themselves in 5, 10 and 15 years' time. In order to elicit internalised and possibly tacit understandings of the profession, responses to questions were explored both in open discussion and by asking respondents to write descriptions and to draw what came into their minds when, for instance, they thought of solicitors. The sessions lasted around two and a half hours.

This focus-group work was followed by semi-structured interviews with students, largely drawn from the full-time cohort but including some part-timers. Interviews are now being conducted with selected members of the cohorts at staged intervals during their training contract and into their first two years after qualification. The project is also tracking selected respondents who have not yet obtained a training contract.

Another sample comprised representatives of the local legal employment market. The research methodology adopted with these employers is similar to that deployed with the students. At the time of writing, a questionnaire, which includes questions many of which correspond to those asked of students, had been administered to 50 per cent of local law firms, and this is being followed by focus groups and interviews. To date, around 25 questionnaires have been returned and reminders are being sent out, and five employers have been interviewed. All the qualitative research is being recorded and then transcribed.

Findings and discussion

THE LEGAL PRACTICE COURSE

The gender balance of the research sample corresponded to the national law student average (55 per cent female). However, 41 per cent of students were drawn from black and ethnic minority (BME) groups, compared to a national figure for all BME students in 2004 of 23.9 per cent (Cole 2005). The other striking differential was the high proportion (45 per cent) of students who could be categorised as working class. The erosion of occupation as a basis for social categorisation has complicated the concept of class; for some theorists it is now obsolete, a 'zombie category' (Beck & Beck-Gernsheim 2001). Yet the related proposition that we are seeing an increase in transformative agency is undermined by the decrease in social mobility in the UK. Instead, following Savage (2000), we might view class as increasingly related to cultural practice, and it may be argued that the entire system of informal barriers and benchmarks erected by the legal profession turns on the resilience of the concept of class, as revealed in educational institution attended (Abel 2003) and, of course, other signifiers such as dress and speech.

In order to establish the class background of the sample, we therefore deployed a mixture of indices including postal code, parental occupation, students' self-categorisation, school attended, patterns of familial attendance at university, and the university where the students had studied for their first degree. For only a quarter of the student body was it common for their family to have attended university; for half, either they or their siblings were first-generation students, and these results corresponded with attendance at state schools; and 55 per cent had studied for their first degree at a new university (most at the university under study). As one respondent said:

> [Y]ou're at a disadvantage because you didn't sort of go to a...not a proper university...I never really thought it would make any difference where you did [the law degree]...but it does.

The enactment of socio-economic background in cultural practices was manifest in other ways that make it difficult for outsider students to 'pass' as potential lawyers. For instance, the dress codes of some female students distinguished them from their middle-class colleagues, resulting in an aesthetic that could be coded as 'common'. One student said of an interview at a law firm: 'They sort of looked at me as if "What are you doing here? You should be working in a hair salon or something"'. A mature student who had had a previous career as an accountant made the following observations about her colleagues:

> I can envisage some of them as being lawyers, but others I look at them and think, 'What are you doing here?'...Their whole demeanour... Some of them look very dolly-birdy...the ones that you can tell will get a training contract...the women are young, attractive, thin, blonde...flirty, but dressed very subtly...they are aware and confident.

On the other hand, the Islamic students' dress highlighted the additional problems they would face in seeking to enter a profession that reflected 'the particular biographies, beliefs and expectations of...white(s)' (Wilkins 1998a: 141).

Speech remains one of the most powerful signifiers of class. A primary function of legal training is to achieve enculturation in the profession's official language; in addition to specific legal terms and the frequent use of Latin, this includes the use of the passive voice and modal markers to signify detachment, which working-class students tended to find alien (Edensor 2000). Many such students had also become conscious of the need to acquire a vocabulary, intonation and accent that would 'bear the imprint of a professional attitude' (Lingard et al. 2003: 612) and spoke of the disadvantage they perceived as flowing from their regional accents.

Although students' reflections on law as a discipline revealed that they had internalised law's cultural paradigm and discourse, and were aware of and took pleasure in the cultural capital this gave them, this socialisation could not compensate for the differential between these outsiders and the professional template, and, perhaps most significantly, for their ignorance of the profession. Whereas many law students in old universities come from 'legal dynasties', and therefore possess not only a network of contacts and cultural capital, but also that intuitive understanding of what the profession requires, the knowledge of many outsiders was originally grounded in films and television programmes such as *Ally McBeal* and *LA Law*. As a result of these media-generated images, students' lack of clear understanding was combined with an illusion of a limitless possibility of entry and progression, which many claimed had been bolstered by the universities at which they had studied for their degree: 'It was like, all the firms would be offering us jobs; it's such a con'. As this last remark indicates, by the LPC stage the NT students were beginning to appreciate the difficulties in gaining entry into the profession. Unless they had established contacts through work as, say, paralegals, it was not uncommon for them to have applied to at least 50 firms without success, engendering deep anxiety and bitterness.

The reasons for the difficulties in obtaining contracts varied according to professional sector. The decline in the small-firm/high-street sector of the profession extends to their intake of trainees: nationally, sole practices and firms with up to 10 partners take only 37 per cent of trainees registered with private practice (Williams & Goriely 2003). Furthermore, as a result of the partial persistence of quasi-kinship structures (Burrage 1996) in this sector, contacts remain a primary means of obtaining a contract, with the result that ethnicity and gender are far more determinant of students' chances of success. This has led to the development of niches in the market, where small high-street firms or sole practices run by minority solicitors can provide a refuge for those who would have difficulty finding places with larger (often all-white) firms (Shiner 2000).[9]

The corporate sector's dominance of the profession extends to training contracts: nationally, 31.4 per cent of all training contracts registered with private practice are with the small number of corporate firms with 81 or more partners, and a further 15.8 per cent with those firms with 26 to 80 partners. This is unfortunate since, in addition to their preference for the graduates of elite universities, they also tend to have specific links with a particular university; for instance, Bristol University was described by one employer as 'a feeding tube to [name of a 'magic circle' firm]'. The following comment is therefore typical: 'There's elitism among the institutions...it borders on discrimination. If you've gone to a new university, not one of the red-brick, top-level institutions, then you're not fit to work for their firm – I've had that said to me.'

A further obstacle for many NT students is the corporate sector's tendency to recruit within a very narrow age band (26 is the preferred age for a trainee). This is despite the fact that the attributes employers cite as desirable always include 'people skills', good communication, time management and (by corporate firms) entrepreneurialism (Sommerlad & Sanderson forthcoming), all of which an older graduate with more life experiences might be more likely to possess. A careers adviser who had worked at both old and new universities made the following comment:

> There's a pecking order...Some [employers] won't be interested in [new university] students, they look at UCAS points[10]...I saw someone at [an old university] and her CV is really scanty compared with students I've met here [new university] who've already had a couple of jobs, so if you look carefully at their CV they've got a lot of skills...but it's back to this snobbish ranking of universities against other universities.

She was also bemused by the enthusiasm both the elite universities and the profession maintained for conservative pedagogies:

> [A] wiser employer might judge people on competencies, well, [new university] students could compete equally on that...Here they learn good team skills, it's a less academic-style teaching.

This sort of pedagogy was experienced as profoundly alienating by one NT student who started a law degree at an old university:

> It was very academic…They made it feel completely alien, the first sort of thing we had to do was…registered and unregistered land…but you didn't really feel you could ask for help if you were struggling…It was more a case of 'go and learn it for yourself and if you haven't understood then there is no point in your being here'.

As a result, she left, returning to study law several years later at a new university, where she encountered a conscious attempt to deconstruct the mysteries of the law, to make transparent the opaque 'rules of the game': '[Y]ou were eased into it more gently from the start and…the tutors are definitely approachable'. Arguably, however, this approach has facilitated the evaluation of new universities by the professional elites as less rigorous and 'dumbed down'.

PROFESSIONAL SOCIALISATION AFTER ENTRY

The 'incomplete and idiosyncratic foundation' (Boon 1998: 168) offered by traditional legal education intensifies the professional socialisation process that trainees undergo during their training contracts. As experiential learning, in which practices (both technical and cultural) are modelled by the master, it serves to break down trainees and remake them in the image of the firm. The formal training in legal skills is designed to inculcate those dispositions that embody the culture of an organisation. The process entails the acquisition not only of practice skills but of a fully embodied new identity, as the following comments by employers emphasise:

> [W]e look at how they walk and how they are dressed.

> [T]rainees today just don't seem to have a sense of what it is to be professional and yet that is so important – learning how to be a professional, what clothes to wear, what to say, how to say it and so on. I would say that's almost more important than the legal skills, knowing how to behave appropriately.

Thus trainees must learn how to display, effortlessly and therefore convincingly, a professional demeanour (Goffman 1957; Entwistle 2001), which, as the comment by a middle-class white man training in an expanding commercial firm suggests, is rigidly bounded: '[It's] conformist…people believe they have to act in a certain way to be looked at as lawyers'. This view was echoed by a (white) trainee, who, as a part-time student, had also worked as a paralegal and therefore described himself as 'already habituated': '[T]o succeed, or just survive, it's vital to show that you fit in, play the game, mix socially and look the part'.

Nonetheless, the socialisation process will differ significantly depending on the extent of the neophyte professional's outsider status and the ecology of the law firm in which he or she is based. In her study of women engineers, in which she describes a three-stage process involving adaptation to professional culture, internalisation of professional identity and demonstration of solidarity with other professionals, Dryburgh (1999) reveals how acquisition of professional identity requires women to enact masculine norms and values in masculine professions. The concomitant need to undergo a process of disassociation, involving the shedding of aspects of her previous (inferior) identity, in coming to terms with the gendered, raced and classed identity of the profession, is echoed in the concerns expressed by a prominent black Caribbean barrister that black lawyers risk becoming unrecognisable to their communities (see Wilkins 1998b). As Carbado has argued, black trainees must 'act white' or 'cover' and suppress aspects of their identity that mark them out as 'other' (cited in Yoshino 2007). A comment by a mature woman trainee about her experiences gives a flavour of what this involves: '...going into court with some young jerk aged 20...all that posturing, body language'.

This woman nevertheless stressed the importance of learning how to perform the posturing, and to speak and embody authority, to develop the 'manner of certitude' and confidence essential to passing as a professional (Goffman 1957): '[S]howing you're confident is an essential skill. You must be able to assert yourself physically, intellectually.' However, the continuing question mark over women's status as 'authoritative knowers' (Thornton 1996) is revealed in the difficulties she found in convincing others of her mastery of these attributes:

> Most of the judges are blokes and I think sometimes they don't listen
> to me because I'm not a bloke – this feeling that they won't accept my
> argument whereas if it had been a man making it, it would have been
> 'oh yes, Mr Prat, I see what you are saying'...Maybe some of the skills
> are irredeemably male...A lot of women are aware of what a reasonable
> settlement would be and I think that constrains you, whereas the men just
> go for it...

As her account suggests, whereas the male trainees (all white) quickly learned 'to play the game', the women, as outsiders, continued to suffer from 'imposter complex', with the result that, in the words of another trainee, they were 'always angsting'. Consequently, for outsiders professional socialisation involves learning to negotiate the various hazards intrinsic to the dissonance that exists between their professional identity and their primordial identity. The obstacles faced by BME trainees are, of course, mediated by gender and class and the firm with which they are training. Evidently the experience of the British Asian trainee in a British Asian firm will be very different to her experience in a firm where her difference is likely to be constructed as inferiority, and where to survive, like white women, she must 'mimic the majority group' (Vignaendra et al. 2000). A firm that was prepared to argue that 'everyone is given an equal chance to conform and if you don't you won't succeed... (Asians) don't conform' encapsulates the racialised nature of the field as depicted by research into white women and black men lawyers in the US (Pierce 2002). Echoing Essed (1991), Pierce's account of white resistance to the black male lawyer in her study reveals the cumulative impact of continual repetition of, for instance, devaluing remarks and 'jokes'.

However, as a status project, the maintenance of law's classed nature is fundamental to the reproduction of professionalism. Hence, of all the intersecting forms of identity that differentiate a subject from normative legal professionalism, class remains the key structuring principle. While middle-class white and BME women and men can successfully adopt a professional identity, albeit at the cost of personal tensions with this role, and often within circumscribed locations or temporalities, *all* signs of working-class identity must be internalised in terms of lack of identity or intrinsically illegitimate forms of identity for a solicitor to inhabit, as the following comments confirm:

> [I]f you were clearly working class…that would be very difficult…I can't think of anyone…

> [T]o be a solicitor you couldn't do it…The persona you have to present must be a bit posh…even if you're doing legal aid.

Implications for training

These findings of the difficulties NT students face in gaining entry into the legal profession, the processes of professional socialisation undergone by those who do gain entry, and the extensive evidence of the stunted career progression such entrants experience suggest a poor prognosis for the WP/diversity agenda in the legal profession. They indicate that unless both the stratified nature of HE and the prejudices of the profession are addressed, its culture, especially of its elite sector, will remain largely white and middle class. It is therefore important to consider how the education and training process at the undergraduate stage might address NT students' current difficulties in entering the legal labour market, and open employing organisations to more public scrutiny, thereby reducing the information asymmetry that market theorists see as one of the key dysfunctions of the current state of affairs.

Evidence suggests that work experience is the most effective means of enabling outsiders to gain entry into the legal profession (Francis & Sommerlad 2008).[11] Work experience can provide NT students with contacts, enable them to come to understand the hidden rules of the field and develop case-handling skills.[12] However, not all law students are able to obtain work placements with law firms. It is therefore important to consider ways in which this experience can be simulated, and also at least some links with the profession developed, in order to raise the profile of NT students. However, in order to make progress on the diversity project, we need to go beyond simply teaching NT students how to mimic the professional norm and raise critical awareness among the student body of the current composition of and power hierarchies within the profession. At the same time, we need to sensitise the profession to diversity issues, including the exclusionary nature of its current conceptualisation of merit, by engaging both with key professionals and policy-makers.

One of the most important strategies should be increasing the accessibility of the elite universities to a more diverse range of students and at the same time ending the explicit stratification that government policy has endorsed. Assuming that WP policies do become more widespread across the sector, research indicates that for these to be successful they must be fully integrated into an institution's strategic goals (Bagguley & Hussain 2007) and remain significant throughout the student life cycle. They also require the development of institutional structures and processes that value diversity, and an approach to the curriculum, learning and teaching that reflects diversity (Thomas & May 2005). This is supported by Carr and Tunnah, who found that the design of law curriculum should be approached with 'an appreciation of the ethnic dimension to learning' (2004: 18). This in turn requires that law schools must know their students – their interests, demographic background, motivation for undertaking the subject, level of knowledge, and previous learning experiences (O'Donnell & Johnstone 1997).

The CRDP is seeking to accomplish these objectives by building on Leeds Metropolitan's long experience in creating work-integrated learning curriculum interventions and electronic professional portfolio developments designed to enhance students' preparedness and their ability to 'read the rules' on transition into and within employment, particularly in the professions. For law students, it is envisaged that these interventions will comprise three interlocking practical approaches: firstly, undergraduate curriculum change; secondly, work with employers, through their continuing professional development programmes; and thirdly, engagement with senior policy-makers with a commitment to diversity and equality.

The curriculum development will comprise a pedagogical instrument that can be embedded within the law degree programme and contains three elements: research, critical analysis of the profession and experiential learning. The research element is based on the work with the postgraduate LPC students reported above (therefore including a questionnaire administered at the beginning of year one of the LLB) and aims to ensure that tutors acquire the necessary in-depth knowledge of the demographic background, motivations and aspirations of the undergraduate student body. The second will be tutor led and will include lectures and workshops given by lawyers, and sessions on self-awareness, interpersonal perception, the psychology of dress, CV development and presentation skills. Students will also research the profession's structure and culture; analyse the skills and other attributes legal practice requires; map the local legal labour market; and develop a personal career strategy including practical steps to meet not only those employer needs that are explicitly stated, but also some of the implicit, unstated expectations discussed above. Students will also be encouraged to arrange visits to courts and law firms and, if possible, mini-placements.

This element also comprises a 'real work' project throughout which students will operate under the same codes of practice and legal and commercial constraints as in a real work situation. The employers will be sought to act as mentors, communicating with the students mainly by email and having occasional scheduled meetings with their group, thus providing continuous support. The resulting project work will be assessed as a group project. Further, as far as possible, assignments will culminate in a presentation, which must be performed as a work simulation.

The second strand of this employability programme aims to increase the law school's engagement with the local legal community. Again, this entails an element of the research project on which this chapter is based in that focus groups will be held with practising lawyers with the following objectives: to obtain their views on diversity and equality and the 'ideal' trainee/lawyer, which can then be fed back into the design and delivery of the curriculum; to sensitise them to the issues involved in seeking to diversify the profession; to raise the profile of the university's student body; and, where possible, to develop partnerships with individual firms or lawyers. Such partnerships would then facilitate the curriculum work outlined above, such as the research exercises into the local legal labour market and the real work projects. In addition, the partnerships would, it is hoped, provide students not only with an insight into law practice culture, but also with networking opportunities.

A primary aim of these two elements of the employability programme is to facilitate reflection on the part of the profession and the student. The insight that reflective practice is essential to the development of professional identity and hence effective learning (Moon 1999) is fundamental to Leeds Metropolitan's workforce development programmes (Stapleford et al. 2006). However, an important aspect of the reflective element is also to encourage a critical perception of the profession by both students and lawyers. This in turn is fundamental to the final strand of the programme, which is constituted by the links the CRDP already enjoys with national policy-makers as a result of its research into diversity. It is currently building on these to highlight the current barriers faced by NT law graduates, and views contributing to and influencing the national debate on diversity as central to its role.

Conclusion

Various forces are combining to produce what would appear to be a real opportunity to transform both HE and the elite professions into more diverse and open institutions. In addition to the policy discourse of diversity and equality, there is the concern to ensure that labour markets operate rationally in accordance with human capital theory, rather than on the basis of characteristics such as class, gender and race. At the same time, traditional pedagogies and philosophies of education are facing significant challenge from neo-liberal discourses of competencies that argue for modes of training of demonstrable value to work performance (see, for example, Bennett et al. 2000). However, there are tensions between these different forces – for instance, the potential conflict between the social justice focus of WP strategies and the primarily economic concern behind some employability policy. It is also important not to underestimate either the investment the middle class have in 'traditional' qualifications, or the necessarily closed and elitist nature of the professional project. The effect of either of these factors could be an erosion of the potential for a more diverse legal profession by the processes of professional socialisation. Equally, if legal education becomes dominated by a narrow competency model, the current tendency to professional fragmentation could be intensified, producing a stratified profession with deskilled niches 'reserved' for the NT aspiring lawyer. These difficulties, however, make it even more vital to respond to the increasing diversity of the law schools by engaging in curriculum reform to make it more possible, not just for more NT law graduates to enter the profession, but also to make the profession a space that is more open to the contributions of different kinds of lawyers.

Notes

1   We would like to thank Sophie Goodeve for her research help, Lisa Geary and Darren Shaw for their assistance, and Dr Peter Sanderson for his invaluable comments.

2   It is difficult to find an appropriate term for students who come from a social group who have previously not attended HE or who do not fit the occupational norm or are otherwise marginalised. The usual term is 'non-traditional'; however, this implicit construction of such students as outsiders (a term also used to describe those who gain entry into previously closed occupations) can be read as pathologising them and constructing them as responsible for their prior absence from these fields. Nevertheless, in view of the difficulty of finding an appropriate alternative we use this term here.

3   This goal has also generated a growing stress on employability in the curriculum and the development of closer links with employers (NCIHE 1997).

4   For the NCIHE (1997) the participation of 'disadvantaged' social groups in HE was also posited as a means to enhance social equality and inclusion.

5   The legal profession's crucial legitimating role has generated great concern on the part of the Department of Constitutional Affairs (now the Ministry of Justice) that it should become more socially representative (DCA 2005).

6   The new universities were formerly polytechnics or colleges of HE that were generally local-authority funded and primarily focused on higher technical, professional and vocational education. In 1992 the Further and Higher Education Act ended the binary divide between these and universities.

7   For instance, McGlynn writes: 'Gender informs many aspects of the law school, from admissions policies, to mooting, to the inclusion of gender perspectives in the...curriculum... to the inculcation of the values, ethics and principles of the law and legal profession and to the recruitment, retention and promotion of women academics' (1999: 89).

8   The resulting gap between academic law and law in practice has been the subject of comment for almost a century (Pound 1910), and the relatively unchanging nature of legal education is demonstrated by the fact that this remains a recurring theme among practitioners.

9   This strategy, however, is under increasing threat due to the accelerating changes in the structure of the market.

10 UCAS is the UK clearing system for entry into HE that provides a standardised tariff system for assessing the value of matriculation qualifications.

11 The strongest single message the NCIHE received from employers was the value of work-related experience (1997).

12 That is, it enables them to develop what Bourdieu (2001) would describe as a 'feel for the game'.

References

Abel R (2003) *English lawyers between market and state: The politics of professionalism.* Oxford: Oxford University Press

Ainley P (2003) Towards a seamless web or a new tertiary tripartism? The emerging shape of post-14 education and training in England. *Higher Education Quarterly* 51(4): 390

Archer L (2007) Diversity, equality and higher education: A critical reflection on the ab/uses of equity discourse within widening participation. *Teaching in Higher Education* 12(5/6): 635

Bagguley P & Hussain Y (2007) *The role of higher education in providing opportunities for South Asian women.* York: Joseph Rowntree Foundation

Beagan B (2001) Micro inequities and everyday inequalities: 'Race', gender, sexuality and class in medical school. *Canadian Journal of Sociology* 26(4): 583

Beck U & Beck-Gernsheim E (2001) *Individualisation: Institutionalised individualisation and its social and political consequences.* London: Sage Publications

Bennett N, Dunne E & Carre C (eds) (2000) *Skills development in higher education and employment.* Buckingham: Open University Press

Blanden J & Machin S (2007) *Recent changes in intergenerational mobility in Great Britain.* Report for the Sutton Trust. London: London School of Economics

Bolton S & Muzio D (2007) Can't live with 'em; can't live without 'em: Gendered segmentation in the legal profession. *Sociology* 41(1): 47

Boon A (1998) History is past politics: A critique of the legal skills movement in England and Wales. *Journal of Law & Society* 25(1): 151

Boon A & Duncan N (1990) An elite profession and elite institutions facing demographic change. *Journal of Access Studies* (Spring): 47

Bourdieu P (2000) *Pascalian meditations.* Cambridge: Polity Press

Bourdieu P (2001) *Masculine domination.* Cambridge: Polity Press

Braithwaite J (2007) Explaining diversity policies in large London law firms. Paper presented to the International Sociological Association XV World Congress of Sociology, Berlin

Brennan J & McGeevor P (1990) *Ethnic minorities and the graduate labour market.* London: Committee for Racial Equality

Brennan J & Shah T (2003) *Access to what? Converting educational opportunity into employment opportunity.* London: Cheri

Burrage M (1996) From a gentlemen's to a public profession: Status and politics in the history of English solicitors. *International Journal of the Legal Profession* 3(1/2): 45

Carr H & Tunnah E (2004) *Examining the effectiveness of the undergraduate law curriculum in preparing black Caribbean students for entry into the legal profession.* Coventry: UK Centre for Legal Education. Accessed 30 March 2009, http://www.ukcle.ac.uk/research projects/tunnah.html

Centre LGS (2005) *Increasing diversity in the judiciary.* Response to the DCA's Consultation Paper. Kent: Centre LGS. Accessed 30 March 2009, http://www.kent.ac.uk/clgs/consultation_responses.html

Chevalier A & Conlon C (2003) *Does it pay to attend a prestigious university?* London: Centre for the Economics of Education

Cole B (2005) *Trends in the solicitors' profession.* Annual Statistical Report, 2004. London: Law Society

DCA (Department of Constitutional Affairs, UK) (2005) *Increasing diversity in the legal profession: A report on government proposals.* London: HM Stationery Office

DfES (Department for Education and Skills, UK) (2003) *Widening participation in HE.* London: HM Stationery Office

Dhavan R (1989) Legal education as restrictive practice: A sceptical view. In W Twining, N Kibble & R Dhavan (eds) *Access to legal education and the legal professions.* London: Butterworths

Dryburgh H (1999) Work hard, play hard: Women and professionalisation in engineering – adapting to the culture. *Gender and Society* 13(5): 664

Edensor T (2000) A welcome back to the working classes. *Sociology* 34(4): 805

Entwistle J (2001) The dressed body. In J Entwistle & E Wilson (eds) *Body dressing.* Oxford: Berg

Essed P (1991) *Understanding everyday racism: An interdisciplinary theory.* New York: Sage Publications

Francis A & Sommerlad H (2008) Access to legal work experience and its role in the (re) production of legal professional identity. Paper presented at the Annual Conference of the Social Legal Studies Association, Manchester (March)

Goffman E (1957) *The presentation of self in everyday life.* New York: Doubleday

Goriely T & Williams T (1996) *The impact of the new training scheme.* Research Study No. 22. London: Law Society

Hagan J & Kay K (1995) *Gender in practice: A study of lawyers' lives.* New York: Oxford University Press

Halpern D (1994) *Entry into the legal profession: The law student cohort study, years 1 and 2.* London: Law Society

Hayward C & Mac an Ghaill M (1997) A man in the making: Sexual masculinities within changing training cultures. *Sociological Review* 45(4): 576

HEFCE (Higher Education Funding Council for England) (2000) *Statistical bulletin.* London: HEFCE

Kennedy D (1992) Legal education as training for hierarchy. In I Grigg-Spall & P Ireland (eds) *The critical lawyers' handbook.* London: Pluto Press

Larson MS (1977) *The rise of professions: A sociological analysis.* London: University of California Press

Lingard L, Garwood K, Schryer C & Spafford M (2003) A certain air of uncertainty: Case presentation and the development of professional identity. *Social Science and Medicine* (56): 603–616

McGlynn C (1999) Women, representation and the legal academy. *Legal Studies* 19(1): 68–92

Mirza HS (1998) Black women in education: A collective movement for social change. In T Modood & T Acland (eds) *Race and higher education.* London: Policy Studies Institute

Moon J (1999) *Reflection in learning and professional development: Theory and practice.* London: Kogan Page

NCIHE (National Committee of Inquiry into Higher Education, UK) (1997) The Dearing report. Norwich: HM Stationery Office

Nicolson D (2005) Demography, discrimination and diversity: A new dawn for the British legal profession? *International Journal of the Legal Profession* 12(2): 201

O'Donnell A & Johnstone R (1997) *Developing a cross-cultural law curriculum.* Sydney: Cavendish

Pierce J (2002) Not qualified? Or not committed? A raced and gendered organisational logic in law firms. In R Banakar & M Travers (eds) *An introduction to law and social theory.* Oxford: Hart

Pound R (1910) Law in books and law in action. *American Law Review* (44): 12

Reay D, Ball S & David M (2002) It's taking me a long time but I'll get there in the end: Mature students on access courses and higher education choice. *British Educational Research Journal* 28(1): 5–19

Rochette A & Pue W (2001) Back to basics? University legal education and 21st-century professionalism. *Windsor Yearbook of Access to Justice* (20): 167

Rolfe H & Anderson T (2003) A firm choice: Law firms' preferences in the recruitment of trainee solicitors. *International Journal of the Legal Profession* 10(13): 315

Sandefur R (2007) Staying power: The persistence of social inequality in shaping lawyer stratification and lawyers' persistence in the profession. *Southwestern University Law Review* 36(3): 539–556

Savage M (2000) *Class analysis and social transformation.* Buckingham: Open University Press

Shiner M (1999) *Entry into the legal profession: The law student cohort study, year 5.* London: Law Society

Shiner M (2000) Young, gifted and blocked! Entry to the solicitors' profession. In P Thomas (ed.) *Discriminating lawyers.* London: Cavendish

Sommerlad H (2002) Women solicitors in a fractured profession: Intersections of gender and professionalism in England and Wales. *International Journal of the Legal Profession* 9(3): 213

Sommerlad H (2007) Researching and theorising the processes of professional identity formation. *Journal of Law and Society* 34(2): 190

Sommerlad H (2008) That obscure object of desire: Sex equality and the legal profession. In R Hunter (ed.) *Rethinking equality.* Oxford: Hart

Sommerlad H & Sanderson P (1998) *Gender, choice and commitment.* Aldershot: Ashgate

Sommerlad H & Sanderson P (2002) Exploring the limits to the standardisation of the expert knowledge of lawyers: Quality and legal aid in the United Kingdom. *Syracuse Law Review* 54(4): 987

Sommerlad H & Sanderson P (forthcoming) *Training and regulating those providing legal advice services: A case study of civil provision.* Report for the Ministry of Justice

Stapleford J, Beasley L & Palmer S (2006) Developing PDP to support employability: An institutional perspective. In R Ward (ed.) *Personal development planning and employability.* York: Higher Education Academy

Thomas L & May H (2005) *From the margins to the mainstream: Embedding widening participation in HE.* London: Universities UK

Thornton M (1996) *Dissonance and distrust: Women in the legal profession*. Oxford: Oxford University Press

Thornton M (1998) Technocentrism in the law school: Why the gender and colour of law remain the same. *Osgoode Hall Law Journal* 36(2): 369

Tong D & Pue W (1999) The best and the brightest? Canadian law school admission. *Osgoode Hall Law Journal* 37(4): 843–876

Vignaendra S (2001) *Social class and entry into the solicitors' profession*. Research Study 41. London: Law Society

Vignaendra S, Williams M & Garvey J (2000) Hearing black and Asian voices: An exploration of identity. In P Thomas (ed.) *Discriminating lawyers*. London: Cavendish

Walkerdine V, Lucey H & Melody J (2001) *Growing up girl: Gender and class in the 21st century*. London: Macmillan

Wilkins D (1998a) Fragmenting professionalism: Racial identity and the ideology of bleached-out lawyering. *International Journal of the Legal Profession* 5(2/3): 141

Wilkins D (1998b) Identities and roles: Race, recognition, and professional responsibility. *Maryland Law Review* 57(4): 1502

Williams T & Goriely T (2003) *Recruitment and retention of solicitors in small firms*. London: Law Society

Witz A (1992) *Professions and patriarchy*. London: Routledge Kegan Paul

Yoshino K (2007) *Covering: The hidden assault on our civil rights*. New York: Random House

9 Research on Canadian teachers' work and learning

Paul Tarc and Harry Smaller

Introduction

In this chapter, we reflect on a decade-long (1997–2007) government-funded research study[1] on Canadian teachers' work and learning to highlight some key insights related to the study's empirical findings and methodological approaches. Given the level of importance which teachers themselves place on their informal learning, and the growing prominence of informal modes of learning across multiple and transnational discourse communities, we focus particularly on this aspect of teachers' overall engagement in their own learning. We examine how teachers involve themselves in their own learning and how they perceive the obstacles affecting their learning practices and intentions. Finally, we consider some challenges to investigating teachers' informal learning.

In writing this chapter for an international audience, we are certainly aware of the relative privilege of teachers in the Canadian context, where there is significant material investment in public schooling and teachers' professional development. However, as we hope to demonstrate, within these materially beneficial contexts many teachers experience increasing pressures over the nature and control of their work, and the quality of their engagement in their professional learning. There is little question in our minds that these pressures are symptomatic of more recent neo-liberal inspired restructurings of state school systems (Carnoy 2000; McNeil 2000; Stromquist 2002).[2] To the extent that these Western-induced changes are being transmitted and taken up in other regions of the world, we hope that some description and analysis of their effects (positive and otherwise) in Canada may be useful to others.

Overview of the study

The research group undertaking this decade-long national study first came together in 1997, and over the interim period has included university faculty members, graduate students, and professional development specialists from teachers' unions and municipal boards of education. The overall purpose of the project was to canvass teachers working in publicly funded elementary and secondary schools across Canada about their own informal and formal learning, and the intersections of this learning with the social and material relations of their workplaces and government policy and programmes related to professional development. From the outset, three distinct but related themes have served to underlie and inform this study: schooling reform, teacher knowledge and informal learning. More than 10 years later, each of these themes is even more significant in the discourse and realities of public schooling than they were when the study began.

Schooling 'reform' and 'restructuring'

There is no question that both the discourse and the reality of *change* continue to dominate most aspects of the schooling agenda today, and this theme informed our study as well. As critical educational historians on several continents have long noted (Katz 1971; Curtis 1988; Gardner 1984; Spaull 1997), demands (whether popular, political and/or academic) for schooling reform have been issued almost from the inception of state schooling itself. Historically, these pressures for change have often been based – at least by dominant voices – on the 'need' for schooling to be linked more closely to the economic 'wants' and 'needs' of the nation (Althouse 1929/1967; Royal Commission on Education 1950; Goodman 1995). However, schooling reform is now linked even more closely to transformations in the larger political economy of provinces and nations – a movement consistent with globalising, neo-liberal economic trends, including tighter control over, but less funding for, public sector social institutions (Ranson 2003; Carnoy & Rhoten 2002; Dale & Robertson 2002). Students and school systems are increasingly being pressured to be more 'competitive' in the global (education) market. These pressures intensify in spite of increasing evidence that direct correspondences between education, employment opportunities and national advantage are tenuous.[3]

More specifically, while the recent demands for reforms in education continue to range across the many dimensions of schooling – funding, governance, curriculum, resources, facilities, etc. – teachers themselves (at least those in Western nations) seem to have been singled out for special attention in unprecedented ways. Traditionally, teachers have typically been addressed as an entity, and improvements to education were often associated with the need to improve conditions for teachers collectively – class sizes, resources, salaries, benefits, pensions and job security. Even where teachers were seen to be in need of further education themselves, governments at various levels often moved to expand and improve teacher education programmes, and/or to offer incentives for teachers to engage in further study, whether in pre-service or in-service models (Hopkins 1969; Robinson 1971; Fleming 1972).

In the past two decades, in the Anglo-West at least, there has been a dramatic shift from this more collective approach to one of individualisation. This change dominates the ways in which teachers' work is being restructured and controlled.[4] Moreover, individualisation is an equally dominant mode in which teachers are increasingly being educated, trained, evaluated and tested.[5] Often, these individualising initiatives are promoted through the rhetoric of a 'need' for increased professionalism. In at least two jurisdictions in Canada (British Columbia and Ontario), government-initiated and controlled 'colleges of teachers' have been established, with a mandate to control the training, certification and practice of teachers (Popkewitz 1994; Ontario Government 1995). At another level, in many areas of the US, salaries, promotion and even basic job tenure for individual teachers are increasingly being determined by teacher testing regimes, increased external evaluation of teacher practice, and/or by student 'scores' on standardised examinations (OSSTF 1999). While these particular measures have yet to gain a foothold in Canada, in at least one province (Ontario) student results from external examinations now appear in the public press, displayed on a school-by-school basis. The implications for individual teachers in these schools seem clear: individual performance, based on student standardised testing, will determine their ultimate worth as 'professional' workers.

In addition to these more recent controls over teachers' classroom practice, there have also been increasing calls to introduce compulsory 'professional development' programmes for teachers, as well as the closely related phenomenon of regular, and compulsory, teacher recertification programmes (Ontario Government 1995). While few teachers, and none of their unions and associations, argue against the need for or the benefits of ongoing professional development, questions are rightfully posed about the intentions behind and the forms of such state-initiated and controlled interventions. For example, who would be involved in the development and implementation of these programmes? What would be the assumptions made about necessary or important knowledge? Would such assumptions be based, and built, on existing teacher knowledge? These are not trivial questions. Indeed a compulsory, province-wide, in-service teacher professional development programme introduced unilaterally by a Conservative government in Ontario in 1999 was found so odious to teachers in the province that an official boycott was implemented almost immediately by all of the province's teacher unions. The unions' response served to mobilise teachers to campaign successfully against the government in the ensuing provincial election in 2003. Not surprisingly, the new Liberal government was quick to announce the demise of the programme, and to promise to work with teachers to develop an alternative.

Teacher knowledge

In the political context of teachers' work, the second underlying theme informing this study is reflected in the increased interest among educational researchers in the concept of 'teacher knowledge'. This research has taken a number of directions in recent years, including explorations about what teacher knowledge is, what it should be, how it is acquired and/or enhanced, and the nature of its relation to student and school success (Briscoe 1997; Klein 1996; Gibson & Olberg 1998; Donmoyer 1995; OCT 1999). Although there is a considerable body of literature covering these themes, to date there has been little attention paid to how teachers themselves see these matters – what they think is important to know and to learn, how they would like to engage in this learning process and what they are already doing in this regard.

Informal learning

This study has also been motivated and informed by the concept of 'informal learning', which refers to how learning is undertaken outside of formal structures of classes and courses, instructors and regulations. As with other categories in the overall study of 'education', investigators of 'informal learning' also share a variety of agreements and differences about its meaning and place (Colley et al. 2003; Straka 2004). Given that our method relied on quantitative surveys as the first stage of data collection, we defined informal and formal learning as conceptually distinct categories. Further, in the quantitative survey we defined informal learning as *explicit,* drawing on David Livingstone's definition of informal learning as

> any activity involving the pursuit of understanding, knowledge or skill which occurs outside the curricula of institutions providing educational programmes, courses or workshops…Explicit informal learning is distinguished from everyday perceptions, general socialisation and more tacit informal learning by people's own conscious identification of the activity as significant learning. The important criteria that distinguish explicit informal learning are the retrospective recognition of both a new significant form of knowledge, understanding or skill acquired on your own initiative and also recognition of the process of acquisition. (Livingstone 1999: 51)

Nevertheless we were made aware of the complexity of the relationship between formal and informal learning, and between the explicit and implicit dimensions of informal learning, through the responses from teachers and through the wider literature. Additionally, we tried to link the increasing attention to informal modes of learning across multiple work settings to our research findings by examining multiple uses of informal learning in the contemporary moment (Tarc 2007).

In national and transnational contexts, informal modes of workplace learning are gaining attention by policy-makers, practitioners and academics. For example, informal learning has become a key stratagem in the regime of 'lifelong learning' employed as a form of governmentality (self-regulation) of worker-citizens by organisations such as the European Commission (Tuschling & Engemann 2006).[6] In parallel, under the imaginary of the 'learning society', management theorists and consultants envision informal learning as a favoured modality for organisational efficiency, human/intellectual capacity building, and maximal flexibility in knowledge-intensive workplaces according to the needs of the 'new' economy (Garrick & Usher 2000; Marsick & Volpe 1999). In the literature of adult education, informal learning is often theorised as an undervalued and under-supported mode of professional/worker learning, where formal learning is represented as only the 'tip of the iceberg' of adult learning (Livingstone 1999; Tough 1979). Recognition and support of workers' informal learning can be framed towards the aims of democratising workplaces and reducing underemployment (Livingstone 2003). Yet 'formalising' informal learning can also become a technique of managing subjectivities according to organisational goals, 'empowering' workers while increasing surveillance and regulation (Garrick & Usher 2000). Some uses of the term 'informal learning' centre on the degree of intentionality and awareness of one's learning (Eraut et al. 2000). Others suggest that the organisational context, rather than the learning, distinguishes formal from informal learning (Straka 2004). In the field of education, informal modes of learning and leadership, such as action research and 'learning communities', also have increasing purchase in the literatures of teachers' professional development and school change.[7]

In the case of teachers, each of the distinct meanings of informal learning is helpful in illuminating the wider dynamics at play under which teachers learn and are expected to learn. A large part of teachers' 'know-how' remains tacit, embedded in their practices. To be a 'reflective practitioner' (Brookfield 1995) requires an examination of one's practices to make more explicit one's learning and pedagogical knowledge. Hoekstra et al. (2007) argue that overly rationalistic approaches to teacher learning, which focus primarily on deliberate and cognitive learning, can have very limited effects on improving practice. Further, contemporary professional development discussions have drawn on management discourse, highlighting the importance of the active, empowered teacher-learner as an agent of change for organisational improvement.

By these discourses, teachers are also constructed as self-regulating subjects. For example, Smyth (1992) illustrates how, despite its emancipatory rationalisations, teachers' 'reflective practice' in the context of neo-liberal school restructuring can effectively act as a technique of control under the guise of devolving autonomy. In this scenario, teachers are reflecting and responding to administrative and classroom demands and needs, engineered not by them, but by the emergent conditions of intensifying workload in underfunded school boards. Illuminating a similar (and troubling) process of 'steering from a distance' under the new capitalism, Gee et al. (1996) highlight how 'empowered units' internalise organisational 'values and goals – often without a great deal of negotiation or conscious reflection and without the exercise of very much top-down authority' (cited in Fuller et al. 2005: 53).

Research methodology

Over the length of the project, empirical data for this study were collected from teachers in a number of ways:[8]

- *Survey questionnaires*: Two similar pencil-and-paper survey questionnaires were mailed out across Canada, the first in 1998 (n = 1 500) and again in 2004 (n = 2 098). Names and home addresses were randomly and proportionately sampled from the membership lists of provincial teachers' unions,[9] resulting in response rates averaging about 50 per cent.
- *Time-study diaries*: During November 1999 and again in February 2000, 13 Ontario secondary school teachers completed week-long time-study diaries[10] – recording, for seven consecutive days, every activity in which they engaged over the 24 hours of each day of that time period. In particular, the informal learning aspects were emphasised, with the request to note, wherever possible, 'when you believe that you have gained any new knowledge, understandings and/or skills, as a result of your activity during any specific activity'.
- *Telephone interviews*: During September 2000, lengthy (up to one hour) telephone interviews were conducted with four teachers randomly selected from those who had completed time-study diaries. These interviews followed closely

on a time of significant government restructuring of schools, including the universal imposition of several new initiatives (curriculum-related, assessment, etc.). Teachers were asked to explore the ways in which they and their colleagues had engaged in acquiring the new knowledge and skills necessary to implement (or mediate or resist) these new requirements.

- *Focus groups*: From 2004 to 2007, a number of teacher focus groups were held in four provinces across Canada. Some groups involved participants randomly sampled, while others involved specific types of teachers: those new to the profession, those internationally trained and those working as 'occasionals' (i.e. daily employment, without a contract).

In our subsequent analysis of the research findings, we found considerable congruence in the data, regardless of the various methods by which they were collected. What follows, then, is our analysis and discussion of these findings, organised by major themes related to the overall purposes of the study – teachers' formal learning, informal learning, workload intensification and teachers' autonomy.

Findings and discussion

Teachers' engagement with formal learning

Overall, Canadian teachers seemed very invested in their work-related formal learning. The two national surveys (1998 and 2004) indicated that a very high percentage (over 90 per cent) engaged in workshops, seminars and courses over the course of the year. In the focus-group interviews, teachers spoke positively about a number of formal courses they had taken, with diverse content and forms of delivery. Most indicated that they would likely continue to take courses to support their ongoing development. While teachers differed considerably on their various interests in formal learning, one of the few positive themes that they held in common was the preference for courses whose content was directly applicable to their classrooms.

The criticisms that teachers had of their professional development, however, were more unified. In general, teachers often spoke critically of prescribed professional development activities that had a 'one size fits all' approach. Teachers who felt that they already had the expertise, or that the particular professional development focus was not relevant to their particular teaching assignment, spoke very negatively of such mandatory experiences. Professional development 'trends' were also spoken about a number of times. While some teachers felt that formal workshops stressing 'literacy' (as one example of a trend) were directly helpful to their work as teachers, others saw these trends as diminishing their own professional development interests and autonomy as learners. Some teachers with many years in the classroom reported that the trends tend to repeat themselves over time, or spoke of the 'swinging pendulum'. From their historical perspective these trends seemed to diminish the autonomy of teachers, who had to constantly adapt to the latest trend making its way down to the classroom teacher. It was noted that these trends were often politically rather than educationally motivated. The following teacher's comment exemplifies teachers' concerns generally with rigid forms of professional development:

And the major obstacle I see to this kind of PD [professional development] is that they tell you what you have to do and they do not rely on you to trust your own instincts and know what you have to do yourself. It is being challenged by the [teachers' union] for that very reason: that it is rigid, it is top-down and it is unprofessional because it does not allow the teacher to choose the direction that professional development needs to go.

Teachers' engagement with informal learning

Although teachers provided mixed responses in their accounting of the value of their experiences with formal modes of learning, virtually all respondents reported on the necessity and value of informal modes of learning. In the 2004 survey almost all of the full-time teachers[11] reported that informal learning was either 'very helpful' (51 per cent) or at the least 'somewhat helpful' (46 per cent). On average, teachers reported engaging in 4 hours of informal work-related learning per week. In addition to work-related informal learning, respondents averaged 5.7 hours per week on community, household or other informal learning. A significant number (78 per cent) indicated that this informal learning in other domains was helpful in their work as teachers.

When asked *how* this workplace informal learning took place, respondents indicated that significant amounts took place collaboratively with colleagues (70 per cent), administrators (8 per cent), students (10 per cent) and parents (4 per cent). Nearly half of the respondents (48 per cent) also indicated that they engaged in informal workplace learning on their own. When considering their informal learning generally across multiple domains of their lives, collaboration with others remains a dominant approach to learning.

In the focus-group interviews, teachers typically began by discussing their learning in courses and workshops, but as the discussion probed deeper into the day-to-day dynamics of teachers' work, the importance of informal learning emerged as dominant. Collaboration with colleagues was the most often cited example of teachers' informal learning. The following quotes are representative of the teachers interviewed:

> Okay, well, I was in great need of professional development this year. And actually my greatest source was another teacher who became a partner to me...

> I think the best professional development I have ever had, that I had gotten the most from, is talking to people in my own school, and having the time to do that...

Even in the context of discussing formal learning in conferences or workshops, teachers often highlighted the importance of meeting and talking with other teachers in the in-between times (for example, during coffee breaks). While a few teachers spoke of enjoying or valuing contact with teachers across different contexts – for example, elementary teachers with secondary school teachers – the majority consistently privileged 'teacher talk' or collaboration with colleagues having similar teaching assignments (whether by grade level or subject discipline). Use of terms such as 'relevance', 'usefulness', 'hands-on' and 'things to take in the class tomorrow' signified the importance of sharing ideas around one's immediate context of learning under the demands of teaching. Similarly, a number of teachers spoke of the enhanced learning when collaborating around shared tasks, such as evaluating a common set of exams or building curricula units. However, a few teachers spoke very negatively about situations where their collaboration had been mandated by authorities around a specific predetermined educational theme, bringing teachers together in (prescribed) groups.

When pressing teachers to speak about the most salient contexts for learning from collaboration, a number of specific recommendations surfaced. Several teachers spoke highly of the chance to observe their colleagues teaching. They valued both the chance to see other ways of approaching a lesson or a class, as well as the shared context to discuss teaching methods and ideas. This opportunity was sometimes made available by a teacher's individual request, suggested by a supportive administrator, or was readily available in team-teaching assignments.

Another common suggestion for supporting informal learning, especially in the context of beginning teachers, was 'mentoring'. Many interviewees described an increase or decrease in mentoring over the years, or from one school to another, but typically all spoke of its positive value. A few of the less experienced teachers spoke of a mentor-colleague as the single most valuable support for their informal learning. Some of the more experienced teachers expressed that the mentoring role also provided a context for their own further learning.

Reading and surfing the internet were also commonly mentioned modes of informal learning. While internet use was not emphasised by all teachers, those who reported utilising it stated that they did so extensively and found it very helpful. A number of teachers echoed the following comment:

> I do not know how I taught before the internet. I take so much material off of there, especially because I have had such a turnover in the subjects that I taught.

Similarly, some teachers talked about their use of books, magazines and journals, television and videos as a way to keep up with pop culture or world events and in order to make connections between students, the world and the curriculum. Some teachers also reported increased use of email to collaborate with colleagues across distances. For a few teachers working in more remote areas or in smaller schools, email was an essential way of getting help, and they spoke of this medium as a way of continuing conversations started in conferences or meetings.

Workload intensification and its challenges for learning

Workload intensification was also a dominant finding of the project analysis. On the one hand, the 2004 survey results indicated only a small but significant quantitative increase in weekly hours worked over the previous five years (50.2 hours, up from 48.9 hours). On the other hand, in the same survey, almost 80 per cent of respondents reported that their workload had increased (44 per cent said it had 'significantly increased' and 35 per cent reported that it had 'increased') over the previous five years, and this perceived workload intensification also appeared as a dominant theme in the focus-group interviews. This apparent discrepancy between the quantitative and qualitative findings was largely clarified, however, in the overall focus-group discussion, where many teachers talked about the increasing devolution of administrative duties, more paperwork, heightened reporting on students, increased supervision, and so on. Clearly, teachers saw these tasks as a diversion from, and an addition to, what they understandably considered to be their central responsibilities – working with students on curricular objectives. The focus-group interviews provided some illustrative examples of this 'compression of work' and increased non-teaching-related tasks. The accompanying stress levels and their negative impacts on teachers' health or wellness also became apparent in some of the interviews.[12] In addition, and clearly related to the larger issues of teacher learning, several respondents reported that this intensification of work impacted negatively on their time (and energy) to engage in learning, both formal and informal.

As previously stated, most of the interviewees emphasised the importance of informal learning as an indispensable and ongoing part of the work of teaching. While the level of participation in *formal* learning seemed to be contingent on a greater number of factors, such as costs of courses, career stage, course availability and relevance, by comparison *informal* learning was presented by many teachers as more constant and continuous, albeit somewhat contingent on structures and processes affecting contact and collegiality.

Lack of time was consistently reported in teacher interviews as the primary obstacle to informal learning (and one of the most emphasised constraints for participating in formal learning as well). This finding is consistent with Lohman's (2000) research on inhibitors to teachers' informal learning, where lack of time was found to be the predominant impediment.[13] And, as in the Lohman study, the problem of insufficient time was typically explained in the context of work intensification as related above.[14] For some, the time pressure created by the increase in workload seemed to impact directly on the quantity and quality of collaboration with colleagues. In addition, some teachers spoke about other impediments, such as work schedules that did not include common planning times or the lack of a common meeting area. An anecdote often repeated was of the teacher working alone while eating lunch rather than going to the staffroom. Another obstacle was the delegation of administrative work to teachers, diminishing both time and infrastructural supports for learning. One quote for illustration will suffice here:

> The paperwork. It impacts on the time that you might do some of that informal learning after school or at lunch because you are busy filling out forms in triplicate or putting together yet another referral package for an assessment.

Another effect of this workload intensification was reflected in how some teachers spoke of informal learning – almost as a survival mechanism, learning how to manage amid all the challenges, rather than as a more autonomous activity directed proactively by the teacher in an area of pedagogical interest. The following quote illustrates well this 'survival' aspect of informal learning:

> And I think because the working conditions have changed so much, the
> formal learning has decreased and the informal learning has skyrocketed
> because you are constantly learning. You have to learn that new
> curriculum, you are just moving along, moving along, so it's never-ending.

This 'on the go' and 'getting by' informal learning leans towards the 'reactive' rather than the 'deliberative' learning categories in Eraut et al.'s (2000) typology of 'non-formal' learning. While some teachers clearly recognised the existence and pervasiveness of this 'survival' mode of learning in response to intensified workload with insufficient supports (lack of upfront training, learning new software in the process of doing report cards electronically, teaching new courses before textbooks have arrived, repairing photocopiers, etc.), many teachers also emphasised the more proactive meanings and uses of informal learning in their work. For example, the teachers interviewed did not typically associate their 'learning' (and their desires for learning) with the technical or administrative demands impacting their workload to which they clearly were responding. Even when the interviewer drew out this connection for some of the groups, in the context of exploring possible obstacles to the teachers' learning, the teachers downplayed the 'survival' aspect of learning across the wider dimensions of their work, quickly refocusing their discussion on what they perceived as the needs of the classroom.

In a sense, two conceptions of learning emerged from teacher discussions in the focus-group interviews. When responding most directly to the interviewer's set question, teachers explained their learning practices and preferences in relation to improving their teaching practice in the classroom. However, in more spontaneous and engaged conversation about the day-to-day challenges of teaching, teachers' more reactive modes of learning became very prevalent once the interviewer drew attention to these modes of learning. This prevalence resonates with the findings of Hoekstra et al. (2007) that a significant proportion of teachers' learning occurs in the reactive or tacit modes.

Teachers' learning and 'autonomy'

It is a challenge to illuminate the structure–agency relation in the context of teachers' work and learning. On the one hand, teachers recognise that, as professional employees largely responding to the demands placed on them legally and contractually, they have little control over the organisation. On the other hand, teachers generally understand themselves as having considerable autonomy at the micro-level of classroom pedagogy (Livingstone & Antonelli 2007). Complicating a top-down control versus bottom-up autonomy/creativity[15] dichotomy are the multiple and complex relations between social ideologies embedded in discourses of professional development, professionalism, and more general social values and norms, as compared to the individual teacher's 'own' sense of acting agentically.

There are increasing calls to accentuate 'professional learning' for teachers (see, for example, Hargreaves 2000; Hannay et al. 2006) against the prior dominance of compulsory, top-down professional development regimes. However, these new discourses of teacher reflection and empowerment also represent new regimes of self-regulation. Thus (teacher) autonomy is a very elusive and complex concept to theorise. Not only is there no 'outside of' control in the context of work, it remains unlikely that 'autonomy' (as with 'freedom') can ever be defined in wholly positive terms. Rather it is often only possible to consider shifts in relative autonomy given changing conditions of work. Clearly, very real constraints such as limited time and material supports can restrict how creatively, reflectively or deliberatively teachers can practise. Nevertheless, changing contexts for professional learning present both new possibilities and new dynamics of control – even under new initiatives promoting informal modes of teacher learning.

As already mentioned, there is growing interest in supporting informal modes of teachers' growth and learning. Most of these recommended practices rest on the assumption that greater teacher autonomy leads to improved working conditions and improved student learning. Autonomy, however, can be envisioned more as means than as ends.[16] For example, under (neo)human capital paradigms, worker autonomy or 'empowerment' can be a tool for shaping workers' subjectivities to correspond with organisational goals (Garrick & Usher 2000). 'Governmentality' and critical theorists who analyse 'lifelong learning' and 'worker empowerment' warn that these approaches can effectively work more as subtle forms of control rather than as liberating or democratising initiatives (Garrick & Usher 2000; Smyth 1992; Tuschling & Engemann 2006).

Based on our focus-group interviews, there is a definite institutional impediment to optimising teachers' collaboration and 'flexible mobilisation' for the purpose of building and sustaining 'learning communities'. In spite of the interest in promoting and supporting teaching as the 'learning profession' (Darling-Hammond & Sykes 1999), the limited material support and sometimes limited social/administrative support for teachers' informal learning suggests that schools do not necessarily represent a 'knowledge intensive work context' for teachers, as characterised by Belanger and Larivière (2005: 20) in their belief that '[t]here is a direct relationship between knowledge intensive work context and organisational support of informal learning activities'. While many teachers spoke of the value of mentoring and of observing colleagues teaching, these valued learning activities came with obstacles that mitigated their take-up. For example, a number of times teachers cited the difficulty of leaving one's 'own' classroom or students. A few teachers also explained that their colleagues (and, presumably, they themselves) could 'lose' their planning periods if they were to take the initiative to observe a colleague teach. Other teachers explained the difficulties of finding common planning times in complex and full schedules, and of extensive student supervision time that interfered with the possibilities for collaboration. Further, teachers noted that in more recent years department heads and administrators have diminishing time to support or engage in peer observation.

Teachers' anecdotal reporting during our research suggests that while collaborative modes of learning are possible and even sometimes promoted by administration, the rigidity of the timetable, the teacher's traditional role (that one teacher needs to be sovereign over their class(es) for the duration of the year or semester), and the curriculum and testing regimes, among other factors, limit teachers' participation. In some sense, the interviews revealed the contradictory space teachers have to negotiate – for example, jumping on board as team players in accord with the latest professional development trend, but with limited material and administrative supports. Teachers have to negotiate the devolving of accountability in the contradictory spaces of educational reform (Dehli & Fumia 2002). On the one hand, they are invited to initiate learning activities such as peer coaching, but, on the other hand, they understand that their absences should not affect their day-to-day routines and supervision, nor how 'their' students perform.

Based on our focus-group interviews with full-time teachers, they generally are not the optimally flexible (Tuschling & Engemann 2006) knowledge workers of the postmodern learning organisation (Garrick & Usher 2000). The more experienced teachers, while 'stressed out' by work intensification and obviously adapting to change, generally resisted envisioning themselves as 'adaptable' or 'flexible'; rather, they articulated more established notions of themselves as professionals and learners. These teachers were quite aware of the educational restructuring taking place in their provinces and criticised aspects of neo-liberal reform and rhetoric. In their critique of these new imperatives, teachers employed terms such as 'accountability', 'data-driven' reform, 'compressed' working schedules, 'expediency' as an operating principle, and 'conservative ideology-driven' reform.

Nevertheless, more nuanced analysis of the survey data offers some correspondences with premises emerging from the 'governmentality' theorists who suggest workers are taking on 'for themselves' learner dispositions, such as 'flexibility', that are conducive to reaching the larger goals of the organisation. In a previous paper (Tarc et al. 2006), we compared teachers who reported more than 10 hours of informal learning weekly ('high informal learners') against teachers who reported one hour or less. High informal learners also reported higher levels of formal learning, higher levels of working hours, higher stress and *greater* job satisfaction. This result, although tentative, does connect with Garrick and Usher's (2000: 12) description of the ' "seduction" at work and by work – a seduction through empowerment'. In other words, being empowered as a 'lifelong learner' and a more productive employee is 'seductive' in the sense of garnering a greater sense of autonomy and productiveness (job satisfaction), even where it tends towards greater levels of work intensification and stress.

Moreover, a few teachers interviewed *do* seem to be taking on some of the characteristics of the flexible, enterprising self – especially teachers with little seniority or teachers who are un(der)employed, as in the case of some of the small sample of occasional teachers interviewed. One full-time teacher, who reported constantly engaging in informal learning, exemplified the subject position of the flexible, lifelong learner. He was highly engaged in both formal and informal learning and able to respond to his frequently changing assignments. This same teacher described himself as 'very flexible', explaining how he constantly has been shifted ('pink-slipped') from one school to the next, and from one teaching assignment to the next. Had we interviewed more teachers with little seniority, we might have heard similar narratives about the need to stay current and be permanently updating.[17] We also heard these narratives from the more contingent occasional ('supply') teachers interviewed.

Informal learning, especially as a means for constructing the 'adaptable worker', can become the responsibility of the individual worker who has to maintain his or her relevancy for a changing economy. At the extreme, funding or opportunities for (formal) professional development could be intentionally minimised where individuals take it on themselves to engage informally to be current and employable. At this extreme, informal learning becomes a form of ongoing, unpaid overtime, exerting pressure on contract teachers who try to maintain reasonable work–home boundaries, and on teachers who are trying to secure full-time contracts. Even for teachers with job security, the following comments are illuminating in terms of the blurring of boundaries between work and home, heightened in an age of interconnectivity and competitiveness. One teacher remarked:

> So we are constantly on call…Last night I got an email telling me that I better review something that I had taught yesterday, because this woman felt that her child didn't learn it properly and she and her husband struggled to teach him, and the email was sent at 9:30 last night. I had a phone call from a parent this year; she left the message at 3:40 a.m.

In the words of another interviewed teacher:

> And now that's just so commonplace. I mean now with the email we have teachers that are going berserk because there are parents emailing and saying we want a report every week on how their kid is doing in high school – every week. And they feel entitlement to that, and it's like where is our boundaries or whatever.

These examples, among others, illustrate the changing working conditions with the blurring of work–home boundaries and pressures for continuous communication and responsiveness to the clients and stakeholders in schooling. These changing conditions, in turn, shape what and how teachers are learning and can further diffuse the focus of teachers' learning from the domain of classroom pedagogy.

Research limitations

As stated, the dominant example given of teachers' engagement with informal learning was collaboration with colleagues. Although the research clearly indicated that teachers learn from and value collaboration with their colleagues, it is less clear *how well* teachers were learning. On this latter point, it would seem that focus-group interviews might not be the optimal method to illuminate teachers' engagement with learning, for two reasons. First and most significantly, it may be necessary to be embedded at the teaching site and interview teachers alongside observations in classrooms and in staff and departmental meetings, to get better insight into the dynamics of teachers' professional learning, whether proactive or reactive. It was hoped that the interviews could probe below the levels of intentional learning on which the survey had to settle. Certainly, the interviews drew out the 'reactive' learning teachers had to perform in order to manage the changing demands of their work. However, other methods embedded within a teacher's day-to-day practice would likely be more useful in illuminating the deeper (more tacit) levels of learning. They might also provide a more realistic picture of the actualities and specificities of teachers' learning and resistances to learning. (Of course, increased levels of intimacy, such as observing and interviewing teachers in the classroom setting, would produce new methodological challenges.)

Second, the focus-group interview seemed to enact a space where teachers performed as good team members and 'active learners'. While teachers were critical of institutional aspects of increased workloads and the public scrutiny of teachers, they were unanimous in their high regard for collaboration with colleagues. Clearly, however, as the attention to *building* 'learning communities' implies, collaboration among staff is not a given. Anyone who has taught in schools knows that conflict as much as cooperation is part of the dynamics of staff relations. Further, working in the 'privacy' of one's own classroom with the 'door shut' can offer teachers – as much as they are team players – a sense of autonomy in their practice. Yet these layers did not arise in discussion under the focus-group arrangement.

Care, then, has to be taken to find methodological approaches that can begin to make explicit much of the practical knowledge of teachers that remained largely opaque under the focus-group interview format used. Interviews embedded in the worksite might have greater potential to uncover the more reactive and implicit modes of learning. To probe more deeply into the actualities of teacher collaboration and conflict, job-embedded and individual interviews would be helpful.

Conclusions

This chapter has presented and contextualised a few key findings from our research study on Canadian teachers that are potentially useful to researchers, policy-makers, and educators from other nations. Globalisation has produced common pressures to rationalise schooling across many national contexts, pressures that set new demands on teachers and their professional development and learning. How educational actors respond to these pressures varies across jurisdictions. In the Canadian context, the ubiquity and value of teachers' informal learning was a dominant research finding. However, 'informal learning' proved to be a messy category – in the literature (contextually), in our findings (empirically) and in our research approach (methodologically). In an individualist, market-oriented society the increasing attention to supporting teachers' professional learning offers both possibilities and new dangers. Clearly teachers understand the importance of informal modes of learning and are highly engaged in informal modes. How to structure and support teachers' informal modes of learning that privilege teacher autonomy over flexibility and adaptability are key challenges facing educational policy-makers and administrators. For professional development regimes in struggling economies there are likely to be complicating and additional challenges. Further research is needed to illuminate the complexity of informal learning and how teachers can be best supported to sustain and improve upon their practices through this mode of learning.

Notes

1 Funding for the first phase of this project (1997–2002) was provided by the 'New Approaches to Lifelong Learning' (NALL) research network project (funded by the Social Sciences and Humanities Research Council [SSHRC] of Canada) and by the Canadian Teachers' Federation and all of its provincial affiliates. Funding for the second phase of the project (2002–2007) was provided solely by the SSHRC-funded 'Work and Lifelong Learning' (WALL) research network project.

2 Neo-liberal restructuring privileges market logics and solutions for the provision of state schooling, manifesting in a whole set of processes towards privatisation, including providing 'school choice' such as magnet and charter initiatives, standardised testing to provide school rankings, pressures for schools to compete and to market their 'product' to their 'clients', and so on.

3 Herbert B, Education is no protection, *New York Times*, 26 January 2004.

4 See, for example, Gleeson & Husbands 2003; Mahony et al. 2003.

5 See, for example, Holmes Group 1990; Labaree 1992; Darling-Hammond 1998; Darling-Hammond & Ball 1998; OECD 1998; Ontario Government 2000.

6 'Governmentality', which owes much to the oeuvre of Michel Foucault, refers to the 'conduct of the self' and, in this case, how organisations (can) control or influence worker subjectivities, not by overt methods of rewards and punishments, but by shaping the worker-learner's individual desires and actions that are ultimately productive in the context of organisational efficiency and output. It is the individual that appears to choose for himself or herself the conduct that is also useful to the organisation.

7 See, for example, Darling-Hammond & Sykes 1999; Fullan 1995; Harris 2003; Hoekstra et al. 2007; Katzenmeyer & Moller 1996; Williams 2003.

8 For a more detailed description of the methodology and findings, see http://www.wallnetwork.ca/resources/Smaller_Clark_Teachers_Survey_Jun2005.pdf.

9 By government legislation, virtually all teachers in publicly funded elementary and secondary schools in Canada must belong to a teacher union; this ensured relatively accurate sampling of all such teachers.

10 For further explanation of this research method, see, for example, Peters & Raaijmakers 1998; Michelson 1998; Michelson & Harvey 1999; Harvey 1984; Harvey & Spinney 2000.

11   Most of the teachers we interviewed were teachers with 10 or (many) more years of experience; a number of the beginning teachers we contacted indicated that they were too busy to volunteer to participate in the focus-group interviews.

12   In spite of these pressures, however, among full-time respondents 29 per cent reported that they were 'very satisfied' with their job, while a further 56 per cent were at least 'somewhat satisfied'. By comparison, only 9 per cent were 'dissatisfied' and 2 per cent 'very dissatisfied' with their job.

13   This finding also aligns with research in adult education on workplace learning more generally (Livingstone et al. 2003).

14   As found in the Lohman study, increased administrative tasks and the perception of having to support students with greater needs were two of the most significant changes reported by teachers in their working conditions in recent years.

15   Storey (2007) suggests that we may want to consider teacher 'creativity' rather than 'autonomy', given that the traditional 'control versus autonomy' construct might have diminishing relevance under new contexts of performativity.

16   Although we do heed postmodern insights that trouble the separability of means versus ends, the point here is that at least conceptually we can differentiate between valuing increased autonomy as a good in itself as opposed to a tool for increasing efficiency.

17   It is worth noting also that Storey (2007) finds that new 'mid-career' entrants to teaching seem more aligned with 'new professionalism' with its 'target setting' and performance-management techniques. Her study in the UK finds that these teachers may find ways to be creative (rather than 'deskilled', as the traditional critique goes) within the new demands of professionalism.

References

Althouse JG (1929/1967) *The Ontario teacher: The historical account of progress, 1800–1910.* Toronto: Ontario Teachers' Federation

Belanger P & Larivière M (2005) *The dynamics of workplace learning in the knowledge economy: Organisational change, knowledge transfer and learning in the pharmaceutical and biotechnology industry.* Accessed 4 October 2007, http://www.wallnetwork.ca/resources/Belanger-Lariviere_Workplace_Learning_Jun2005mtg.pdf

Briscoe C (1997) Cognitive frameworks and teacher practices: A case study of teacher learning and change. *Journal of Educational Thought* 28(3): 286–299

Brookfield S (1995) *Becoming a critically reflective teacher.* San Francisco: Jossey-Bass

Carnoy M (2000) Globalisation and educational reform. In NP Stromquist & K Monkman (eds) *Globalisation and education: Integration and contestation across cultures.* Lanham, MD: Rowman and Littlefield

Carnoy M & Rhoten D (2002) What does globalisation mean for educational change? A comparative approach. *Comparative Education Review* 46(1): 1–9

Colley H, Hodkinson P & Malcolm J (2003) *Formality and informality in learning.* London: Learning and Skills Development Agency

Curtis B (1988) *Building the educational state: Canada West, 1836–1871.* London: Falmer Press

Dale R & Robertson S (2002) The varying effects of regional organisations as subjects of globalisation of education. *Comparative Education Review* 46(1): 10–36

Darling-Hammond L (1998) Teachers and teaching: Testing policy hypothesis from a national commission report. *Educational Researcher* 27(1): 5–15

Darling-Hammond L & Ball D (1998) Teaching for high standards: What policymakers need to know and be able to do. ERIC Document ED426491

Darling-Hammond L & Sykes G (eds) (1999) *Teaching as the learning profession: Handbook of policy and practice* (1st edition). San Francisco: Jossey-Bass

Dehli K & Fumia D (2002) *Teachers' informal learning, identity and contemporary education 'reform'*. Accessed 25 September 2007, http://www.oise.utoronto.ca/depts/sese/csew/nall/res/56KariDehli.pdf

Donmoyer R (1995) The very idea of a knowledge base. Paper presented at the Annual Meeting of the American Education Research Association, San Francisco (April)

Eraut M, Alderton J, Cole G & Senker P (2000) Development of knowledge and skills at work. In F Coffield (ed.) *Differing visions of a learning society*. Bristol: Policy Press

Fleming WG (1972) *Ontario's educative society*. Toronto: University of Toronto Press

Fullan M (1995) The school as a learning organisation: Distant dreams. *Theory into Practice* 34(4): 230–235

Fuller A, Hodkinson H, Hodkinson P & Unwin L (2005) Learning as peripheral participation in communities of practice: A reassessment of key concepts in workplace learning. *British Educational Research Journal* 31(1): 49–68

Gardner P (1984) *The lost elementary schools of Victorian England*. London: Croom Helm

Garrick J & Usher R (2000) *Flexible learning, contemporary work and enterprising selves*. Accessed 8 July 2007, http://www.epe.lacbac.gc.ca/100/201/300/ejofsociology/2000/v05n02/content/vol005.001/garrick-usher.html

Gee JP, Hull GA & Lankshear C (1996) *The new work order: Behind the language of the new capitalism*. Boulder, CO: Westview Press

Gibson S & Olberg D (1998) Learning to use the internet: A study of teacher learning through collaborative research partnerships. *Alberta Journal of Educational Research* 44(2): 239–242

Gleeson D & Husbands C (2003) Modernising schooling through performance management: A critical appraisal. *Journal of Education Policy* 18(5): 499–511

Goodman W (1995) Change without difference: School restructuring in historical perspective. *Harvard Educational Review* 65(1): 1–30

Hannay L, Wideman R & Seller W (2006) *Professional learning to reshape teaching*. Toronto: Elementary Teachers' Federation of Ontario

Hargreaves A (2000) Four ages of professionalism and professional learning. *Teachers and Teaching* 6(2): 151–182

Harris A (2003) Teacher leadership as distributed leadership: Heresy, fantasy or possibility? *School Leadership and Management* 23(3): 313–324

Harvey A (1984) *Time budget research*. Frankfurt and New York: Campus Verlag

Harvey A & Spinney J (2000) *Life on and off the job: A time-use study of Nova Scotia teachers*. Halifax: St Mary's University

Hoekstra A, Beijaard D, Brekelmans M & Korthagen F (2007) Experienced teachers' informal learning from classroom teaching. *Teachers and Teaching* 13(2): 191–208

Holmes Group (1990) *Tomorrow's schools: Principles for the design of professional development schools*. East Lansing, MI: Holmes Group

Hopkins RA (1969) *The long march: The history of the Ontario Public School Men Teachers' Federation*. Toronto: Baxter Publications

Katz M (1971) *Class, bureaucracy and schools*. New York: Praeger Press

Katzenmeyer M & Moller G (1996) *Awakening the sleeping giant: Leadership development for teachers*. Thousand Oaks, CA: Corwin Press

Klein P (1996) Preservice teachers' beliefs about learning and knowledge. *Alberta Journal of Educational Research* 42(4): 361–377

Labaree FD (1992) Power, knowledge and the rationalisation of teaching: A genealogy of the movement to professionalise teaching. *Harvard Educational Review* 62(2): 123–155

Livingstone DW (1999) Exploring the icebergs of adult learning: Findings of the first Canadian survey of informal learning practices. *Canadian Journal for the Study of Adult Education* 13(2): 49–72

Livingstone DW (2003) Hidden dimensions of work and learning: The significance of unpaid work and informal learning in global capitalism. *Journal of Workplace Learning* 15(7/8): 359–367

Livingstone DW & Antonelli F (March 2007) *How do teachers compare to other workers? Professionally speaking*. Accessed 1 October 2007, http://www.oct.ca/publications/professionally_speaking/march_2007/how_do_teachers_compare.asp

Livingstone DW, Stowe S & Raykov M (2003) *Annotated bibliography on the changing nature of work and lifelong learning*. Accessed 12 April 2008, http://www.wallnetwork.ca/resources/wallwp02.pdf

Lohman M (2000) Informal learning in the workplace: A case study of public school teachers. *Adult Education Quarterly* 50(2): 83–101

Mahoney P, Menter I & Hextall I (2003) Edu-business: Are teachers working in a new world? Paper presented at the Annual Meeting of the American Educational Research Association, Chicago (April)

Marsick VJ & Volpe M (1999) The nature and need for informal learning. *Advances in Developing Human Resources* 1(3): 1–9

McNeil LM (2000) *Contradictions of school reform: Educational costs of standardised testing*. New York: Routledge

Michelson W (1998) Time pressure and human agency in home-based employment. *Society and Leisure* 21(2): 455–472

Michelson W & Harvey A (1999) Is teachers' work never done? Time-use and subjective outcomes. Paper presented at the Annual Meeting of the American Sociological Association, Chicago (August)

OCT (Ontario College of Teachers) (1999) *Standards of practice for the teaching profession*. Toronto: OCT

OECD (Organisation for Economic Co-operation and Development) (1998) Staying ahead: In-service training and teacher professional development. *What Works in Education Series.* Paris: OECD

Ontario Government (1995) Province to proceed with Ontario College of Teachers. *Ministry of Education News Release*, 21 November. Document available from the author

Ontario Government (2000) *Ontario teacher testing programme.* Toronto: Ontario Ministry of Education

OSSTF (Ontario Secondary School Teachers' Federation) (1999) *A report on teacher testing.* Toronto: OSSTF

Peters P & Raaijmakers S (1998) Time crunch and the perception of control over time from a gendered perspective: The Dutch case. *Society and Leisure* 21(2): 417–433

Popkewitz T (1994) Professionalisation in teaching and teacher education: Some notes on its history, ideology, and potential. *Teaching and Teacher Education* 10(1): 1–14

Ranson S (2003) Public accountability in the age of neo-liberal governance. *Journal of Education Policy* 18(5): 459–480

Robinson SGB (1971) *Do not erase.* Toronto: OSSTF

Royal Commission on Education in Ontario (1950) *Report 1950.* Toronto: Ontario Government

Smyth J (1992) Teachers' work and the politics of reflection. *American Educational Research Journal* 29(2): 267–300

Spaull A (1997) 'A law unto themselves': Victorian state school teachers and the federal 'labour power.' *Discourse: Studies in the Cultural Politics of Education* 18(2): 185–196

Storey A (2007) Cultural shifts in teaching: New workforce, new professionalism? *Curriculum Journal* 18(3): 253–270

Straka GA (2004) *Informal learning: Genealogy, concepts, antagonisms and questions.* Accessed 29 September 2007, http://itb.uni-bremen.de/downloads/Publikationen/Forschungsberichte/fb_15_04.pdf

Stromquist NP (2002) *Education in a globalised world: The connectivity of economic power, technology, and knowledge.* Lanham, MD: Rowman and Littlefield

Tarc P (2007) Informal learning in 'performative' times: Insights from empirical research on Canadian teachers' work and learning. *Canadian Journal for the Study of Adult Education* 21(2): 71–86

Tarc P, Smaller H & Antonelli F (2006) *Illuminating teachers' informal learning: Shaping professional development and schooling reform.* Accessed 6 June 2007, http://www.wallnetwork.ca/resources/Tarc_Teachers_Inf_Learning_AERA06.pdf

Tough A (1979) *The adult's learning projects: A fresh approach to theory and practice in adult learning.* Toronto: OISE Press

Tuschling A & Engemann C (2006) From education to lifelong learning: The emerging regime of learning in the European Union. *Educational Philosophy and Theory* 38(4): 451–469

Williams A (2003) Informal learning in the workplace: A case study of new teachers. *Educational Studies* 29(2): 207–219

10 Migration and organising: Between periphery and centre

Anannya Bhattacharjee

Introduction

Migration of economically, socially and culturally oppressed people is an increasingly significant phenomenon in the contemporary world. Yet, although migrants keep the economic engines running, they are largely invisible in the political and social fabric of societies. Their political and social visibility falls within the large cracks between the home region that loses their presence and the host region that ignores their concerns. While migrants may be viewed as being on the periphery of collective belonging, their roles in any society far exceed their perceived position. This is true regardless of whether the migration takes place within national boundaries (domestic migration) or across national boundaries (international migration). For the most part, migration is not a product of individual choice or freedom but rather a forced necessity: most migrants are economic and political refugees of a destructive, undemocratic and extractive development model, and their conditions are the barometers of what is going wrong.

My instinctive closeness to migration is shaped by my own forced personal and later political journeys – from India to the US, back to India, and now between the two. My political commitments have been greatly influenced by the phenomenon of migration or immigration, especially forced migration driven by economic necessity.

In this chapter, I reflect on my learnings and experiences with organising in migrant/ immigrant and socially oppressed (by race, gender, caste, region, nationality) working-class communities in the US and India. I hope to establish that organising among migrant communities requires frameworks and tactics that are distinct, and that such strategies may well lead us to new modes of organising that are needed for building a stronger movement for social and economic justice and for imagining a new type of working class nationally and internationally. Ultimately, we have to try to answer the question, what is the working class today, and how can we create solidarity in a world that expertly divides the working class within and across nations?

South Asian communities in the US

My relationship to work, movement building, identity and politics has been deeply influenced by my own journeys – involuntary and voluntary – within national boundaries and internationally. Politicised during my adult years in the US through that country's invasion of Central America and the anti-apartheid movement, I, like many foreign students, primarily identified myself with left-wing struggles against US imperialist foreign policies. Coming as I did from a post-colonial country (India) and from a lower-middle-class background, anti-imperialist spaces allowed me to locate myself in a landscape in which I felt otherwise invisible.

However, I became increasingly dissatisfied with the limits of my participation in these struggles, mainly because I did not think such activities could mobilise large numbers of people at the local level. Yet, at the same time I believed that change could only come about through mass mobilisation. It began to dawn on me that being locally relevant is key to building any kind of movement that can mobilise people on a substantial scale. It became clear that while solidarity with remote communities, even with my home country, was crucial, it could not be the anchoring force of my work and I had to fight for justice where I was – in the communities where I lived, studied, worked and played. Based in the US as I was then, solidarity with oppressed and 'Third World' nations necessarily involved suffering people who lived elsewhere. And while anti-imperialist solidarity struggles have the potential to translate into significant and important work, being removed from the situation in these places means that one remains materially disengaged from an analysis of organising and power. *Anti-imperialist struggles need to be built from the inside out.* Engagement with this principle led me to see the importance of working for change among the people residing in the US.

Engaging community struggles in New York

Although I had never before self-consciously called myself South Asian, when I arrived in New York City after my student years I identified myself as a new immigrant/foreigner in the city's South Asian community. This was a community that was only starting to be recognised as a growing and significant immigrant community. Between 1960 and 2000, the Asian population in the US increased considerably and, according to census figures, people of Indian origin constituted the largest Asian immigrant group at this time. However, there was a considerable difference between those immigrants who had come to the US in the early 1900s and had struggled against anti-immigrant sentiments in California, while at the same time actively supporting India's nationalist struggle for freedom from British colonial rule, and the professional wave of immigrants, post 1965, who were engrossed in their individual economic and professional pursuits. In the 1980s, around the time when I started organising, there ushered in a new wave of working-class Indians and people of Indian origin from India, East Africa and the Caribbean.

I became involved in social justice issues with such immigrants in the metropolitan area of New York City in the thick of the Reagan–Bush years and the rise of the American right. It was a time when the left/progressive social justice movement in the US was at a generally low point and a period of massive change in the South Asian immigrant community. As I soon discovered, militancy and organising around US foreign policy and organising in one's own community are two different worlds of knowledge and skills. I knew little about immigration history in the US and, although I could sense things were changing, I did not have the historical insight into the significance of the moment that I was experiencing. In retrospect, I realise that any new immigrant would typically have little meaningful knowledge of present or past histories of struggles or movements in the US.

It is not difficult to see how new immigrants have to interface most frequently with dominant forms of oppression and power – in other words, the ruling class. But it may not be immediately evident that new immigrants also interface with dominant forms of *resistance*, which may or may not be the most transformative. Accessing those who are similarly exploited and who are resisting (strategically and militantly) is one of the hardest tasks during a right-wing upsurge. Because of their lack of connection to, and understanding of, the host country's politics, new immigrants tend to engage with what is most visible and accessible. As Marx said in a different context:

> Men make their own history, but they do not make it just as they please;
> they do not make it under circumstances chosen by themselves, but
> under circumstances directly found, given and transmitted from the past.
> (Tucker 1978: 595)

Finding my community

I was first confronted by the question of how to locate the community of South Asians with which I identified historically. As yet, I was unfamiliar with the idea of immigrant people forming communities from scratch, a history particular to the US and a process that I will call here 'communities-in-formation'.

From my limited exposure to the Civil Rights struggle, the Black Power movement, the American Indian movement and the Chicano movement, I had absorbed the notion that ethnically/racially defined (although indigenous communities do not exactly fit this categorisation) and politically self-conscious communities are one of the building blocks for social justice and change in a country like the US. However, as a first-generation Indian immigrant I was unschooled in the concept of immigration and had little understanding of immigration and immigrant communities as a political phenomenon. I took it for granted that there was a 'community-in-existence' – a number of people loosely called a community of Indians, if not South Asians – and that it was only a matter of finding them. In fact, my mission was to discover such a community, one in which I would find my place. But as I went about trying to locate this community, it became clearer that I was actually defining this so-called community for myself. Through the work I was doing, I in turn was helping to form this community.

Crisis intervention and its limitations

As I engaged with South Asians in New York, I discovered that many of the women confronted situations of violence within their families. This was my first indication that the community I was looking for faced a particular crisis internal to it. And this crisis resonated with my own closeness to issues of gender oppression. In addition to imperialism, I had also been shaped by feminism, although at the time I was not yet fully conversant with the divisions and tensions within it.[1] As a result, a number of us decided to develop a domestic violence crisis organisation in the New York metropolitan area, seeing this response as providing a window through which we could find, serve and engage with the South Asian community. It became the first such women's organisation in a metropolitan area that was the largest home to South Asians.[2]

In the absence of more familiar signs of what constitutes political activity – a broad spectrum of political parties, mass-based organisations and labour unions – there was a range of newly emerging non-governmental organisations (NGOs) in New York. These included a number of well-established organisations responding to domestic violence and offering services to women, and these organisations provided mentoring for us. This consisted mainly of 'issue-based' technical assistance and training to enable us to respond to the women caught in violent situations or crises. Thus we received the support we needed to set up an NGO with access to resources including funders, technical assistance providers, non-profit-related libraries, and pro bono legal organisations well versed in non-profit law.[3]

While initially enthusiastic about reaching out to these well-established organisations, in later years I became critical of much of their approach. I began to feel that the service-oriented, professional, domestic violence organisations were narrow and issue-based and that this actually hindered the process of movement building.[4] What seemed to be missing was a historically informed perspective of the movement, a critical analysis of its successes and failures, comparisons with organising strategies in other social movements, and open discussion of the conflicts within the movement. I struggled to find others who shared my critique and yet, despite my misgivings, this crisis response to domestic violence actually served as a point of entry for us into what we thought were communities-in-existence, but that were actually processes of communities-in-formation.

Several issues for reflection emerge from this intervention. Firstly, while domestic violence was indicative of a problem requiring a response within the community, the positive side was that it presented the opportunity to engage in building the strength and power of women within the community, which could be a step towards constructing an alternative community to the one in formation, and from which to engage with the larger US landscape. This is not the logic that usually drives the formation of a crisis response, except in a highly submerged sense. However, if this logic were to be followed, then our approach to the crisis could be seen as an entry point for constructive community building as opposed to defence fortification – from building women-power to women-led community building. This could have an opening-up, as opposed to a closing-down, effect.

Secondly, the crisis intervention response addressed a key fault line internal to a community – in this case, patriarchy within the community. While we were making a very important intervention in this community-in-formation, over time if such an intervention, which at its core was a defensive mechanism modelled on crisis management as opposed to social transformation, did not engage in constructive building as well, then it ran the risk of becoming self-referential rather than expansive and unifying. This would have serious implications for the process of communities-in-formation. Such efforts are ultimately unable to leverage the power of the work for forming the community, and continue to relegate that task to other regressive or value-neutral forces.

Thirdly, it was tempting to initiate crisis response efforts, imagining them to be building and not just defending, and hope that they would ultimately lead to constructive community building. This is highly unlikely, even in politically mature communities. Turning defensive organisations into constructive organisations at a later stage is extremely difficult.

Finally, given the lack of community organisation (except for male-dominated cultural and value-neutral formations), much work had to be undertaken by unorganised groups attempting organisation. When a crisis response occurs in the absence of a larger mass formation or organisation, it can reinforce the belief that a group of individuals can come together, start from scratch and develop a comprehensive solution to a crisis internal to that very community. But this approach works against collective solutions where the collective is a historical and political formation carved out of a process of negotiation. In the absence of a broader agenda of mass formations, this approach also promotes narrow problem solving. In new immigrant communities choices are limited, however, and engaging in a minority community formation through a crisis reinforces a sense of marginalisation and victimhood, which, without the broader organised fabric, can be ultimately draining. Placed within a larger context of political activity, it soon begins to define certain formations and preclude others.

These experiences among the immigrant community made me question how one would measure 'success' in community organising. The quest for upward mobility, which is the hallmark of the immigrant bourgeoisie and which drives working-class migration in search of employment, could well become the defining mark of success in work for social justice. America's projected image of democracy, individual freedom and economic opportunities provides the illusion of inclusion and the possibility of achieving this American dream, with some adjustments. But, as I witnessed during my years in New York City, the reality for most is quite different: on an early morning in the Washington Heights area one can see Latino day labourers lining up. Bosses drive up in their vehicles to choose them and pick them up. The labourers, desperately needing the slave-like wages, compete with each other for the boss's attention. They know that for the kind of jobs they are going to, the boss is looking for a muscular physique – so those labourers who have them wear clothing that displays their muscular arms and strength. This is not unlike scenarios in books and movies that I have read and seen about the African slave trade – a cruel and dark chapter in migration history to the US.

I am reminded that today's fight is not all that new, but it is harder to see because capital and government have got better at hiding exploitation in the pages of dense legislation, and at segregating its population and isolating its oppressed so that the oppressed cannot meet each other except on the oppressor's own terms. As James Boggs and Grace Lee Boggs (1970) suggest: 'The truth is that the democracy of which Americans have been so proud is based on the worst kind of class system in the world, a class system that is based on the systematic exploitation of another race' (1970: 125). Elaborating on the so-called American dream, they say:

> This is what the American 'classless society' is – using others, and particularly those of other races, to advance yourself materially and socially, without regard for right and wrong and without regard for social responsibility. What has been boasted about as the 'opportunity' to see above your class in America has been, in reality, opportunism. What has been boasted about as the 'freedom of the individual' has been, in reality, the freedom to purchase material goods regardless of human values. What has been boasted about as 'government of the people' has been, in reality, the evasion by the people of the social responsibilities of self-government. (Boggs & Boggs 1970: 126)

Immigrants and working-class people of colour in the US

Through my experiences in organising in later years – in the broader working-class communities of colour, with immigrant workers (such as those in restaurants, vending and taxi driving), women workers (such those as in domestic work and retail), and around attacks on civil rights of people of colour (both immigrants and native-born, through border enforcement, policing and imprisonment) – it became clear that the three categories – race, immigration status and nationality/nation-of-origin – are central to defining immigrant policies and practices and therefore to any kind of organising work in the US.

Citizenship laws and labour controls

Central to immigrant policies and practices in the US are two notions: one is the clarification of US citizenship, and the other is the control of cheap labour. It is about making the country run profitably but allowing visibility and a decent life only to those who fit a certain economic and political profile. I use the term 'citizenship' not just to indicate the holder of a US passport, although that is certainly a powerful document, but also to signify who is privileged, who is seen to have rights and who is indeed visible as a public member of the US nation state. Anti-immigrant rhetoric and laws, denouncing immigration and advocating for stricter law enforcement, are ultimately not just about immigrants. Etienne Balibar and Immanuel Wallerstein (1991: 20) describe '[t]he functioning of the category of immigration as a substitute for the notion of race' as an aspect of neo-racism. In other words, the anti-immigrant discourse provides an alibi for the real object – that is, people of colour.

The more citizenship is contested, the more cheap labour goes underground. Government takes over the work of regulating labour on behalf of capital: whereas workers outside the US find employers enticing them to enter the US and work, the government (mainly through immigration authorities and law enforcement) makes sure their invisibility and vulnerability are maximised. It is not only immigrants who are trapped in this continuum, but also people of colour, because the distinction between the two is not clear. As an organiser I repeatedly saw this conflation causing a common state of terror among communities of colour and at the same time a rift between native-born people of colour and immigrants of colour.

Asian immigrant communities (including working-class Indian, Pakistani, Bangladeshi, Chinese, Korean, Vietnamese and Cambodian communities) provide services to the city and the country. Their legal status, livelihood and living conditions are controlled by their employers, and their safety and security are controlled by the police and the criminal justice system. As immigrants and people of colour form a continuum of oppressed people in the US, we must assume that anyone from this group, especially if she or he is working class, is vulnerable to deportation, exploitation, physical danger and criminalisation.

The illusion of democracy

Manning Marable's (2004) comments in the context of African Americans resonate for other communities of colour as well:

> Not too far in the distance lies the social consequence of these policies: an unequal, two-tiered, uncivil society, characterised by a governing hierarchy of middle- to upper-class 'citizens' who own nearly all property and financial assets, and a vast subaltern of quasi- or subcitizens encumbered beneath the cruel weight of permanent unemployment, discriminatory courts and sentencing procedures, dehumanised prisons, voting disfranchisement, residential segregation, and the elimination of most public services for the poor. (Marable 2004: 1)

Thus, I realised that organising in immigrant communities would have to contend not just with service provision, but also with the larger context of a false sense of democracy that helps to mystify subjugation of entire communities originating from former colonised nations. As Bill Fletcher (2003) puts it: 'Any illusion, accepted by workers, can become a material obstacle to the development of class consciousness and the blocking of forward motion.'

At the same time, democracy and economic promises in a capitalist economy are counter-posed with dictatorship and economic failures elsewhere. Thus, organising in communities of colour in the US needs to simultaneously integrate a critique of contemporary US imperialism that fuels this false sense of capitalist promises and democracy at home, and of backward dictatorships elsewhere, leading to a continual pursuit of the ever-receding American dream.

Global worker struggles

As I moved into civil rights and immigrant rights, and simultaneously into immigrant worker struggles, these lessons steered me towards understanding and practising different modes of organising. My next challenge was how to link local organising to the larger, anti-imperialist global framework, not just theoretically but concretely. This necessarily involved articulating local struggles to other struggles and developing an overlapping or intersecting analysis. As Laclau and Mouffe suggest:

> The political meaning of a local community involvement…is not given from the beginning: it crucially depends upon its hegemonic articulation with other struggles and demands. (Laclau & Mouffe 1985: 87)

Global capitalist aggression and imperialist adventurism, the attendant large-scale migration in search of work and the exploitation that such migration allows, provide the twin engines for developing articulations that can provide us with the inspiration for this larger framework.

Migrants in Gurgaon, India

Several years later, when I moved back to India, I found myself living in northwest India in one of the largest urban industrial hubs today. The National Capital Region (NCR) – straddling the three states of Delhi, Haryana and Uttar Pradesh – is among the fastest-growing industrial hubs in India and one of the world's largest built-up urbanised zones. The population has grown to over 14 million with the migration of people from states all over India, providing the area with a steady supply of cheap labour for production for the global market. The central government is located here, giving the illusion of access.

Gurgaon, a fast-growing developing area, has a highway cutting through it, creating its two 'faces'. One side is residential and consumer driven, with shopping malls, modern apartments, and so on. The other side is a huge industrial area manufacturing products for the global consumer market; this side of Gurgaon is the focus of my discussion. It is a grindingly desolate place where words like 'beauty', 'culture' or 'identity' seem luxurious; where fairness and justice seem like a dream; and where only brute force and survival are real. It is here that we have been confronting questions about community, organisation and resistance.

Workplaces in Gurgaon are places of dislocation operating within newly developing capitalist regimes. They are places of dislocation in several ways: workers are migrants, and even if long-time migrants they have never managed to stabilise their living and family arrangements; employers are building new factories and restructuring production increasingly to align themselves with global modes of production; the government is staffed by old political and bureaucratic hands who are committed to the employers taking the lead in the exercise of global economic alignment and who are mostly experienced in the feudal handling of disputes. Gurgaon is, therefore, a mix of new capitalist structures and feudal powers and practices.

The vast majority of the migrant workers are Dalits, tribals and Muslims from poorer states reeling under rapid mining developments, industrialisation, urbanisation, a high degree of landlessness and limited ownership of alternative productive resources. The primary source of livelihood is wage labour; thus people are forced to migrate in search of work. The migrant workers in these new industries connected to global production – both formally and informally – are unorganised and heavily exploited by employers, labour contractors, landlords, law enforcement, and so on. In fact, the NCR is one of the most unorganised regions outside of the Delhi city area, with very few social service organisations, unions or other organised groups.

Organising workers

Organising in Gurgaon means organising workers who come from the eastern states of India, which have had a long history of revolutionary struggles. They come from the communities that have been the subject and object of these struggles. They are now 'communities-in-formation'. The majority of the workforce is not unionised and is socially fragmented, making it possible for employers to use social divisions to exploit their labour further. Workers identify not solely as workers but through other identities as well: class, caste, sub-caste, gender, religion, region, semi-rural/urban, and so on. They often live in precarious housing conditions with poor infrastructure, and their survival needs go beyond issues of wages and benefits. In the few instances when workers have stood up to demand their basic rights, they have been brutally crushed by the employers. These workers have no legal work contracts on which to fall back in the event of intimidation by the employers. In public places and housing colonies, they endure inhuman treatment from local landlords. In effect they are voiceless citizens within the workplace or outside of it. They live a life that is isolated and invisible from the rest of the society. We have seen that such workers have a strong desire to fight back, but they are overpowered by their sense of helplessness. In this particular situation an urgent task lies ahead of us.

Politically and culturally desolate, such places of dislocation with their single focus on production and profit need multiple and simultaneous activities for building organisation. These are places where the words 'local' and 'working class' have to be redefined as very few are really 'local' in the way the term has been traditionally used. The varied structures of work (from organised factories to home-based work, from regular workers with benefits to contract workers) and the varied communities of workers (from diverse states and villages, with diverse religions, castes and cultures, loyalties and politics) all result in a working class that is anything but monolithic and which demands new organising strategies. The location for organising may need to be the workplace, but equally it needs to be the colonies in which workers live, the streets they walk between work and home, the markets they shop in, and so on. The issues that arise in these locations – housing, service agencies, schools, markets, transportation, and so on – are just as relevant as issues of wages, hours and benefits in the workplace.

While a unified working-class consciousness may seem to be a receding dream, it is not an abstract failure due to lack of some kind of intelligence. I believe it is not possible to develop meaningful strategy without intentionally and systematically delving into the problems that obstruct community building and unity of purpose. A workers' organisation needs to be woven out of various threads of organising efforts that reflect the diversity of the workers themselves, situated within the context of production that is the central force bringing the diverse workers together at a given place and time. As Marx said:

> What they [men] are, therefore, coincides with their production, both with what they produce and with how they produce. The nature of individuals thus depends on the material conditions determining their production. This production only makes its appearance with the *increase of population*. In its turn, this presupposes the *intercourse* of individuals with one another. The form of this intercourse is again determined by production. (Tucker 1978: 150; italics in original)

Conclusion: Periphery is central, centre is peripheral

The combination of issues that I have struggled with – violence against women, institutionalised racist violence, exploitation of low-wage and migrant workers – has given me the opportunity to understand the interconnectedness of issues and the importance of simultaneous attention. The result is the development of various tributaries of the organising process, needing attention simultaneously before they can connect with each other.

As Laclau and Mouffe suggest:

> [I]n order to advance in the determination of social antagonisms, it is necessary to analyse the plurality of diverse and frequently contradictory positions, and to discard the idea of a perfectly unified and homogenous agent, such as the 'working class' of classical discourse. The search for the 'true' working class and its limits is a false problem, and as such lacks any theoretical or political relevance…[T]here are no privileged points for the unleashing of a socialist political practice; this hinges upon a 'collective will' that is laboriously constructed from a number of dissimilar points. (Laclau & Mouffe 1985: 84)

This organising process has necessarily involved constant redefining of periphery and centre while not forgetting the anchoring force of the process. The periphery can move to the centre and the centre to the periphery – contingent on the moment, the phase, the priorities and the strategy.

In the contemporary world, where global connections and attention are needed, we also need to discuss global North–South dimensions. In my work today, I try to maintain an integrity to local struggles and at the same time explore grassroots strategies for linking working-class organisations across borders in the global North and South. The question is, what should be the basis of international relationships at this time of nascent but significant changes in our movements struggling for social and economic justice? The architecture of what such relationships would actually look like is not clear, but it can only emerge through developing models of working together and achieving concrete gains.

International solidarity between the global North and South is also deeply complicated by the inherent inequalities of the imperialist global capitalist system. To borrow Balibar's words in the context of racism, 'the destruction of the racist complex presupposes not only the revolt of its victims, but the transformation of the racists themselves and, consequently, *the internal decomposition of the community created by racism*' (Balibar & Wallerstein 1991: 18; italics added). How can we build common relevance in a non-imperialist way? Global North organisations have the advantage of mobility, greater resources and access to technology, but an imperialist relationship can very quickly be created under these circumstances. Developing a mutually beneficial non-imperialist strategy based on common relevance requires patience, dialogue and mutual respect. This raises many other questions.

How do we practise democratic learning? A meaningful international relationship requires establishing intimate working relations over a period of time and engaging each other in ways that help to transfer lessons that are most useful. A global North organisation, with access to resources and technology, may decide what the global South needs to learn, rather than engage in a democratic learning process. The former process builds a patronising one-sided relationship in which the learning process does not fully achieve the results that would help the struggles of both countries.

How do we build through strength, not weakness? An organisation that is weakening in the home country can be tempted to go to outside sources in order to build strength. However, strength cannot be imported. If an organisation cannot build strength at home, it is unlikely to help build strength outside. International solidarity between the global North and South must come from the premise that both must find their strengths at home, and only in that process can one build a powerful relationship.

How do we incorporate the best of both worlds? A learning relationship requires both sides to explore lessons and strategically suspend prejudices. For example, the US is a country where ideologies, especially on the left, are present below the surface, unlike India, where ideologies are visible and often of paramount importance. US organisations are more trained in pragmatic action and tactical methods, and since they operate in a country that is far more politically repressive than India, they have also learned to disguise their ideological positions. On the other hand, Indian organisations have a tradition of training their cadres through explicitly ideological camps and may pay scant attention to strategy and tactics. We need both in order to fight the assault of imperialist globalisation. Instead of dismissing one side for being pragmatic and the other for being rigidly ideological, we need to create learning mechanisms that bring the best of the two worlds together. The global South and

North both occupy the centre and the periphery from different perspectives and at different times, and therefore global strategies have to contend with the changing positions and cannot indulge in fixing either the centre or the periphery in a rigid and ideological manner.

Notes

1   By the time I entered the women's movement, feminist practices had moved far away from notions of transformation and building power and instead had become focused on bourgeois and individualistic concerns. Other forms of more radical feminism – African American, Latino, indigenous, revolutionary – were not immediately accessible.

2   For more analysis, see Bhattacharjee (1992).

3   For a deeper analysis, see Bhattacharjee (1997).

4   See Bhattacharjee (2002).

References

Balibar E & Wallerstein I (1991) *Race, nation and class: Ambiguous identities*. London and New York: Verso

Bhattacharjee A (1992) The habit of ex-nomination: Woman, nation and the Indian immigrant bourgeoisie. *Public Culture* 5(1): 19–44. Republished (1998) in S Dasgupta (ed.) *A patchwork shawl: Chronicles of South Asian women in America*. Rutgers, NJ: Rutgers University Press

Bhattacharjee A (1997) A slippery path: Organising resistance to violence against women. In S Shah (ed.) *Dragon ladies: Asian American feminists breathe fire*. Cambridge, MA: South End Press

Bhattacharjee A (2002) Putting community back in the domestic violence movement. DifferenTakes Issue Papers Series No. 15. Population and Development Program, Hampshire College, Amherst, MA. Accessed 24 March 2009, http://popdev.hampshire.edu/projects/dt/15

Boggs J & Boggs GL (1970) Democracy: Capitalism's last battle-cry. In J Boggs (ed.) *Racism and the class struggle*. New York and London: Monthly Review Press

Fletcher B (2003) Transcript of speech given to Labor Notes Conference, USA (September). Accessed 24 March 2009, http://www.labornet.org/news/0903/fletch.htm

Laclau E & Mouffe C (1985) *Hegemony and socialist strategy: Towards a radical democratic politics*. London: Verso

Marable M (2004) *The new racial domain*. ZNet commentary, 30 April. Accessed 24 March 2009, http://www.zmag.org/zspace/commentaries/1924

Tucker R (1978) *Marx–Engels reader* (2nd edition). New York and London: WW Norton and Company

11 Peripheralisation, exploitation and lifelong learning in Canadian guest worker programmes

Peter H Sawchuk and Arlo Kempf

Introduction

The subject of guest worker programmes has been emerging in diverse scholarly literatures for some time. Known by different names, these programmes refer to the importation of temporary labour under specific conditions. In various guises such programmes are increasingly prevalent in core capitalist countries. Across North, Central and South America, as well as the Caribbean and beyond, their impact on national economies has been dramatic. Despite the recent focus of debate around guest worker programmes in the Americas and elsewhere, these forms of the planned development of peripheral, transnational labour markets have been around a long time, producing networks that have touched virtually every region of the globe.

As distinct from the literatures of migration studies, international human geography, international labour market economics and post-colonialism, to name a few, the amount of lifelong learning and work scholarship devoted to the topic of guest work is slight. Our perspective – shared with those committed to the notion that work and learning always take place within a contested political landscape – is that an informed understanding of the phenomenon of guest worker programmes is long overdue.

Superficially, however, the work and learning relations of guest worker programmes hold few mysteries: they simply represent a highly exploited instance of these relations that involves little, if any, skill and knowledge of consequence to the evolving future of work. How on earth, it might be asked, can such forms of work, with their echoes of the twentieth, nineteenth and even eighteenth centuries, be considered a relevant topic as we enter the twenty-first century of advanced knowledge work, expansive technologies and globalised production and trade? Our position in this chapter is that, in a rapidly globalising and polarising world, guest work and its variants are increasingly central to the labour and learning of the twenty-first century. As all work and learning relations are deeply shaped by cultural, political and economic histories, and as skills, learning and knowledge can remain so well hidden in the occupational lives that constitute the experience of peripheral labour markets such as those produced by guest work, we feel compelled to address these learning dynamics despite their rawness, entangled as they are in employment so basely human as to be confused with the sheer act of survival.

We begin our discussion with a brief summary of the historical context that seeks to register the long pattern of what we call 'infrastructure building'. In our view, this long building process has established the virtual inevitability of guest worker programme expansion across the Americas. Moreover, we claim that the situation in Canada cannot be adequately understood without a vision of its origins in broader political/military histories, such as US continental hegemony and Canada's relationship with the British Commonwealth. Our analysis focuses on agricultural guest work and draws on both secondary analysis of popular education initiatives as well as our own series of visits to the field/worksites, preliminary interviews and conversations with guest workers in the agricultural sector in central (Ontario) and western (British Columbia) Canada.

The historical trajectory of guest worker programme expansion

Our ultimate concern in this chapter is to develop an understanding of lifelong learning and work in the context of guest worker programmes in Canada, and for this establishing some historical context is crucial. In many ways, the establishment of the contemporary North American guest worker programme infrastructure begins with US continental action in relation to the Mexican–American War (1846–1848) (Chacón & Davis 2006). Following on a variety of informal and formal policy periods – that is, periods of official closed-border policy and open-border practices encouraging undocumented migration alternating with formalised guest worker programmes – among the results of this conflict was the establishment of Mexico as a permanent peripheral labour market first for the US. In Canada, guest worker programmes were originally established vis-à-vis the British Commonwealth colonial network leading first to Caribbean–Canadian arrangements. Over time, however, Canadian policy has become increasingly oriented towards US-dominated dynamics across the Americas through which Mexico has become the leading origin country while experimentation, most recently with Thai communities, is now emerging (see Sawchuk & Kempf 2007). In brief, we maintain that the context of work and lifelong learning lies in the dynamics of both long, relatively independent trajectories of peripheral labour market infrastructure building and North American (US/Canadian) policy synchronisation in relation to the near and far global South.[1]

The economic sector that has traditionally been at the centre of guest work issues has been the agricultural sector, although this situation is rapidly changing. Nevertheless, in both Canada and the US the agricultural sector has been the origin of guest worker programmes. In Canada specifically, such programmes flourished under long-established labour legislation that explicitly excluded farm workers from union organising. These sections of labour code were fundamental to establishing labour market peripheralisation so central to the viability of agribusiness/factory farms and their growing dependence on guest worker programmes. Indeed, this legislation has only recently been challenged through the June 2007 Supreme Court of Canada ruling that allows, in principle, the right to organise labour unions inclusive of farm workers.[2]

Over the last decade, accentuated further by recent labour market needs in western Canadian oil boom regions, three other sectors have found a home in guest worker policy discussions: hospitality (hotels, seasonal resorts), transportation (trucking) and light manufacturing (food processing, plastics and other consumer products). Following the argument of Vogel (2007), if guest work is expanded significantly into these sectors, the economic effects on broader labour market conditions in host countries would likely multiply, spreading well beyond these sectors. The US government's recent (bipartisan) proposals for guest worker programme expansion, and similarly its attempts to deregulate cross-border trucking in the North American Free Trade Agreement (NAFTA) region, seek to formalise existing experimentation in the transportation sector. How this discussion proceeds in Canada will likely show some distinctions: differences in union density and, obviously, the proximity/cost issues (e.g. distance from Mexico) will likely play some role. In contrast with Canada, the engagement of guest worker programmes within, for example, pockets of light industry across a range of southern 'right-to-work' (i.e. anti-union) states in the US depends on an already highly integrated Mexican–American border integration history shaped also by the effective establishment of *macquiladoran*[3] economic zones.

To summarise at this point, our claim is that capitalist economic imperatives – the need for cheap, vulnerable labour imported from international peripheral labour markets – have historically driven the processes of guest work programme expansion. But we add that such processes both actively produce impoverishment and macquiladorisation in origin countries while negotiating and incorporating worker insecurity as well as traditional nativism/racism in the host country.[4]

Canadian guest work

Without rights to health and safety, social benefits or freedom of movement, and with the help of unceremonious, state-enforced cancellations of contracts with few if any avenues of appeal, guest worker experiences in North America offer perhaps the closest contemporary approximation to the original system of US chattel slavery. Moreover, guest worker programmes function as a parasitic phenomenon: families and communities in origin countries bear the costs of social reproduction while host countries claim the profits and enjoy unfettered labour control (Burawoy 1976).

Building on its immigration policy that effectively targeted specific national/ethno-racial groups during the late nineteenth and first half of the twentieth century, Canada in the 1960s experienced increasing wage pressures against a backdrop of more generalised pressure to reform its immigration system, as well as demands for change from Canadian agribusiness. Anticipating the initiation of the country's immigration 'points system', which would be established in 1967 to shift legal entry to economic and educational factors, in 1966 the Canadian state instituted its Seasonal Agricultural Workers Programme (SAWP), a programme that remains in place today. The SAWP brings particular foreign workers to the country for periods of between six weeks and eight months. Built on formal agreements with origin countries, the programme is formally predicated on 'labour market complementarity and bilateral co-operation that provides benefits to all participants' (Preibisch & Binford 2007: 9). Largest in the provinces of Ontario, British Columbia and Quebec, the SAWP has been established in nine provinces over the past five years and is growing at an unprecedented rate:

in 2001 there were 20 000 guest workers nationally (Weston & Scarpa de Masellis 2003); by 2007 this number had grown to 166 000.[5] Building on its roots in the British Commonwealth, the SAWP originally targeted Caribbean, and specifically Jamaican, men to come and work on fixed-term labour contracts on Canadian farms (Satzewich 1991). Caribbean men constituted the bulk of these workers until the late 1980s, when the state, alongside eager growers, came to establish Mexico as the dominant origin country for the SAWP (Cecil & Ebanks 1991; Bolaria 1992; Smart 1998; Basok 2002; Binford 2002; UFCW 2002; Preibisch 2004; Sharma 2006; Preibisch & Binford 2007).

What sense do the different economic actors make of the programme today? Certainly, beyond the support for the programme found among growers, the local businesses of the host communities also see economic benefit. In terms of guest work programme expansion, activists and organised labour in Canada see a serious organising challenge interwoven with concerns for the possibility of radiating, downward pressure on wages generally. In the case of the Caribbean and Mexican guest workers themselves, they are compelled to embrace an opportunity to work and send remittances to family at home, while occasionally making positive, sustained community linkages locally as well as in nearby city centres where previously established cultural communities are found. The *compelled* dimension of this embrace is a direct artefact of the subjugation of the Mexican economy that has increasingly produced new and wider gaps between labour market segments that take in ever-wider swaths of the labour pool of the Americas.

At the level of the labour process specifically, traditional divide-and-conquer strategies are virtually universal in the agricultural guest worker programmes in Canada. Roots of these employer strategies are found in racist ideologies and in beliefs regarding genetics that intertwine with a basic capital-accumulation calculus that play out in complex relationships between growers, workers (both new and returning), workers' families, and the local communities of both the host and origin countries. A core feature of guest work divide-and-conquer strategies is spatial-linguistic organisation of production and racialised divisions of labour. Workers are separated by virtue of culture, language and/or race, which combine with locally derived traditions revolving around the working of specific crop types (e.g. Caribbean workers for tree picking and sustained ditch work versus Mexican workers for weeding and planting and low crop harvesting) [see Preibisch & Binford 2007]). Moreover, it is regularly the case that Mexicans are supervised by Jamaicans, or by Mexicans from other regions in Mexico, and so on, a situation fraught with language differences. Workers are also separated based on their ability to understand and work well with one another. Language use is regularly the object of control in guest work – what is termed in the literature as employer control of 'backchat' – a practice with a rich historical lineage in managerial thought regarding matters of labour control and resistance (Chacón & Davis 2006; Palmer 2004; Livingstone & Sawchuk 2004; Sawchuk 2009a, 2009b). Thus, far from a simplistic work and learning environment, guest work can be seen to be a deeply historical, political and economic process that produces a highly complex and conflictual form of lifelong learning transcending local time and space.

Our own research with guest workers shows that the structures, resources and processes of control in Canadian guest work are powerful.[6] Our discussions with guest workers have suggested that efforts by Mexican guest workers to respond to these processes of control have been met with extraordinary resistance from Mexican consular authorities. Workers report consular pressure to stay away from the United Food and Commercial Workers (UFCW) support centres. They say that they could access the services of this union, but that it would mean forgoing any further assistance or representation from the local Mexican consulate. Other workers describe confrontations with consular officials in which they have been directly told to stay away from the centres. Some workers refer to surveillance of after-work activities relating to the UFCW support centres.

However, despite efforts to control them, groups of guest workers can and do generate cultures of solidarity on a local scale, with some dispersed instances of open revolt as has been seen in each of the core receiver provinces in Canada. Moreover, often with the aid of local community groups, activist organisations such as Justicia/Justice for Migrant Workers (J4MW) and organised labour (e.g. UFCW), there is a developing potential for expanding cultural alignment and struggle. This cultural alignment with host communities appears latent but growing (Preibisch 2004). It is seen, for example, in relations between the various Caribbean communities in the city of Toronto and Caribbean guest workers. Furthermore, through the sheer force of time and numbers, local businesses and services in nearby communities are increasingly geared towards guest worker populations. As Preibisch (2004) and others have noted, in some locations Mexican workers, for example, can now find staple Mexican foods at many local shops, Mexican beer is kept well stocked and international services (such as wire transfers and phone/internet services) are increasingly easy to find. These services no doubt provide some level of material comfort.

Importantly, these services constitute the most public face of guest work in Canada. Culturally homogeneous, white, and English- or French-speaking, small town-Canada tends to notice signs in Spanish as well as groups of Mexican or Jamaican Sunday shoppers in stores, bars and restaurants, and international money-wiring desks. On the whole, however, guest work has gone largely unnoticed in Canada for all but those communities hosting guest worker operations. Cultural and material resources are scarce for guest workers in Canada, and provide little counterbalance to the institutional, structural and cultural forms of control (as well as the resulting alienation) generated by employer practices and contracts, and by the efforts of both origin- and host-country governments.

Beyond the labour process: Guest worker lives, control and alienation

Our research brings into sharp relief how control is exercised through a number of formal, informal and tacit ways in the life of guest workers. The work week generally consists of six to seven 10- to 12-hour working days, week in and week out for the duration of the contract, leaving little time or energy for non-work activities including forms of organising and resistance. Indeed, one challenge in the research has been finding the time to talk to people whose lives are dominated by long hours and physically draining labour. Within these 60-, 70- or 80-hour work weeks, guest work is mediated by constant job insecurity. Workers report the precarious nature of almost all aspects of work. Work proceeds with (and control proceeds from) constant fear of injury, deportation, transfer and a bad '*patron*' (boss). From season to season, workers do not know if they will return. Coming back requires luck, strategy and what the workers we spoke with referred to as 'God's grace' on both the Canadian and source-country side. Sometimes workers come to establish lasting relationships with local citizens (many workers have been coming to Canada for well over a decade), and in some cases there exist sympathetic host-community groups that together offer important resources for support. However, from season to season, employers can decide to hire particular workers, or to give a worker a poor recommendation and thereby severely limit future opportunities for hiring within the programme as a whole.

Outside of the farms, greenhouses and other workplaces, workers are further regulated via surveillance and monitoring of both personal time and space. Workers generally live on employer property, in small (overcrowded) apartments, dormitories or trailers.[7] As we experienced in the course of our research, many workers are permitted visitors in their residences until 9 pm on weekdays and 11 pm on weekends. A sign in one trailer informed residents that this rule would be enforced by a roving security force who reported any violations to the employer – those in breach becoming more vulnerable to the threat of deportation. Further control of 'domestic space' was evidenced in one house by a small broom spray-painted gold and tacked to the wall. We were told that the household had won the 'Golden Broom Prize' for the tidiest home based on the results of regular employer inspections. Indeed, at the annual company dinner (the proceedings were in English), the women who had won the prize did not know they had won it until an English-speaking co-worker prompted them to go up to the front of the room to accept their award. In many ways, language becomes an additional means of control as it divides workers from each other, from supervisors and growers, and, in the case of Mexican guest workers, from the surrounding community.

Beyond the alienating features of the labour process itself, the broader structures of experience of life as a guest worker produce profound alienation. First-time guest workers typically come with the idea that they will get to know a new town, region or even country. Upon arrival few get to know even the small communities in which they reside. In the small town of Virgil, Ontario, when one worker was asked if he was getting to know Canada, he answered that he had not even had the opportunity to know the town let alone the country. Indeed, in our research it became clear that guest workers were frustrated at rarely leaving their workplace. This, combined with the dislocation from family and community at home, creates an intensified alienation that leaves workers in a state of depression.

In addition, our conversations with neighbouring local residents revealed a tension between 'guests' and 'hosts', which often proceeds along racialised as well as class lines when relatively wealthy and largely white communities find relatively poor workers of colour in their midst. Preibisch and Binford (2007) have described the nativist racism that mediates worker interaction with their surrounding communities. Combined with the separation from community-support networks of their home country, workers rely on one another. Despite their limited free time, workers sometimes manage to form tight communities with others from their home community, region and/or country. Longing to go home as a result of the difficulty of the work, the isolation in Canada, and the poor treatment by employers and not infrequently by the host community as well, there is a profound hurt caused by separation from family and specifically children that informs what we may call the broader pedagogy of guest work life. Many workers, on meeting each other for the first time, will, before anything else, show photos of children back home. There is a common currency of social displacement and thus a shared common pedagogy of getting through it.

The transnational element of the Canadian guest worker programme allows for a hyper-exploitation of workers – both within the labour process and within the broader, lived experience of guest working – with a parallel and related reduction in employer and government accountability. With health and safety concerns off the employer's plate and citizenship rights no longer the host government's problem, this transnational model creates a revolving non-citizen population – a population welcomed neither formally nor informally, a population disempowered by design. This is, in essence, a carefully scripted tragedy requiring substantial employer/transnational government collaboration. Profound alienation within and beyond work finds its parallel in the production of the alien 'other' for the Canadian government and portions of the citizenship through which terrible working conditions are not only experienced by workers but come to be thought of by many Canadians as deserved. Capitalism's apologists argue that Canadians simply don't want these jobs; it is perhaps more accurate to say that Canadians feel they do not deserve these jobs – as evidenced by their refusal to do them – while Mexican, Jamaican, Thai and other foreign guest workers do.

The workers, of course, understand this better than anyone else as they live the role of lightning rod in dangerous workplaces, unwelcoming communities and cramped bunk beds. These guest workers live and learn a deeply troubling form of transnational labour, and as such create understandings and articulations thereof through pedagogies of deprivation, discrimination, adaptation and survival. Our discussions with workers suggest that although many wish to acquire Canadian citizenship, few wish to move to Canada. For most workers we met, the push to become Canadian was generally driven by the will to subvert their non-citizen status within a system to which they have already contributed a great deal but which entitles them to few benefits. In other words, the workers understand the game, but their willingness to play should not be confused with an endorsement of the rules.

Deepening the analysis of the labour/learning processes

Having painted in broad strokes the nature of contemporary guest work in Canada, we can now more effectively outline what we see as the complex circuit of communication, participation and learning that shapes Canadian guest work as a transnational labour process.

Circuits of learning relations

Organised training in guest worker production is virtually non-existent and is entirely dependent on ongoing, worker-to-worker on-the-job training and direct supervisory edict, which provide the most prominent form of immediate, production-based learning. However, when considering the expansive portrait of learning both within the labour process and within guest work life experiences, these practices represent merely the tip of the learning iceberg. In other words, intertwined with immediate production learning is a second dimension in the form of the dense fabric of 'intercultural learning' surrounding guest work. This learning is multidimensional: it takes place across relations between workers and growers, but also implicates bureaucrats (both Canadian officials and origin-country consulates) as well as residents of host communities. In the case of each example, it features some moments of cross-cultural pleasure[8] but is more often characterised as conflictual. Third, and again closely intertwined, there is the intercultural learning that takes place between different workers within and between ethno-linguistic/national groups (e.g. Mexican and Caribbean workers) as well as learning and communication between those from different regions of the same country. Fourth is the learning and exchanges between host country activists, such as those from J4MW or the UFCW, as well as those from community- and university-based organisations. Finally, and perhaps one of the least-understood dimensions of this complex circuit of learning, is the extended, transnational lines of development constituted vis-à-vis family and community units across borders and, with the passage of time, generations. Across these five dimensions a 'curriculum of experience' is generated, redeveloped, stored, taught and learned.

Materiality of learning

Having summarised our understanding of the dimensions of learning and guest work, we now turn to a brief, secondary analysis of these dynamics based on popular education work carried out by J4MW (Hinnenkamp 2004).[9] Based on our own research, we have suggested the vital role of material resources in shaping workers' experiences. The effects of the material dimensions of traditional industrial control are in full force here, including those related to strict divisions of labour, and divide-and-conquer labour process organisation; but unlike the vast majority of work and learning literature, additional physical conditions were important factors that shaped experience, interests and learning needs of guest workers. In other words, work and learning in guest worker programmes in Canada is infused throughout with a pedagogy of cold, heat, wet and outdated: that is, sub-standard housing, tools, boots, transportation, pesticide protection, and so on. Workers in Hinnenkamp's discussion groups clearly articulate how acute injuries and chronic health dangers stand as central themes around which their thinking, reaction and strategising – and hence learning strategies – revolve (Hinnenkamp 2004). Summarised under a broad notion of health and safety concerns, these challenges deeply shape the directions of learning amid agricultural production and sub-standard on-site living conditions. Moreover, necessarily implicated in these conditions are underlying relations with the state and citizenship vis-à-vis the virtual absence of legal right to protection under legislation.

Tensions in learning

Like Freire (1970), Hinnenkamp's (2004) method of investigation involved the workers' selection of images (from magazines, etc.) to facilitate dialogue. One such example was the selection of a magazine picture of a marathon runner. This image formed the basis of dialogue about the labour process. Gazing upon the picture, one worker comments: 'This also represents a job. Some people work in this way and others – the Mexicans – that come here, we do it in a different way, helping Canada to progress' (Hinnenkamp 2004: 14). From this statement, Hinnenkamp reports how the dialogue sparked off a variety of additional themes. There are two lines of enquiry that we pursue here. The first is a (underdeveloped) thesis that Mexican workers bring with them specific patterns, orientations and cultural constructions of work life that may be distinct from Euro-American labour processes and workers. One way to understand this may be to pursue the notion that in an era of concern about 'overworked workers', 'work/life balance', and so on, Mexican workers may sustain a different orientation that, while clearly not eschewing hard work, may nevertheless subsume hard work within an orientation that sees paid work as only part of the fulfilment of individual and collective needs. (Hinnenkamp's focus groups also revealed a specific understanding that differences among workers in terms of distinct skills, abilities and work interests should be taken into account in the design and execution of the labour process, and a questioning of the tried-and-true technical and social division of labour held sacrosanct in Euro-American industrial design.) This orientation, if it exists, would in principle stand as an alternative to the manic, economically conditioned neurosis of segments of Euro-American workers. Assuredly, this is more complex and requires an explanation of elaborate figuring of relations between self, work, family and society – orientations, we emphasise, that must be actively reproduced and learned – that increasingly eludes major segments of Euro-American society. Another layer of this first line of enquiry is that there are likely specific forms of work-based knowledge and skill, at this point hidden from academic research, related to agricultural work and the social relations that shape it that are distinct from, if not in conflict with, what now constitutes Euro-American industrial-capitalist farming.

A second major line of enquiry emerging from this portion of Hinnenkamp's work deals with the conflict between older and newer (often younger) workers, who, in classic industrial sociology terms, would be understood as 'rate busters' – those who work particularly fast to garner supervisory approval. Hinnenkamp (2004) specifically comments on this, noting that workers were hesitant to fully articulate these dynamics.

The learning of how fast to work, how to subtly resist and control production speed, also would not surprise classic industrial sociologists, but unique aspects of guest work in Canada further shape and sharpen these dynamics. Building from our basic description in the previous section, this learning is mediated by the brutality of the work. Indeed, over dinner with a number of workers during our own research one mentioned his other job at home in Mexico – he was a factory worker in a town near the US border and produced light electronics. He described it as a *maquiladora* and then said, 'You know, a sweatshop'.[10] It soon emerged that many of the workers had similar jobs in the off-season. When asked to compare the work in Canada with that in the sweatshop, the workers around the table unanimously agreed that if the pay were equal, they would prefer the sweatshop, citing the difficulty of the work in the guest worker programme. They went on to praise the relative 'stability' of sweatshop employment. In Canada, growers exercise the right to hand-select workers for return work in following seasons, and if the grower were to identify collective resistance, he can also choose to, as Preibisch and Binford (2007) put it, 'surf' a country or region for whole new intake communities. Further shaping and sharpening tensions is the poverty of Mexico, constructed, as we saw earlier, across an almost two-century trajectory of concerted political and military actions in which, in the last decades, the Canadian state has been both tacitly and actively complicit. Here we see a structure that sets specific dynamics of labour and learning at once familiar but also archaic – a work system in twenty-first-century Canada the equivalent of which one must look back more than a century to chattel slavery to find (Genovese 1974).

Learning and resistance

A too-often-ignored element in work and learning research is the skills, knowledge and learning that grow out of workers' needs and interests rather than those of management and production (see Sawchuk 2006, 2007). The most intense and obvious examples of these are the structures and moments of (organised and spontaneous) resistance. Beyond the material conditions outlined above, fuelling the conflict/resistance are the perceived attitudes of host-country residents toward workers. As one group of workers in Hinnenkamp (2004: 16) agreed, 'In Canada they like dogs better than they like Mexicans.' Others went on to describe their treatment as 'animals', as 'machines', and so on. As we have indicated, outright racism shapes many of the workers' experiences, both within the production process and within the surrounding community. The ethno-linguistic differences – revolving around the absence of Spanish-language capacity of the supervisory staff and the ethnocentric presumptions that continue to reproduce this inadequacy – produce a degenerative feedback loop of events in which half-understood English-only instructions and ineffectively directed work are followed by supervisory criticism (and not infrequently racialised claims of laziness and neglect), while workers themselves become increasingly frustrated, and on it goes. However, the resulting forms of and ruminations on resistance among guest workers in Canada appear to express distinct dynamics. Reflecting on poor conditions, a worker quoted in Hinnenkamp (2004: 19) comments: '[I wonder] if this is really what the Canadian people or the bosses we have want us to do – hold a demonstration…to express what's wrong with our houses, how we are treated, and the benefits that we should have a right to'. Where else in the Canadian economy, we could ask, would this question be asked? It signals yet another unique feature of work and learning endemic to contemporary guest work.

Conclusion

Guest worker programmes are poised to undergo significant expansion implicating a host of countries across the Americas. In this chapter we have sought to establish a historical foundation for understanding the labour/learning dynamics that shape these programmes in Canada specifically. These dynamics have radiant causes and effects on workers, employers, and origin and host communities, and will undoubtedly reverberate across labour markets more broadly.

We have also sought to begin to articulate the broader context and then the complex circuits of learning as well as the cultural, political and economic forces at play within the core 'curriculum of experience' that is contemporary guest work. We have offered a basic programme of investigation for such circuits, and then provided an introductory analysis of related themes based on previously published popular education work as well as our own preliminary research.

We maintain that these dynamics are reflective of labour processes of both the previous century and the current one. Indeed, if the work of the twenty-first century is to be more deeply characterised by globalisation and polarisation hand in glove with the continued development of peripheral, international labour markets, then the complex and conflictual work and learning endemic to guest worker programmes such as those we have discussed will continue to grow in relevance. The work and learning relations of guest work may hold few mysteries if dealt with in a narrow, decontextualised fashion. However, in undertaking efforts at contextualisation – and in engaging the perspectives of workers themselves – we see how complex these circuits of work and learning can and do become. Consciously and less self-consciously, in explicit and implicit ways, the experience of guest work teaches employers, government agencies, host and origin communities, organisers and, above all, workers themselves. It teaches not merely the skills and knowledge central to guest work agricultural production but the broader (positive and negative) skills and knowledge of the transnational life of guest work. Shaping these dynamics is a particularly powerful confluence of race, class and citizenship relations from which reproduction, intensification and contestation flows.

Notes

1   See Sawchuk and Kempf (2007) for a more complete discussion of the historical trajectory of guest worker programmes in North America, including the roles of the General Agreement on Trade in Services (GATS), the North American Free Trade Agreement (NAFTA) and, most recently, the US Homeland Security policy.

2   At the time of writing, the Canadian province of Manitoba, under New Democratic Party governance, has been the first provincial jurisdiction to apply this finding of the Canadian Supreme Court to its own labour code, explicitly extending rights to migrant/guest workers as

well, and publicly calling for other provinces to do the same. With a range of court challenges pending, the United Food and Commercial Workers (UFCW) of Canada has been particularly active in the use of this landmark decision. Prior to this, in Ontario, Canada's most populated province and home to the largest proportion of migrant farm labourers, the Agricultural Employees Protection Act 2002 (Bill 187) was passed on 18 November 2002. This Act allows farm workers to form associations and make representations to their employers, though not the right to unionise or strike, and farm workers remain excluded from provincial health and safety legislation.

3   Macquiladora refers to free-trade economic zones established at the border between the US and Mexico.

4   In Canada, these dimensions are particularly well laid out in Sharma's detailed examination of Bill C-11 – Canada's border security and citizenship law that was actively debated and laid bare the active construction of preferred citizens and their 'others' (Sharma 2001, 2006).

5   The temporary workers pouring into Canada are often exploited, *The Economist*, 22 November 2007.

6   Research based on multiple visits to farming operations in Ontario and British Columbia, including informal discussions with 12 key informants.

7   On a quiet street in Edmonton, Alberta, the franchise owner of a McDonald's restaurant has purchased a small three-bedroom split-level house in which resides a group of young Filipino guest workers (his employees at the restaurant). The mortgage is paid through source garnishing of the workers' wages.

8   Indeed, for workers, learning about Anglo-Canadian culture is one of the enjoyable features of guest work (Hinnenkamp 2004), and there are similar examples of enjoyment for host-community members as well (Preibisch 2004). As noted, forms of ethno-racial-class conflict largely overshadow these instances.

9   Based in southern Ontario, the J4MW involved Sunday meetings held over the course of four weeks with 18 male and 3 female farm workers aged 20 to 60. All were citizens of Mexico and part of the Canadian government's SAWP. The project eventually produced not simply data but striking artwork, dramatic scripts and interpretation.

10   All translations in the Sawchuk/Kempf research done by Kempf.

References

Basok T (2002) *Tortillas and tomatoes*. Montreal: McGill-Queens University Press

Binford L (2002) Social and economic contradictions of rural migrant contract labour between Tlaxcala, Mexico, and Canada. *Culture and Agriculture* 24(2): 1–19

Bolaria B (1992) Farm labour, work conditions, and health risk. In *Rural Sociology in Canada*. Toronto: Oxford University Press

Burawoy M (1976) The functions and reproduction of migrant labour: Comparative material from southern Africa and the United States. *American Journal of Sociology* 81(5): 1050–1087

Cecil R & Ebanks G (1991) The human condition of West Indian migrant farm labour in southwestern Ontario. *International Migration* 29(3): 384–404

Chacón J & Davis M (2006) *No one is illegal: Fighting racism and state violence on the U.S.–Mexico border*. Chicago: Haymarket Books

Freire P (1970) *Pedagogy of the oppressed*. New York: Continuum

Genovese E (1974) *Roll, Jordan, roll: The world the slaves made.* New York: Pantheon Books

Hinnenkamp K (2004) *The experience of Mexican seasonal agricultural workers in Canada: A collaborative multimedia project.* Toronto: J4MW. Accessed 14 January 2007, http://www. justicia4migrantworkers.org

Livingstone DW & Sawchuk P (2004) *Hidden knowledge: Organised labour in the information age.* Toronto: Broadview Press

Palmer B (2004) Race and revolution. *Labour/Le Travail* 54(Fall): 193–222

Preibisch K (2004) Migrant agricultural workers and processes of social inclusion in rural Canada: *Encuentros* and *desencuentros. Canadian Journal of Latin American and Caribbean Studies* 29(57–58): 203–239

Preibisch K & Binford L (2007) Interrogating racialised global labour supply: An exploration of the racial/national replacement of foreign agricultural workers in Canada. *Canadian Review of Sociology and Anthropology* 44(1): 5–36

Satzewich V (1991) *Racism and the incorporation of foreign labour: Farm labour migration to Canada since 1945.* New York: Routledge

Sawchuk PH (2006) 'Use-value' and the rethinking of skills, learning and the labour process. *Journal of Industrial Relations* 48(5): 593–617

Sawchuk PH (2007) Understanding diverse outcomes for working-class learning: Conceptualising class consciousness as knowledge activity. *Economic and Labour Relations Review* 17(2): 199–216

Sawchuk PH (2009a) A Canadian union perspective on education and citizenship: The role of labour markets and work in the 21st century. *Revista Educação e Cidadania (Review of Education and Citizenship)* 7(1): 33–54

Sawchuk PH (2009b) Anti-colonialism, labour and the pedagogies of community unionism: The case of hotel workers in Canada. In A Kempf (ed.) *Breaching the colonial contract: Anti-colonialism in the US and Canada.* London: Peter Lange

Sawchuk PH & Kempf A (2007) Labour market internationalisation and guest worker programmes in the US and Canada. Paper presented at the 5th International Researching Work and Learning Conference, Cape Town, South Africa (3 December)

Sharma N (2001) On being not Canadian: The social organisation of 'migrant workers' in Canada. *Canadian Review of Sociology and Anthropology* 38(4): 414–439

Sharma N (2006) *Home economics: Nationalism and the making of migrant workers in Canada.* Toronto: University of Toronto Press

Smart J (1998) Borrowed men on borrowed time: Globalisation, labour migration and local economies in Alberta. *Canadian Journal of Regional Science* 20(12): 141–156

UFCW (United Food and Commercial Workers) (2002) *National report: Status of migrant farm workers in Canada.* Ottawa: UFCW. Accessed 14 January 2007, http://www.ufcw.ca/cgi-bin/ download.cgi/National+ReportENG.pdf?id=231&a=v&name=National+ReportENG.pdf

Vogel R (2007) Transient servitude: The U.S. Guest Worker Program for exploiting Mexican and Central American workers. *Monthly Review* (January): 1–23

Weston A & Scarpa de Masellis L (2003) *Hemispheric integration and trade relations: Implications for Canada's seasonal agricultural workers programme.* Ottawa: North–South Institute

Section II

Recognising knowledges

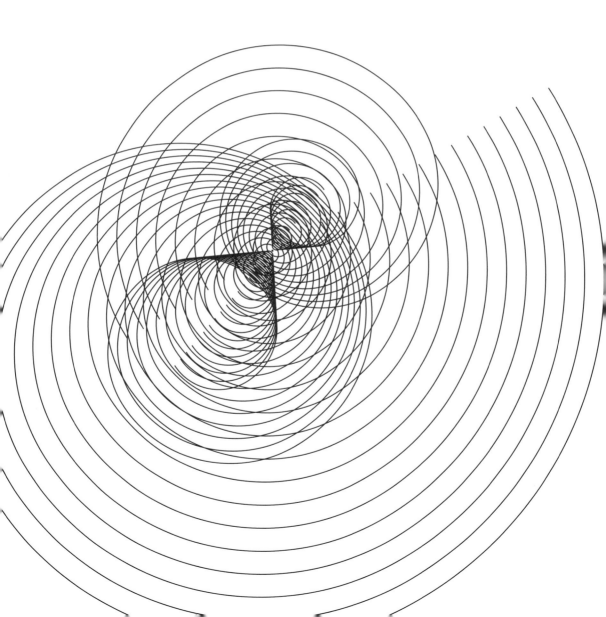

12 Learning in emotional labour and emotion work

John Field and Irene Malcolm

Introduction

The idea of emotional labour has been widely debated in recent years. Interest in the concept arises from wider debates about occupational change in what has been loosely labelled the 'new economy', as well as from growing academic interest in workers' subjectivity and agency. First, the transformation of work in the established industrial nations has led to significant increases in various kinds of service work that require direct or technologically mediated human interaction. This, it is argued, places a growing premium on affective competences that were hitherto ignored or taken for granted. In turn, the globalisation of service industries, and indeed of consumer travel and demand, has brought Western expectations to the rest of the world. Second, the transformation of everyday life in Western societies – above all, the decline since the 1950s of inherited routines and established support systems – has disrupted many of the scripts that once governed social encounters. Instead of relying on habit and established guides to etiquette, individuals must fall back on their own resources. Abroad, in a world characterised by informality and apparent spontaneity, people may have to read and navigate each social encounter afresh (Misztal 2000). Finally, the cultural turn in the social sciences has brought renewed attention to workers' feelings and their emotional qualities as significant factors that will shape how they engage with the job. Trade union and political campaigns over gender equality and against low pay have asserted the value of emotional labour, particularly among women workers (Franzway 2000).

While the emotional labour debate has attracted widespread attention in sociology, feminism and management studies, it has only recently started to interest educationalists, including those who study adult learning and worker development. This chapter, based on research in Scotland, explores the ways in which the experiences and meanings of emotional labour can be said to relate to recent changes in how adults learn, specifically how they learn for work. The empirical research that we draw on in this chapter was conducted as part of the Learning Lives project, a large-scale multi-method study that aims to deepen understanding of the complexities of learning across the life course, drawing on longitudinal data to understand identity, agency, change and learning in adult life, including adult working life.[1] Our research in the Learning Lives project involved life-history interviews with workers in a range of contexts that included interactive services, such as call centres and social work – occupations in which women usually form a significant proportion of the workforce and which are seen to be associated with a 'feminisation' of work (Colley 2006b).

We start by summarising the current debate over emotional labour, emphasising particularly its relevance for researchers interested in lifelong learning. We then present cases of two women interviewees employed in call centres. While much other writing about this sector has dealt with organisational perspectives, our analysis is based on biographical research which focuses on the women's lived experiences of work, contextualised in the telling of their life stories. While this sets limits to our findings, not least because we present only two individual narratives, it allows us to explore what interviewees say about their experiences of emotional labour and how they learned to do emotional labour. We will argue that they learned from emotional labour, but we will also examine their responses to tensions between surveillance and discretion and the ways in which experiences of both work and learning are shaped by gender as they interact with the worker's sense of self. We conclude with comments on the relevance of the emotional labour debate to recent trends in adult learning.

Emotional labour and the new economy

In her influential book *The Managed Heart*, Arlie Hochschild addressed the 'emotional labour' that employees are required to perform as an everyday part of their job (Hochschild 1983). Hochschild argued that, due to their position of social subordination, women perform most emotional labour and are required to take responsibility for the feelings of others. According to Hochschild, emotion management in employment is to be distinguished from similar processes in kinship-based caring or other relations of affect, since it is scripted by company management and directed and supervised by others for payment, a process which is highly gendered. The 'soft' skills that women use in emotional labour have been 'mislabelled as "natural" ' and presented as inherently feminine in nature, rather than arising from gendered processes of socialisation (Hochschild 1983: 167).

Hochschild argues that emotion management comes at a price. When the emotional performance works well, the worker feels 'somehow satisfied in how personal her service actually was' (1983: 136). However, when pressure and workload increase, the management of emotions can become an act of alienation in which the worker engages in 'surface acting' (pretence) in a way that is inauthentic and potentially harmful. When the gap between 'natural self' and performing self becomes too wide, she argues, the personal authenticity of the worker is challenged, leading to stress, anxiety and burn-out.

Hochschild's account has been increasingly influential, as service employment has continued to replace manufacturing and extractive work. While initially a feature of Western societies, globalisation of both consumption and production is extending similar trends across the planet. The jobs that Hochschild took for her case studies are service occupations, such as airline cabin crew. It is often argued that in an expanding service sector, as well as in many knowledge-intensive occupations, communication and interaction play a central role in determining client satisfaction and competitive advantage (Du Gay 1996). Workers in the new economy, then, experience increased emphasis on new skills and qualities, such as their physical appearance and demeanour (aesthetic labour) and their control of overtly affective behaviour (emotional labour). And while workers must learn how to manage their identity through competent, visible and audible performance in the workplace, their managers are required to balance worker autonomy with new types of surveillance.

Hochschild has argued that the demands placed on workers in the new economy pose considerable identity challenges for women, a point affirmed in more recent research conducted by Wajcman and Martin (2002) into the career narratives of managers in large companies in Australia. Hughes argues that the management of emotional competences may well 'signal a further move towards totalising regimes of organisational domination in which employee identity becomes effectively subsumed within the workplace and opportunities for resistance are greatly limited' (Hughes 2005: 613; see also Du Gay 1996). There is, then, more at stake in the debate than recognising the value of a waiter's smile or a cashier's 'Have a nice day'.

Hochschild's initial theorisation has its limitations when applied to twenty-first-century work, hardly surprisingly given that it was published more than twenty-five years ago. Before considering subsequent work, however, it is important to stress the real conceptual and empirical gains that have arisen in the course of the debate. First, the debate has shone some analytical light on the role of emotion in the labour process and on expectations of women's work, a topic which previously had been largely neglected. Second, it has challenged some of the dominant accounts of skill and skills development. Third, it has drawn attention to the low status and rewards associated with jobs involving emotional labour. Fourth, it has connected the analysis of emotional labour to debates over occupational well-being and workplace stress. Finally, the debate has generated a significant body of new conceptual and empirical work, much of which has focused on testing the claims made by Hochschild and others.

Other feminist writers have sought to develop Hochschild's theorisation by highlighting the positive uses of emotion in constructing and sustaining identity. Colley's study of trainee nursery nurses shows how this group of young women increasingly came to see their management of feeling as a marker of maturity and personal as well as professional worth, and as a departure from their former, presumably 'immature' selves (Colley 2006a). While there may be risks (for example, of over-identification), Colley's study suggested that these were stronger for the teacher than the learner (Colley 2006a). So one point to emerge from recent research is that when emotional labour is performed, it is not always susceptible to measurement and control; a degree of worker autonomy and discretion remains. Workers are agentic and can adopt coping strategies of different kinds; they may even deploy emotional competence in strategies of resistance.

As well as studies that broadly conform to Hochschild's approach (e.g. Cullingford 2006), others have challenged or, perhaps more accurately, qualified Hochschild's depiction of emotional labour. Some question what they perceive to be a rather one-dimensional portrait of the worker engaged in emotional labour. Payne (2006) and Hughes (2005) dispute what they see as Hochschild's view of the worker as a passive subject who simply suffers alienation as a result of the demands made, arguing that workers must be seen as creating as well as reflecting their circumstances, and not portrayed as 'cultural dupes' pursuing an imposed managerial agenda. Studies of caregivers, for instance, report that these service workers often go way beyond their contracted obligations, yet still feel in control of the 'bounded emotionality' that they perform in their work (Payne 2006; Ashforth & Tomiuk 2000). Indeed, workers may even see emotion management as part of who they are, as a way of supporting their authenticity and expressing their identity (Ashforth & Tomiuk 2000). Some experience the performance of competent emotion work as an important part of building identity and developing agency.

Some researchers further challenge what they see as narrow and excluding definitions that set boundaries around emotional labour. Hochschild's account is confined to service work, but emotion management appears to be pervasive in different forms across a wide range of workplaces. Hochschild is concerned with emotional labour performed for pay in capitalist relations of production, yet a number of ethnographic studies of workplaces show workers managing emotions autonomously as a 'gift' – be it to other workers or to clients and customers (Bolton 2000; Callaghan & Thompson 2002). In a study of staff and volunteers in a not-for-profit organisation, Callaghan noted that while there were broad differences in the nature of emotion work carried out by different groups of workers, including between men and women, all were involved in one way or another; indeed, even members of the armed services carried out emotion management, albeit expressed through humour and other practices of disguise (Callaghan 2000).

There is also a risk that the emotional labour debate overemphasises novelty and neglects continuity. Some workers have always performed 'emotion work'. Butlers and footmen, domestic workers and waiters, shop assistants and hairdressers, tailors and dressmakers: all these occupations, which flourished in pre-industrial, proto-industrial and industrial society, involved a high level of emotion management. As we will discuss, what has changed is not so much the ubiquity of emotional labour, but the systems of control used in the scripting and surveillance of some performances of it.

While emotional labour certainly has implications for adult learning, they are rather ambiguous. Some question whether emotional competences are indeed skills, and whether they can be deliberately taught and learned, particularly in adult life. Payne, for example, sees affective competences as the product of primary socialisation:

> Even if we accept the argument that such emotion work is incredibly complex and has become more so over time, this may still be seen as an ability that *most* people learn to perform (often unconsciously) during the course of their early socialisation. Thus, although this process may appear extremely complex at a very deep level, at another level it might also be seen as a relatively mundane or ordinary accomplishment. (Payne 2006: 16)

He goes on to ask whether it is 'possible, for example, to train genuine empathy or compassion given that such personality traits are deeply wired into the emotional circuitry of the brain through a combination of genetic imprinting and primary socialisation' (Payne 2006: 19).

Such doubts are widely shared. Among our interviewees, Sue Martin[2] took a similar view. In recruiting new workers, she preferred

> to recruit someone with more customer service skills and train them in the technical because it's easier to train technical knowledge than it is to train good customer service skills.

Yet there is a small industry of consultants and trainers who make a living from developing emotional capabilities (e.g. Dulewicz and Higgs 1998), while self-development handbooks on developing one's emotional intelligence are available from almost any bookshop. The subject has also found its way into the curriculum, particularly in management development programmes. So how do experienced emotion workers develop and build their skills, and do they regard them as arising from imposition or from construction?

Two learning/working lives

As part of the Learning Lives project we undertook a series of extended life-history and life-course interviews with a group of 30 working adults. The sample included workers in the new economy (call centres), the service economy (community and social work) and manufacturing (engineering): the workers all faced change, and all were required to perform identity work. In this chapter we focus on the work and learning of two call centre workers, who are part of an industry which represents an important new form of employment in Scotland, both in terms of the size of the sector and the nature of the labour process (Callaghan & Thompson 2002).

Call centres have attracted significant attention from academics, mainly focusing on labour processes and forms of control. Relatively limited attention has so far been paid to learning identities or to recruitment and training, and in so far as the latter have been studied (Callaghan & Thompson 2002) it has been from a critical organisational perspective. This chapter, by contrast, presents biographical evidence that places workplace experiences in the broad narrative of the worker's life and learning; our fieldwork gives us limited insights into the wider organisational context. We present the experiences of two women who worked in the same medium-sized call centre company, performing and managing emotional labour – their own initially, and subsequently also that of others – as they developed their working identity and their learning.

Sue Martin, in her late twenties at the time of our interview, works in the human resources (HR) department of the call centre. She presented her current work in HR as involving very significant levels of interpersonal contact: 'I guess the kind of thing I deal with on a day-to-day basis are, it's most[ly] people, mostly managers at all levels in the business'. She summarised her role as 'about 90% problem solving and dealing with people's issues and concerns'.

Sue Martin came from a working-class background and had left school at age 16. She was attracted to her present job because 'I had a bit of call centre experience and I like the environment, 'cause it's a very young, a very busy, a very fun environment'. She had not worked 'on the phones' and had no desire to. She recalled her fears when she first joined the company:

> I came here and I knew nothing, I knew nothing. I hadn't worked in the call centre industry for four years so the technology and the way things were done had moved on in leaps and bounds…and it's a very different type of environment as well. This is not a high-volume call environment, it's customer service, it's low-volume calls, it's deal with the customer, resolve the issue. It's nothing like what I worked in before, and I was terrified, absolutely terrified.

Sue also described anxiety as part of her work in relation to the responsibilities and consequences of her job: 'I've got someone who's really not performing, I don't know how to deal with it, I want them out the business'.

Sue thus conformed to one of Hochschild's negative patterns, in that she experienced profound anxiety over her ability to perform emotion work. Yet Sue had sought out this job, partly as a way of avoiding what she saw as the mindless repetition and stress of sales work. She had worked in sales in an earlier job, and 'hated it with a passion'. Sue seems to have resented the intrusion and attempt to control her emotion work, blaming a management who operated by bureaucratised routines.

Sue's role in her current job involved supporting those who managed the call agents and ensuring that their actions were in accordance with company policy and company ethos. She clearly experienced some anxiety in the role, but expressed no concern about her authenticity, or tension between her 'performing self' and her 'authentic self'. On the contrary, she emphasised her confidence in her strong sense of expertise rooted in experience, relishing the way that company managers consulted her and sought her advice. This recognition in turn informed her sense of self: 'now they'll come to me with anything, and that's trust that you build through proving that you do have the ability and you do have the knowledge and you do have the legislation experience'. In short, emotional labour was part of her identity work that was harnessed by the company.

Sue's positive view of the kind of emotional labour she performed seems to derive from the value she places on learning from experience. She stated unambiguously that experience was a better teacher than formal training. A previous employer had sent her to university to study for a part-time diploma in human resource management, and while she enjoyed some of it, other parts were 'a complete waste of time because sometimes you're standing in front of a lecturer who's been in HR ten years ago, and you're like, yeah, your theory's great but that doesn't work in an office environment'. She had dropped out, resuming study some years later with a different university, aiming to move on – and upwards – when she had the diploma.

Sue viewed her skills of emotion management as aspects of her controlled, professional identity. She described one example, taken from her family life. Her fiancé's mother had visited Sue on the morning of her wedding:

> [Sue's mother-in-law] was crying and I said 'What's wrong with you?' [Her mother-in-law said,] 'Oh, I'm just emotional' and I said, 'Well, I'm sorry but I'm really calm, and I don't really need you to be like that with me...I don't really need anyone round about me who's upset or who's emotional.'

For Sue, then, the wedding was the staging of an emotional performance: competent emotion management was to be admired and, conversely, the uncontrolled outpouring of emotions indicated a lack of personal (and professional) control.

Our second case is that of Jeannie Taylor, in her mid thirties at the time of our interview. Jeannie went straight into university from school and took a degree in French with marketing; her educational trajectory therefore followed what might be called the standard biography for middle-class girls of her generation. She had entered telephone banking in her mid twenties and was now working as a call centre manager, supervising the work of call agents.

Jeannie's role included recording calls and coaching agents on their techniques, a position she moved into after working as an agent herself. She described her role as follows:

> When you call a call centre...there's usually a wee announcement that'll say, 'For quality and training purposes your call may be monitored'. That's what I do, I record the calls and I listen to them and I give feedback based on the recorded calls.

Jeannie's customers (usually global companies) outsourced customer care to her company and she described how the details of the commission, including the script for call agents, were discussed:

> [W]e will also sit down with the clients and the business and say, 'Well, what is it you want your guys to be doing?' So we'll have certain guidelines that say you are supposed to use this script, you have to ask that question, and then when I listen to the calls that's what I must bring out, or do they comply to what we need them to do, are they using the systems the way that they should be using them.

While Sue's job was to support managers through face-to-face communication, Jeannie focused on managing the scripted emotional performance of call agents in technically mediated communication. When giving feedback, Jeannie sat down with the call agent

> and because the calls are recorded or most of the calls get recorded, so we can play that back to the agent and say, 'What did you think of your performance, what would you have done differently, what did you do well?' and we can coach them on their performances.

Having worked as an agent herself, she knew the pressures: 'you personally get the blame'. But she described it as pretty straightforward: 'a brain-dumb job, it's not really a brain-dumb job but there are certain tasks that you can do very, very easily'.

Jeannie, unlike Sue, did express concern over authenticity. Even as a team leader, 'you get really bored doing that, so you have to keep your own motivation up, you have to not sound robotic, but when you've got a hundred calls in the queue it's kind of hard to do'. In a previous job where Jeannie also had a supervisory role she had taken calls when 'the customer's a screamer and they demand to talk to a manager'. At one stage she had even been 'taking over calls for sport'. She drew on her own experience, but whereas Sue took pride in exercising control and achieving consistent emotional management, Jeannie saw it as an everyday method of handling the pressures of emotional performance:

> I know I'm a weeper, when things get far too much for me I know that I just cry, so when I start to recognise those signs then I know that I need to do something different.

Like Sue, Jeannie had learned by observation of fellow workers, as well as from family life. So, in her management approach, she admired and had learned from a colleague who was managing three or four projects:

> [A]nd he will still make the time to come in and say to people, 'How are you getting on, how did you get on with your house purchase, did your wee boy pass his exams?' He's got great people skills.

She also gave a counter-example, describing her mother's head teacher as 'a career person and not a people person, and she's obviously been on a feedback course and she's learned a feedback sandwich that you give two bits of positive feedback, then you give the negative and then you finish with a positive'. Needless to say, Jeannie thought this an incompetent and mechanistic way of giving feedback, lacking in authenticity and inadequate to the emotional demands of the industry in which she worked.

Nevertheless, Jeannie expressed a clear commitment to training in interpersonal skills. As well as giving direct feedback in her current role, she had become a trainer in her previous job, which involved 'a mix of soft skills and hard skills'. The soft skills included 'things like listening and questioning', much of which was taught through role-play and other activities. Her present employer used neurolinguistic programming as the basis for soft skills training, and developed this to include attention to the body's posture and gestures such as smiling, or 'how would they sound and getting them then to emulate that, so that they can fake that confidence on the phone'.

Jeannie was an active learner, pursuing courses on coaching and hypnosis (including self-hypnosis), and learning about tarot. At the time of the fourth interview, she had just taught a taster course in belly dancing as part of the company's participation in learning-at-work day. When her job came under threat as a result of a takeover, she was actively considering teaching adults as a career.

As well as some differences, there were similarities in the way the two women viewed training. Like Sue, Jeannie valued personal disposition and life experience. Describing her previous job, she said that

> one of the best workers we ever, ever had in there was actually a retired teacher. It was just because he had the life experience that he was bringing to it, so he knew, he knew how to talk to people and he knew. Yes, he was maybe that little bit slower on picking up the technical side of things, but the softer side of things made up for that.

Ultimately, she treated interpersonal skills as part of identity: 'a lot of that does cross over into the who-you-are aspect'. She presented good call centre skills as a form of 'acting', so that in the end 'some people can and some people can't'.

Like Sue, Jeannie's anecdotes of work reflect a concern for professionalism, distance and control. Even when her job ended as a result of company relocation, Jeannie took what she called the 'professional' approach to handing over to the incoming supervisor:

> It was nothing personal, it was the situation, it was the company...Maybe it's just about this is my legacy, but I mean it's something over the years that I think is just...reputation and dignity are kind of big ones for me.

At the time of our sixth interview, Jeannie was working as a client administrator in another company that had a call centre as part of its business. Much of this job involved administrative tasks, which she thought of as 'mind-numbingly boring'. She seemed to miss direct contact with customers or agents.

So Jeannie saw her competence in emotion management as part of her wider skills set, and she also spoke of it in more general terms as part of a person's identity. It was important to preserve professionalism at all times, as a sort of personal ethos that underpinned appropriate behaviour in the company. She seemed comfortable with her account of herself as someone who enjoyed listening to others and interacting with them, and she told admiring stories of call agents who were good at 'faking it'. While Jeannie noted marked gender differences in the call agents' ways of dealing with emotional labour, she did not view it as involving intrinsically female attributes, and she thought that skilled and less-skilled workers could be found among men and women alike.

We do not wish to suggest that emotional labour is unproblematic. Clearly, Jeannie's story in particular illustrates that it involves a degree of colonisation of the self, and a mobilisation of qualities and attributes that have often (not always) been treated predominantly as part of the private rather than the public sphere. But these accounts are consistent with critical analyses that emphasise worker agency. Sue and Jeannie are not passive cultural dupes, assenting submissively to an imposed process. In particular the informal policies of emotional support among the call agents were initiated and implemented by the workers themselves. Those who are skilled emotion workers seem aware of their ability to manage their emotions, and understand it as part of a process of professionalism that binds the skilled together and promotes professional pride in a high standard of performance. It is also built into people's processes of identification, becoming a strong part of their sense of who they are.

Learning to 'fake it'

Relatively little attention has been paid to the implications of emotion work for education and training. In so far as it has been discussed, it is usually with respect to the management of emotion in formal classroom settings or in early career development (Colley 2006a, 2006b; Cullingford 2006). By contrast, the two cases in this chapter concern adult women who have reached managerial positions, albeit relatively modest ones that are also vulnerable to changing market forces. While there were similarities in the emotional labour described by Sue and Jeannie, there were also differences. Both valued good emotional performance and competent emotional management which preserved professionalism in all circumstances, including when the job that has required it has been removed and the worker (Jeannie) made redundant. Sue operated in a more 'traditional' work format that relied mainly on face-to-face communication and was subject to less direct management surveillance. Jeannie, on the other hand, had worked as a call agent and then supervised those call agents who undertook technically mediated communication that was scripted and monitored by management. Where differences in emotion work and emotional labour existed, these were likely to have implications for workers' learning and identities – for example, in sustaining identity and preserving a worker's sense of authenticity and in the performance of gender.

In identifying with the company, workers were required to use strategies of resistance with customers to overcome gendered expectations (for example, of the women call agents' product knowledge). However, the way in which such forms of resistance interacted with identity, agency and gender requires further analysis in relation to developments in technology (Faulkner 2007) and in the surveillance of 'soft' skills. Learning about the self in the world and management of one's role and identity were significant to worker survival and to possibilities for resistance.

Lastly, emotional labour was not a purely individual activity and, in survival and resistance, interviewees drew on mutual support among fellow workers. This was particularly important when workers were pushed to the breaking point in customer interactions. Both interviewees had experience of training in aspects of emotion work, and while they had reservations about its effectiveness for some people, it did not evoke particular anxieties within their narratives.

Workers are not just 'docile bodies' inhabiting a quasi-Foucauldian world of surveillance and discursive power (Du Gay 1996). While they perform emotional labour in capitalist relations of production, workers also draw on their emotion work to develop narratives of identity that express their confidence in their abilities. We concur with Scheere and Solomon (2006) in suggesting that there is a tendency sometimes simply to portray 'contemporary work practices as oppressive and disempowering, particularly for women workers' (2006: 103), overlooking the ways in which workers actively deploy their emotional and other resources to position themselves more securely within the context of the new economy.

Conclusions

How does this analysis affect the practice of teachers and trainers in workplace and adult learning? Two sets of implications spring immediately to mind – for the self-reflective practices of teachers and others concerned professionally with supporting adult learning; and for the identities of the learners with whom we work.

Turning first to implications for teachers' practices, we suggest recognition of the fact that teachers are also knowledge workers in the 'new' economy for whom emotion work is significant in their everyday teaching labour. There are always attempts to regulate and routinise the behaviour of teachers – for example, through centralised target setting or the use of competency-based standards as the primary basis for the curriculum. Nevertheless, the classroom or workshop remains something of a 'black box' in which teachers and trainers exercise considerable discretion over the ways in which they carry out tasks. This discretion extends to the emotion work that teachers undertake; and we would suggest that where adult and workplace learning move towards more interactive and practice-based forms of instruction, so the significance of emotion work and emotional labour increases.

Second, teachers and trainers need to be conscious of the role of affect in learners' everyday working lives. Recognition of the agentic self of the learner does not mean denial of structure and even less of systemic hierarchies of privilege and dis/advantage, but rather implies an appreciation of the individual's ability to negotiate meaning and help create 'real life' institutional cultures and processes that make work and organisations possible. The question then arises as to how educators should react to increasing demands for emotion skills in the workplace. What, for example, are the long-term implications for learning and identity of the scripting of workers' performance, and how are we as adult educators and trainers to understand and deal with these? What pedagogies are needed in the face of technically mediated work whose immediacy requires emotional labour that challenges worker control and sometimes worker identity?

Since workers are not simply 'docile bodies' who embody the requisite skills in a passive and unreflexive manner, then it follows that affective competences can be an important aspect of people's occupational identities. Being good at managing one's emotions becomes an important part of who people believe themselves to be and provides a basis for their self-judgement of their professionalism and self-respect. The development of identities in this way has implications for gender and the adult educator's role in preparing learners to sustain their identities, and strategies of resistance must involve an awareness of the gendered aspects of emotional labour.

This raises a further question, relating to the wider Learning Lives project. This chapter focuses particularly on the accounts of two female participants, but we also draw on the stories of other workers who took part in our research. Yet, while many call centre agents are men, those who volunteered to take part in this research were predominantly women (in a ratio of 5 to 1). This raises the issue of possible implications of emotional labour for the gendering of women's work and for forms of masculinity. Are there ways in which emotional labour constrains identity and learning? Would men have been so open about the anxieties of emotional labour in their work? What might be the effects on learning and identity of seeming gender differences in the way workers deal with emotional labour? This reinforces the significance of gender in initial education, particularly for learners' evolving sense of their mature capabilities as competent adults (see Colley 2006a). However, emotion and gender are equally relevant to continuing learning in the adult life course, for workers' active engagement in the processes of negotiating control in their everyday working lives, as well as for their evolving sense of professionalism and autonomy.

Emotion work can be read both as context and as practices. Colley is surely right to insist on a social rather than an individualised understanding of how emotion work is learned and practised. But this should encourage us to understand emotion work as arising out of processes of biographical learning, which are intrinsically iterative in nature; blend aspects of formal, informal and non-formal learning; and involve workers in an active engagement with their world. This in turn affects workers' views of and engagement with workplace learning and job-related learning, within the wider context of how they handle change and learning across their lives.

One approach, based on defining workers as the passive victims of emotional exploitation, might logically suggest that we should shore up existing, frequently gendered learner identities, protecting learners from the threats and anxieties of exposure to stress-inducing technologies of the self. As Ecclestone puts it, the core curriculum in such approaches becomes 'the self and learning about the self as a "subject" in both senses of the word' (Ecclestone 2007: 130). An alternative might be to engage more fully with the demands of emotional labour while applying older, critical traditions of learning that examine and challenge classed and gendered relations of inequality to new and highly technological contexts of the twenty-first-century economy where adults learn and work. This seems to us the more fruitful approach.

Notes

1   Further details of the Learning Lives project, including accounts of data collection and analysis, are available on http://www.learninglives.org.

2   We do not use real names in this chapter; instead we invited interviewees to choose pseudonyms, so as not to compromise their identity.

References

Ashforth B & Tomiuk M (2000) Emotional labour and authenticity: Views from service agents. In S Fineman (ed.) *Emotion in organisations.* London: Sage Publications

Bolton S (2000) Emotions here, emotions there, emotional organisations everywhere. *Critical Perspectives in Accounting* 11(2): 155–171

Callaghan G & Thompson P (2002) 'We recruit attitude': The selection and shaping of routine call centre labour. *Journal of Management Studies* 39(2): 233–254

Callaghan J (2000) Emotion management and organisational functions: A case study of patterns in a not-for-profit organisation. *Human Resource Development Quarterly* 11(3): 245–267

Colley H (2006a) From childcare practitioner to FE tutor: Biography, identity and lifelong learning. In C Leathwood & B Francis (eds) *Gender and lifelong learning: Critical feminist engagements.* London: Routledge

Colley H (2006b) Learning to labour with feeling: Class, gender and emotion in childcare education and training. *Contemporary Issues in Early Childhood* 7(1): 15–29

Cullingford C (2006) Mentoring as myth and reality: Evidence and ambiguity. In C Cullingford (ed.) *Mentoring in education: An international perspective.* Aldershot: Ashgate

Du Gay P (1996) *Consumption and identity at work.* London: Sage Publications

Dulewicz V & Higgs M (1998) Soul researching. *People Management* (October): 42–45

Ecclestone K (2007) Editorial: An identity crisis? Using concepts of 'identity', 'agency' and 'structure' in the education of adults. *Studies in the Education of Adults* 39(2): 121–131

Faulkner W (2007) 'Nuts and bolts and people': Gender-troubled engineering identities. *Social Studies of Science* 37(3): 331–356

Franzway S (2000) Women working in a greedy institution: Commitment and emotional labour in the union movement. *Gender, Work and Organisation* 7(4): 258–268

Hochschild A (1983) *The managed heart: The commercialisation of human feeling.* Berkeley: University of California Press

Hughes J (2005) Bringing emotion to work: Emotional intelligence, employee resistance and the reinvention of character. *Work, Employment and Society* 19(3): 603–625

Misztal BA (2000) *Informality: Social theory and contemporary practice.* London: Routledge

Payne J (2006) *What's wrong with emotional labour?* SKOPE Research Paper 65. Oxford and Coventry: University of Oxford and University of Warwick

Scheere H & Solomon N (2006) The moving subject: Shifting work(ers) across and beyond organisational boundaries. In S Billett, T Fenwick & M Somerville (eds) *Work, subjectivity and learning: Understanding learning through working life.* Dordrecht: Springer

Wajcman J & Martin B (2002) Narratives of identity in modern management: The corrosion of gender difference? *Sociology* 36(4): 985–1002

13 Recognising *phronesis*, or practical wisdom, in the recognition of prior learning

Mignonne Breier

Introduction

In his *Nicomachean Ethics*, Aristotle presents the concept of *phronesis* (often translated as 'practical wisdom') and juxtaposes it against scientific and craft knowledge. He says it is acquired with experience and makes one wise as well as informed:

> [T]hough the young become proficient in geometry and mathematics, and wise in matters like these, they do not seem to become practically wise. The reason is that practical wisdom is concerned also with particular facts, and particulars come to be known from experience; and a young person is not experienced, since experience takes a long time to produce. (Crisp 2000: 111)

Noel (1999) has noted the many ways in which education researchers have used the concept of *phronesis* as a means to guide the improvement of teaching practices. Flyvberg (2001: 135) has argued for a 'phronetic' social science that emphasises the particular, case studies and 'practical rationality'.

Research on a teacher-upgrading programme in South Africa called the National Professional Diploma in Education (NPDE) has shown the potential significance of this concept for the increasingly common practice of recognition (assessment) of prior learning (RPL).[1] In this research, teachers with limited formal qualifications manifested knowledge and competences that defied categorisation in the dualistic terms in which RPL is commonly conceived. This mastery was neither purely formal (or abstract, general, universal, etc.) nor purely informal (or abstract, particular, local, etc.). It carried a strong sense of morality and of community and emphasised the particular in the light of general – and crucially, ethical – ideals. It was, in brief, a form of practical wisdom.

In this chapter I consider accounts of the life experiences, personal qualities and knowledge of selected teachers in the light of various definitions of *phronesis* as well as opposing forms of knowledge. I begin with a description of the rise of RPL in South Africa, and the particular form it took in the teacher-upgrading programme, while also providing background on education under apartheid. I then consider the role that practical wisdom might play in future conceptualisations of RPL, and in particular the recognition of the pastoral role of teachers.

The promise of recognition of prior learning

RPL was placed on the South African education policy agenda in the early 1990s shortly before the dawn of the country's new democracy. Championed by the trade unions, it was mooted as a means of redress whereby workers who had been oppressed by the old regime could have their competences acknowledged and rewarded in the new regime or could gain access or credit in formal institutions of learning. Given that millions of people were deprived of even a basic formal education under apartheid, and experienced all the economic disadvantages attached to that deprivation, the notion of recognising the knowledge and skills that they had acquired non-formally (through trade union courses, for example) or informally (through life experience) was very seductive. 'From sweeper to engineer' was the popular slogan.

However, the promise encompassed a number of dilemmas, such as:
- How does a formal education programme recognise non-formal or informal education unless that non-formal or informal education led to knowledge and skills that are equivalent – even broadly so – to that which is demanded in the formal programme?
- How do individuals acquire, in an informal context, the type of knowledge and skills that is associated with formal education?

Although these are issues that face RPL practitioners anywhere in the world, they are particularly relevant in the South African context because of the extent of educational disadvantage in the country, which means that many RPL applicants do not have the underlying level of formal literacy and numeracy that is often assumed in the international literature on RPL. It is not surprising that in higher education at least the form of RPL that prevails is for access rather than credit (Breier & Burness 2003).

Education under apartheid

Until little more than a decade ago, the education system in South Africa was split along racial lines: there were separate education systems for whites, coloureds, Indians and Africans, with the latter group receiving the least resourced and most inferior form of education. The mission schools that some were able to attend were an exception, but they were systematically dismantled after the National Party came to power in 1948. The Nationalist government introduced mass schooling for Africans, but its 'Bantu education' was designed to ensure a 'black urban underclass of semi-skilled labourers' (Cross & Chisholm 1990: 56).

Teacher education was also unequal. In the early decades of the twentieth century, teacher training was seen as synonymous with secondary schooling and the few Africans who did reach secondary school were trained as secondary teachers. By 1939, only 2 per cent of African students at school had reached post-primary classes. At the same time, white teacher training was located in post-matriculation colleges or university education departments (Cross & Chisholm 1990).

With the development of apartheid came the development of African and coloured teaching colleges, many of them in the so-called homelands created in terms of the government's separate development policy. Welch (2002) reports that these colleges provided many African students with their only access to tertiary education, as the state provided teaching bursaries to students who did not have matriculation exemption (that is, the necessary combination of subjects and grades in the school-leaving examination to qualify for entrance to university).

In the early 1990s, as South Africa entered the period of transition to democratic rule and began to develop a new education policy, there were more than 100 teacher colleges, most of them geared for Africans and providing qualifications that were below the official minimum of M+3.[2] Within white teacher education the norm was M+4 (NEPI 1992).

A further concern was the pervasive education theory known as 'fundamental pedagogics' (FP), the strange mix of abstract phenomenological theory and highly prescriptive teacher manuals that shaped the teacher education programmes at the University of South Africa (UNISA), most of the Afrikaans universities, most of the universities that had been set up for Africans, and the colleges of education set up for Africans or coloureds (NEPI 1992).

In trying to develop a 'science' of education, FP-inclined academics (many from UNISA) produced textbooks containing lists upon lists of uncontextualised items to be learned by rote. But the most important deficiency is that FP was (and still is) absolutely silent on context. A report on teacher education by the National Education Policy Investigation (NEPI) stated:

> Fundamental Pedagogics is intellectually harmful in that it neutralises and depoliticises educational discourse, and does not provide students and teachers with the concepts necessary to assess critically its (or any other) claims about education. (NEPI 1992: 17)

A number of reforms were introduced post 1994 in order to overcome the worst effects of apartheid education. One of the most important of these was the introduction of outcomes-based education (OBE), which was meant to displace the previous emphasis on content and rote learning, make explicit what learners should attend to, and direct assessment towards specified goals. The ultimate purpose was to encourage the development of (economically) useful skills by all sectors of the population (Mason 1999).

However, OBE received heavy criticism for, among other things, its failure to take account of the shortages of personnel and resources in black (particularly African) schools, its complicated and obscure terminology, and its problematic claims and assumptions about the relationship between curriculum and economic growth (Jansen 1998). A review committee was appointed that suggested a number of improvements, which resulted in a Revised National Curriculum Statement (DoE 2000b).

The National Professional Diploma in Education

When the NPDE was introduced in 2001, there were about 40 000 under-qualified teachers in South Africa. Many were middle-aged African women who were teaching in mother tongue at foundation phase (the first three years of schooling in the South African education system) and who had studied at colleges that offered qualifications that were now regarded as insufficient for registration as a teacher.

They had been teaching for more than a decade and had been trying to upgrade their qualifications for some time.

The NPDE catered for two categories of teachers, of which one was slightly more qualified than the other (M+3 versus M+2) and consequently in a higher pay class (REQV 12 rather than REQV 11),[3] although their teaching duties might be the same. The NPDE had a limited budget and was designed as a two-year (maximum) part-time programme for all students. In order to retain the distinction between REQV levels while keeping within these time constraints, the less-qualified teachers were offered 'credit' through 'RPL'. As the programme unfolded at the 17 institutions offering it, it became clear that the Department of Education (DoE) regarded the RPL component as little more than a bureaucratic exercise in which all candidates would inevitably be successful. But educators still had to put together programmes that offered at least a semblance of the practice as it is conventionally understood. RPL usually occurs prior to commencement of a programme and requires the candidate to demonstrate competences practically, or to show them indirectly in a portfolio in which they reflect on prior experience and their learning derived from it. This proved to be very difficult in the NPDE programme.

The institutions were not able to offer RPL prior to the commencement of the NPDE programme, because this would have meant extending the length of the programme and their budgets did not allow for this. Most of the programmes did not conduct systematic classroom observations because of the time, financial and logistical obstacles involved. Many of the teachers were in rural schools situated many kilometres from the university concerned and often on poor-quality roads. The institutions generally resorted to the portfolio method as a means to determine prior learning, but this presented further difficulties, for reasons that will be elaborated below.

Many of the older teachers were at a particular disadvantage in the NPDE programme. They had trained in the apartheid era under the conditions described previously, and had received insufficient or inappropriate instruction in the content of the subjects they were required to teach. Their teacher education was limited largely to a set of procedures and methods (including rote learning) that are now largely discredited. They were also given little opportunity to develop the type of English language and literacy skills necessary to meet the demands of the English-medium NPDE programme. Trained in terms of fundamental pedagogics, which required extensive learning by rote, they had little preparation for the type of reflection usually associated with RPL and commonly featured in teacher education curricula. Reflection was also a particularly important feature of the NPDE.

The research noted the conundrum or paradox at the heart of the NPDE programme:

- RPL is about recognising and affirming prior learning based on informal or non-formal (usually practical) experience.
- Many of the teachers received an education that is now considered to be inadequate and have developed practices (such as rote learning) that are known to be unsound and inappropriate.
- How do you recognise and thereby affirm the prior learning of such a teacher?

The study found that this paradox, combined with the limited, bureaucratic aims of the DoE, militated against any form of RPL as it is generally known. The three university programmes that were studied in depth mostly provided extra exercises that the RPL teachers were required to perform alongside the mainstream NPDE tasks. These involved the preparation and presentation of lessons and subsequent reflection on the lessons. Alternatively, they were asked questions that encouraged them to reflect on particular incidents in their teaching career. This was the closest attempt to RPL, but not all students took the task seriously and we found several instances in which students had copied each other's work – in other words, produced the same personal experience, to the letter in some cases. Only one of the three institutions did systematic classroom observations making use of local tutors (Ralphs 2006).

While the research exposed the inadequacies of the RPL offered in the NPDE programme and argued that it should not be called RPL at all, these were not its major conclusions. The empirical research[4] raised familiar questions about the soundness of the academic knowledge (including content knowledge and English literacy) of some of the teachers, particularly the foundation phase teachers, but it also exposed their very great strengths and another dimension of knowledge which the researchers found difficult to describe.

This dimension is captured to some extent in the words of one of the teacher educators who was interviewed for the research. This teacher educator was sceptical that one could 'RPL' the rural teachers in his NPDE programme when one knew their experience and knowledge (of formal subjects) was lacking, but he did concede that they had competences suited to the conditions under which they had to work:

> They need to manage a very different teaching/learning situation. There are areas with HIV/AIDS, and traditional leadership, the school blows over and they have to rebuild it out of mud again. There are large distances to travel, resources are not available, kids' social problems – these are the things that teachers have to deal with more than with teaching and learning, and it's kind of identifying those needs really is probably what RPL should be about, and recognising that people have competencies and building on them.

The dimension is also echoed in the words of Harley et al. (2000: 294) in reporting on a study of 'effective' teachers in six KwaZulu-Natal schools where they refer to a 'something extra', which, quoting Barber (1995: 76), is 'that part of all education that does not obey the laws of physics, that defies logic, but at the same time is the key to educational success'. Barber was referring specifically to classroom practice and 'the extraordinary ability of [some] teachers to generate sparks of learning, even in the most inauspicious circumstances'.

The research found examples of teachers working against great odds to further their qualifications while teaching full-time. Of those interviewed in depth, all came from impoverished homes and most had to curtail their education to earn money for their families. They spoke of moral and religious values that had shaped their attitudes to life. And it appeared from their accounts that they had gained great strengths in the course of their difficult lives (Ralphs 2006). One teacher, Ms M, had drawn on such strengths to teach traumatised children in a community wracked by faction fighting and, at another particularly poor school, to improvise science equipment. Another teacher, Mr B, the son of an Anglican minister, experienced many moves in his childhood, exposing him to many different communities. He also had to drop out of university and find work to support his mother and siblings after his father died. Later he used these strengths

> to stand on my feet, be responsible and considerate to my family
> members. This kind of endurance helps me to give support to my learners
> as well as my colleagues during sorrowful times, encourage them to be
> strong and face up to the challenges.

What kind of knowledge?

The accounts above demonstrate a number of qualities: innovativeness, compassion, independence, responsibility, ingenuity and endurance, moulded in the spirit of personal and religious values. They suggest particular types of disposition but also much more. Beneath those qualities are indications of a form of knowledge and reasoning that enables the individual to be described as such: that which enabled Ms M to deal compassionately with children in a violent community and to innovate in the absence of classroom equipment; and that which enabled Mr B to learn from different cultural experiences and difficult personal times. I contend that Aristotle's concept of *phronesis*, or practical wisdom, provides a name and description for this type of knowledge.

What is phronesis?

In the translations of and commentaries on Aristotle's concept of *phronesis*, there is some confusion over whether the authors mean a form of knowledge, a form of reasoning or understanding, a form of disposition or a personal quality.[5] For example, Gadamer (1985) speaks of *phronesis* as a kind of 'moral knowledge'; Saugstad (2005), as a form of 'practical' knowledge; Gustavsson (2007), as 'knowledge'; Nussbaum (2001), as a kind of perception or understanding; Kristjansson (2005), as 'an intellectual disposition'; while Noel (1999) presents a range of interpretations from numerous authors, including *phronesis* as a 'state of capacity' or 'characteristic of a person' to *phronesis* as a form of practical reasoning or perception. There is one common denominator, however, across all these definitions. *Phronesis* has a moral or ethical component.

Flyvberg (2001) refers to *phronesis* as one of three 'intellectual virtues', the others being *episteme* and *techne*. But his detailed characterisation of these virtues suggests they are all forms of knowledge:

- *Episteme* Scientific knowledge. Universal, invariable, context-independent. Based on general analytical rationality.
- *Techne* Craft/art. Pragmatic, variable, context-independent. Oriented towards production. Based on practical instrumental rationality governed by a conscious goal.

- *Phronesis* Ethics. Deliberation about values with reference to praxis. Pragmatic, variable, context-dependent. Oriented towards action. Based on practical value-rationality. (Flyvberg 2001: 57)

It is probably significant (and indicative of the values that our society currently prizes) that there is no direct English translation for *phronesis,* while there are terms that relate to *episteme* (epistemic, epistemology) and *techne* (technique, technical and technology). The term 'practical wisdom' is used in modern translations and commentaries,[6] but it does little to clear the confusion over whether *phronesis* is a form of knowledge or a disposition. Wisdom, as the *Concise Oxford Dictionary* tells us, can be both 'the quality of being wise' and 'the body of knowledge and experience that develops within a specified society or period' (Soames & Stevenson 2004).

In this chapter I argue for a definition of practical wisdom that accommodates both knowledge and reasoning, in the same way that philosophy, mathematics, physical science or other disciplines encompass both forms of reasoning and bodies of knowledge. Furthermore, practical wisdom has the following features:

- It is flexible. Quoting Nussbaum, Gustavsson (n.d. a: 4) says it brings 'a kind of complex sensitivity to the outstanding features of a concrete situation'. Like the flexible ruler used to measure building columns with curves and grooves on the Greek island of Lesbos, *phronesis* 'adapts to the form of the stones and yet keeps its own direction'.
- Its gaze is one of 'intellectual virtue' rather than intellect alone (Gadamer 1985: 22). It is also 'no cold ray', as is the Kantian vision of reason, but is imbued with emotion and imagination (Gustavsson n.d. b: 9) and has a strong ethical, moral component.
- It is oriented beyond the self towards a wider community and in the interests of that community. In this respect it embraces the notion of *sensus communis,* which Gadamer (1985: 21) has defined as 'the sense that founds community', and it 'seeks the good life, with and for others' (Gustavsson 2007: 83).

Richard Bernstein (quoted in Gustavsson 2007: 8) provides the following useful definition, which notably refers to *phronesis* as both reasoning and knowledge:

> *Phronesis* is a form of reasoning and knowledge that involves a distinctive mediation between the universal and the particular. This mediation is not accomplished by any appeal to technical rules or method...or by the subsumption of a pregiven determinate universal to a particular case. The 'intellectual virtue' of *phronesis* is a form of reasoning, yielding a type of ethical know-how in which what is universal and what is particular are codetermined.

Different forms of practical wisdom

The research not only revealed the importance of practical wisdom, but also made it clear that there are different forms of it, some more abstract or 'epistemic' than others. In the terms used by educational sociologist Basil Bernstein (2000), some forms are more closely associated with 'vertical discourses' (abstract, usually disciplinary knowledge) and some with 'horizontal discourses' (the knowledge and competences of everyday life), although *phronesis* always involves both types of knowledge to varying extents. It is essentially a form of knowledge and reasoning that enables an individual to negotiate the particular in the light of a general, ethical understanding.

The following account of the experiences of Ms T shows that *phronesis* can draw on both horizontal and vertical resources:

> Ms T is a Zulu-speaking teacher at foundation phase who teaches in Zulu and seldom needs to speak or write in English in the school context. She was in her late forties at the time of this research. Her portfolio, which, following the norms of the NPDE at her particular university, was written in English and had many grammar and spelling mistakes, spoke repeatedly of her love and care for her learners. It also mentioned several times that she has four children for whom she has full responsibility as her husband has a 'misordered mind'. In an interview she revealed that her children ranged from Grade 1 to a first-year technikon engineering student. And the 'misordered mind' of Mr T had once even led to him to trying to kill her with an axe.

In my observations of her teaching, I found that Ms T was indeed a loving, caring teacher who tried to attend as much to the spirited and gifted as the slow and needy. Interviews with her head of department and principal confirmed and reinforced my impressions. They both spoke of her love for the children, the extra care she took with those who needed it, and her success in teaching Zulu even to students from higher grades. Both were adamant that she had more to offer the school and its pupils than a young graduate fresh out of college or university. The latter might know more about the Revised National Curriculum Statement (an important focus of the NPDE), but in theory only – and anyway, they said, the new RNCS was nothing more than a restatement of what they had been doing for years.

Although her qualities of love and care equipped her for many of her classroom situations, they did little to assist Ms T in negotiating with the bureaucracy of the university at which she was studying. It would appear that Ms T's particular form of practical wisdom was drawing mainly from her horizontal or common-sense repertoire. As the following anecdote illustrates, she had far fewer epistemic resources at hand:

> In the Mpumulanga province where Ms T worked, schools had been warned that their underqualified teachers would be redeployed and replaced if they did not pass the NPDE. It was thus of vital importance to Ms T that she obtain this qualification. Yet at the time of the research the university was refusing to allow her to graduate, even though she had completed and passed all the necessary courses, because it had discovered that she had been admitted without the necessary entry qualifications. She needed a full two-year diploma and she had not completed hers. Instead of accepting responsibility for their own mistake, the university was

refusing to allow her to graduate and requiring instead that she re-register for another course for which she was eligible. Of the qualities that Ms T displayed in the classroom, only her tenacity prepared her for her battle with the university authorities. Here she also needed – and lacked – a different, shrewder kind of practical wisdom that could not be exercised without greater mastery of the language (English) and discourses of authority. Her letters, telephone calls and countless photocopies of mostly irrelevant documents failed to bend the university and nearly two years after completing her studies she had still not been allowed to graduate.

Ms T's experience demonstrates a range of forms of *phronesis*, including that which demands complex mastery of vertical discourses as well as that which draws on horizontal resources alone. The latter amounts to a form of pastoralism.

There is a danger one might discount the latter as much less important than the former, given the growing concern that South African teachers lack sufficient knowledge of the subjects they teach, with severe consequences for the academic performance of their learners. At the same time there is increasing recognition that in the context of the HIV/AIDS pandemic, the pastoral role is of great importance even if it has received little attention in education policy. Bhana et al. (2006) note the enormous amount of pastoral work that teachers in under-resourced schools in poor communities have to perform. This work

> does not count towards promotion nor is it noticed in any public way by the teacher hierarchy. But, we argue, it is this work that is cushioning learners from the trauma of loss that many are confronting. It is thus vital for the well-being of schools, even as it is hidden from public recognition. (2006: 5)

The importance of the pastoral role in teacher education curricula is recognised internationally,[7] but in the South African *Norms and Standards for Educators* (DoE 2000a) it is mentioned only once. The DoE's tall order presents the following roles of the teacher (in these exact words and order):

- Learning Mediator.
- Interpreter and Designer of Learning Programmes and Materials.
- Leader, Administrator and Manager.
- Community, Citizenship and *Pastoral role* (italics added).
- Scholar, Researcher and Lifelong Learner.
- Assessor.
- Learning Area/Subject/Discipline/Phase Specialist.

The DoE defines all seven roles in terms of practical, foundational and reflexive competences. The term 'pastoral role' is not mentioned again but would seem to be best located in reflexive competence

> [w]here the learner demonstrates the ability to integrate or connect performances and decision making with understanding and with the ability to adapt to change and unforeseen circumstances and explain the reasons behind these actions. (DoE 2000a: 13)

As part of their community, citizenship and pastoral role, teachers are urged to reflect on ethical issues and also critically analyse the degree to which the school curriculum promotes HIV/AIDS awareness, among other requirements. Yet, none of these injunctions captures the qualities of love, compassion, care, and so on that the teachers in our study manifested. But it is unlikely that practical wisdom in all its many facets can ever be captured in neat lists of bullet points.

Harley et al. (2000) have noted that an effective teacher is not one who plays all of the roles or who demonstrates all the competences underpinning each of the roles, but 'one who [makes] an appropriate weighting of the roles and a selection of competences in response to specific contexts'. These teachers, as noted earlier, have 'something extra'. This 'something extra' cannot be fully disaggregated or apprehended by means of description of discrete roles. In the view of Harley et al., any attempt to 'neatly "package" the education enterprise by means of technical specifications' creates 'an unattainable ideal and in doing so fails to capture the heart of the profession' (2000: 295).

Conclusion

Aristotle has suggested that one should seek practical wisdom by 'considering the sort of people we consider practically wise' (Crisp 2000: 107). The accounts of teachers in this chapter contain references to the sort of people and the kinds of qualities that encourage one to think of knowledge as more than just *episteme* and *techne*. They are qualities emanating from practical wisdom but are not to be equated with it directly. They provide a *sense* of the practical wisdom that underlies these qualities, rather than manifestations of the knowledge and reasoning itself. We would need to conduct further research involving more detailed interviews (preferably in mother tongue) in order to speak directly of that knowledge or reasoning.

In giving emphasis to *phronesis*, I do not wish to imply that the qualities and knowledge described in the accounts of Ms T and others should necessarily be exchangeable for access or credits in a teacher education programme that demands 'hard' propositional knowledge, nor even in a programme such as the NPDE, which is largely about (pedagogical) process knowledge. To do so would be to disadvantage even further those schoolchildren who are struggling to escape the legacies of educational apartheid and need the knowledge and skills associated with the vertical discourses (in other words, the epistemic knowledge) in order to gain status and material success. The point is that by giving recognition to practical wisdom, by acknowledging that such a form of knowledge exists, one also accords the respect that is due to persons who have not had the opportunities or any of the advantages of formal education but have managed to survive under the harshest of conditions in a way that few of the formally educated would have been able to do. If one considers that teaching is a moral activity (Noel 1999) and recognises that practical wisdom is as important for good teaching as the specific propositional and process knowledge that is taught in formal programmes, then one can understand, for example, why the school in Mpumulanga was so concerned that it might lose a loved and experienced teacher like Ms T.

Is it possible to recognise practical wisdom in an RPL context? It probably is, in the context of an individual process with few time constraints (which rules out the NPDE entirely). It would probably need to be recounted and recognised in narrative. Whether it could ever be assessed, judged and given a mark out of 100 is another question entirely. But readings on practical wisdom should certainly form part of any teacher education curriculum and any RPL portfolio development course. One needs to be reminded that the 'good'[8] life is achieved not only through intellectual knowledge and practical skills but also through the fine art of bringing ethical ideals flexibly to bear on the complex circumstances of daily lives.

Notes

1   This research is reported in detail in Breier (2008). The contribution of Alan Ralphs (2006) and Michael Gardiner (2006) is gratefully acknowledged. The research formed part of the Teacher Education Project funded by the Royal Netherlands Embassy.

2   Within the South African system this means matriculation, the school-leaving certificate that one attains after 12 years of schooling, and a three-year teaching qualification.

3   REQV stands for relative education qualification value.

4   The empirical research included observations of teaching practice, perusal of portfolios and course documentation, and semi-structured interviews with teachers and teacher educators.

5   Like Bourdieu's practical knowledge, which has Aristotelian origins according to Flyvberg (2001).

6   Some examples are Crisp (2000) and Nussbaum (2001).

7   See, for example, Cleave et al. (1997).

8   'Good' is used here in the Aristotelian sense to refer to a life that seeks to be virtuous as well as comfortable, with an orientation towards a wider community.

References

Barber M (1995) Reconstructing the teaching profession. *Journal of Education for Teaching* 21(1): 75–85

Bernstein B (2000) *Pedagogy, symbolic control and identity* (revised edition). London: Taylor and Francis

Bernstein R (1983) *Beyond objectivism and relativism: Science, hermeneutics and praxis.* Philadelphia: University of Pennsylvania Press

Bhana D, Morrell R, Epstein D & Moletsane R (2006) The hidden work of caring: Teachers and the maturing AIDS epidemic in diverse secondary schools in Durban. *Journal of Education* (38): 5–23

Breier M (2008) *The RPL conundrum: Recognition of prior learning in a teacher upgrading programme.* Cape Town: HSRC Press

Breier M & Burness A (2003) *The implementation of recognition of prior learning at universities and technikons in South Africa 2003.* Bellville: Education Policy Unit

Cleave H, Carey P, Norris P, Sloper P, While D & Charlton A (1997) Pastoral care in initial teacher education: A survey of secondary teacher education institutions. *Pastoral Care* 15(2): 16–21

Crisp R (trans. & ed.) (2000) *Nicomachean ethics.* Cambridge: Cambridge University Press

Cross M & Chisholm L (1990) The roots of segregated schooling in 20th-century South Africa. In N Mokubung (ed.) *Pedagogy of domination: Toward a democratic education in South Africa*. Trenton, NJ: Africa World Press

DoE (Department of Education, South Africa) (2000a) *Norms and standards for educators*. Government Gazette 415 (20844). Pretoria: DoE

DoE (2000b) *Revised national curriculum statement*. Pretoria: DoE. Accessed 22 July 2008, http://www.mml.co.za/revised_national_curriculum_statement.htm

Flyvbjerg B (2001) *Making social science matter*. Cambridge: Cambridge University Press

Gadamer H-G (1985) *Truth and method*. London: Sheed and Ward

Gardiner M (2006) Research in the Limpopo province for the project on RPL in teacher education, with a focus on the NPDE. Case study report for the Teacher Education Project 13. Document available from the author

Gustavsson B (n.d. a) *Phronesis* as knowledge. Document available from the author

Gustavsson B (n.d. b) The meaning of *Bildung* in contemporary society. Document available from the author

Gustavsson B (2007) Negotiating the space for democracy between the universal and the particular: The role of phronesis. In C Odora Hoppers, B Gustavsson, E Motala & J Pampallis (eds) Democracy and human rights in education and society: Explorations from South Africa and Sweden. Örebro, Sweden: Örebro University Press

Harley K, Barasa F, Bertram C, Mattson E & Pillay S (2000). 'The real and the ideal': Teacher roles and competences in South African policy and practice. *International Journal of Educational Development* (20): 287–304

Jansen J (1998) Curriculum reform in South Africa: A critical analysis of outcomes-based education. *Cambridge Journal of Education* 28(3): 321–331

Kristjansson K (2005) Smoothing it: Some Aristotelian misgivings about the *phronesis*–praxis perspective on education. *Educational Philosophy and Theory* 37(4): 455–473

Mason M (1999) Outcomes-based education in South African curriculum reform: A response to Jonathan Jansen. *Cambridge Journal of Education* 29(1): 137–143

NEPI (National Education Policy Investigation) (1992) *Teacher education*. Cape Town: Oxford University Press and National Education Coordinating Committee

Noel J (1999) On the varieties of *phronesis*. *Educational Philosophy and Theory* 31(3): 273–289

Nussbaum MC (2001) *The fragility of goodness: Luck and ethics in Greek tragedy and philosophy* (revised edition). Cambridge: Cambridge University Press

Ralphs A (2006) RPL in the NPDE at the Nelson Mandela Metropolitan University: Case study report based on teachers from the Bizana district in the Eastern Cape. Case study report for the Teacher Education Project 13. Document available from the author

Saugstad T (2005) Aristotle's contribution to scholastic and non-scholastic learning theories. *Pedagogy, Culture and Society* 13(3): 347–365

Soames C & Stevenson A (2004) *Concise Oxford dictionary* (11th edition). Oxford: Oxford University Press

Welch T (2002) Historical overview of teacher education. In J Adler & Y Reed (eds) *Challenges of teacher development: An investigation of take-up in South Africa*. Pretoria: Van Schaik Publishers

14 Learning indigenous knowledge systems

Jennifer Hays

Introduction

The South African Department of Science and Technology (DST) policy on indigenous knowledge systems (IKS), introduced in 2004, is a major step forward in the recognition of the legitimacy of systems of knowledge other than 'Western' or 'scientific' knowledge, and reflects a growing shift in consciousness among academics, policy-makers and practitioners in a number of fields as to the value and the legitimacy of IKS. The way that this shift is interpreted and applied, however, is still in the process of being worked out. IKS are (practically by definition) mutable, integrated and informally transmitted, and thus difficult to formalise and fit into the hierarchical and highly compartmentalised systems of modern governments and other organisations. Training and qualifications authorities across southern Africa are working to develop ways to recognise informal skills in a way that will bestow on them the recognition and legitimacy that formal qualifications do. There are two general aspects to this: integrating IKS into existing formal structures and recognising the legitimacy of informal structures. I argue in this chapter that both of these angles are of critical importance; however, the emphasis is often on the first one (incorporating indigenous knowledge into formal structures), leading to an imbalance in the approach. This imbalance can jeopardise the success of otherwise well-thought-out approaches.

There are many arenas in which these issues are pertinent. In this chapter, I focus on the particular challenges faced in integrating IKS into the formal education system. Again there are some basic sets of problems to be solved: How can IKS be integrated into the formal curriculum? How can someone who has gained extensive knowledge and skills but who has no formal education be recognised? In order to fully integrate IKS into any education system, it is critical to involve the elders who are the bearers of the knowledge. However, integrating experiential, orally transmitted knowledge – usually held by someone who has little or no formal education – into an education system that privileges easily compartmentalised and written information and formal qualifications presents many challenges. This chapter highlights some of these complicated issues as they take shape in southern Africa.

When discussing the concept of 'indigenous' in southern Africa, we must also keep in mind that there are layers of indigeneity. The DST policy states that IKS in South Africa have been 'marginalised, suppressed, and subjected to ridicule' (this is true as well for its neighbours to the north – Botswana and Namibia). While the IKS of most Africans have been seriously marginalised, it is the 'most indigenous' group, the San (also called Bushmen, or Basarwa in Botswana), who occupy the furthest fringe. This chapter will discuss the relationship between indigenous knowledge and education, looking primarily at the San of Botswana and Namibia. The arguments and conclusions in this chapter are based on several different forms of research, including long-term anthropological fieldwork (and several short field visits); involvement in development projects and other education and language efforts in southern Africa over several years; and a review of the literature on indigenous knowledge, indigenous education, and ethnographic accounts of the San.

From July 2001 to May 2002, I conducted fieldwork in the Nyae Nyae Conservancy on issues of language and education with the Ju|'hoansi,[1] who are indigenous to that area. The conservancy is the site of the Nyae Nyae Village Schools, a mother-tongue education project that was begun in the early 1990s and which will be discussed below. This research included participant observation, classroom observation and interviews with Ju|'hoansi parents, teachers, youth and children. This chapter also draws on my year-long work as a consultant for the Regional San Education Project of WIMSA (the Working Group of Indigenous Minorities in Southern Africa). This position involved researching and developing potential areas of collaboration and support for San education projects across Botswana, Namibia and South Africa; conducting extensive interviews with a wide variety of national, local and international stakeholders in indigenous education; and organising workshops and conferences at both country and international levels. My extended experience as a consultant for the Botswana-based organisation Letloa, which provides support to several community-based projects serving San communities in the northwestern part of the country, also informs my conclusions here. Working closely with the University of Botswana, Letloa has been working to develop a comprehensive and collaborative approach to San education, and this will also be described below.

The extended and shorter-term fieldwork, as well as the practical work to which it has sought to contribute, has involved identifying and describing the specific ways in which the indigenous knowledge of the San and its transmission strategies differ from (and sometimes clash with) those of the formal education system, and evaluating the relevance of both to the daily lives of community members. Finally, both the academic and applied work described above has involved research into the extensive existing literature on the indigenous knowledge, socialisation processes and knowledge transmission of the Ju|'hoansi and other San. All of these forms of research inform the arguments made here.

I begin with a brief description of the San and then outline what is meant here by IKS. Next I discuss some specific characteristics common to the IKS of the San, and highlight the contrast with formal education. I then briefly describe some ongoing educational projects (existing and proposed) in Botswana, Namibia and South Africa, and the relevance of this discussion to those efforts. In the final section of the chapter, I address the question, why maintain indigenous knowledge? I argue that this maintenance is important for communities themselves and for humanity in general. While formal recognition is an important part of maintenance efforts, we must also recognise its limitations.

Background

The San

The San are former hunter-gatherers living today in Botswana and Namibia, and to a lesser extent in South Africa, Angola, Zimbabwe and Zambia. Residing primarily in small, scattered settlements in remote areas, or as workers on farms, the San participate only marginally in national politics and the cash economy. While other groups in South Africa have also experienced dispossession and violence and are today economically, politically and socially marginalised, the San are everywhere at the bottom of the socio-economic hierarchy. In many places San students are doubly marginalised. African IKS are marginalised within the global context in general, and the indigenous knowledge of hunters and gatherers is further marginalised within the national contexts of both Botswana and Namibia. There are distinct differences in the forms of knowledge, environmental ethics, child-rearing techniques and social values between, on the one hand, agriculturalists and pastoralists and, on the other hand, hunters and gatherers (see Le Roux 1999; Hays 2007). Thus education and language initiatives designed to accommodate the home culture and language of local Bantu-speaking groups, for example, do not help the San, but often add an extra layer of alienation.

Many San see the formal education system as their only hope for accessing greater economic opportunity and gaining control over their lives. In practice, the experience of San children in government schools across southern Africa has been characterised largely by very high drop-out rates. There are many interrelated reasons why this is so, and an important one has to do with the enormous disjuncture between the IKS, transmission strategies and supporting social ethos of the San, and the knowledge, transmission strategies and social values associated with the formal education system. This will be discussed in greater detail below, but first I outline some important characteristics of indigenous knowledge.

What are 'indigenous knowledge systems'?

> Indigenous knowledge is a complete knowledge system with its own concepts of epistemology, philosophy and scientific and logical validity...[which] can only be learned and understood by means of pedagogy traditionally employed by these people themselves. (Battiste & Henderson-Youngblood 2000: 41)

> The underlying fact is that IK has always been and continues to be the primary factor in the survival and welfare of the majority of South Africans. (DST 2004: 5)

There is no universally accepted term for the category of knowledge referred to in this chapter. It is variably referred to as *traditional knowledge, local knowledge, indigenous knowledge, traditional environmental knowledge* or *indigenous knowledge systems*. Each term has a somewhat different emphasis, but the essence of the category is knowledge that is specific to a particular place and a particular group of people. Often the focus is on environmental knowledge. For the purposes of this discussion, I will use the term *indigenous knowledge systems*, or IKS, as used in the DST policy.

The category of 'local/traditional/indigenous knowledge' is frequently misrepresented. Understandings of it are often built on a conception of homogeneous communities and can be misunderstood to connote a 'rigid systematised version of knowledge, abstracted from individual agents' rather than a knowledge that is historically determined and flexible (Green 2000: 73). In fact, fluidity, diversity and adaptability are among the defining characteristics of IKS. Scott (1998) argues that the discourse of 'high modernism' has been so successfully structured 'that all other kinds of knowledge are regarded as backward, static traditions, as old wives' tales and superstitions' (1998: 331).[2] As Scott and many others have convincingly argued, however, far from being 'backwards' or 'static', the practical knowledge of someone who has made his or her living – indeed, has survived – through a lifetime of 'exceptionally close and astute observation' of his or her environment is often superior to anything that can be discovered easily through 'scientific' methods.

In her discussion of traditional environmental knowledge (TEK), McGregor (2004) makes an important distinction between 'Aboriginal' and 'non-Aboriginal' conceptions of what this kind of knowledge actually 'is':

> Aboriginal views of TEK are 'verb-based' – that is, action-oriented. TEK is not limited, in the Aboriginal view, to a 'body of knowledge'. It is expressed as a 'way of life'; it is conceived as being something that you *do*. Non-Aboriginal views of TEK are 'noun-' or 'product-based'. That is, they tend to focus on physical characteristics. TEK is viewed as a *thing* rather than something that you do. (McGregor 2004: 78)

This is a critical distinction, one with important implications for educational efforts focusing on indigenous populations. McGregor proposes the following description of TEK, based on Johnson (1992):

> a body of knowledge built up by a group of people through generations of living in close contact with nature. It includes a system of classification, a set of empirical observations about the local environment, and a system of self-management that governs resource use. The quantity and quality of traditional environmental knowledge varies among community members, depending upon gender, age, social status, intellectual capability, and profession (hunter, spiritual leader, healer, etc.). With its roots firmly in the past, traditional environmental knowledge is both *cumulative and dynamic*, building upon the experience of earlier generations and adapting to the new technological and socioeconomic changes of the present. (McGregor 2004: 77; italics added)

The understanding of TEK as 'cumulative and dynamic' is key, for it both encompasses the intense and long-term relationship that people have had with their environment and allows that knowledge to become 'updated' in a rapidly changing world as new information is acquired.

Indigenous knowledge, formal education and the San

Indigenous knowledge and its transmission in San communities

The IKS possessed by the San vary according to language group, geographical location, local availability of resources and, increasingly, legal restrictions on traditional practices – especially hunting. However, all are based on a recent hunting and gathering lifestyle and ethos. Although living solely from hunting and gathering is no longer a real option for the vast majority of San communities, many do still gain a substantial portion of their subsistence through these methods. The complexity of the skills required for tracking and hunting is described by Blurton Jones and Konnor (1976), who compare the intellectual processes required to those associated with modern science. They report that the !Kung demonstrated an 'advanced ability to observe and assemble facts about behaviour and to discriminate facts from hearsay and interpretation' and that in these areas their ability surpassed not only 'lay observers' but 'many professionals in western society' (1976: 344).

Draper (1976) points out that although the hunting and gathering lifestyle is technologically simple, this simplicity can be deceptive, for the subsistence activities themselves are quite complex. In more stratified societies, food production is broken down into tasks that can be carried out by individuals of varying levels of competence. This is especially true for agricultural and pastoral societies, where children can participate in maintenance chores such as taking care of animals or weeding crops (Draper 1976). In hunting and gathering societies, the process of food gathering requires detailed and integrated knowledge about a large variety of plant and animal species and sophisticated problem-solving skills; furthermore, the activity itself can be dangerous. Deadly snakes, carnivores, elephants and other dangerous animals populate a relatively undifferentiated bush environment in which getting disoriented and lost could mean death. There is thus little work that children can do on their own until they are fully competent adults; until that time they accompany the adults, watching and learning according to their own desire to do so, and with increasing frequency as they mature.

The IKS of San communities are connected to their experience with school in different ways. The transfer of children to formal school settings is one of the primary ways in which such knowledge is undermined. Simultaneously, the incongruence between different knowledge systems and their transmission is one of the biggest barriers to indigenous students' success in mainstream education systems. A literature review of research on child-rearing approaches, learning and teaching styles, and the traditional knowledge of the Juǀ'hoansi and other San groups reveals a number of consistent themes, including a general discouragement of competitive and aggressive behaviour and self-promotion; a tolerant child-rearing style that respects individual mood, will and personality; a general absence of physical punishment; an informal socialisation process in which children and adults interact freely; and observational and participatory (as opposed to instructional) learning styles (Draper 1976; Konner 1976; Blurton Jones & Konner 1976; Marshall 1976; Tanaka 1980; Guenther 1976, 1999; Le Roux 1999, 2002; Hays 2007). The egalitarian ethic that characterises adult social relationships also characterises children's play, which is generally cooperative in nature; likewise the lack of hierarchical social structures is also reflected in an approach to children that places very little emphasis on obedience. In small-village settings, Ju|'hoansi children observe their parents at close range and imitate them from a young age, but they do not begin participating in adult work until they are adolescents.

Blurton Jones and Konnor's (1976) observations of the transmission of knowledge relevant to hunting also support the findings of both Marshall (1976) and Draper (1976); they note that there seems to be 'relatively little transmission of *information* from one man to another, even from old to young' (1976: 344; italics added). These authors state that much of the knowledge is gained 'informally' and suggest that such knowledge is thus 'assimilated more easily and rapidly than knowledge gained under pressure or direct instruction' (1976: 345). As children get older, they choose when and how they wish to participate in the subsistence activities of the group. In this self-motivated fashion, with virtually no direct pressure from their parents or other adults, by the time they are in their early teens both boys and girls are competent to find and recognise plant foods, and by young adulthood they are, as Marshall described them, 'fully competent botanists' and gatherers of edible and useful plants (1976: 96). All of these characteristics differ sharply from what Ju|'hoansi students are expected to adapt to in the formal education system.

Formal education and indigenous knowledge

The formal education system has devastating effects on the transmission of IKS for two primary reasons. First, formal education often requires separation of children from the environment in which they learn the knowledge systems of their community. Since many indigenous communities still reside in places that are considered 'remote' from the urban centres of mainstream society, children often must attend boarding schools that are far from their communities. Indigenous children's experiences in schools are often characterised by long periods of separation from parents and communities and from the context in which their knowledge is communicated. Away from their families, children are taught foreign systems of knowledge, usually in a language variety other than their own. Second, even for those whose schools are in their communities, the emphasis on the skills associated with formal education is so strong that all other forms of knowledge are implicitly devalued. A fundamental problem with formal education systems is that they tend to emphasise indigenous students' incompetencies, rather than the areas in which they are already competent or developing competence. This undermines both the learning process of the students and the transmission of indigenous knowledge.

Relevance to current projects in southern Africa

Given all of this, the increasing recognition of the validity of diverse forms of knowledge is welcome, and incorporating indigenous knowledge into education efforts is crucial for many reasons. It is critical to the success of the students, for community integrity, for the maintenance of IKS, and to provide the widest possible range of economic and social opportunities for students and communities. However, translating it into official practice presents numerous challenges. In this section, I briefly describe current efforts in Namibia, Botswana and South Africa to officially recognise the indigenous knowledge of San communities and/or to incorporate IKS into the formal or non-formal (but government-recognised) education systems.

The Village Schools, Namibia

The Village Schools in northwestern Namibia are the only place where San children in southern Africa have access to education in their own language for the first three years of schooling; they are also the only place where conscious efforts have been made to incorporate indigenous knowledge into the requirements for a teacher-training programme. The Village Schools Project (VSP) was designed in the early 1990s to combat the high drop-out rate of Ju|'hoansi students in the (now) Nyae Nyae Conservancy of Namibia, and was initiated in an enthusiastic and supportive environment. Developed by a local NGO in close consultation with the community, with the support of the Ministry of Education and with the input of experienced anthropologists and linguists, the original defining goals of the project included mother-tongue instruction, the incorporation of traditional knowledge and transmission strategies, and the employment of Ju|'hoansi teachers. The Village Schools were set in several small villages, allowing students to remain in their home communities *and* have access to formal education.

At that time, there were no Ju|'hoansi who had attained the Grade 12 certificate required for entry into the course towards the Basic Education Teacher Diploma. Working closely with the community and involved NGOs, the Ministry of Education designed an equivalence programme for the Ju|'hoansi that allowed them to enter into the programme with a Grade 10 certificate plus two years of teaching experience. Furthermore, the Grade 10 subjects that they were required to pass were chosen, and altered, to allow for maximum recognition of the teachers' existing competence based on their cultural knowledge. Thus, at the early phases of the project, the IKS of the Ju|'hoansi were acknowledged and respected, although no formal qualifications were given specifically for traditional knowledge and no explicit standards were set.

If the Village Schools had been designed to remain a private initiative, the teachers would not have been required to have nationally recognised certifications. However, obtaining certification for the teachers was considered desirable for two main reasons. One was sustainability of the school: donor funding was not indefinite and the Village Schools had eventually to be taken over by the government. In addition, official accreditation would allow the teachers to receive the same status and benefits as other teachers, and also to teach in other schools elsewhere in the country if they decided to do so. After the certification of the initial group of teachers based partly on their traditional knowledge, subsequent groups of trainee teachers were required to follow the standard course for teacher training. The Nyae Nyae Village Schools Project was taken over by Namibia's Ministry of Education in 2004 and is no longer considered a 'project'. As of 2006, there were no specific plans to incorporate indigenous knowledge into the teacher-training programme.

Although an important initial focus of the project was on providing schooling closer to home and incorporating the language, knowledge and skills of the home communities, the goal of preparing children to be successful in the government schools soon became – and remains – the central goal of the Village Schools. The successful transfer of children to the government school in Grade 4 is viewed as the primary determinant of the success of the Village Schools. However, the vast majority of students do *not* transfer successfully; in fact, no student from the Village Schools passed Grade 4 at the Tsumkwe school until 2007, when three did. The reasons for this are numerous, complex and interconnected, and I have discussed them in detail elsewhere (Hays 2007). In part, however, this 'failure' to transfer has to do with the enormous gap between the IKS and transmission strategies of the Ju|'hoansi – and the culture in which they are embedded – and those of the government school.

Simultaneously, we can view the students' decision not to remain at the Tsumkwe school as a strategic choice about which kind of knowledge and activity will afford them the best social and economic options later in life. While at the Village Schools, children spend time with elders and parents, participate in activities appropriate to their age, and gain knowledge and understanding of the bush. When children go to the government school in the central town of Tsumkwe, however, they are away from their parents and elders for significant periods of time and there is little occasion for them to learn or practise traditional skills. Significantly, the vast majority of students do not remain at the government school in Tsumkwe but choose to return to their home villages (sometimes repeating another year or two at the Village School).

Although the emphasis of evaluations of the Village Schools has been largely on the transition of the students to the formal government school, and on achieving formal qualifications for students, in practice the students, teachers and communities also recognise other benefits of the project. Moreover, many of the students are choosing traditional knowledge and activities over participation in the government school. For any effort to address the educational situation of the Ju|'hoansi to be successful, these decisions must be understood and respected, and the best way to balance traditional knowledge with access to mainstream opportunities must be determined.

Botswana

I have argued that formal education and IKS are fundamentally incompatible in some ways. A more obvious place to integrate IKS is into informal or vocational training programmes. Government bodies responsible for non-formal education and vocational training in Botswana are moving rapidly in this direction. The Botswana Training Authority (BOTA) has developed standards by which traditional skills in a variety of areas are formally recognised, even if they have not been attained by formal training. Standards developed for traditional knowledge thus far have been developed primarily in areas related to crafts, music/dance and tourism.

Although the assessment standards developed thus far do not link directly to teaching qualifications, the certification of specialised skills, such as tracking, may facilitate efforts to incorporate elders into community-based education efforts. The Department of Non-Formal Education (DNFE) has also drafted some progressive programmes for working with rural populations that build on local culture and languages; however, the implementation of these is hampered by the lack of a government policy on using languages other than Setswana or English in education. Both BOTA and the DNFE are in theory open to the incorporation of non-dominant cultures and languages into their curriculum if policy would permit. 'Indigenous knowledge systems' is not yet a key phrase in their discourses.

Also in Botswana, a collaborative effort has been under way since 2004 to develop an educational approach that will provide remote populations, many of whom are San, with educational options that match their language, culture and needs. Spearheaded by the local NGO Letloa and the University of Botswana, extensive consultations with the Ministry of Education, the DNFE and BOTA have been an important part of defining the approach, and support for the effort is strong within these institutions. An important focus of this project is how to involve San parents and communities more fully in the education of their children, and also to recognise and validate the ways that they are already involved, including in the transmission of IKS. These efforts have faced many obstacles, in terms of both funding and political support, but they are ongoing. The success of these and any related efforts will depend on the extent to which the community and its elders are involved in the process of defining and implementing the project.

South Africa

South Africa's IKS policy is far more progressive and comprehensive than approaches in either Botswana or Namibia, and it is hoped that this policy will provide an example for neighbouring countries and set the stage for a more productive approach to knowledge and learning. However, there are still some gaps, especially in terms of practical implementation. The policy discusses the need to integrate IKS into the education system but does not propose how this can be done, although the policy does discuss the transformation of a 'content-driven' syllabus to a 'problem-solving' one as creating impetus for the recognition of IKS (DST 2004: 17).

The South African National Qualifications Framework (NQF) includes the certification and qualification of trackers, which is one of the skills most relevant to indigenous knowledge maintenance for San communities. Tracking is included under the Tourism, Hospitality and Sport Education and Training Authority (THETA) and three tracker-training courses are currently registered. The Indigenous Peoples of Africa Coordinating Committee (IPACC), a networking organisation based in Cape Town, actively works to promote the certification of traditional knowledge for San communities in southern Africa. IPACC works with local communities in South Africa as well as Botswana and Namibia to increase awareness of their rights regarding indigenous knowledge, and to help them to determine the potential benefits of formal recognition and how indigenous knowledge can be used both for income generation and as a cultural resource (IPACC 2006). IPACC works to ensure that San communities and individuals can be involved at all levels of the development of assessment and accreditation standards. Ideally, the certification of trackers will allow greater employment opportunities for those who have little formal education but extensive environmental knowledge, which will in turn further validate the knowledge systems and skills in the eyes of outsiders and will increase the economic incentive for communities to continue to transmit them.

Ongoing challenges

A persistent problem with – and potential pitfall for – education projects seeking to incorporate 'indigenous knowledge' into the curriculum is that they tend to focus on the information itself rather than on the forms of knowledge transmission. However, according to the understandings presented above, the information that forms the basis of IKS cannot be divided into discrete units and taught for segmented time periods; rather it must be communicated over sustained periods of close contact with the environment and with the community made up of the bearers of this knowledge. Alternative approaches that mimic instructional styles of Western education thus do little to maintain such knowledge systems and have limited success in facilitating transitions to the mainstream schools. Such approaches are generally short-sighted and ultimately unsuccessful. What is needed is a deep restructuring of our conception of 'knowledge', and how it is communicated, in order for us to recognise the legitimacy of IKS. In the example of the Village Schools Project in Namibia, the *intent* to recognise IKS – on their own terms – is present, but without either the long-term funding to support a 'private' school or a clear recognition of IKS by the government, this element is difficult to maintain. Where that recognition does occur, as in South Africa, links between education and indigenous knowledge are lacking.

Why maintain indigenous knowledge?

Given the 'obvious' importance for indigenous peoples of participating in mainstream political and economic systems, the necessity of formal education in order to be able to do so, and the growing environmental, economic and legal restrictions on practising traditional skills, we might reasonably wonder if making efforts to include IKS in educational approaches, formal and non-formal, is a worthwhile endeavour. In this section, I present various perspectives on this question.

One argument in favour of incorporating indigenous knowledge into education systems is pedagogical: children 'learn better' if information is presented to them in a language and context that they can relate to and if their areas of competence are valued rather than denigrated. This approach is gaining increasing recognition in mainstream educational movements, along with increasing recognition of the value of mother-tongue education. Virtually always, however, the ultimate goal is a transition to the dominant language and culture, through success in mainstream educational institutions. Relating education to the home language and culture is seen as more of a stepping stone than an end in and of itself (as described above for the Village Schools). For many indigenous peoples, however, these forms of knowledge *are* valuable in and of themselves, and efforts to incorporate them into education efforts are an important element of maintenance strategies.

Another perspective recognises the sophistication of indigenous knowledge and argues that, far from being obsolete, such knowledge is in fact extremely valuable to humanity in general, for a number of reasons:

> The depth of indigenous knowledge rooted in the long inhabitation of a particular place offers lessons that can benefit everyone, from educator to scientist, as we search for a more satisfying and sustainable way to live on this planet...[I]ndigenous knowledge and ways of knowing are beginning to be recognised as consisting of complex knowledge systems with an adaptive integrity of their own. (Barnhardt & Kawagley 2005: 9)

New directions in science are revealing that many indigenous cultures and philosophies are based on deep understandings about the interconnectedness of life that modern science is only now beginning to grasp. Many indigenous peoples today live in marginal environments such as the Arctic and the Kalahari that are among the first to experience the effects of climate change. The keen observational skills and deep environmental awareness of indigenous peoples can provide an insight and an angle on problems that modern science could not achieve. Indigenous knowledge is thus valuable in its own right and should be nurtured; recognising, validating and incorporating IKS into formal and non-formal education projects will be an important part of efforts in this direction.

Ultimately, the maintenance of indigenous knowledge will rest primarily in its usefulness and relevance to the lives of the indigenous peoples who 'own' it. Simply extracting pieces will not maintain the understanding in which it is embedded. Most indigenous peoples today, especially those in developing countries, are still eking out an existence on the margins of survival. Regardless of the value of their knowledge to the rest of humanity, it will survive only if the bearers of the knowledge themselves see it not abstractly or romantically but as contributing towards their survival. The extent to which TEK is still valuable to indigenous peoples' physical survival varies greatly depending on their circumstances. For many indigenous peoples today – especially those living in marginal environments remote from urban centres, as do most San – this knowledge is still very much alive and crucial to their survival. In such circumstances, to undermine these skills through their non-recognition – as happens in large part through formal education – is to deprive the people themselves of a crucial resource.

Clearly it would be misguided to argue that *only* knowing how to survive in the bush, and in social isolation, is education enough for San people today; that option is rapidly diminishing for them everywhere. However, in many communities, at least at some times, the majority of the community food intake may be through these means. Although it may not be adequate, in these circumstances it is still crucial to survival. Unless and until other means of obtaining food are secure, maintaining the skills that allow them to live from the veld are critical, and people will maintain this as an option to the extent that they are able. Moreover, many San report that they like and want to practise these skills. While parents do want their children to learn how to read and write and to speak English, they also want them to learn how to track and hunt animals and to be able to gather plant foods and to make crafts. People depend on all of these things for survival.

Even if there is agreement on the validity of the effort, a host of practical questions remains. Can IKS be formalised to fit into the hierarchical and compartmentalised systems of modern governments and other organisations? How can the bearers of IKS – usually community elders who have extensive experience, knowledge and skill but who rarely have formal qualifications – be recognised as qualified teachers? Do their transmission strategies match what is expected by outsiders? How does formal recognition impact community dynamics? And, importantly, do they *need* to be formally recognised by outsiders in order for community members to perceive their own knowledge as legitimate? How do we achieve a balance between efforts to formally recognise IKS and a respect for the informality of the transmission strategies and social systems in which they are embedded? These issues require further discussion and debate, and southern African attempts to address the issues described in this chapter will benefit from an understanding of what has worked and what hasn't worked elsewhere. Most important, however, will be a deep understanding of and appreciation for complex local dynamics, and a commitment to involving the community in decision-making processes.

Conclusions

I have argued here that there is a fundamental incompatibility between IKS and the ways that modern education systems (both formal and non-formal) evaluate and measure 'knowledge' and its transmission. Although this is true, it does not mean that formal recognition of IKS should not take place at all. There is a place for formal qualifications, and bearers of IKS should have the opportunity for their skills to be recognised. Formal qualifications will be required in some areas – for example, for indigenous elders or youth who wish to become qualified as teachers in the formal education system – and if these qualifications recognise the knowledge that potential teachers bring with them, this is a positive development.

At the same time, the insistence on formal qualifications can have undesirable consequences, shifting community dynamics and undermining their existing efforts to maintain their own skills and knowledge. For example, gaining certification in a particular skill is generally associated with increased monetary income, or with a new expectation of being financially reimbursed for an activity or service that previously was practised as a normal part of community life. This can create numerous complications, especially in egalitarian communities. If not carefully managed, such situations create enormous tension within the community, and in some cases can lead to refusal to practise traditional skills.

Finally, it must be recognised that San communities and individuals do not, in fact, *require* the validation of outsiders in order for them to perceive their own knowledge as legitimate. For many, their knowledge is important on its own terms – as a means of survival, identity or community cohesion. The decisions of indigenous peoples to remain outside the formal systems – of education, economy and others – are as valid as efforts to incorporate them.

Notes

1   The Ju|'hoansi are one of the San language groups. The | symbol represents one of the click sounds that characterise San languages.

2   Scott argues that those such as modern research institutions, international corporations and development officials have 'made their successful institutional way in the world' through the systematic denigration of the practical value of local knowledge (1998: 331–332).

References

Barnhardt R & Kawagley OA (2005) Indigenous knowledge systems and Alaska native ways of knowing. *Anthropology and Education Quarterly* 36(1): 8–23

Battiste M & Henderson-Youngblood J (2000) *Protecting indigenous knowledge and heritage: A global challenge.* Purich's Aboriginal Issues Series. Saskatoon, SK: Purich

Blurton Jones N & Konnor M (1976) !Kung knowledge of animal behaviour. In R Lee and I DeVore (eds) *Kalahari hunter-gatherers.* Cambridge: Aldine

Draper P (1976) Social and economic constraints on child life among the !Kung. In R Lee and I DeVore (eds) *Kalahari hunter-gatherers.* Cambridge: Aldine

DST (Department of Science and Technology, South Africa) (2004) *Indigenous knowledge systems.* Policy document. Pretoria: DST. Accessed 30 March 2009, http://www.dst.gov.za/publications-policies/strategies-reports/reports/IKS_Policy%20PDF.pdf/view?searchterm=IKS%20policy%20document

Green M (2000) Participatory development and the appropriation of agency in southern Tanzania. *Critique of Anthropology* 20(1): 67–89

Guenther M (1976) From hunters to squatters: Social and cultural change among the farm San of Ghanzi, Botswana. In R Lee and I DeVore (eds) *Kalahari hunter-gatherers.* Cambridge: Aldine

Guenther M (1999) *Tricksters and trancers: Bushman religion and society.* Bloomington: Indiana University Press

Hays J (2007) Education, rights and survival for the Nyae Nyae Ju|'hoansi: Illuminating global and local discourses. PhD dissertation, University at Albany, State University of New York

IPACC (Indigenous Peoples of Africa Coordinating Committee) (2006) *IPACC southern African workshop on the formalisation of the traditional knowledge of tracking.* Accessed 30 March 2009, http://www.ipacc.org.za/uploads/docs/Tsumkwe_English.pdf

Johnson M (ed.) (1992) *Lore: Capturing traditional environmental knowledge.* Ottawa: Dene Cultural Institute and the International Development Research Centre

Konner M (1976) Maternal care, infant behaviour and development among the !Kung. In R Lee and I DeVore (eds) *Kalahari hunter-gatherers.* Cambridge: Aldine

Le Roux W (1999) *Torn apart: San children as change agents in a process of assimilation.* Windhoek: WIMSA

Le Roux W (2002) *The challenges of change: A tracer study of San preschool children in Botswana.* The Hague: Bernard Van Leer Foundation

Marshall L (1976) *The !Kung of Nyae Nyae.* Cambridge, MA: Harvard University Press

McGregor D (2004) Traditional ecological knowledge and sustainable development: Towards coexistence. In M Blaser, H Feit & G McRae (eds) *In the way of development: Indigenous peoples, life projects and globalisation.* London and New York: Zed Books

Scott JC (1998) *Seeing like a state: How certain schemes to improve the human condition have failed.* New Haven, CT: Yale University Press

Tanaka J (1980) *The San hunter-gatherers of the Kalahari.* Tokyo: University of Tokyo Press

15 Domestic workers and knowledge in everyday life

Jonathan Grossman

Introduction

Historically, domestic workers in South Africa were 'pioneers of precarity'. Even legally, they could be hired and fired under any terms, or in fact no terms. Their legal precarity was mirrored by a generalised social denigration in which the commonest defining adjective for a domestic worker was either 'only' or 'just'. Over years of struggle, aspects of the legal situation have been changed to afford formal limited protection, but there remain striking continuities in lived experience.

The women of the backyard worked, and continue to work, as caregivers, confidantes, nurses, childminders, secretaries, cleaners, security guards, therapists and in many other jobs. They straddle the apparent divide between workplace and home, their workplace being a home and much domestic work being unpaid. They are placed in a daily struggle of resistance, for survival, for hope and happiness at the barricades of everyday life. All of this and more involves learning and teaching – processes of knowledge production and sharing. It could not be otherwise, given the range of experience that it involves and the forms and techniques of survival that it requires. Yet in the context of deeply structured social inequalities, which are replicated in hierarchies of knowledge, much of this is devalued, denigrated and thereby wasted. It seems that, at most, we have the recognition of a level of experiential learning, increasingly often tied to an overriding concern with a 'skills deficit'. This focuses on the presumed limitations of what is known, and on what is apparently not known, rather than on the depths, range and content of what is known.

My engagement in organisational, political and educational work with domestic workers has been a set of encounters with centres of knowledge generation, production and sharing. The academic works from which I have most effectively learned and from which I can most easily teach have that same character of engagement in and with everyday struggles of ordinary working-class people.

In her examination of 'post-Vygotskian perspectives', Cooper (2005: 57) presents Engestrom's view that 'everyday thinking has, in principle, the same theoretical potential as the consciously elaborated concepts of science'. We know that workers can learn from the experiences of everyday life. But do we allow for the possibility that a domestic worker, using everyday thinking, can produce analytical insights into the complexities of everyday life and social context? It is possible to identify the emotional responses of domestic workers with the complexities of relations between people. But do we allow for the possibility that a domestic worker, using everyday thinking, can produce analytical insights into those complexities? Can profound analytical insights be conveyed through forms other than the scientific ordering of data? Or, in this era of neo-liberal globalisation, do we recognise profundity only in the forms and structured hierarchies of knowledge production of class society? Could profound insight not also lie within the domestic worker and her thoughts, discussions and engagements with other domestic workers? Can we recognise this if it is happening – do we have the 'research capacity'?

My point of departure in this chapter is that learning, sharing knowledge and knowledge production should be recognised as aspects of what happens in the context of the everyday experience of domestic workers. What follows is an outline of some encounters with domestic workers and their ideas in order to explore the questions I have raised above. In doing so I will suggest ways of seeing and hearing that acknowledge systematisation, analytical explanation and insight from these workers.[1]

Abolition, beetroot, claims and denials, ignorant educators and changed relations between people?

Imagining abolition

In 1986, in the midst of a state of emergency, the then new South African Domestic Workers Union (SADWU) produced a manifesto. Many of its demands could be assessed as limited reforms, but among them, however, is the apparently unlikely demand for the abolition of domestic work. A critique of the limited nature of the reforms demanded might easily lead one to argue that we are dealing with the limitations of trade unionism, reformism or low levels of political consciousness. When such critiques are made, they do not encompass the demand for the abolition of domestic work – so it is not commented upon. By itself, it is a demand that could be challenging the very roots of commodification, alienated labour, patriarchy and structured social inequality in class society. It could be about the total transformation of the way in which people treat each other, such that domestic work is not imposed, forced, alienated, exploited. It could be read as the demand for an end to everything that domestic workers most hate about their situation – the demand for at least a minimum utopia; it could be an extraordinary act of imaginative vision.

Beetroot and utopian thinking

More than 10 years later, in the early days of democracy in the new South Africa, a group of domestic workers was discussing possibilities for the future. I asked specifically what they would most love to be doing. Of the approximately 20 workers involved in the discussion, all except one said they would most love either to have a small shop or to have a small cooking or sewing business. These options reflect rather than challenge many of the continuing problems of structured social inequality in the new South Africa. While they may provide some women with opportunities for clawing their way out of the worst of poverty, they leave untouched and in some aspects replicate structures of patriarchy and class society. In the character of the meetings, each of the participants was required to speak and describe her dream. It was the turn of the last participant – the oldest woman there. She announced that she would most love to grow beetroot. There was some laughter but no directed discussion and the workers continued to talk about other issues.

I have never had the opportunity to ask the domestic worker about this dream,[2] but I like to think that at some stage in her life she had grown beetroot and found peace and happiness and satisfaction in doing that. Maybe she had been able to derive some sort of income. Yet the dream was puzzling, especially in its contrast to the pattern of the other dreams. I have thought more about it since then and wondered what would need to happen for her dream to be realised. It may be part of an achievable middle-class dream to be able to escape the rat race and go grow things on a smallholding, although this means that daily life remains unchanged for the many and in some respects must necessarily be unchanged for such escapes to be possible for a few. But for this woman it would mean confrontation with the whole range of power relations and structures of inequality that allow some people from the middle class to escape to smallholdings, but that make a million working-class women, including this particular woman, a domestic worker and not a beetroot grower. More than that, instead of this domestic worker's dream being a bit strange, couldn't this be a case of utopian thinking, challenging and breaking socially constructed boundaries of oppression and exploitation?

Claiming and denying knowledge

A group of domestic workers had been meeting over many months around the period of South Africa's first democratic election in 1994. They were invited to address the issue of 'wage negotiation' by acting out a play and so chose the characters accordingly – the worker, the woman employer, the employer's husband, the employer's mother and the employer's children. As they acted out the scene, they presumed but did not explicitly name another character – a group of domestic workers. The play showed insights into complex family dynamics, power relations within the family, psychologies of different characters, structured processes of breaking the isolation of the worker by invoking the unnamed additional character – the group of workers. At the actual negotiations, the worker made no demands. She adopted an apparently meek and submissive attitude. When the employer responded by invoking power and aggression, the worker went silent. Afterwards she went to different members of the family, acting out hurt, fear and some desperation. They responded to this by demanding more sympathy from the employer. At different stages, there were appeals to the additional character for advice and support. Eventually the husband demanded peace and quiet in his home and insisted that the fighting be stopped with a meaningful pay increase. The worker had both survived and 'won'.

It is possible to have seen the play, or a real-life version of it, and have reached two very different conclusions. One would focus on the worker's meekness, silence and lack of aggressive pursuit of her rights. A second would focus on the depths of her insight into the power dynamics and how to survive in them. It could be argued that it was precisely this insight that led her to consciously adopt a demeanour of meekness and silence as weapons of survival. The same situation, in other words, may be read as a reflection of the worker as victim, or as a reflection of the depths of the worker's knowledge in negotiating successfully in a situation that would otherwise make her simply the victim. Put differently, it could be seen as reflecting the reality that each domestic worker is her own shop steward. The former reading presents the analytical knowledge of the viewer. The latter reading recognises and analyses analytical knowledge of the worker.

Feigning ignorance

In the process leading up to the 1994 democratic elections, Adelaide, herself a domestic worker, was an educator responsible for training other domestic workers, through the union and an African National Congress (ANC) branch, in the technicalities of voting. On the day of the elections, her employer approached her. Speaking English in a slow, deliberately simplified way much as one might use with an uncomprehending child, she said: 'Adelaide, it's elections today. Did you know about that? Do you know about voting?' Adelaide continued to portray ignorance. It was a carefully made strategic choice: run the risk of confronting the employer with her mistaken presumptions of ignorance, or reassure the employer by confirming the presumptions. Adelaide chose the latter. It is safer, in the experience of many domestic workers, to confirm the stereotype of ignorance rather than risk being branded and possibly victimised as 'too clever'. So, for the employer, Adelaide the educator became Adelaide, just a domestic worker, Adelaide the ignorant. When Adelaide recounted this story to other workers, she did so with humour and pride, mocking the utter stupidity and social ignorance of the employer. She did this in the context not of an isolated encounter with the employer, but at a union meeting with other domestic workers. Other workers listening acknowledged both her humour and pride, recognising in her story an assertion of dignity and strategic thinking through silence.

Wisdom and the denigrated compassion of the backyard

I have used the moments sketched above to illustrate an underlying question that they pose: are the limitations that we might identify analytically (the problems) in the story, in the storyteller; or are they in the way in which we make sense of the story and the storyteller? That is, are they embedded in the story and storyteller, or are they embedded in the frameworks through which we see and hear them? In the next section, I want to probe this question, drawing on a story – some might say the analysis – provided by Mama Ethel.

The story was told in 1996 as South Africa was beginning to immerse itself in the Truth and Reconciliation Commission (TRC) process. A group of domestic workers, meeting within the framework of an ANC branch and SADWU, decided that they also wanted to tell their stories. They knew that these stories were not going to be part of the

TRC process. Instead they told them to each other and sometimes to a researcher who was asked to come and record them. One such story was told by Mama Ethel.[3]

Mama Ethel described in vivid detail how doctors and students had discussed in front of her whether or not to remove her womb. She says:

> They didn't know that I understand English. Because most of the people from Transkei or from home talks little English or some of them even don't understand English. One of the doctors argued that they should perform the operation because 'there's so many students who need this operation of taking wombs'. Another argued: 'But can't we just give her chance to have because maybe she – every woman would like to have a chance. So why don't we give her one chance because she will always come back to us.' So this doctor said, 'But where will we get somebody to help us [meaning someone on whom to perform the operation as part of student training]? We have got students now. They are waiting here.' They just tell me there are students who must see this operation. No permission. You don't ask apparatus what you are going to do. Because they don't talk. Here, we are just…apparatus for the white doctors because there was no black doctor, no, not even a coloured doctor. It was only white students. So they used, it's how they learn from us. You, you are like animals.

Mama Ethel listened to this discussion among the staff and then took a decision. She refused to have the operation in those circumstances; she waited until the medical staff were gone and, without telling them, left the hospital. She told her story shortly before she died of cancer of the uterus.

At a different point in the interviews, she explains something of her approach to dealing with an employer who repeatedly took out 'her frustrations' on Mama Ethel:

> They can't stand to be unhappy, to have no money. But even that I come to understand. She is a woman looking after a small child. A divorced woman. She is young. She wants life but she has got a child to her. She is working. She must share her pay. It's me, it's the house; it's her and her child. I mean, I come to understand why does she – something upset her, she comes and take out her frustration because she has got no husband to share the hard – the hardship. So I used to put myself into her place, and I decided not to leave her. I must look after this woman. She needs someone. She is a woman looking after her child; she must have a house for the child and her. But she must work so she needs someone to look after the child… She has got so much responsibility. So she has to take it out to someone. So I'm the only person around she can take out all her frustrations.

Then Mama Ethel expresses the regret that the employer never was able to see her as a friend:

> Because if you have got something, you can just call a friend. Just talk. While you talk it out, it's boiling down to you. Then afterwards, you are

relieved and you have got new plans for it. But [me] being a black woman, she couldn't do that to me. And yet that would have helped her.

The first part of the story was an account of her own denigration and suffering at the hands of the medical profession. Having told that story, Mama Ethel went on to talk about more ordinary everyday experiences at work. She also had some views about hope. Talking about her white employer specifically and white employers in general, she said:

> You are not used to suffering. To have nothing and depend on neighbours. Once you have got no money, you think it's the end or the end of the world. Whereas, we still have the hope. We just go to the neighbours and tell them you have got nothing. Then you share what she have got. In return, once you get something you bring it and say, I'm lucky this month. I've got this, then we are also free. Give it back by sharing.

For me, Mama Ethel is explaining her knowledge as an expression of what Gramsci (1926), in apparently very different circumstances, may have called 'the organic capacity of the working class'. In the context of the individual isolation of the domestic worker, she is invoking a form of collectivism. She is grounding it in lived experience – the lived experience of suffering and struggle. Her argument is that it generates sharing among the victims. That sharing is the basis for a different and better future, grounded in survival of the intolerable present. Some might call it central to utopian thinking.

Bloch and the hieroglyph of hope

Some years later, I was trying to do some work around the issue of 'hope'. I was specifically interested in hope as a crucial component of mass struggle, and the relationship of hope to socialism. Internet searches gave me very little – usually taking me to the *Christian Science Monitor* and/or writings about religion. Then a colleague referred me to Ernst Bloch's 'hieroglyph of hope', discussed in his book *The Principle of Hope*. I was quite excited and I tried several times to read this work. But I found it impenetrable, obscure and unhelpful. I turned instead to commentaries about it and found two (Aronson 1999; Roberts 1990), which for me were absorbing, clear and stimulating. I extracted two quotes that have profoundly inspired me and that I have used in some of my academic work. I do so without pretending that they come from a comprehensive reading of Bloch.

Bloch says that 'thinking means venturing beyond' (quoted in Roberts 1990: 29), and that 'to be human really means to have utopias' (quoted in Aronson 1999: 472). To me there is an enormous amount of knowledge embodied in each of these short quotes. I wonder what is in the rest of the dense, obtuse and impenetrable work – but I have taken more than enough.

Elevating and denigrating knowledge

I have translated what Mama Ethel said, as someone else would have done had she been speaking in her home language, isiXhosa. I have used accounts of Bloch to

213

do the same for me – translate the dense and impenetrable into accounts that I can understand, and that take me to some of the knowledge that was already there in his dense and impenetrable work. In academic terms, this is often what is done to the knowledge of domestic workers. It is there already but it is spoken in languages that the academic may not immediately understand. Sometimes it is silenced. There is translation of different kinds and the translation gets published. At my and other universities, if it is in a peer-reviewed subsidy-generating journal, that publication is called research. There is likely to be an acknowledgement and statement of thanks to the worker/s who shared their stories, even knowledge. But as far as new knowledge goes, that is signified by the peer-reviewed publication and its forms and packaging, not the content of the workers' knowledge. Without that form and packaging, there is at best knowledge and learning, not even the possibility of new analytical insights. With that form and packaging, it is necessarily only deemed to be knowledge when located in and produced by the academic.

I don't know of domestic workers who write dense, impenetrable works. But I have heard many workers say things that are profound and rich and that embody an enormous depth of knowledge. Is what Mama Ethel says a simple description, embodied in a story? Or is it a complex understanding, involving complex processes of knowledge production about complex issues – simply expressed at each point? Is this story told by Mama Ethel the description of experience, reflection, interpretation and analysis? Or is it just storytelling? It is surely all of these performed through storytelling. She describes, ordering and organising as she does so. She reflects, reviewing what she has described. She explains, accounting for what she has described, and in the process provides an analysis of class, race and gender. Then she connects, using her analysis to develop her insights on social experience, action and hope. Why is it that Mama Ethel may be so easily construed as speaking only 'common sense' whereas the major written work from Bloch constitutes knowledge? We consider the two quotes from Bloch knowledge on their own – as they were for me. Why do we afford them that character? And why are they considered to be knowledge more than two insights from a domestic worker? Is it because of where they come from, what surrounds them, how they are presented and who speaks the words? In the case of Mama Ethel, are we looking at emotional sensitivity, or are we also looking at a depth of understanding of a complex situation? Are we looking at kindness or wisdom? Could it be that we are looking at both? What makes one richer than the other? Why is some knowledge elevated as one, and some knowledge denigrated as the other?

Knowledge, power and the academy

The answers lie partly in the power of the academy to authorise some knowledge as 'new'. Although this begs the question of the power of the academy itself, there are forms and conventions that determine what is new knowledge. The university and the academics within it are the authorising power of what constitutes knowledge and new knowledge. 'Research' is the authorised embodiment of new knowledge. How much of it, however, is simply myth, fabrication, nonsense, propaganda, ideological obfuscation and/or packaging of what was already known? After many years at a university, I am increasingly struck by how little of what is portrayed as knowledge *is* knowledge, let alone new knowledge. The entire academic enterprise would come crashing down if it were the case that 'simple, ordinary, uneducated' people – people who are 'just' domestic workers – could also think and produce complex thoughts and ideas; that different sites of everyday life might be centres of the intellectual universe. This in addition to – or, maybe even more threateningly, instead of – the authorised centre: the academy.

What makes everyday thinking everyday? The answer to this question is as circular as suggesting that scientific thinking is scientific because it is thought by scientific thinkers. Too often, embedded in the question is a hierarchy of knowledge which relegates everyday knowledge to secondary status – not because it is everyday, but because it does not follow the forms or reside in the person of the scientific thinker. The knowledge, ordering, making sense of a domestic worker is very often either not conveyed because she is denied an audience, or dismissed because it is conveyed in a story. In scientific knowledge we are concerned with validation. When a domestic worker tells a story to other domestic workers, I have seen and heard the signs of recognition and affirmation. When workers affirm a story, they can be doing something beyond relating to it emotionally or recognising it through experience. They are also moving intellectually through time and space to make sense of something that they did not personally experience. Put differently, they are thinking abstractly. If they relate to the immediacy of the story, which is not immediate in their own experience, it is not simply because it is similar to what they know from experience. It is also because they can make sense of what they do not know from immediate experience by abstract thinking – by ordering, interpreting and making sense of the story. In the everyday knowing of the domestic worker, there are processes of systematisation (Fischer 2005), reflection, organisation of experiences, and ordering of what is encountered. All these processes constitute analytical abstraction and explanation, and are not appropriately understood either as formalised scientific thinking or as simply common-sense everyday experiential learning.

If a great novelist writes a story, it is searched and researched for profound meaning and analytical insight. Although some scientific thinkers might have a problem with the form, it is usually enough to point to the greatness of the novelist to allow for the possibility that there is an insight for which to search. If a domestic worker tells the story, we seem to be able to allow for the fact that there is everyday, experiential knowledge in the story, but not for the possibility that there is a great intellectual insight. For that to happen, the story must be taken from the worker, deciphered, translated, and transformed into the forms with which the academy is secure. If knowledge production and specifically new knowledge production is deemed to exist, it becomes the knowledge production of the academic and not the knowledge production of the storyteller in whose story the knowledge is embedded. This is often turned into a problem of levels of knowledge and knowledge production versus new knowledge production. Those may be issues, but it is in fact a problem of knowledge appropriation and expropriation, packaging and formal certification – a problem of the politics of knowledge, not its closeness to or distance from the truth.

It is testimony to a deeply diseased society when it can only trivialise the knowledge and skill involved in being a domestic worker, and draw out of it only recognition of ignorance and lack of skills. It is equally a sign of disease when a society limits the enormous amount of knowledge, exemplified in what I have been discussing, to the task of survival and 'survival skills'. Most progressives would accept, and even insist, that domestic workers have everyday knowledge. The problem is simply deepened when attempts to assert and recognise that knowledge carry with them imposed boundaries and limitations on how far that knowledge could possibly extend. There is nothing trivial about practical everyday knowledge, but the way that it is recognised suggests that only a trivialised version of that knowledge is possible. Simply put, the domestic worker knows how to boil an egg, but could she ever reflect on which came first, the chicken or the egg? She knows how to deal with her employer, but could she ever imagine a future in which she did not need to do this and instead could use her capacities for something else, something more? She can make sensible suggestions about practical childcare, but can she tell us anything about love and compassion? She survives oppression and exploitation, but could she develop analytical insights that help us understand them?

Researching knowledge

How do we research knowledge itself? What do we actually know about the knowledge of domestic workers? Does anyone ask? And if and when we do, do we presume that we must ask only about the immediate, concrete and practical, and not about the abstract, complex and immaterial? There are unfortunate echoes of this reductionism and effective denigration in the autonomist ethos inspiring much current thinking on the left. Some of that thinking insists that ordinary workers are concerned only with the immediate and the concrete – jobs, houses, water, electricity – and not with the abstract and the less immediate – such as 'politics' and 'theory', and love and hope. It is as if there is a stages theory of humaneness, which is complemented by an identity politics when it recognises the domestic worker as human subject only when she leaves/arrives (migration studies) and/or brings difference (diversity studies).

Of course there are alternatives and resistances to this even in the academy. There are important bodies of academic work within and across different disciplines that insist on recognition of the lived experience and knowledge of everyday life. The problem is the context of the power relations in which such work is swallowed, smothered and absorbed into the forms and structures of academic production. In recognising, asserting and affirming the knowledge of the storyteller and the form of the story through academic work, the problem in the real context is always going to be that it requires and rests on the authority of the academic. This reproduces rather than challenges the notion that the academic person and the academic form are inherently closer to truth on a hierarchy of knowledge. The very process of assertion and affirmation can end up replicating, rather than challenging, when it comes through structures and in forms that insist on and/or presume hierarchy.

The conjunctural window: Challenges and possibilities

In the ideological hegemony of 'market thinking', politics is ordinarily reduced to economics, and economics to arithmetic. It becomes primarily about relationships between and the distribution of things. Through those processes, the power relations between people, and the possibilities of challenging these, become obscured. This chapter has sought to examine how this applies to domestic workers, ordinary working-class people, and their knowledge in general. Domestic workers are working in a context that excludes almost no issues or instances of relationships between people. In the South African context, there are additionally conjunctural features of domestic work making for a particularly complex experience of change and continuity amid structures of oppression and exploitation, and, partly as a result, for a particularly rich site of learning and knowledge production. These features include:

- Transition from informality and lack of regulation to formality and regulation through the extension of legislation.
- A sector with a majority of women employers in the context of a gender division of labour.
- An increasing number of black employers in the context of a racial division of labour.
- Working-class employers in the context of structures of occupation based on class.
- A massive sector of paid employment in the context of mass unemployment where much domestic work is unpaid.
- Work activities that are often uniform despite very rigidly structured socio-historical divides between, for example, the employed domestic worker, the unemployed woman doing domestic work, and the publicly funded 'community health worker'.
- Beyond that, domestic workers fit into the growing category of the working poor of the global village. They are likely to be inhabitants of the 'planet of slums' (Davis 2006).

Domestic workers and domestic work are rich sources of intellectual life. There is much to learn about the ways in which people relate to each other in the contexts of deeply structured multiple oppressions and exploitation, and the ways in which these could be challenged. For those of us located in the academy, the possibility and challenge is there to do this in ways that are grounded in recognition of the knowledge domestic workers carry with them.

Several points flow out of my discussion in this chapter:

- Those who believe that there are distinct hierarchies of knowledge, which order everyday, common-sense, experiential knowledge further from truth and insight than academic, abstract, scientific knowledge, have to say so and make the intellectual argument – rather than simply rely on the structures of power that have already confirmed their belief.
- Some of us may believe that there is a distinction between different forms of knowledge but no necessary hierarchy of proximity to truth and depth of complexity in that distinction. If so, we must actively resist the implicit and

explicit affirmation of exactly those hierarchies even in the ways in which we seek to question them.

- We are challenged to find better ways of seeing and hearing that move beyond the obfuscation of domestic workers as silent and invisible. Put differently, we are challenged to find better ways of 'researching' domestic work, domestic workers and their knowledge.

- To do this, and other important things, we have to be able to imagine. Specifically, we have to be able to imagine people other than academics, forms other than peer-reviewed publication and sites other than the university as centres of knowledge production and of the intellectual universe. Beyond that, we have to allow for the possibility that they may be better, more productive, more penetrating and more socially useful centres.

- In seeking to do that, we need to look for the appropriate ways to participate in, try to contribute to, and learn from the processes of collective organisation, mobilisation, action and sharing that are centres of the intellectual universe of everyday life for people outside the academy. I mean this as a matter of regular, ongoing practice, not an historical once-off from the past.

Conclusion

As simple as all this may be, none of it sits easily within the academy. I have recounted the story of Mama Ethel to progressive colleagues and listened to responses that recognise that it is a sad story but see in her decision a reflection of the passivity of the domestic worker. As one colleague put it, 'She just decided to go and die.' Mama Ethel was faced with a choice – between her health and her dignity. She chose her dignity. It came to mean that she was going to die from cancer when that may have been delayed through medical intervention. With differing specificities, it is a choice facing millions of multiply oppressed and exploited people every day. In the reality, she did something very different than simply accept that choice. She took an additional decision – something that, had it been written by Bloch, might have been a profound dictum within a hieroglyph of hope: 'No one else should ever have to face the same choice between their health and their dignity.' It took her to the founding conference of the domestic workers union, to the founding meeting of a branch of the newly unbanned ANC, to other domestic workers in a set of organisational activities that she pursued quietly and resolutely. All of this was based on her making sense of her own experience, and using that knowledge as the guiding basis to further action. She was explicitly determined to tell her story; determined that it should be heard, and that it be understood not just as an account of how things were, but as a call to action about changing them.

I am not sure where exactly this falls in terms of the orthodox dichotomies and hierarchies of knowledge. It is not new knowledge, even less does it become new when this chapter is published. Although I have been involved in sharing the knowledge and it has been shared in part through an academic conference and publication, it was generated in a very different process. Hopefully its validation will lie in advances in the struggles of everyday life, rather than merely in peer review and publication.

Whatever else it may or may not be, that knowledge seems to be deeply socially useful, valuable and important. It becomes more so, not less, because in various ways and forms it is knowledge generated in the everyday experience of millions of ordinary working-class people. Its extraordinariness lies in its ordinariness. It is happening millions of times over all over the place, every day. If it is apparently silent, it is because of ears that too often cannot hear. If it is seemingly invisible, it is because of eyes that too often cannot see. If it is apparently individualised and atomised, it is also part the struggle of everyday life embracing millions. When it is used by people to coalesce into united demands and action, history is made. When it is organised into assertive mutual solidarity, it offers surely the best prospects for that 'other world' that must be made possible. With their work and their lives placing them in such centres of learning, we should approach domestic workers to learn what they have to tell us and teach us about those issues. Perhaps there will indeed be no knowledge to elevate as 'new'. If we allow the possibility that there will be rich knowledge, deep knowledge, socially valuable, useful and insightful knowledge, that it may be about complexities and abstractions as well as the concrete and immediate, we may be rewarded. There are illuminating, socially useful hieroglyphs of hope already existing, already known, and waiting to be newly respected, shared and used.

Notes

1   Thanks to the domestic worker collectives of SADWU Sea Point, Masiphathisane and East London. Thanks also to Jane van der Riet.

2   This was many years before beetroot became notorious as a method of dealing with HIV/AIDS according to the health minister. So this dream was not about a niche in the market!

3   Interviewed by Jane van der Riet, June and July 1996. Mama Ethel requested that we use her name, and is quoted with her permission.

References

Aronson R (1999) Hope after hope? *Social Research* 66(2): 471–494

Cooper L (2005) Towards a theory of pedagogy, learning and knowledge in an 'everyday' context: A case study of a South African trade union. PhD thesis, University of Cape Town, South Africa

Davis M (2006) *Planet of slums.* London: Verso

Fischer MCB (2005) The methodology of 'systematisation' and its relevance to the academy. In J Crowther, V Galloway & I Martin (eds) *Popular education: Engaging the academy.* Leicester: NIACE

Gramsci (1926) Once again on the organic capacities of the working class. Accessed 1 August 2006, http://www.marxists.org/archive/gramsci/1926/10/organic_capabilities.htm

Roberts RH (1990) *Hope and its hieroglyph.* Atlanta, GA: Scholars Press

16 The gender order of knowledge: Everyday life in a welfare state

Gunilla Härnsten and Ulla Rosén

Introduction

Sweden is often presented as a country that has succeeded in establishing a high degree of gender equality within society, and in many ways this is true. However, the time has come to critically examine the results of efforts made during the last century in this regard.

Social citizenship as a dimension of citizenship can be regarded as affording basic security to people. By being citizens we have the right to a fundamental level of security, but we also have certain obligations to fulfil. Historically, the Swedish welfare system developed two ways of dispensing welfare benefits: through insurances and through allowances. Payment of insurances was attached to wage labour and as a consequence the power order of gender was built in. Women's participation in the labour market has always been less than men's and women's work has always been paid less than men's work, and this is still the case. Unpaid labour, associated predominantly with women, the private sphere and informal learning processes, is not considered valid for claiming the full benefits of social citizenship. Thus women have been the predominant recipients of welfare as allowances throughout Sweden's history and this continues to be so, although they also are producers of welfare in the sense that they are responsible for the health and well-being of their families and others.

This chapter reflects on some of the work being done by a newly established interdisciplinary project in Sweden that is investigating the gender relations that prevail in working life and in education, with a view to challenging and transforming them. Our focus is on the processes that have contributed to marginalising the experience-based knowledge of women, and which have led to its classification as domestic and humanitarian rather than political. We are interested in the daily life issues that women experience and the knowledge that women have acquired through their experience – knowledge that is often undervalued and in many cases has been discarded or lost. In this chapter, we highlight the consequences of this silencing for the construction of women's social citizenship, and their unequal access to rights and opportunities. Within the concept of gender order we also include aspects of class and ethnicity.

Analysis of gender relations is extremely important when examining the content and design of education at all levels in Swedish society. In reflecting on the social changes that have taken place in Sweden, we also see parallels with the erosion of so-called indigenous knowledge in other contexts (Odora Hoppers 2002) in the face of attempts at standardisation and mass production of education. We see an urgent need to develop ways of preserving such knowledge, and believe that some of the lessons from the Swedish context may be of interest within the wider international perspective, and may perhaps give rise to some comparative research.

In this chapter, we provide some background on the concept of citizenship and on the Swedish welfare state in order to situate our analysis of the gendered nature of social citizenship. We then discuss the gendering of knowledge and analyse this phenomenon from a feminist critique. Finally, we propose some ways for making this silenced, gendered knowledge visible within the Swedish context in the hope that it will resonate with other contexts.

Social citizenship

In order to understand the mechanisms that have resulted in the marginalising and silencing of women's experience-based knowledge within the Swedish welfare state, two key concepts need to be discussed: citizenship, and the private and public spheres.

Citizenship

In the 1950s, British sociologist TH Marshall (1950, 1964) defined citizenship as consisting of three different dimensions: civil, political and social. Civil citizenship gives citizens the right to certain individual freedoms – for example, freedom of speech, ownership, and equality of justice – and these are guaranteed by the juridical system. Political citizenship provides the right to participate in elections and is associated with citizens' roles in influencing parliament and local government. Social citizenship guarantees basic security independent of income but also includes certain rights – for example, the right to education. Marshall also maintained that democratisation implies a historical development of citizenship: the civil dimension occurred first, during the eighteenth century; the political, during the nineteenth century; and the social, during the twentieth century. Marshall did not, however, question the fact that the citizenship he was discussing referred exclusively to men, and suggested that 'the status of women, or at least married women, was in some respect peculiar' (1964: 78). Despite his gendered perspective, Marshall's ideas have remained uncontested for a long time and continue to have significant influence on researchers who are engaged in analysing and designing different types of welfare states.

However, since the mid 1980s, researchers have begun to critique his views, mainly from feminist perspectives. Wendy Sarvasy (1997) claims that Marshall regards women as second-class citizens and that he completely ignores the significance of women's unpaid work on their social citizenship. For Marshall and many others, the masculine construction of citizenship is unproblematic. Carole Pateman (1988) argues in her book *The Sexual Contract* that Marshall has uncritically adopted John Locke's account of the social contract between man and master. She claims that in Locke's thinking the citizen was undoubtedly a man. This idea has been entrenched and, in many respects, has had considerable influence on the construction of notions of both society and citizenship. By introducing the concept 'sexual contract', Pateman demonstrates that citizenship for women is not only different from the way it is constructed for men, but it also appears differently in the private and public spheres. The citizenship rights of women are regarded in different ways depending on whether the context is the private or the public domain (Pateman 1988).

Private and public spheres

In contrast to men's activities, women's activities have been located largely in the private sphere and generally are not attributed any value for social citizenship. And yet, during times of social and economic crisis it is often women who have mobilised an alternative welfare system by conducting their 'private' commitments –such as cooking, childcare and healthcare – in the more public arena. In considering this social pattern, Barbara Einhorn (1999) warns about 'the trap of civil society', where women's role is marginalised as humanitarian rather than political. Both historically and currently, the struggle for social citizenship has been a central issue for women as political actors (Björk 2000; Florin 2006; Leira 1992; Lister 2003; Sainsbury 1999; Wikander 2006).

Ruth Lister (2003) also focuses on the gendered nature of social citizenship. Unlike civil and political citizenship, social citizenship includes, in addition to rights and obligations, the demand for access to resources. Therefore a perspective on gender power relations is necessary in order to expose these inequalities. She draws a distinction between 'the citizen – the worker' and 'the citizen – the carer', which gives a more complex view of the private/public border. As suggested, regardless of which welfare regime has been in power, the wage-earning citizen has still been privileged at the cost of the caring citizen (Sainsbury 1999). This distinction continues to make social citizenship different for those who are wage earners than for those who are not.[1] It is also possible to turn the discussion the other way round and to argue that unpaid work, particularly in the private sphere, is not considered proper work, and that those who perform such work do not accrue the same benefits as 'the citizen – the worker'.

Background on the Swedish welfare state

The development of the Swedish welfare state was preceded by three significant changes within the society: proletarianisation, democratisation and urbanisation. The process of proletarianisation coincided with the rise of industrialisation and with it a decline in the rural population and a corresponding increase in an urban working class dependent on wage labour. With the growth of capitalism, investment in land became less attractive as the importance of capital increased. This implied changes in the political order as more and more men passed the wage limit to become eligible for participation in national elections. This levelling of political power occurred in tandem with the new socio-economic order in society. Eric Hobsbawm (1962) refers to these economic and political changes as the 'double revolution'. In Sweden these processes developed fairly smoothly as political citizenship with the right to vote had been established earlier on – for men in 1909, and for women in 1919. Thus, with both civil and political citizenship achieved, the claim for social citizenship could begin.

Decisions to establish a welfare system that would be accessible to everyone were taken early on. Further developments resulted in what Gösta Esping-Andersen (1990) has called 'the social-democratic welfare state'. This meant that welfare was organised within the growing public sector and distributed on an individual basis, in contrast to other systems that prioritise the family or the market. In Sweden, welfare was made available both in the form of social insurances, which were attached to wage labour (e.g. old-age, unemployment, sick- and parental-leave benefits), and in the form of allowances to the needy. Child allowances were one exception: since 1948 mothers of all Swedish children have received this allowance, regardless of their class position.

Under the Swedish social-democratic welfare state the public sector expanded and with it the extension of the labour market to women. One of the first employment sites for women was the public school, where they were employed as teachers, school canteen cooks and clerical assistants in school administration. The health sector also expanded and employed many Swedish women, and today this sector is the largest employer of women. In short, the development of the Swedish welfare state led to the creation of a separate sphere within the public sector that absorbed women's labour. Ironically, it was the work that they had been used to doing as unpaid workers in their homes that women now performed as wage labourers.

Women's entry into the labour market, mainly as producers of welfare, can account to some degree for why knowledge transfer between generations has diminished. In order to benefit from the social security system, women were required to work full-time outside the home. As more and more women joined the ranks of full-time workers, and because of their working conditions that required them to work long hours outside the home, significant aspects of the knowledge that had characterised their earlier work in the home were lost. Another contributing factor was the way that the transfer of practical knowledge became 'schoolified' and professionalised in different forms of education, such that the transfer now took place between expert and pupil. Within the field of 'domestic education' in particular, this so-called professionalising was considered essential in order to achieve the recognition of this everyday knowledge as 'real knowledge'. Towards the end of the nineteenth century, moves were made to introduce scientific approaches to the management of domestic work (Aléx 2000). These changes were evident in the educational institutions established around this time, where the distinction between what was considered to be 'expert knowledge' and the knowledge that had been traditionally transferred and practised was clearly made. This shift is evidenced in the emphasis on rational and scientific thought, including the use of technology and references to scientific results in subjects such as hygiene, nutrition, physiology, technology and other areas (Aléx 2000; Berner 1996). As a result, knowledge that had previously been transferred through generations in the home was in some way transformed. At best it was professionalised, but it in many cases it was discarded, lost or silenced.

Everyday knowledge

We begin this section with an illustration from contemporary Sweden:

> Customer: 'Excuse me, but how do you know that a Sharon fruit is ripe?'[2]
>
> Employee in the shop: 'Sharon fruit? Well, I suppose you check the bounce. If it bounces it's probably ripe...'
>
> *It wasn't ripe!*

This dialogue between a customer and an employee is part of an advertising campaign for the food-store chain ICA. The subsequent remark made by the employer concerning the employee's behaviour is, 'Yes, I know. We must have a fruit and greens position.'

Many of us in Sweden find this scene highly amusing, but more significantly it indicates what happens when knowledge that no longer constitutes a part of everyday life is silenced or is no longer communicated. And this, we suggest, is a consequence of an increasingly rationalising and mass-producing society. With regard to our example, the Swedish Food Industry Workers' Union is currently very concerned that food industry workers' knowledge has diminished considerably, which in the long run will weaken the workers' influence on their work.

How, then, does the would-be fruit and greens employee acquire his or her knowledge? Today this would take place through some sort of education programme, possibly arranged by the food-store chain. Although we would not have seen Sharon fruit in Swedish stores 50 years ago, if the same discussion had been about a more common fruit or vegetable, the employee would very likely have acquired the necessary knowledge at home, conveyed by a member of the older generation. What we are seeing now is that the decision about whose and what knowledge counts, and what is regarded as important and valuable, has to a large extent moved from the private to the public sphere.

Gendered knowledge processes

It is no coincidence that the previous illustration, about which so many people joke, refers to a knowledge domain that has traditionally belonged to women and the domestic sphere. It is this kind of knowledge that has been lost in the process of establishing the welfare state, as the public sector has taken over the responsibility for acquiring as well as transmitting it. This knowledge has been scientifically transformed and professionalised, and furthermore it has become a different sort of knowledge, something other than that which was used at home. This process of both silencing and transforming knowledge cannot be understood without questioning from a gender perspective the notion of citizenship and, in particular, social citizenship. It also raises questions about what is happening within the education system, not least in the universities.

An example of the process of gendering knowledge is the way research and knowledge about home technology used to be reported. In the mid twentieth century, the Swedish *Hemmens Forskningsinstitut* (Home Research Institute) conducted a number of investigations, including testing machines for household use. The findings were generally reported in language not usually associated with research. Mostly, what was referred to was 'testing, trying out and assessment', whereas the term 'research' was reserved for activities associated with institutions where more masculine-designated research was conducted (Rosén 2008). US historian Ruth Oldenziel claims that both feminine technology and technology focused on the feminine sphere have not been valued as highly as the masculine machine culture. In her book *Making Technology Masculine* she demonstrates how technology as a relatively young academic discipline has gradually become more and more defined as masculine. Of special note is her discussion of the concepts 'useful knowledge' and 'useful arts', which she claims have had a strong feminine coding throughout history but which after the Enlightenment became increasingly defined as masculine (Oldenziel 1999).

The story of the creation of the famous Swedish Västerbotten cheese is another example. This cheese was created in the late nineteenth century by the dairymaid Eleonora Lindström. She deliberately transformed an established processing method and, as a result, produced a unique and now very popular cheese. But Lindström did not receive full acknowledgement for her product or her knowledge, and the story of the creation of this cheese is sometimes conveyed as the result of an unsuccessful cheese-making process (Sommestad 1992: 53). While Lindström used both her theoretical and practical knowledge to develop this new product, in the story of the cheese's creation both her theoretical knowledge and her skills have been denigrated. How different this account would be if Eleonora Lindström had been a man![3]

Another aspect to consider is the way that the learning process itself is gendered. Understanding this may help to explain why women's knowledge is less valued on every level in our society. The socially constructed notions of what constitutes 'male' and 'female' are gendered. Over time, ways of being and identities have been characterised as male or as female. We are so enmeshed in stereotypical patterns that we even talk differently to a newborn baby depending on whether the baby is a girl or a boy. In our daily lives and even more so in (social) science, 'gender' more often than not means 'female', as the neutral standard is male; anything challenging it is gendered.

Swedish historian Yvonne Hirdman (2001) draws attention to the patriarchal Western way of thinking when she says, 'In the beginning there was the man'. The other sex is defined as 'not a man'. In many ways and in many contexts, women have not even been acknowledged as human beings. This worldview has had a huge impact on every single aspect of our lives, and in particular it has defined what counts as real knowledge, what is personal and what is public, and what knowledge is given the highest value in society.

Plato (427–347 BC), one of the first writers on knowledge and education, is often referred to as having introduced this dualistic thinking in his distinction between body and soul, reason and feelings, the self and others. Many feminist writers, for example Jane Roland Martin (1985), have identified this Platonic thinking as fundamentally contradictory to feminist ways of looking at learning. The most reasonable explanation for this perspective would be to see it emanating from Plato's social position as an upper-class male within ancient Greek society, and to acknowledge that many of the interpreters of his writings have been philosophers and intellectuals who have occupied similarly privileged positions within their social hierarchies.

What is labelled female is valued less than what is labelled male, and this unequal valuing applies to knowledge as well as to the person who carries this knowledge. This gendered ordering of knowledge has had severe consequences for the whole educational system, not least for higher education, as well as for working lives and social citizenship.

Understanding and challenging the gender order of knowledge

The theoretical framework that informs our research includes scrutinising both material and symbolic expressions of power relations. An important dimension, which is fundamental to all participatory action research (PAR), is that apart from principles of justice or fairness, research knowledge is more grounded if it is developed in cooperation with the people concerned (see, for example, Nowotny et al. 2001; Reason & Bradbury 2001). The approaches that we use have been shaped partly within the framework of research circles (see below), where the content that is covered is analysed in cooperation with all the people involved.

A common aim of both feminist and participatory research is to contribute to democratic change in the lives of the people who are involved. Another central tenet of both research paradigms is that knowledge construction – the inquiry – should be conducted in cooperation with the people who are affected by this work. Thus, the latter are regarded as important knowledge sources and not as passive spectators or objects who might eventually be given the opportunity to take part in the usually quite arranged and filtered research findings. Instead, by including in the process the groups that are concerned about the research, the resources are not only considerably enlarged, but the research itself is also democratised. In addition, the hierarchical relationship between the researcher and the researched is radically changed.[4]

Feminist critique of mainstream science

Our theoretical position critiques the control that mainstream academia exercises over which theories are to be used, as well as over the interpretation of empirical data. It is also concerned with the question of object and subject in research, and the relationship of the academy to those groups and individuals in society whose issues, problems and perspectives may not be taken into consideration. The relevance of this kind of critique of the academy is highlighted in an article by Mona Eliasson (2004) in which she points to different forms of resistance to change that continue to characterise the mainstream academy. This resistance is mainly expressed as passivity, where, for example, gender issues are given a token space within universities but are not regarded seriously as a relevant knowledge area. On the other hand, Eliasson also emphasises that external forces are putting pressure on institutions for more fundamental change.

Nancy Fraser (2003) advocates a policy that is founded on both redistribution and recognition – that is, material as well as more symbolic expressions of power relations. She stresses that the struggle for recognition 'has exploded everywhere', but that all too often it has fallen victim to the current spirit and thus been reduced to individualism. She also claims that a more critical attitude to the terms 'private' and 'public' is needed and points to that 'rhetoric concerning the private attempts to exclude certain issues and interests from the public debate by personalising them and/or familising them' (2003: 164). In our experience, we can see clear examples of how this applies to women's knowledge within, as well as outside, the world of the university. What is counted as knowledge is men's knowledge with its established concepts and perspectives and which has been gathered for centuries (Hirdman 1992, 2007).

Historical materialist feminism

In the early stages of feminism there were strong advocates in universities for what Fraser calls 'redistribution', or a fundamental critique of the capitalist system and its consequences. Nancy Hartsock (1983) proceeds from Marx's distinction between appearance and essence, and claims, among other things, that women's lives constitute a favourable position for vigorously criticising the institutions and ideologies that supply the foundation for the capitalist form of patriarchy. Hartsock takes her point of departure from the Marxist postulate that not only are human beings active, but reality itself consists of 'sensuous human activity, practice' (1983: 288). However, instead of focusing on men's work, her emphasis is on whether the life activities of women and the institutions that structure them can fulfil the claims of representing a feminist standpoint:

> My focus is instead on institutionalized social practices and on the specific epistemology and ontology manifested by the institutionalized sexual division of labour. (1983: 288)

Dorothy Smith (1996, 2005) demonstrates how the ruling group's concepts and theoretical order contribute to keeping control over science. She also points to the obstacles and difficulties that obstruct cooperation between women's movements and feminists at universities. The need is mutual but university feminism has developed at the cost of cooperation:

> But there is a cost. There are powers operating at a less-visible level in the university that pull our feminist work in unseen ways…we have also become increasingly detached from our former linkages and activism and organisation outside the academy. (Smith 1996: 51–52)

She also emphasises something that resonates with our experiences within the academy:

> I've sometimes thought that faculty members could be as radical as they wished in their writing and in the classroom so long as radicalism did not lead to an activism that built relationships between a university intelligentsia and a society's marginalised and exploited people. (1996: 53)

This serves as an important reminder for us today as we deepen cooperation with a more and more interactive base. It is a challenge to keep the radicalism that once upheld the idea of cooperation and not get stuck in what Smith describes as '[t]he academy creeps up upon us!' (1996: 57). Our contention is that women's experience-based knowledge was silenced not because it was unnecessary or obsolete, but because it did not fit into the exploitative schema of capitalism's ruling groups.

Making silenced knowledge visible

We would now like to describe two approaches that are currently being used in an attempt to retrieve the knowledge that has been silenced or discarded. One approach is through the documentation of such knowledge, which is being done consciously or unconsciously by different institutions in Sweden. The Nordic Museum, the Labour Museum, the archives of the Swedish Broadcasting Corporation, the Life in Sweden association and many other organisations have rich collections of life histories that are significant in this context. By analysing them, the picture of events from the 1930s and some decades previously emerges. The second approach is through encounters (for example, in research circles) with those who are still carriers of this unique knowledge – by engaging with their experiences and exploring them from a cross-disciplinary and integrated perspective.

Documentation

From a number of archives, material containing a range of examples of knowledge that is no longer practised can be retrieved. Most of this material consists of different kinds of records and a large number of diaries, mainly of male writers. There are also collections of material consisting of questionnaires that ethnologists have produced. In a dialect archive there are also stories that have been recorded for the purposes of preserving samples of dialects but where further analysis of the content could be fruitful. The Life in Sweden association has published a sample of all the memories that have been sent to the organisation, and those that have not been published have been filed in the Nordic Museum.

The Swedish Broadcasting Corporation archives hold material that could reveal some of the knowledge that we no longer consider necessary. Initiators such as the TAM (the Swedish Salaried Employees' Archives and Museum) and the Labour Museum have also collected workplace stories and a large number of these have been published, with stories of social counsellors as the most recent publication.

Practising 'knowledge care'

Research circles are also a form of research that has proved useful for retrieving and documenting knowledge and experiences that have hitherto been tacit, unformulated and perhaps even silenced (Holmstrand & Härnsten 2003). In research circles, methods and tools for drawing out elusive, unspoken and hidden knowledge have been applied. Some examples include oral history (Hansson & Thor 2006), memory work (Haug 1985, 1998; Widerberg 1995; Esseveld 1999) and different forms of life-history approaches (Härnsten 1994). In our former studies we have used these tools as well as more traditionally designed interviews. There is huge potential to deepen knowledge care if a number of basic conditions (see below) are met.

Research circles provide the space for an encounter between one's own experiences and critically grounded theoretical analysis in a challenging and collective forum. In-depth pedagogical analyses have shown that the critically scrutinising eye needs the security, trust and recognition of its own experiences in order to be able to see more deeply. A considerable degree of trust is required to understand and reveal the hidden ideologies that mystify our real living conditions. This trust and mutuality is also a basic condition for what we have started calling 'democratic knowledge processes' (Härnsten 1996; Härnsten & Holmstrand 2002). As noted previously, Fraser (2003) claims that redistribution is more absent today than recognition. For this reason we believe it is important to be explicit about content as well as methods in order to see through the ideological smokescreens that surround us. Thus our approach is built on a combination of research work in a more general sense and the advantages that can obtain in participatory-oriented research.

Whose knowledge counts?

As mentioned previously, views about knowledge and knowledge construction within the school system and in universities are of utmost concern. What is counted as valid knowledge and is considered worthy of being on the literature lists for university courses as well as forming the basis for dissertations is mainly defined by male conceptions. Ever since compulsory schooling was established in Sweden in 1842, the content of girls' and boys' education has been different (Isling 1993). Although the form may have changed and it is sometimes concealed, in essence the pattern remains whereby that knowledge regarded as belonging to women's domains is marginalised as subordinated knowledge. And this trend is certainly present within the academy. In a recently completed research project with several researchers from different disciplines (Härnsten & Wingård 2007), we concluded that historically women were first excluded, and then have not been taken seriously in the world of the university. Although there is currently much talk about gender equality, the focus is mostly on head-counting the representation in the two gender categories. That this is far from the core of the issue is seldom put forward as a problem.

This project focuses on the view of knowledge and the experiences that most often do not count. In several subdivisions of the project, memory work and life stories have demonstrated the power and challenges contained in bringing out and making visible the memories of the participants. Where participants have worked deeply over a long period, these experiences have provided a basis both for personal strength and for challenging their contexts. Participating pre-school teachers, for example, have understood their double subordination as women and as teachers furthest down the age hierarchy of the education system (Siljehag 2007). Now they are able to take action in a new way. But this ability is the result of long-term work.

Other parts of the programme have given us tools for understanding the main trends in the universities. Our application of Bernstein's (1977) conceptual model of framing and classification (control and power) in a life-history course at Växjö University (Härnsten et al. 2007) has helped us further clarify what is happening. The free word – the feeling of freedom – that is the foundation of all creative activity, whether in working life, at school or in society at large, is under threat. In Bernstein's terminology, we clearly see this trend as a return to a 'strong classification' as well as a 'rigid framing'.

The *control* exercised over universities today is without parallel in modern times. The state exercises its controls through regulations, evaluations and decrees that emanate from a number of different levels within the system. This results in rigid and incredibly time-consuming procedures that affect all academic tasks. The time and energy that is used to shape, scrutinise, illuminate, make accessible on the internet, and control all course syllabi and study plans is enormous. The time spent by teachers and scholars could be more fruitfully devoted to meeting with students in an open and mutually constructive spirit. Course curricula that allow for the spontaneous or unknown to occur during the educational process are conspicuously absent. Researching ways of working (during ongoing courses), which we partly have been able to apply within the framework of projects, now struggles for space. The regulating state documents that recommend diversity in order to achieve a more solidly founded knowledge are rapidly becoming obsolete. All this contributes to limiting core tasks of both teachers and students and to a work environment that largely nips creativity in the bud.

The *power* over universities is exercised by the state and the market through the prevailing economic system. Here, investment in what is familiar is favoured: the knowledge that colleagues and the right receiver will appreciate and feel comfortable with. More time-consuming, creative and collaborative knowledge production is not favoured by such a system (Gibbons et al. 1994). Research funding is allocated to already established and secure environments that are not too challenging. Resources for gender research with the potential to challenge are often distributed to areas that do not deepen the knowledge about or challenge gender power structures, but instead fit into the patterns that in essence maintain the system we are in (Berggren 2002).

During a certain period in the 1970s, we were able to use Bernstein's concepts of power and control to describe the situation of weakened control over schools and particularly the universities in Sweden. To a large extent, teachers and pupils at that time decided the form and content that should shape schooling. To a certain degree even power was challenged – the division into subjects was loosened and universities had a relatively high degree of autonomy. The financial conditions meant that at least university professors could conduct their own research and doctoral students could be admitted on the basis of their interests and merits. Now, however, everything is governed by the market. Even the international context, to which we are all connected, has decreased the space for creative and challenging activities of our own. The adaptation to the Bologna model has, in our country, been taken to its limit. Ultimately, global capitalism is the cause of this standardisation and adaptation to the influence of market forces. Where can we find perspectives, challenges and free thinking today? There seems to be little space for this at universities.

Conclusion

In this chapter we have highlighted the connection between domains in everyday life where knowledge has been silenced and the power order of gender in society. The impact of this order on women's social citizenship is extensive. It is clear that women are not regarded as full and worthy citizens. We have also scrutinised the way this power order is entrenched in the educational system, and not least in research and conceptions of what is recognised as 'real knowledge'. Our focus has been mainly on Sweden, with the aim of developing a deeper understanding of the processes at work in our society. At the same time, we have drawn attention to some of the ways we believe we can challenge these processes in the light of the past. And here we also welcome the experiences of other countries. Our conviction is that our cross-disciplinary work will benefit from a more global view, both from countries with a different history and political tradition as well as from those that are similar to Sweden.

Our interest is not primarily academic; rather it prioritises the very important task of seeing how the knowledge of all people, not least the lost or hidden knowledge of women that has been built up through experiences, has lived on and survived from generation to generation. It is also imperative that this knowledge building is done in cooperation with the people concerned, as well as challenged by critical perspectives from relevant research. We are convinced that knowledge obtained this way is better knowledge. But more importantly, if the research is to have any significant impact, it is because the people involved have also acquired the strength to take action and contribute to changing the conditions. A society where more than half of the population does not feel that their knowledge counts or is not regarded as valuable is not a human society. And yet, sooner than we think, such knowledge other than the kinds of knowledge that are now given the most surplus value may be needed. In times of catastrophe, when modern technology is knocked out quite suddenly, the silenced knowledge is needed. How to get warmth and water, how to maintain hygiene and how to prepare cooked food – all these presuppose this knowledge. But perhaps even more important is the ability to maintain human relations in order to survive. If memories, experiences, emotions and thus everyday knowledge are regarded as feminine and irrelevant for citizens and power holders, what kind of society do we have? And if problems connected to poverty, economic failure and racism are addressed by people who do not even see the need for this knowledge, where are we today?

Notes

1   In developing this argument, Alice Kessler-Harris (2001) introduced the term 'economic citizenship'. However, as this focuses on access to resources and is linked to political issues concerning economic democracy, which has not yet been achieved in Sweden or anywhere else, in this chapter we use the term 'social citizenship'.

2   Sharon fruit is also known as persimmon.

3   Even today the advertisements about this cheese depict it as a mysterious product that can only be produced at the original location in the north of Sweden. Factors other than Eleonora Lindström's theoretical and practical knowledge continue to be the ones that count!

4   One of the pioneers in feminist PAR is Patricia Maguire (see, for example, Maguire 1987, 2001). More recently the number of feminist participatory-oriented researchers has grown considerably.

References

Aléx P (2000) Skolkökslärarinnorna och kunskapen om hemmet. In A Hatje (ed.) *Sedkelskiftets utmaningar: Essäer om välfärd, utbildning och nationell identitet vid sekelskiftet 1900.* Stockholm: Carlssons

Berggren A (2002) Objektivitet och vetenskaplighet: Genusperspektivet i vetenskapsvärlden. *Häften för kritiska studier* 35(2–4): 88–95

Berner B (1996) *Sakernas tillstånd: Kön, klass, teknisk expertis.* Stockholm: Carlssons

Bernstein B (1977) *Towards a theory of educational transmissions.* Vol. 3 of *Class, codes and control.* London: Routledge and Kegan Paul

Björk G (2000) *Att förhandla sitt medborgarskap: Kvinnor som kollektiva politiska aktörer i Örebro 1900–1950.* Lund: Arkiv

Einhorn B (1999) Gender and citizenship in the context of democratisation and economic transformation in east central Europe: Equality, democracy, and the welfare state. In SM Rai (ed.) *International perspectives on gender and democratisation.* New York: St Martin's Press

Eliasson M (2004) Genus i akademin – om motstånd mot förändring. *Socialt perspektiv* 4: 11–21

Esping-Andersen G (1990) The three worlds of welfare capitalism. Cambridge: Polity Press

Esseveld J (1999) Minnesarbete. In I Sjöberg (ed.) *Mer än kalla fakta: Kvalitativ forskning i praktiken.* Lund: Studentlitteratur

Florin C (2006) *Kvinnor får röst: Kön, känslor och politisk kultur i kvinnornas rösträttsrörelse.* Stockholm: Atlas

Fraser N (2003) *Den radikala fantasin: Mellan omfördelning och erkännande.* Göteborg: Daidalos

Gibbons M, Limoges C, Nowotny H, Schwartzman S, Scott P & Trow M (1994) *The new production of knowledge: The dynamics of science and research in contemporary societies.* London: Sage Publications

Hansson L & Thor M (eds) (2006) *Muntlig historia.* Lund: Studentlitteratur

Härnsten G (1994) *The research circle: Building knowledge on equal terms.* Stockholm: LO

Härnsten G (1996) Demokratiska kunskapsprocesser. In I Hammer & L Holmstrand (eds) *Arbetarrörelsen och demokratin.* ALFOFAK report, Uppsala

Härnsten G, Ahlbäck T, Alm M, Carlsson M, Dettner-Arvidsson A, Frithiof E, Gillberg C, Hellgren I, Klinthäll E, Ljung I, Pong K, Sjöblom B & Söderlund-Wijk B (2007) *Levt liv som kunskapskälla: Livsberättelser i högre utbildning.* Report no. 1–2007, Centre for Educational Development, Växjö University, Sweden

Härnsten G & Holmstrand L (2002) Research circles in Sweden: Strengthening the double democratic function of trade unions. In B Spencer (ed.) *Unions and learning in a global economy: International and comparative perspectives.* Toronto: Thomson Educational Publishing

Härnsten G & Wingård B (eds) (2007) *Högskoleutbildning javisst, men för vem och för vad? Genusperspektiv i praktiknära forskning i högre utbildning.* Växjö: Växjö University Press

Hartsock N (1983) The feminist standpoint: Developing the ground for a specifically feminist historical materialism. In S Harding & MB Hintikka (eds) *Discovering reality: Feminist perspectives on epistemology, metaphysics, methodology, and philosophy of science.* Dordrecht: Reidel

Haug F (1985) Memory work. *Psyke och Logos* 6: 85–115

Haug F (1998) Minne och frigörelse. *Socialistisk debatt* 3: 4–15

Hirdman Y (1992) Introduktion. In G Åström & Y Hirdman (eds) *Kontrakt i kris.* Stockholm: Carlssons

Hirdman Y (2001) *Genus: Om det stabilas föränderliga förmer.* Malmö: Liber

Hirdman Y (2007) *Gösta och genusordningen: Feministiska betraktelser.* Stockholm: Ordfront

Hobsbawm E (1962) The age of revolution. New York: New American Library

Holmstrand L & Härnsten G (2003) *Förutsättningar för forskningscirklar i skolan: En kritisk granskning.* Stockholm: Myndigheten för skolutveckling

Isling Å (1993) Patriarkat och könsskräck i skolan. In G Härnsten (ed.) *För barnen, med barnen och bland barnen: En vänbok till Eva-Mari Köhle*r. Stockholm: Carlssons

Kessler-Harris A (2001) *In pursuit of equity: Women, men, and the quest for economic citizenship in 20th-century America.* Oxford: Oxford University Press

Leira A (1992) *Welfare states and working mothers.* Cambridge: Cambridge University Press

Lister R (2003) *Citizenship: Feminist perspectives.* New York: Palgrave Macmillan

Maguire P (1987) *Doing participatory research: A feminist approach.* Amherst, MA: Center for International Education, University of Massachusetts

Maguire P (2001) Uneven ground: Feminisms and action research. In P Reason & H Bradbury (eds) *Handbook of action research.* London: Sage Publications

Marshall TH (1950) *Citizenship and social class and other essays.* Cambridge: Cambridge University Press

Marshall TH (1964) *Class, citizenship and social development.* Garden City, NY: Doubleday

Martin JR (1985) *Reclaiming a conversation: The ideal of the educated woman.* New Haven, CT: Yale University Press

Nowotny H, Scott P & Gibbons M (2001) *Rethinking science: Knowledge and the public in an age of uncertainty.* Cambridge: Polity Press

Odora Hoppers C (ed.) (2002) *Indigenous knowledge and the integration of knowledge systems: Towards a philosophy of articulation.* Claremont, South Africa: New Africa Books

Oldenziel R (1999) *Making technology masculine: Men, women, and modern machines in America, 1870–1945.* Amsterdam: Amsterdam University Press

Pateman C (1988) *The sexual contract.* Stanford, CA: Stanford University Press

Reason P & Bradbury H (eds) (2001) *Handbook of action research*. London: Sage Publications

Rosén U (2008) *Rational solution to the laundry issue: Policy and research for day-to-day life in the welfare state*. Scandinavian Working Papers in Economics. Accessed 27 March 2009, http:// swopec.hhs.se/cesisp/abs/cesisp0133.htm

Sainsbury D (1999) *Gender and welfare state regimes*. Oxford: Oxford University Press

Sarvasy W (1997) Social citizenship from a feminist perspective. *Hypatia* 12(4): 54–73

Siljehag E (2007) *Igenkännande och motkraft* (Recognition and counter power). PhD dissertation, Stockholm University, Sweden

Smith D (1996) Contradictions for feminist social scientists. In H Gottfried (ed.) *Feminism and social change: Bridging theory and practice*. Urbana and Chicago: University of Illinois Press

Smith D (2005) *Institutional ethnography: A sociology for people*. Walnut Creek, CA: AltaMira Press

Sommestad L (1992) *Från mejerska till mejerist: En studie av mejeriyrkets maskuliniseringsprocess*. Lund: Arkiv

Widerberg K (1995) *Kunskapens kön: Minnen, reflektioner och teori*. Stockholm: Norstedts Förlag

Wikander U (2006) *Feminism, familj och medborgarskap. Debatter på internationella kongresser om nattarbetsförbud för kvinnor 1889–1919*. Göteborg: Makadam

17 Urban mindset, rural realities: Teaching on the edge

Barbara Barter

Introduction

In 2005, I taught a distance education course on current issues in rural education at a Canadian university. Most participants were graduate students with teaching experience in rural schools. However, some were teachers who taught in urban schools. Since the course was Web-based, most students were professional full-time teachers. Over the duration of the course, a number of participants recounted that there is a need for rural research and that system administrators, such as those who work within government departments, institutions responsible for teacher-training programmes, and school district offices, need to understand the value of rural education and of rural schools. Although many of the students in the course were from one Canadian province, some were from other parts of Canada or from other countries and had diverse, yet similar, rural teaching and living experiences. In listening to their discussions, I heard narratives that were systemic in nature and that expressed participants' feelings of being recognised not as educators in rural communities but as rural teachers forced to fit urban realities. The graduate students in the course consistently maintained that 'alternative epistemological and pedagogical approaches in teaching, leading, and learning are required that will benefit rural education and rural educators' (Barter 2008: 468–469).

This is the backdrop against which I began a research study in 2006. Although several issues emerged through this research, this chapter addresses two of these. The first is the significant and persistent urban/rural line of inclusion and exclusion experienced by teachers and administrators in rural environments. The second is a double-edged 'hidden dimension' of knowledge – that which suppresses rural knowledge and advances urban knowledge, and that which suppresses the knowledge of rural teachers as professionals. Both issues draw attention to a neglected part of the education system. In this chapter, I address these two issues through a literature review and a brief analysis of what participants had to say about them.

Overview of the study

The study centred on learning about rural education, specifically for graduate students enrolled in a distance education course at a Canadian university. The thesis questions were: (1) What are the current issues in education within the community in which you teach? (2) How do these issues compare to the literature? (3) What do you think supporting agencies such as governments and universities need to be doing to advance rural education? The inquiry design and implementation were grounded in theories of constructivism (Schwandt 1997) and personal practical knowledge (Connelly & Clandinin 1988). Both theories 'position teachers as holders and makers of knowledge' and shift 'teaching and its relationship to curriculum and instruction' (Barter 2008) to a more research-in-action-based professional development.

The data were derived from three sources: electronic conversations among the 15 consenting participants, small-group postings and instructor responses. This was made possible by the university through a designated Web-based forum designed specifically for distance education courses. Each week groups of four students were presented with a specific unit focus for which they had to cover assigned readings, do a Web search and respond to a set of guiding questions. Each group was responsible for posting a composite answer that invited responses from other members of the class. These forums were left open until the end of the course, and students were encouraged to reflect, question and return to their postings to share their thoughts and create a knowledge base of experiences connected to the readings. Topics were derived from issues that students raised, and I followed up at the end of each unit with an instructor's response to which students in turn responded.

The approximately 750 pages of data were collated, colour-coded according to the research thesis questions and labelled as the intended outcomes. It was at this stage that I discovered the need for a fourth category, that of unintended outcomes. These themes emerged from what students added through reflection once responses were placed online and were open for discussion with other groups. It is two of these outcomes that set the context for this chapter – a need for research in rural education and a need for system administrators to understand the value of rural education and rural schools.

Limitations and strengths

The study relied on responses from students working towards a graduate degree. This placed students in dual roles as both students and participants in research. Traditionally, there is something inherently different between these two roles. According to Bogdan and Biklen, teachers are normally astute observers, do systematic inquiry and draw conclusions (1998: 36). But they also point out that teachers are different from researchers in that a researcher's primary responsibility is to the research whereas a teacher's primary responsibility is to teaching, developing curriculum and managing students. Yet if one takes the epistemological position that knowledge is social and that it is inherent in teacher practice to work out ways to communicate with others, to learn from one another and to validate one another's experiences, then using such dialogue to advance research may be viewed as part of the natural progression of learning.

A second limitation was my role as instructor and researcher. According to Carson and Sumara, the actions of researchers 'are driven by...a moral/ethical impulse, founded on an attentiveness to our own complicity in affecting events that range from emerging individual perceptions to broader collective activities' (2001: 308). They found in their own research that they deliberately inserted themselves 'into the space that Jerome Bruner calls "culture making" through such actions as making suggestions…and introducing theory as a means of making sense of things'. Similarly, I found myself engaging in class discussion with responses of my own, creating 'inevitable participation' (Carson & Sumara 2001: 309). To balance the teacher–researcher role, I attempted to maintain a split existence. My responsibility between 9 January and 9 April 2006 rested with teaching the course. Once all the required course evaluations had been submitted to the university, I revisited the postings of consenting students as a researcher and used research procedures to collate and analyse the discussion areas as data.

Third, the research was mainly North American based, both in its literature and in its findings. Given this limitation, the intent was not to generalise the data but rather to ask readers to accept the work as one localised instance of teacher narratives that may be shared and expanded to the narratives of others in the field. As Altrichter points out, 'participating in a professional discussion is a means of validating and developing the insights of individuals' (1993: 52). Exposing one's practice and theory of rural education to academic discussion increases one's chances of linking insights and broadening the knowledge base.

Engaging the literature

Research in rural education, as a part of rural sociology, has a long history dating back to the classical social theories found in the works of Tönnies (1957), Durkheim (1984) and Weber (1964, 1970). Profound changes in a shift from rural to urban styles of living stimulated the need to explain the impact of these structural changes. For Tönnies (1957), society as *Gemeinschaft* and society as *Gesellschaft* are interdependent. *Gemeinschaft* (community) is often used to define an 'ideal type' of society in which social bonds are personal and direct and there are shared beliefs and values characteristic of small-scale, localised societies. *Gesellschaft* refers to a society where social bonds are usually complex, impersonal, instrumental and narrow. In this type of society there is a strict division between private and public spheres of life that is more apparent in larger, more urban societies. Weber (1970), on the other hand, was concerned about the impact the growth of capitalism would have on rural areas, in particular as they related to farming in Germany. His research focused on what social factors had brought about the rationalisation of Western society. Two of his distinguishing terms were *traditional authority*, that which defines the 'everyday actions to which people have become habitually accustomed' (Weber 1964: 116), and *legal rational authority*, which is based on specialisation, the division of labour and the growth of large-scale corporations through bureaucratic leadership. Durkheim's principal thesis was to explore what holds society together (Jaffee 2001). Similar to Weber (1970), he focused on the division of labour, which he categorised into two types: mechanical and organic solidarity. Mechanical solidarity is 'based on the similarity in life experiences which derived from common activities' (Jaffee 2001: 11) in rural communities. The organic is found in more industrial, urban societies.

Although the writings of Tönnies, Weber and Durkheim demonstrate epistemological differences, these researchers share a common interest in the way economic, political and social changes have impacted on modernisation. Their challenge was to understand what was happening as a result of the growth of industrialisation, and how it affected personal relationships and community life. Theirs may well have been the first call for a rural sociology. As Weber ascertained, 'of all communities, the social constructions of rural districts are the most individual and the most closely connected with particular historical developments' (1970: 363), and therefore they warrant attention. Although the United States took up the call, critics (Hofstadter 1966; Newby 1980) claim that US research has been primarily oriented either towards urban society as ideal or towards rural issues from a social policy perspective. Hence, Newby (1980) found it to be research that is more reactive than proactive. This is evidenced in the works of many Western writers.

DeYoung, for example, asserts that there is an increase in the volume of 'in-house' literature on the needs of rural schools, but that most of it focuses on 'more and better data-based studies on rural schooling dynamics' or 'on administrative issues and problems in the operation of these institutions' (1987: 129). He also argues that the current literature exhibits an 'urban bias' (1987: 128) and that this exists as a worldwide phenomenon. Writers point out that much of the quality research on issues in rural schooling is being carried out by anthropologists and historians (DeYoung 1987), ethnographers and sociologists (Khattri et al. 1997), and through literary sources, both fiction and non-fiction (Chambers 1999). DeYoung claims that this work has been done within 'the framework of understanding culturally different populations rather than ruralness per se' (1987: 131). And although research from these fields may prove to be beneficial to rural educators, he argues that educational researchers need to take the lead in advancing such research. Theobald and Nachtigal (1995) and Bauch (2001) claim that research has been directed towards urban schools, and that rural and urban schools are not one and the same. As such, rural schools need to 'attend to [their] own place' (Theobald & Nachtigal 1995).

Mulcahy's (1996) work on rural education in one Canadian province verifies this with reference to his research on multi-grade classrooms. At the beginning, his participants, mostly rural teachers, raised questions such as why the issue of rural teaching was not being addressed through the university's teacher-training programme; why curriculum guides produced by the provincial ministry provided no guidance on how to implement the prescribed programmes in multi-grade environments; and why presenters at professional development workshops were unable to provide answers when rural teachers asked questions about how to do something in a rural school. Many of these teachers felt ignored by the agencies responsible for education in their province.

Some writers (Herzog & Pittman 2002) point out that one of the problems facing rural education is its lack of definition, and that existing definitions are weighted heavily towards economic capital and view 'rural areas as sectors of a national economy' (Budge 2006: 2). On the other hand, Stern's (1994) notion of 'rural' defined as culture – including strong connections between family, church and school; the importance of regional differences; and a strong sense of place – is not as common. The latter view positions 'concern with personal, family, and community relations on a higher level of priority than legal, contractual, and formal bureaucratic conventions' (Kincheloe & Pinar 1991: 13). As Coupal explains:

> The people of [rural communities], who share a heritage, common locale and homogeneity of economic activity, often develop a strong sense of community…[and]…are able to move from what could be construed as a structural-functionalist to a constructivist definition of community. That is, they define themselves as different from other social groups because of geographic location; however, they also distinguish themselves through their consciousness of boundary, their distinctive social discourse that expresses commonality and identifies those who are 'outside' the community. (2005: 1)

In focusing on urban bias, Wallin questions the hegemonic domination of urbanisation on rural Canadian schools and sees rural communities as being on the periphery of the world economy. Under such conditions, these communities have been marginalised and made vulnerable through such threats as degraded resources, out-migration and administrative neglect (2006: 2). Mulcahy's (1999) work outlines what he considers to be the two most serious impediments to the development of education in rural communities: one being 'the urban mindset' and the other being 'the cult of efficiency'. Similar to Wallin (2006), the former implies that decisions are made through larger, more standardised urban school models, which lead to policies and programmes that do not necessarily reflect rural realities or their uniqueness. The latter is hallmarked by fiscal restraints. In attempting to become more efficient, several ministries, including education (at least in Canada), have been forced into budget cutting that has led to the emergence of a 'cuts' culture based on a corporate model. Corbett (2007) takes a look at the role of formal schooling in one rural community that had gone through profound economic changes with the shift from a local to a more global fishery. According to Theobald, Corbett's work 'sheds revealing light on the intellectual poverty of regnant educational policy and practice in both the United States and Canada' (2007: 1).

Findings and discussion

What the literature reveals

Overall, the literature review reveals a vast amount of writing on rural education, rural schools and rural communities, forcing one to consider why there is a call for more research both from the literature and from participants in the research study. First, there are those who claim that, although there is ample research, it is of poor quality and lacks systematic experimentation (Arnold et al. 2005). Second, there is the notion that much of the existing literature comes from disciplines other than education (DeYoung 1987; Chambers 1999) and that researchers of rural education need to be involved in that research. Similar to the literature, participants in the study indicated that those responsible for education need to know more about what is happening in the rural environments in which teachers work and live. Many participants praised the work of 'local' researchers, especially those who seemed to be valuing teachers' work. Third, there are those (Bauch 2001; Theobald & Nachtigal 1995) who say that much of the research on current reform efforts has been directed towards urban schools and that rural and urban schools are not the same. They argue that rural settings need to attend to their own place. Similarly, DeYoung (1987) points to a need for research on rural as a concept rather than rural as an urban problem.

These reasons, coupled with the notion that the existing research may be more reactive than proactive, demonstrate why there appears to be an ongoing call for research in the area of rural education. There is a sense of something lacking. Both the literature and the participant dialogues signal that it may not be that there is not enough research on rural education, but rather that there is not enough of the right kind of research. We require research which supports rather than denigrates rural education and its students and teachers, which studies the impact of ministry policy implementation and which includes rural educators. According to the literature these have been long-standing issues. Hofstadter, for example, once described the research in rural education in the United States as an 'educational jeremiad' (1966: 301). The work of Woods (2003) in exploring the hunting debate of the United Kingdom depicts the 'countryside' as a 'contested space'. For Smith 'all schools are by implication subject to... critique' (2002: 27) but those that have had the most condemnation are rural schools. As urbanisation has begun to dominate societal structures, rural schools have become the 'other schools' that require remediation intended to make them more like city schools. For rural education this dilemma has grown with declining rural populations and the twenty-first-century shift towards globalisation. Hence, there has evolved a legacy of educational reform, and the literature required to legitimate it, rather than a legacy of rural schools supported with rural models and rural values. It is clear that, as researchers, we have not been able to push the boundaries of rural education through proactivity and advance what we know: that rural schools are just as good a place to be as urban schools. There is a need to shift the epistemology of education.

From the literature to participants

Much of the literature portrays rural education as problematic. Hence, as critics point out, the literature is more reactive than proactive. Similar to the literature, study participant responses show a strong sense of awareness that, as professionals in their workplace, they are not valued as highly as their counterparts in more urban areas. They felt there are two working standards – one for rural teachers and another for urban teachers. As one group explained: 'We have found that the majority of our issues point to our system of education being insensitive to the uniqueness of the rural context.' One participant wrote:

> [I]t seems that rural education has little respect from our [district]...
> You can teach [specialty areas] in the smaller, rural schools without the

recommended requirements. However, as soon as you try to transfer to a larger school you are not qualified to teach in these areas. What does this say about the quality of small school education?

Some participants believed that with school closures and consolidation they were losing sight of the meaning of education. Another counterpointed:

> I am not sure we are losing sight…I think it reflects the changing nature of society's expectations and we, as small rural communities, are left to deal with the changes made by [those] who make the decisions on what it means to be educated – our needs are not addressed in that dialogue!

Participants expressed the belief that system administrators not only do not value rural education and its differences, but also do not understand the same. They recounted narratives of system administrators showing insensitivity towards rural issues and rural ways of doing things. One pointed out:

> Through course discussions, course readings and reflection, it has been made abundantly clear that the needs of the rural teacher are unique, and stem from the context in which they work. Equally clear is the fact that those in positions of authority have not attended to those unique aspects to the extent that is needed. Consequently, the needs of the rural educator, the rural student and the rural community are not being addressed.

One wrote: 'So, we become doormats; our opinion and experience count very little towards decisions made at the top.' For participants, policy decisions emanated from 'those who fail to understand the rural setting'. They spoke of rural school values such as community use of school buildings being 'eroded as a result of the ever-increasing litigious nature of society' that was often experienced in larger centres but was also forced onto rural communities through generic policies. Participants described their feelings about the way system administrators seemed to place more value on 'economic capital' than on people and how they found themselves caught in an education reform process framed by school closure and school consolidations. They doubted the reasons given by system administrators for the need for education reform. One participant wrote: '[T]here is no clear conceptual map, or hard evidence, at this point, that illustrates how restructuring will improve how schools operate or how restructuring is positively correlated to increase student achievement and educational equity.' Another participant wrote:

> Your posting states that…small schools are educationally viable. So, why is the promotion of small schools not an issue in [our province]? We hear tell of the benefits, some of us have seen it first-hand…In your paper you have stated many benefits of small schools. I only wish [our government] was more positive about small schools instead of looking at them as being a burden to the education system.

Similar to the calls for more research found in the literature, and probably stemming from their feelings of exclusion from system changes, participants wanted to know why the topic of rural education appeared to be underdeveloped in comparison to other areas of educational study. One queried whether it was because it was a difficult area to explore, or whether there was simply little interest in the topic or 'limited political' will to do so. Many of the participants had a sense that, as rural teachers in rural communities, they were a burden to 'progressive educational reform'. They used words such as 'isolation, inequality [and] targeted for reform, and described a sense of disconnection from the rest of the education system' (Barter 2008). These comments express the feelings of exclusion and of being of less value – the feeling that being rural is somehow not as good as being urban. As one respondent wrote: 'Unfortunately, as long as rural communities exist, there will always be a perception that rural = less.' Another wrote: 'Not only does institutionalisation preserve the will or feelings of the majority and best represent the majority, it marginalises "others", in this case, "rural" schools.' Through such narratives, one discerns not only feelings of exclusion, but also a sense of a possible pathology of the growing 'cult of efficiency' and the 'bigger is better' syndrome. One potential outcome is that this pathology both informs rural education, and impedes it by devaluing it. Not only did participants feel that they were not included, but they believed they were less valued for their expertise as it pertained to their knowledge in rural education. Participants in the study believed that they were unprepared to deal with this urban/rural split, and for these feelings of being excluded from their field as professionals.

Beyond the study

Although participants' stories connect to specific issues within their own localised working environment, their narratives also point to significant issues embedded at the macro-level of society. When participants are asking why the topic of rural education is underdeveloped in comparison to other areas of research and imply that there may be 'little interest' in the issue and a lack of political motivation to address it, and when these themes are supported by long-standing literature, one has to question at a much deeper level than the local situation. Participants' critical discourse motivates me to look towards the larger social, cultural and political dimensions of education in at least two areas: the inclusiveness of rural teachers and their sense of place within the teaching profession, and the effects of the intersection between rural and urban life worlds.

Hodgkinson maintains that education is one of the most complex and profound concepts in language, and that it is 'something very special in the field of human affairs' (1991: 1). It is more than training and more than the 'acquisition of knowledge' (1991: 16); rather, it is a place where we acquire our values or beliefs, and the 'teaching–learning of values is somehow subsumed within the larger concept of education' (1991: 16). Hence, the fundamental work of schools is teaching and learning, and this is special because it 'both forms and is formed by values' (1991: Preface). From this perspective, a teacher's work is unique in that it is cultured as being more than an occupation. Teachers become 'moral agents' who locate themselves in complex and diverse 'historical, personal, communal, and professional landscapes' (Clandinin & Connelly 1995: vii). It is a place where rural teachers in particular live out dual lives. Since teachers contextualise education within a formalised urban system, they live out lives of professional training, standardised by state policy through generic certification. But they also live out lives as workers in a specific community with a history and culture of its own where they rely on their personal practical knowledge, 'that body of convictions and meanings, conscious and unconscious, that have arisen from experience…and is expressed in' their practice (Clandinin & Connelly 1995: 7).

Here evolves the tension between formal education and workplace learning. Teachers-in-training make a transition from a school of theoretical learning to a school of work where their knowledge becomes recontextualised into workplace learning. If we listen to conversations of participants from the study, I think it fair to say that these teachers encountered both a professional and a personal practical knowledge landscape that created epistemological dilemmas. This landscape included how teachers saw themselves valued as workers and identified how the places in which they lived are valued. How they interpret those values may determine how they think others see them, as well as how they see themselves as teachers. From this premise it is an easy step to seeing the school not only as a place of teaching and learning, but also as a place of workplace learning, and it also demonstrates how rural teachers are affected by the theory and practice of their lives and their life worlds.

Weber (1964) recognised that we are immersed in a world 'dominated by capitalism' where urbanisation seems to survive and thrive best. In a world where positive growth is symbolised by large cities and larger corporations it is not difficult to visualise rural as feeling smaller both in geography and in social stature. As such, capitalism and urbanisation have influenced a decline of rural capacity in many areas, including education, leaving such communities sitting on the periphery of what is considered to be acceptable living. This forces the kind of questions that researchers might need to be asking:

• Are rural teachers as valued as urban teachers?
• Is there a positive value placed on rural communities, rural education and rural schooling?
• If there is, what is it and why aren't rural teachers aware of it?
• Is it a hidden dimension?

I believe that there is another point for consideration, which is that there exists in rural communities an intersection between the traditional habits of living (Weber 1964) – that which make them rural – and the contemporary needs dominated by urban environments. In some ways the economic culture of rural communities, influenced by capitalism, has changed, thus changing their social culture. For example, for rural fishers the move from small boats to one-million-dollar vessels, from inshore fishing to deep-sea fishing, from small individual community fish plants to larger consolidated plants employing many communities – all these changes affect the lives of rural people. In that sense, rural communities and schools have given way to powerful, non-local industrial models forcing external control and different values on their lives. The same can be said of rural education. It, too, is tied to the urban mindset that encompasses global competitiveness and economic dominance and the standards that are pervasive in today's demand for education accountability.

For teachers there is a tension between how to live out generic curricula while living rural values. They find themselves caught in a sea change with few, if any, supports. As Foster (2004: 180) points out, 'standards…can often be seen to have their origin in the drive to create school systems that produce effective workers who can compete in a global economy'. Having productive workers is not the issue, says Foster, but 'when it drives out other value ends it becomes much more problematic' (2004: 180). A question that has to be considered is whether urban standards confine the world's ability to diversify. If this is the case, as Chambers (1999) maintains, then it victimises and marginalises any peoples who are living outside those standards and at the same time are trying to live, or are expected to live, within those standards. As a report from the Nelson Mandela Foundation on South African education indicates:

> Rural areas are isolated but also fully part of contemporary South Africa…They are impoverished but also fully monetarised…These areas are not traditional havens cut off from a South Africa that forged ahead without and in ignorance of them, but rather their very traditionalism has been created by a South African society and economy that needed the labour that could be extracted from what misleadingly appeared to be timeless rural enclaves. (NMF 2005: 136)

Now, it seems that rural South African communities 'fall short of national policy' and, like many other rural areas, are struggling to implement new forms of schooling based on national standards. Mellow compares the rural–urban association to a gavotte, a 'Baroque dance movement in duple meter' (2005: 50). Professionals such as rural teachers are drawn into a rural–urban gavotte as 'they try to reconcile their experience of rural society with the standards of professional work that emerge from urban settings. Dancing to this "duple" or double-beat presents unique challenges for rural professionals' (2005: 51). One of those challenges is reconciling rural as being associated with urban society. Part of that reconciliation might be recognising that we are a society that is lacking a topography of rural education theorising.

It is suggested that what rural South Africa requires is a form of teaching and learning that takes the people of those communities into account (NMF 2005). These needs, according to the literature, are remarkably similar to those of other countries. Foster's (2004) remedy is to see US schools as communities: to restructure classrooms, redefine the role of administrators and review the relationships among stakeholders through community. Foster echoes Tönnies's (1957) notion of *Gemeinschaft*, the building of community through kinship, mind and place. It is communal thinking that has traditionally and naturally identified rural life. This was the narrative of participants in my study. And although these solutions are not absolutes, they demonstrate that alternative ways are necessary to shift the existing trends of education.

Conclusion

Two consistent unintended outcomes from the research were the need to establish a theory of rural education and the need to connect rural education to community – that is, rural education that is based on rural models and values. From my perspective, it is a need that not only signifies part of the diversity and complexity of rural living and rural schools but is also a call for more research to develop both as acceptable valued parts of world growth. The literature indicates that the absence of such research is symptomatic of many countries, especially in those where urbanisation has become the societal norm. Such a norm establishes a growth in globalisation that increasingly challenges and marginalises rural life as it currently exists.

On the website call for papers, the theme of the Fifth International Conference on Researching Work and Learning held in South Africa in December 2007 reminds us that we have to 'rethink the "centre" as well as the "margins" of society from a variety of countries and perspectives'.[1] We need to deepen and enrich our understandings about work and learning in rural areas. Similarly, participants in my study added to the mounting evidence that supports the success of smaller schools. The implication of this research is that the focus of the literature should move away from assessing whether or not rural schools are viable to how curriculum and instruction can be developed to support them. There is a need for rural schools as identified spaces. Identified spaces have value – non-identified spaces lose value or have none. I believe there is a difference between, on the one hand, needing research that asks or advises how best to make rural communities more like urban ones and, on the other, trying to find out the place of rural societies within contemporary society and how best to theorise about those changes that occur in rural societies as a result of contemporary society. My research calls for a refocus on schools that is inclusive of rural-based theory with rural-based models, a process that would enhance and legitimise rural knowledge. To do so would be to imbue a neglected area of education with value and provide opportunity to create a knowledge base for people who live in rural areas, especially teachers.

Note

1   For more information on the conference, see http://rwl5.uwc.ac.za.

References

Altrichter H (1993) The concept of quality in action research. In M Schratz (ed.) *Qualitative voices in educational research.* London: Falmer Press

Arnold ML, Newman JH, Gaddy BB & Dean CB (2005) A look at the condition of rural education research: Setting a direction for rural research. *Journal of Research in Rural Education* 20(6). Accessed 15 June 2006, http://www.umaine.edu/jrre/20-6.htm

Barter B (2008) Rural education: Learning to be rural teachers. *Journal of Workplace Learning* 20(7/8): 468–479

Bauch PA (2001) School–community partnerships in rural schools: Leadership, renewal, and a sense of place. *Peabody Journal of Education* 76(2): 204–221

Bogdan RC & Biklen SK (1998) *Qualitative research for education: An introduction to theory and methods.* Needham, MA: Allyn and Bacon

Budge K (2006) Rural leaders, rural places: Problem, privilege, and possibility. *Journal of Research in Rural Education* 21(13). Accessed 15 November 2006, http://www.umaine.edu/jrre/21-13.pdf

Carson TR & Sumara D (eds) (2001) *Action research as a living practice.* New York: Peter Lang

Chambers C (1999) A topography for Canadian curriculum theory. *Canadian Journal of Education* 24(2): 137–150

Clandinin DJ & Connelly FM (1995) *Teachers' professional knowledge landscapes.* New York: Teachers College Press

Connelly FM & Clandinin DJ (1988) *Teachers as curriculum planners: Narratives of experience.* New York: Teachers College Press

Corbett M (2007) *Learning to leave: The irony of schooling in a coastal community.* Halifax, NS: Frenwood Publishing

Coupal LV (2005) Changing the meaning of community: E-learning in rural Newfoundland, Canada. Accessed 10 May 2005, http://www.royalroads.ca

DeYoung AJ (1987) The status of American rural education research: An integrated review and commentary. *Review of Educational Research* 57(2): 123–148

Durkheim E (1984) *The division of labour in society.* New York: Free Press

Foster W (2004) The decline of the local: A challenge to educational leadership. *Educational Administration Quarterly* 40(2): 176–190

Herzog MJR & Pittman R (2002) The nature of rural schools: Trends, perceptions and values. In DM Chalker (ed.) *Leadership for rural schools: Lessons for all educators.* Kent: Scarecrow Press

Hodgkinson C (1991) *Educational leadership: The moral art.* Albany, NY: State University of New York Press

Hofstadter R (1966) *Anti-intellectualism in American life.* New York: Vintage Books

Jaffee D (2001) *Organization theory: Tension and change.* New York: McGraw-Hill

Khattri N, Riley KW & Kane MB (1997) Students at risk in poor, rural areas: A review of the research. *Journal of Research in Rural Education* 13(2): 79–97

Kincheloe J & Pinar W (eds) (1991) *Curriculum as a social psychoanalysis: The significance of place.* Albany, NY: State University of New York Press

Mellow M (2005) The work of rural professionals: Doing the *Gemeinschaft-Gesellschaft* gavotte. *Rural Sociology* 70(1): 50–69

Mulcahy DM (1996) Why rural education? *Morning Watch* 24(11). Accessed 7 January 2005, http://www.mun.ca/educ/faculty/mwatch/fall96/mulcahy.htm

Mulcahy DM (1999) Future directions for rural schools in Newfoundland and Labrador: Is the 'virtual school' the way to go? Accessed 8 June 2005, http://www.mun.ca/educ/faculty/mwatch/fall99/mulcahy.htm

Newby H (1980) Rural sociology. *Current Sociology* 28(1): 1–11

NMF (Nelson Mandela Foundation) (2005) Emerging voices: A report on education in South African rural communities. Accessed 23 September 2007, http://www.hsrcpress.ac.za

Schwandt T (1997) *Qualitative inquiry: A dictionary of terms.* Thousand Oaks, CA: Sage Publications

Smith P (2002) It's déjà vu all over again: The rural school problem revisited. In DM Chalker (ed.) *Leadership for rural schools: Lessons for all educators.* Kent: Scarecrow Press

Stern JD (1994) *The condition of education in rural schools.* Washington, DC: US Department of Education

Theobald P (2007) Review of *Learning to leave: The irony of schooling in a coastal community. Journal of Research in Rural Education.* Accessed 10 February 2008, http://jrre.psu.edu/ articles/22-4.pdf

Theobald P & Nachtigal P (1995) Culture, community and the promise of rural education. *Phi Delta Kappan* (October): 132–135

Tönnies F (1957) *Gemeinschaft und Gesellschaft* [Community and society]. CP Loomis, ed. and trans. East Lansing, MI: Michigan State University Press

Wallin D (2006) Educational priorities and capacity: A summary of research on rural education in Manitoba. Prepared for the Manitoba Association of School Superintendents and the Manitoba Association of School Trustees. Accessed 20 February 2008, http://www.mast. mb.ca

Weber M (1964) *The theory of social and economic organisation.* New York: Free Press

Weber M (1970) [1904] Capitalism and rural society in Germany. In HH Gerth & CW Mills (eds) *From Max Weber: Essays in sociology.* London: Routledge

Woods M (2003) Deconstructing rural protest: The emergence of a new social movement. *Journal of Rural Studies* 19(3): 309–325

Section III

Exploring possibilities, creating change

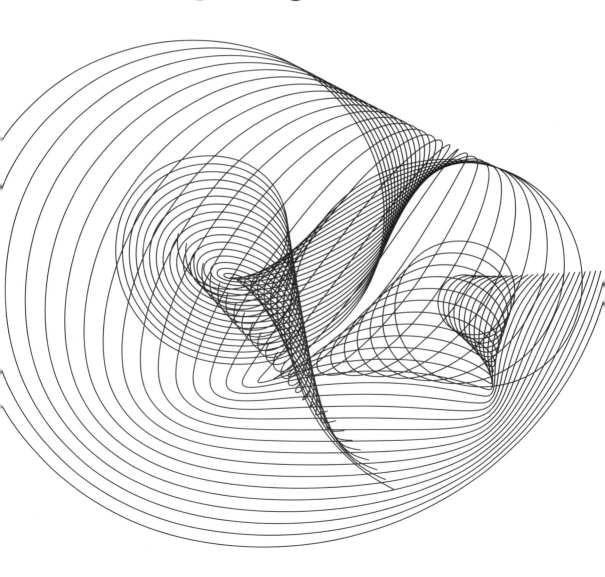

Workers organising/learning

18 Learning democracy from North–South worker exchanges

Judith Marshall

Introduction

In 2001, 10 Canadian workers from the United Steelworkers union (USW) took part in a workers' exchange visit to Mexico, where they were introduced to labour realities by the Authentic Workers Front (FAT), a Mexican confederation of labour unions. During a visit to the export-processing zones straddling the border with the US, one of the Canadians convinced a plant manager that the group included potential investors. This resulted in a lengthy guided tour through an immaculately clean, brightly lit manufacturing plant with state-of-the-art equipment, operated by highly skilled Mexican workers.

During the debriefing that evening, one of the Canadians exploded with frustration at the FAT hosts. 'You've been telling us for years about sweatshops in the *maquilas*.[1] It's a load of crap. That plant today was more modern than my plant in Canada.'

The next day the Canadians visited the community where these Mexican *maquila* workers lived – rife with makeshift shacks, illegally hooked-up power lines, raw sewage, young children without day-care centres or schools. Yet buses with the names of global manufacturing giants – Sony, GE, Westinghouse – plied regularly through the squalor to transport their employees to state-of-the-art factories.

The worker exchange had provided a dramatic 'learning moment'. What could have conveyed more graphically the lure of Mexico for North American manufacturers? The same goods made in Canada for C$16 an hour, a solid benefits package and a pension could – post NAFTA, the free-trade agreement that created a borderless North American market – be produced in a *maquiladora* for a wage bill of C$5 a day in a 'special economic zone', free from taxes and tariffs. When Mexican workers pressurised for higher wages, the company responded with a threat to move to even lower-waged Guatemala or Honduras. Since that visit in 2001, many of these transnationals have transferred their operations to manufacturing platforms in Asia.

Corporate globalisation has forced unionised steelworkers in Canada to rethink 'work' and 'global competitiveness' and invent new forms of building global alliances. In the first section of this chapter, I look at two ways of seeing that make it difficult for Canadian steelworkers to grasp what is happening globally. In the second section, I focus on how workers' exchanges involving rank-and-file union members have become an integral part of USW activities, thanks to the establishment of international development funds within the major private and public sector unions in Canada since 1985. These exchanges have proved to be powerful learning tools for Canadian workers.

In the final section, I focus on stories of individual workers and, using their own words, try to capture how North–South exchanges have turned their understanding of the world upside down. I also look at how they use what they have learned to build new organisational structures and new forms of communication and worker solidarity.

Deconstructing the global South

USW courses on globalisation regularly include resource people from Chile, South Africa or Guatemala. The presentation by the guests is often introduced by brainstorming about the images of their country prevailing in Canada through the media, travel brochures and aid organisations. Almost invariably the images of the South include 'violence', 'poverty', 'corruption', 'backwardness', 'a need for our charity' and 'lacking expertise'. The South is cast as uniformly rural, limited to subsistence agriculture and, if industrialised, using obsolete technology.

Conversations with two USW activists, one who had visited *maquilas* in Mexico and the other who had visited the University of the Western Cape in South Africa, provide reflections on their perceptions of the global South:

> Before I left, my thoughts about the places we were going to visit – the factories, the workplaces – included sweatshop-like atmospheres, dim lighting, old equipment, dangerous working conditions. But I was shocked by the advanced nature of the workplaces. In a lot of ways they were better than what I had worked with here. (Humphrey 2007)

> I envisioned the [whole country] to be extremely poor, and that there would be more violence…I expected the entire area to be what we see on TV. When I landed in Cape Town, I was just flabbergasted by the beauty of the city…we have this preconceived notion that they are not as advanced or educated. When I actually went to the university, I could have been walking into the University of Toronto…I am almost ashamed to admit that I felt that way, but the trip really changed this view. (Gow 2007)

Where do the characterisations of the South operative in Canadian workers' heads come from, and what role does the reproduction of these perceptions play in contemporary configurations of power and knowledge? As neo-liberal globalisation began to assert its hold in the late 1970s, so did new ways of seeing the imperial hold of an earlier era. Edward Said's ground-breaking *Orientalism* reordered the study of colonialism, showing how Western representation of the Middle East as it was produced and circulated in Europe was an active ideological component of colonial power. Said moves beyond narrow understandings of colonial authority based on superior military power and coercive mechanisms to show how colonialism's real strength lay in producing a 'discourse' about the Orient, a structure of thinking to be found in literary and artistic productions, in political and scientific writing and, indeed, in the creation of Oriental studies as such. First and foremost, it was a political vision of the Middle East that propagated a binary opposition between the familiar – Europe, the West, 'us'– and the strange – the Orient, the East, 'them' (Said 1978, 1994).

Said's seminal works focused on the relationship between Europe and the Middle East. Contemporary post-colonial scholars such as Ana Loomba take up the same questions:

> [T]his opposition is crucial to European self-conception: if colonised people are irrational, Europeans are rational; if the former are barbaric, sensual, and lazy, Europe is civilization itself, with its sexual appetites under control and its dominant ethic that of hard work; if the Orient is static, Europe can be seen as developing and marching ahead. The Orient has to be feminine so that Europe can be masculine. This dialectic between self and other, derived in part from deconstruction, has been hugely influential in subsequent studies of colonial discourses in other places – critics have traced it as informing colonial attitudes towards Africans, Native Americans, and other non-European peoples. (Loomba 1998: 45)

Substitute 'North' and 'South' for 'Europeans' and 'colonised people' and one sees readily the way that current discourses about the South have become an active ideological component of North–South relations. For Canadian trade unionists, little in their education or their experiences would prompt them to reflect on the colonial relationship. Indeed, many would claim to be 'perfect strangers' to the First Nations people colonised in Canada itself, despite a historical relationship of subjugation and assimilation (York University 2005).[2]

One of the most effective posters used in anti-racism work in Canada over the years bore this simple message: 'being white means you can choose whether to take on the issues of racism or not'. If enjoying 'white privilege' without connecting it to issues of systemic racism is an option, how much more so is 'Northern privilege' enjoyed without connecting it to the history of slavery, colonialism and corporate pillage that has and does shape the South?

Even less would most workers engage in any kind of critique of the assumptions of modernism that permeate Canadian culture – namely, advocacy of science, technology and rationality as the foundations for equating change with progress; the ethnocentric equation of history with the triumphs of European civilisation; and the globalising view that the industrialised Western countries constitute a legitimate centre for imposing control on the rest of the world (Giroux 1988).

If Canadians in general view the South through an ideological lens skewed even more by Canada's ever-closer cultural proximity to the contemporary centre of imperial power, the US, Canadian trade unionists have yet another way of seeing the South that makes it difficult to build global connections. The whole history of the labour movement is premised on fighting for workers' rights and entitlements that apply across jurisdictions. Collective bargaining is enshrined as a process for bringing dignity, higher wages, benefits and safer working conditions across the workplace. There is resistance to contract workers employed under different conditions, and to the introduction of business systems and quality management programmes that reward individual workers and erode all sense of the collective. At the international level, 'an injury to one is an injury to all' has been a watchword for the labour movement over the years. In practice, this has meant taking solidarity action on labour rights issues, whether in the prolonged struggle to dismantle apartheid in South Africa or in the current struggles around trade union rights in Colombia.

Assumptions about the central role of governments in establishing regulatory regimes are fundamental to the practice of international solidarity. The dilemma today is that the most powerful actors in the global economy share none of this logic of rights across jurisdictions and strong government roles in maintaining them. The transnationals have mounted a massive campaign for deregulation over the past few decades through programmes of structural adjustment in the South and free-trade agreements in the North. Big corporations and big governments think about global spaces driven by supply chains, controlling key resources and strategic markets. They put together networks of operations managed electronically as a single global entity, with the driving logic being maximum profit for shareholders rather than the creation of decent jobs, much less the alleviation of poverty. Indeed, neo-liberal pundits in Canada are so enthusiastic about this new world of 'supply chains' that they actually refer to concepts such as sovereignty and the nation state as 'ephemeral'.

In her extraordinary work *The Shock Doctrine*, Naomi Klein traces the history of neo-liberalism, documenting in thought-provoking fashion the boldness of those promoting market fundamentalism who now use even outright military occupation, as in Iraq, to pursue their goals. As she writes:

> Having been part of the movement against ballooning corporate power
> that made its global debut in Seattle in 1999, I was accustomed to
> seeing…business-friendly policies imposed through arm-twisting at
> World Trade Organization summits, or as the conditions attached to loans
> from the International Monetary Fund. The three trademark demands –
> privatisation, government deregulation and deep cuts to social spending –
> tended to be extremely unpopular with citizens, but when the agreements
> were signed there was still at least the pretext of mutual consent between
> the governments doing the negotiating, as well as a consensus among the
> supposed experts. Now the same ideological program was being imposed
> via the most baldly coercive means possible: under foreign military
> occupation after an invasion, or immediately following a cataclysmic
> natural disaster. September 11 appeared to have provided Washington
> with the green light to stop asking countries if they wanted the U.S.
> version of 'free trade and democracy' and to start imposing it with Shock
> and Awe military force. (Klein 2007: 9)

Governments around the globe have been persuaded under neo-liberal tutelage that their main role is to facilitate business and let market forces prevail. In such a context, the disconnect grows between a worker logic of a strong government role in promoting employment and rights regimes across geo-political spaces, and a corporate logic of profitable, high-tech enclaves and supply chains employing a privileged few amid seas of unemployment and poverty.

To further distance Canadian workers from challenging corporate globalisation, 'labour rights' have been folded into the approach of the modern-day human rights movement. Picking its way between claims and counter-claims in the Cold War climate, the modern human rights movement has opted for an approach that has tried to remain independent of any government, political faction, ideology, economic interest or religious creed. In an effort not to adopt any group's 'political agenda', however, rights activists have tended to focus on minute documentation of rights violations and actions to pressure the governments that perpetrate them, leaving unexamined the political project of these governments in establishing neo-liberal policies, including the role of the transnational corporations in colluding with governments of the South to introduce these new regimes (Klein 2007).[3] This means that even workers actively engaged in international solidarity campaigns often operate within a 'blinkered' version focusing narrowly on rights, without taking on the broader and more complex ideological and political projects of neo-liberal modes of governance.

So while unions in the North continue to engage their members in campaigns pressurising Southern governments to defend labour rights, powerful corporate players erase national borders through trade agreements and create their global supply chains, picking and choosing locations, investment projects and workers of interest to them in their global pursuits. Indeed, as Aihwa Ong brilliantly argues, one of the hallmarks of neo-liberalism is precisely its capacity to operate as a malleable technology of governing, equally at home in liberal democracies and in post-colonial, authoritarian and post-socialist situations. States make exceptions to their usual practices of governing in order to reposition themselves to compete in the global economy and, in so doing, reconfigure the relationships between the governing and the governed, power and knowledge, and sovereignty and territoriality. This means the emergence of an interactive form of citizenship that organises people and defines their rights and entitlements according to their marketable skills in the global economy rather than their membership within national states (Ong 2006: 3).

Ong's anthropological cases studies of workers in Asia – from young Filipino women persuaded that work as 'nannies' in Hong Kong or Canada with remittances to family is a kind of 'national service', to workers in special economic zones in China – document these regimes where sovereignty and citizenship are being pried apart. She extends her critical gaze to the Asian 'tiger economies' such as Singapore, Malaysia, Thailand and Indonesia, which have also been characterised as 'developmental states'. Ong notes the difference between 'developmentalism' – where the national economy is the target of state action with a mix of powerful bureaucracy, public enterprises and state monopolies that result in structural changes in the productive system and steady growth rates – and the 'postdevelopmentalism' that has prevailed in Asia since the 1980s. This she characterises as

> a more dispersed strategy that does not treat the national territory as a uniform political space. Market-driven logic induces the coordination of political policies with the corporate interests, so that developmental decisions favor the fragmentation of the national space into various noncontiguous zones, and promote the differential regulation of populations who can be connected to or disconnected from global circuits of capital. (Ong 2006: 77)

Canadian workers, then, embark on global exchanges with a 'knowledge' of the South shaped by the prevailing structure of thinking within Canada and the trade union movement. This 'knowledge' often enters into sharp contradiction with what they encounter on their journeys.

Global exchanges: Tools for worker learning

The establishment of an international development fund, called the Steelworkers Humanity Fund, within the USW in 1985 was prompted by the dramatic famine taking place in Ethiopia. New communications technology brought heart-rending images directly into Canadian living rooms. The USW responded with a uniquely union strategy: introducing an international development fund into collective bargaining.

By the late 1980s, workers in most USW workplaces had bargained the Humanity Fund into their collective agreements and were contributing a penny from every hour they worked to the fund. While this averaged only C$20 a year per worker, cumulatively it created an annual revenue of about a million dollars. The USW had pioneered the concept, but other unions were soon on board, all with matching dollars from CIDA, the Canadian International Development Agency.

International affairs has historically been an area of union activity carried out at central level by the Canadian Labour Congress, in close collaboration with the senior political leaders of the major affiliates. Local union activists have tended to become directly involved only in campaigns around the most egregious abuses of labour rights, from apartheid in South Africa, to Colombia, to *maquiladoras*. The establishment of multiple labour international development funds, however, has created new spaces for global action designed, funded and staffed by the major public and private sector unions. By the mid 1990s, the Steelworkers Humanity Fund was managing programmes with an annual budget of about C$2.3 million that included funding for long-term development projects, disaster relief, development education and policy advocacy (Marshall 1997).

Creating a labour tool for responding to international humanitarian crises drove the creation of the Steelworkers Humanity Fund in 1985. The funds created in subsequent years were driven by the need to find a tool for responding to corporate globalisation. The Canadian labour movement had fought back against the onslaught of the neo-liberal model in Canada, first through the FTA, a free-trade agreement with the US, and then through NAFTA, an extension of this agreement to include Mexico. Factory workers in central Canada saw their manufacturing jobs disappearing to Mexico. The workers in the mining sector were feeling a strong pull from Chile. The 1973 coup had established a brutal military dictatorship and new economic directions driven by economists trained in neo-liberal fundamentalism under Milton Friedman at the University of Chicago. The combined forces of repression and market fundamentalism had made Chile wide open for business.[4] Canadian mining companies were eager to invest and Canadian mineworkers found themselves packing equipment in Canada to send to mining towns such as Iquique and Copiapo while their managers spent lunch hours working on Spanish lessons.

At a 1992 Humanity Fund Board meeting, the mandate of the fund was expanded to include using the fund to help union members better understand and function in the global economy. As board member Jim Saare, from a smelter in western Canada, put it, unless the board made the fund a tool for union members to deal with the international world as they are experiencing it – and this means globalisation and trade deals such as NAFTA – the fund would lose their support.

On the one hand, this meant more projects working directly with trade unions rather than community groups and, indeed, all of the labour funds soon joined together with the Canadian Labour Congress to form a Labour International Development Committee and to negotiate co-funding from CIDA, specifically for projects with labour organisations.

For the Humanity Fund it also meant sharpening the focus of the education programme. From the earliest days, the fund had carried out an education programme with two main components: the international solidarity courses of varying lengths; and the worker exchanges involving rank-and-file union members who contributed to the fund. The 'Thinking North–South' course became a regular offering on the menu of the week-long USW schools. A shorter course called 'Facing Global Management' was jointly developed with activists and used in area councils or large locals. There were also mini-courses more in the nature of briefings and debriefings for members travelling on visits to projects and worker exchanges.

The participants came to the courses for various reasons. In some cases, a local union opted to send someone with a focus more on growing the fund than on globalisation. They wanted first-hand knowledge of how the fund functioned and what was being supported through the fund to take back to the local. Local union members already interested in international affairs often participated. The fund offered scholarships, which it used to ensure gender and racial diversity among the course participants.

'Thinking North–South' was designed to engage USW members in learning new knowledge, attitudes, skills and behaviours related to the workings of the global economy and how the Humanity Fund could be used as a tool for engaging in it. Using popular education methodology, the course started with the realities of the workplaces and communities of the participants, and how these realities were linked to and shaped by the global economy.

One of the biggest challenges in 'Thinking North–South' was to have the participants begin to discover the knowledge of the South that was already operative in shaping their attitudes and behaviours. Only a tiny handful had actually spent any time in the South, and most of that travel was to well-insulated tourist resorts. Yet they had internalised the discourse about the South that is such an integral part of the contemporary North–South configuration of power and knowledge.

The learning activities in the courses were designed to deconstruct the prevailing images of the South and promote a growing awareness of 'Northern privilege'. One powerful tool was the presence of guests from the community groups and unions supported by the Humanity Fund. Course participants had the opportunity to interact for a week with a South African miner, or with a community kitchen organiser from Peru, inside the classroom and over beers long into the night.

Over the years, participants would often draw me aside at some point to make revealing comments such as, 'I never knew that there were women from Africa who were educated and spoke English'. Indeed, the stereotyping of Africa was perhaps the strongest. An exchange of university workers to South Africa and Mozambique in 2007 pointed to the same phenomenon. The group spent the first 10 days of their visit interacting with vibrant new social movements fighting issues of privatisation, land, jobs, housing and AIDS treatment in and around Cape Town and Johannesburg. They also met university workers in Cape Town, Johannesburg and Maputo struggling with the same issues of privatisation and corporatisation of public education that they faced at home in Canada. Yet they commented to me that they felt they still hadn't seen 'the real Africa'.[5]

In these exchanges, Canadian workers were genuinely moved, sometimes even to tears, by the stories of trade union leaders from places such as Colombia and Guatemala who put their own and their families' lives on the line as union organisers. Yet far from situating this in terms of a history of imperialism and pillage, or contemporary neo-liberal machinations in which our own corporations and government are often actively complicit, the reaction from the Canadian worker was more often about luck:

> The factories were amazing, really as good or even better than what we
> have to work with here. But the poverty was simply unbelievable, children
> without clothes on, people living in shacks by the side of the road or right
> on the highway. I have never seen anything like it. I tell you one thing: it
> really makes you realise how lucky we are in Canada. (Bickell 2007)

One of the tools that proved most effective in triggering deeper examination of existing attitudes is a video called 'Shaping the Image'. The video sets out to explore how the Ethiopian crisis got worked up into a major media event. It starts with the image of an Ethiopian woman – the scene complete with emaciated child, slack breasts, ubiquitous flies – and then cuts to an image of abundance from rural Kenya, where a plump village woman sits amid baskets of produce, bantering with her well-dressed diplomat son who is home on a visit. He suggests that this scene of plenty is far more typical of rural Africa and ponders why Africa is so relentlessly cast as a place of famine and poverty.

The video moves on through a workshop of African journalists lamenting how rarely they get to tell their own story, to a sharp critique of celebrity ambassadors. A corporate executive exults in the huge success of his company's advertisement for the Live Aid concert. Taking an already well-known company jingle, they incorporated Bob Geldof's famine photos with words about 'reaching out' and 'saving someone'. It was a corporate branding triumph. Without even having to mention the company's name, they were able to convey that their company cared!

Course participants are usually groaning audibly after this media critique, realising how much they have accepted these worked-up images of Africa as the real thing, how readily they had been duped into thinking that dipping into their pockets can really 'end hunger now'. They recognise the insidious messaging of the 'charity industry', endlessly projecting images of helpless and needy Africans with Northern donors as their only hope for salvation.

In the early days, the 'Thinking North–South' course was the usual stepping stone for solidarity visits. USW activists contributing to the fund made 8- to 10-day visits to a community kitchen programme in the slums of Lima or to a pig-rearing project in Guatemala, as well as making contact with local trade unionists.

Over the course of the 1990s, the global solidarity courses and worker exchanges became much more strategically focused, laying the foundation for USW involvement in networks of workers in the same sector or with a common transnational employer. Involving rank-and-file workers in global exchanges and networks was new to union culture. Historically, international travel by unions had tended to be limited to formal meetings of the International Labour Organization (ILO) and global union federations (such as the International Metalworkers' Federation and the International Federation of Chemical, Energy, Mine and General Workers' Unions), congresses of well-established unions and the odd conference. For the most part, those representing the union had been senior political leaders and/or staff members with technical expertise (Marshall & Garcia 2006).

Over the past 17 years, more than 200 rank-and-file workers have been involved in solidarity visits and worker exchanges. These have ranged from trips made by one or two members to learn about the work of a particular organisation, to a 10-person Toronto Area Council delegation to Mexico. At times the travel has been linked to the World Social Forum or the various parallel forums, alongside negotiating sessions for the Free Trade Area of the Americas (FTAA). Or the trips have been linked to a particular event, from election monitoring in South Africa, to participation in the congress of a union supported by the fund. Sometimes the local union members have travelled with a staff member of the Humanity Fund responsible for the project, adding more of a monitoring and evaluation dimension to the trip. At other times, the main purpose is education and exchange, with workers bringing to it their own experiences of activism within workplace and community.

In recent years, more and more of these exchanges have been understood as building blocks in constructing networks of workers who share the same transnational employer. Today there are global networks in varying stages of formation with workers from Teck Cominco, Gerdau, X-strata, Tenaris, Mittal, G4S and Vale. There are also sectoral networks, linking university workers, security guards or health workers.

USW security guard workers have carried out exchanges with their counterparts in Mozambique and have participated in global campaigns against the anti-union practices of G4S, the largest security guard transnational. University technical, administrative and service workers from the University of Guelph and the University of Toronto have begun to connect with their counterparts in Mexico, South Africa, Mozambique and the UK.

The follow-up action on the university exchanges has included articles in each other's bulletins and further bilateral visits. In addition, the University of Toronto workers decided they wanted to run a 'Globalisation School' similar to the one they had participated in with grassroots activists in Cape Town. This resulted in a highly successful USW Globalisation School in Toronto in 2007 with 90 participants, including workers from universities in London, Mexico City, Cape Town and Maputo. All of these activities serve to lay the foundations for ongoing networks able to communicate and act together as they face the new challenges of corporate globalisation.

Learning about globalisation: Workers' voices

In the first section of the chapter, I explored the operative understanding of the South that USW members take into their new roles as global activists. In the next section, I outlined a new practice of international work in the Canadian labour movement through labour international development funds. In this section, I explore what kinds of new knowledge, attitudes, skills and behaviours have been learned from these global encounters. Clearly, much more systematic research could and should be done in this area, but in the meantime it is possible to map out some preliminary observations. These are based on my own observations as the coordinator of the Humanity Fund education programme for the past 17 years, and also on interviews with USW members who have participated in Humanity Fund exchanges in an evaluation research project carried out in 2007.[6]

The global exchange visits generate new knowledge ranging from the nuts and bolts of trade unionism to broad questions about global issues. Not surprisingly, Canadian trade unionists have a set of working assumptions about what constitutes a union, all derived from their own experiences of union structures in Canada. One of the first shocks for Canadian miners in their exchanges with Chile in the early 1990s was to discover that in Chilean unions there are neither shop stewards nor health and safety representatives. The five elected executive members were the only official union presence in the workplace, and if they all happened to be on the same shift, there could be entire week-long shifts working the mine site high in the Andes without any union presence. The comparable mine in Canada would have had not only the elected officers, some of whom would work full-time on union affairs, but also a steward for every 20 to 30 members, health and safety representatives and a fully functioning joint health and safety structure.

The construction of a global network of workers from 10 countries employed by the Brazilian steel multinational Gerdau has provided a kind of learning laboratory for comparative studies of trade unions. The Gerdau meetings began from a first gathering in 1998 hosted by the National Confederation of Brazilian Metalworkers affiliated with the CUT labour central, bringing together workers from Brazil, Chile and Canada. Bilateral visits and a second international meeting deepened the relationships and led to a third international meeting and the formation of a Gerdau Workers World Council with recognition by the International Metalworkers' Federation, although not yet by the company itself.

There was considerable learning about the difficulties of comparing unions and workers from one country to those from another because of widely divergent contexts and structures. For example, the strong workplace presence that characterises a unionised steel plant in Canada is not to be found in Brazil. Only the automobile plants in São Paulo have workers' commissions within the plants. Elsewhere, workplaces are grouped together in geographic areas and bargaining and servicing are carried out by a union structure outside the workplace.

There are also big differences in terms of what constitutes a bargaining unit and how unions finance themselves. As Ted Bickell, a Canadian Gerdau worker who attended the third international meeting, plaintively put it:

> It would have been great to sit down and get to know each other [the other Canadian Gerdau workers]. Also, it would have been helpful to have had a briefing on how the unions work in other countries – for example, dues check-offs and whatnot. I spent a lot of time trying to figure that stuff out. (Bickell 2007)

While unions in Canada basically relate to management through their collective bargaining agreements and have a finely honed set of monitoring and grievance procedures to force compliance with the agreement, unions in many other countries do not. On the other hand, many unions in the South play a much stronger role in policy dialogue with their governments, and have much stronger links with workers in the informal sector and the unemployed. Newer network members range from Spanish workers steeped in social dialogue and struggles to defend a 35-hour work week, to Colombian Gerdau workers living amid state terrorism.

Until the USW began to participate actively in global exchanges and networks, transnational managers enjoyed a monopoly of knowledge about what was happening in each of their operations. Management held this knowledge over workers' heads, as if their employees outside of Canada were the competition. Denis Matteau, the local union president in a large smelter owned by a transnational company which also has mining and smelting operations in Chile and Peru, expressed it this way:

> The exchanges also help us here. We need to know and understand about working conditions in the South. Management provides a lot of disinformation about what is happening in its operations in other parts of the world. We have regular meetings with the employer on production

and costs. They always talk of less-costly operations in the South and threaten to move more production there if we do not agree to whatever it is they are asking of us. (Matteau 2007)

After two exchange visits to Chile and Peru, there was a regular flow of information back and forth between the smelter workers in Canada and their counterparts in Latin America. When bargaining in the Chile smelter ended in a strike in 2007, the Chilean workers kept up an information hotline with their Canadian counterparts. The response of the union in Canada went well beyond just the traditional message of solidarity. The Canadian union president also went to his manager, reminded him how much their plant depended on a regular flow of raw materials from this particular operation in Chile and strongly urged his manager to lean on the managers in Chile to break the impasse. A settlement was reached 48 hours later. Was the union intervention a factor? We will never know definitively. What we can affirm with certainty is that the unions in both countries feel much stronger in handling the complexities of their relationships with their transnational managers when they can support each other actively at critical moments.

The new knowledge created by these exchange visits is infinitely variable and very much a two-way flow. Gerry LeBlanc, at the time a miner, visited South Africa as a monitor in the heyday of mobilisation for the country's first democratic elections. He commented:

> You don't teach a South African what it means to be a trade unionist. You learn from them…Despite the fact that we were from different parts of the world and had much different experiences, there was this moment when I was sitting with a group of South African workers and we were talking about safety issues and people dying in the mines. At that point we were no longer conducting a cultural or worker exchange, we were just miners talking about our fallen brothers who had passed away in the mines. There is no greater feeling of solidarity than that. (LeBlanc 2007)

Marlene Gow, who does race and gender training for the USW in Canada, visited South Africa some years later on a trainers' exchange with the Centre for Adult and Continuing Education at the University of the Western Cape, and came back with new insights about AIDS:

> AIDS is an issue in Africa that is affected by class, poverty, power and culture. In some ways men don't use a condom as a show of power. They are often less employed than women. Although condoms are available, men won't use them, just to exert some control over their relationships with women. I had thought that the AIDS issue was a problem of people not being smart enough to deal with it, but I now think that it has more to do with class and power. This has inspired me to be more active in AIDS education. (Gow 2007)

Travel for some members fills in nuts-and-bolts details. For Ray Grant, participation in an event in Argentina where Latino heads of state said a definitive 'no' to the

FTAA, a free-trade deal encompassing the 34 countries of the Americas, prompted new thoughts about the big picture:

> My impression of globalisation after attending this conference and from what I know is this. The rich get richer, the poor get poorer and the middle class get poorer. Regardless of where a person works, the employer will pay just enough for that person to live. We spoke to people who said in Burma they make four cents an hour. That is crazy. When I heard this it really changed how I understood globalisation. (Grant 2007)

Existing attitudes may come under scrutiny as a result of travel or encounters with international guests at home:

> My first exposure to the international world was the Quebec Summit in 2001.[7] I had thought that foreign workers were stealing jobs from us before that. After the summit, I got interested in how it worked overseas. I came to understand that it was not about foreign workers stealing our jobs. It was about employers manipulating our heads with misinformation about foreign workers. (Matteau 2007)

The Teck Cominco network was driven by the USW's need to understand better why Canadian mining investment in Chile was increasing so dramatically. A Chilean political exile who had become a USW activist while in Canada helped map the terrain on his return to Chile. Senior USW leaders began to attend mining and metal union events in Chile and the union decided to bring Chilean miners from two Canadian companies that had started up operations in Chile. Two Chilean miners from Teck Cominco and Placer Dome mines each spent a month in Canadian operations of these same companies and ended their trip at a USW National Policy Conference. This initiative underscored the importance of the human factor. While the Teck Cominco exchange established the foundation for continuing work over the years, the Placer Dome connection was never consolidated. Richard Boyce, the president of the Teck Cominco mine, was very keen for more contact and soon visited Chile himself, along with the health and safety coordinator of Highland Valley Copper.

The first eight-day exchange to Chile was not tightly scripted, giving space for both sides to learn about each other's realities and establish ways to be useful to each other. After returning to Canada, funding was sent for a computer and email hook-up to ensure continued communication. Boyce summarised the exchange as follows:

> We met with individuals, determined through conversation and asking questions of the workers there what they wanted and needed that we could provide. We put on a mini financial course and set it all up ourselves. We also put together a session on organising, put together a plan to get people signed up, and they ended up with 100 per cent of workers at that worksite becoming union members. (Boyce 2007)

At an early stage in the contacts with Chilean unionists, the paternalistic attitudes of the Canadians came under scrutiny. They confessed after the first exchange that they had just assumed their guest from Chile would come from a mine with rudimentary technology and would have few skills himself. Instead, their guest was an experienced electrician and, on their return visit, they found a mine using more sophisticated technology than theirs at Highland Valley.

The exchanges back and forth of the Teck Cominco workers were supplemented by regular conference calls with a translator on the line. Local union leaders began to develop the same capacity for intervention and working the relationship with management on global issues as they did on domestic issues. One of the conference calls brought shocking news of a fatality of a young Chilean miner, left pinned under a massive truck while police inspectors made the four-hour journey up to the mine. Once the inspection was completed, management told the Chileans to get back to work. After the call, Boyce promptly fired off a note of protest to the mine managers in Chile, suggesting that such inhumane treatment had not worked on Canadian miners over the years so why were the Canadian managers now trying to use it on the Chileans? Within hours, there was return communication from managers in Iquique – again, the power dynamic of only management being in the know was broken and workers felt more empowered through their ability to undertake joint action.

Working the global connections has often served to bring the Canadian local unions themselves into closer working relationships. While changes of local union leadership both in North and South – and a host of other factors – make building these networks a rough and uneven process, the Teck Cominco network has recently come together to put out a Teck Cominco Accord that enshrines a set of common principles and issues for the network.

For many, the trip to another country, language and culture took them well beyond their comfort level as travellers. Coming face to face with poverty was difficult, even though it fit with existing stereotypes. The shock of sophisticated urban centres, such as Buenos Aires or Johannesburg, modern production facilities and skilled workers was even harder to process. Few workers had questioned the 'Team Canada' rhetoric when their companies joined Canadian government officials on junkets to promote new investments, widely touted to contribute to 'development'. During the exchange visits, they learned that these Canadian companies were perceived as the exploiters, benefiting from weaker labour and environmental regulations and exacerbating rich–poor disparities.

In some cases, USW members taking part in the exchange did reflect more deeply on North–South differences. Ray Grant put it this way:

> The unions over there are more 'radical' – I am not sure if this is the right
> word, but I cannot come up with a better one. Perhaps they are more
> passionate and act more aggressively, but that comes with the territory
> and their history with employers and government. They have more to deal
> with and they deal with it with more passion than our union at home. Our
> union is great, but at the same time, we have less to deal with, things are
> easier for us and we don't have to struggle as much as they do. (Grant 2007)

Darren Patrick, long active on First Nations issues in Canada, worried aloud about the imposition of Western models:

> Our goals here, I have heard over and over, are to ensure that those in developing countries are brought up to our standards of living, that it is not a race to the bottom. I agree with this but also think that we need to be wary that we do not impose our ideals and systems in places where they will only serve to eliminate the cultures and practices of the people of that country. (Patrick 2007)

The solidarity visits and labour exchanges resulted not just in new knowledge and attitudes but also in new skills. On their return, travellers were asked to do reports and to speak at USW events ranging from local membership meetings to courses and conferences. New writing, photography, PowerPoint presentation and public speaking skills were honed as workers put these reports together and took them on the road.

Finding mechanisms to communicate about the trips turns out to be an important challenge. Ideas run deep within union culture that a trip is always a 'perk' or a reward for loyalty, akin to a Club Med vacation, even if those travelling never see the beach. Local union president Denis Matteau sought ways to involve larger numbers from his plant in briefing and debriefing sessions before and after travel. These helped to break down any perceptions of neglecting the members at home:

> It was important to communicate with my members on my return. We did articles in our newsletters on the three trips and detailed trip reports. We also made photos available. All of this helped the members understand that these were not tourist trips, but there is always a strong sentiment that the president and executive should be staying at home working on members' concerns in the plant. (Matteau 2007)

Usually the reports focused on general descriptions of the country and on organisations visited and projects funded by the Humanity Fund. One trip to Chile included a lengthy workplace inspection and the opportunity to compare health and safety conditions:

> Alto Norte and CCR [X-strata smelters in Chile and Canada] are like twin smelters. I saw a lot of things in the Alto Norte smelter that we would not have allowed in our smelter – emission levels, dangerous procedures, etc. There were very few regulations in place. When I got back I wrote a detailed report about working conditions in Alto Norte and shared it with all the members. The employer improved the standards in Alto Norte after that. We feel sure that the public report to members in Canada prompted them to do so. (Matteau 2007)

New skills are also needed to enable participation in the networks. Some members embark on language courses. Others start working more regularly with email and email list software. Recognising that their counterparts in Mozambique or Peru may have no computers to start with, local unions send funds for computer purchase and internet service. In recent years, many members have learned to use Skype as a tool for cheaper telephone communications.

Over the years, then, globalisation has become a major theme in USW courses and presence of workers from the South has become the norm at USW schools and conferences. Worker exchanges, however, have provided the most powerful learning moments over the years and have become the building blocks for ongoing networks and councils of workers with a common transnational employer.

In the case of the Gerdau network, the decade of working as a network has resulted in a new capacity for joint action. Gerdau began to expand heavily in the US in 2006 and teamed up there with virulently anti-union managers who soon locked out workers in Beaumont, Texas. With workers in one plant locked out and bargaining on indefinite hold in several other plants, the US unions turned to the network for support and embarked on a major lobbying and solidarity campaign. This included frequent exchanges of US and Brazilian workers and lobbying the Brazilian government, where not only President Lula but many ministers as well came from a metalworker background. The campaign also included giant billboards in Brazil questioning how Gerdau was managing its US operations. The subsequent change of management and willingness to go back to the bargaining table are seen as signs of the effectiveness of the network actions.

Network members prepared for the third international meeting of the Gerdau network by filling out a questionnaire and making a study visit to Colombia. Three issues of common concern were identified: contracting out, health and safety, and worker responses to Gerdau business systems. The network has subsequently organised a workshop on health and safety in Uruguay and another on workplace restructuring in Rio, with a follow-up session in 2008 in Houston, which included a visit to the locked-out Texas workers who benefited so greatly from the campaign.

Working the global dynamics is not easy. Each union is embedded in a particular social context, and the North–South power relations do not cease to be operative simply because all those involved are trade unionists. Some in the network were concerned about the optics of such a high-profile campaign to support US Gerdau workers in Texas while the ongoing plight of Colombian Gerdau workers received little attention. In unofficial – and unguarded – moments, some of the Brazilian workers even expressed pride that one of their companies was now a major transnational player, able to give US workers the mistreatment so many Latino workers had suffered over the years from US companies!

Conclusion

The broad goal of the courses on globalisation and the worker exchanges was the invention of new ways for Canadian workers to understand and operate within the globalised economy. The dramatic impact of corporate globalisation on workers' lives in recent years has made it obvious that old ways of engaging in 'international affairs' and 'international solidarity' have to be challenged. Global issues cannot be understood as mere add-ons, at the fringe of the union's continuing central domestic agenda of organising and bargaining. Building global alliances and networks has to become a central component of the union's work, benefiting from new communications technologies that strengthen the capacity of workers at a local level to stay closely connected as they navigate their relationships with transnational managers. It may well become standard practice for workers in future to go to the bargaining table, not just with their own issues, but also with those of their counterparts around the world.

The interviews with workers who have been involved in exchanges and networks provide tantalising glimpses of how the learning from these global connections has turned their views of the world upside down and given them a taste of global citizenship. Yet to be genuinely effective, the alliances and networks that they are now learning to construct have to extend beyond permanent workers to include contract workers, 'guest' workers and the unemployed. Indeed they have to reach beyond the labour movement as such to other social movements of environmentalists, women, aboriginals and the poor if they are to have any hope of seriously challenging corporate power. There is no beaten path to follow in forging these new connections. The Latin American adage was never truer: 'we make the road by walking'.

Notes

1   *Maquilas* is the Spanish word for export-processing zones.

2   York University in Toronto has promoted an important internal discussion process about what it would mean to teach and learn differently about the relationships between aboriginal and non-aboriginal people. They have extended their question to the reality of their own diverse student body and looked at relationships in other equity areas (white people in relation to racism, men in relation to gender, citizens of the North in relation to the South).

3   For a powerful discussion of how this 'human rights' approach can actually serve to hide the link between rights violations and larger political/ideological projects, see Naomi Klein's discussion of Argentina and Chile during the years when neo-liberalism was being established with the help of military coups and dirty wars (2007: 118–128).

4   For a cogent description of how Chile and other Southern Cone countries were subjected to neo-liberal forms of government through this 'shock therapy' combining brutal repression and market fundamentalism, see Klein (2007).

5   The repeated comment in Cape Town and Johannesburg that we had not yet reached 'the real Africa' prompted an article with that title, published in *Amandla*, a new South African publication for social movements, and *Our Times*, a labour publication in Canada (Marshall 2007).

6   I gratefully acknowledge the contribution of Ben Katz in working with me to carry out these interviews during the summer of 2007 as part of his work in the industrial relations programme at the University of Toronto.

7   As part of the People's Summit (parallel to the Summit of the Americas, which brought together heads of state of the Americas), the USW held a Commission of Inquiry on Corporate Conduct in the Americas. This was organised jointly with the FAT (Mexico), the Chilean Confederation of Mining and CONSTRAMET (Chile), and CNM/CUT (Brazil).

References

Giroux H (1988) Border pedagogy in the age of postmodernism. *Boston University Journal of Education* 170(3): 162–181

Klein N (2007) *The shock doctrine.* London: Allen Lane

Loomba A (1998) *Colonialism/postcolonialism.* London and New York: Routledge

Marshall J (1997) Globalisation from below: The trade union connections. In S Walters (ed.) *Globalisation, adult education and training: Impacts and issues.* London: Zed Books

Marshall J (2007) The real Africa. *Our Times* 27(3): 18ff and *Amandla* Experimental (3): 22–24

Marshall J & Garcia J (2006) Building capacity for global action. In P Kumar & C Shenk (eds) *Paths to union renewal.* Peterborough, ON: Broadview Press

Ong A (2006) *Neoliberalism as exception.* Durham, NC, and London: Duke University Press

Said E (1978) *Orientalism.* London: Routledge and Kegan Paul

Said E (1994) *Culture and imperialism.* New York: Vintage

York University (2005) *Voices of diversity and equity: Transforming university curriculum.* Toronto: FES/CST, York University

Interviews

Ted Bickell, 24 July 2007

Richard Boyce, 6 June 2007

Marlene Gow, 12 July 2007

Ray Grant, 25 July 2007

John Humphrey, 31 May 2007

Gerry LeBlanc, 4 July 2007

Pete Mandryk, 9 August 2007

Denis Matteau, 21 August 2007

Darren Patrick, 20 August 2007

19 The desire for something better: Learning and organising in the new world of work

Tony Brown

Introduction

There is an increasing polarisation of income, job opportunities and access to education in the advanced economies. Simultaneously there is a continuing reordering of economic relations between the advanced and the newly industrialising economies, as there is also within the newly industrialising economies. This process is often explained by a too-easy reference to an ill-defined 'globalisation'. However, if the advanced economies are being restructured in such a way that sees jobs in industries such as manufacturing disappear, then we need to examine where and in what conditions those jobs reappear. Changes to the contours of work, employment and education in one part of the world need to be understood in the context of a concomitant reshaping of those same relations in other parts of the world.

While some argue that Taylorist or Fordist work practices are a thing of the past as service industries replace manufacturing in the West, they reappear in much more intense forms in the rapidly growing economies of China, India, other parts of Asia, and in the free-trade zones of Central America, Southeast Asia and southern China. Within the advanced economies there is a contemporary phenomenon of overwork, while in the newly industrialising economies there is both super-exploitation in the new manufacturing plants and mass exclusion from the labour force.

Another way of understanding globalisation is as the extension of the market, and the social relations established by it, into virtually all corners of the globe, or what Mojab refers to as 'the normalisation of capitalism' (Chapter 1, this volume). Therefore, examining the new globalised capitalism requires us to see the restructuring of work as an interconnected process with different expressions in different sites and contexts. The literature that dominates the study of work and learning takes little account of the extent and depth of this restructuring, or of the consequences of polarisation, or of efforts to critically analyse and organise alternatives to it, as the literature remains overly focused on a particular and limited dimension that goes under the headings of 'the knowledge economy' and 'the knowledge worker'.

Where are the challenges to this internationalisation and naturalisation of capitalism? Workers' organisations have been slow to develop their capacity to resist these changes in any unified or systematic way. This reflects both the challenges involved in overcoming bureaucratic and organisational traditions resting on national identities, as well as a slowness to develop political and ideological alternatives.

An important aspect of this development is the educational dimension. Education within the labour movement needs to involve more than presenting a database of facts and statistics, because 'revealing' the extent of the problems associated with polarisation will not in and of itself change consciousness. Education within the labour movement also needs to draw from and build on experience, to develop analytical frameworks and a sense of historical movement and flow. It needs to assist people in developing their stories, their narratives that convey flow, change and interests. Thus an important question to ask is, are unions and related organisations doing this? In recent years there have been signs that within the labour movement new ways to organise are being learned and new ways of making cross-border alliances are being explored.

I begin this chapter by examining new developments in the integration of the global economy that impact on work. In particular, I look at how the restructuring of work and production takes on different shapes in different countries and regions and what this means for workers both within and outside of the formal economy. Next I discuss how unions and non-unionised workers are responding to the challenges of a restructured and integrated world market. I refer to structural responses and examples of strategic campaigning aimed at building labour capacity to confront corporate power and to build cross-border solidarity between workers in advanced and newly industrialising countries, and between workers from newly industrialising countries who are working in the advanced economies. I conclude with a discussion of the need to revive the critique of the market so that alternative, democratic re-visioning can be woven into new stories of a better world.

What's new in globalisation?

In many ways capital has been global since the sixteenth century, and there is a lot of exaggeration and hype in the talk about globalisation today. But there are four developments that are relatively new in the last 10 years or so.

Developments

The first development is that today the world is made up almost entirely of capitalist states integrated into the world market. In the whole of the previous history of capitalism, there have been many countries dominated by pre-capitalist ruling classes and pre-capitalist modes of production, and tied into the world market in very limited and specialised ways. Moreover, for much of the twentieth century there was a 'second world' comprising the Stalinist bloc of command economies. But now, in almost all countries there are true-blue capitalist states well integrated into the world market.

Secondly, almost all countries are integrated into the world market in complex ways. These include substantial sectors integrated into complex production networks stretching over several countries. For a large part of the history of capitalism, the pattern of world trade was one of raw materials being exported from less-developed countries to western Europe or the US, where manufacturing industry was based in the metropolis, and manufactured goods being exported back to the less-developed countries. That pattern has pretty much broken down. Today the biggest exporter of bulk raw materials is the US, the most developed country, while manufactured goods predominate in world trade and in the exports of less-developed countries.

Thirdly, there has been an enormous cheapening and speeding-up of transport and communications. This is also the era of mass international air travel, mass international telephone communication and the internet.

Fourthly, the wage working class, defined as those who sell their labour power to capital and are exploited by capital, together with the children and retired people of that class, probably comprises the majority of the world's population for the first time ever. It is difficult to say precisely, because in many countries large numbers of people are 'semi-proletarians' who have bits of jobs or casual jobs and subsist partly on wage labour and partly on begging or petty trade. Nevertheless, there has been a tremendous expansion of wage labour. Indonesia, one of the less capitalistically developed countries in the world, and where many people live not far from poverty, has probably a higher proportion of wage labour than Germany did in 1918.

These developments did not happen all at once. Capital did not suddenly flip over into new forms in 1990, or at any other particular date. The developments listed above are culminations of tendencies that go back a very long time, but in the 1990s the four developments reached a sort of 'critical mass', and that happened mainly through three processes.

Processes

Firstly, the economic crises of the 1970s and 1980s brought an end to the long boom period following the Second World War. This period saw the gradual knitting together of world trade, the gradual development of autonomous capitalist centres in many of the ex-colonial countries and the gradual rise of transnational corporations. The end of the boom – accompanied by the defeat of the US in Vietnam, the sudden and dramatic increase in oil prices, and the simultaneous emergence of high inflation and unemployment – heralded a new political and economic era. The early 1970s opened a period of major economic crises in which the relations of capitalist states to the world market generated doubt and division, and confronted ruling classes with difficult choices. Instead of choosing the option of raising economic barriers and erecting siege economies on the model followed in the 1930s, they chose the option of reorganising their affairs to attune them better to the gradually more powerful world market.

Those interests within the ruling classes who looked towards the world market won an increasing political hegemony. They were prepared to pay a high price in the restructuring of industries, not only in working-class suffering but also in the ruination of large sections of capital. In the early 1980s in Britain, for example, under the Conservative government of Margaret Thatcher, about one-quarter of manufacturing industry was eliminated in a few years. Despite the opposition from within her party, Thatcher won in the struggle over European integration and monetary union.

Similarly, labour parties in Australia and New Zealand systematically privatised state-owned industries and services, deregulated finance, centralised wage fixing and removed protectionist trade barriers. In China, Deng Xiaoping's rehabilitation in 1978 signalled the end of Maoism personified by the Gang of Four, and Deng's modernisation programme heralded an era of economic liberalisation while confining strict control of the political process to the Chinese Communist Party. In each case those 'globalist' sections were able to establish their outlook as the new 'common sense' of capital.

The second development was the response of governments in less-developed countries to the Third World debt crisis after 1982. Instead of defaulting on the debt and emulating the economic nationalism of the 1930s, they responded by privatisations, anti-inflation policies, welfare cuts, deregulation, export drives – whatever was necessary to restore their credit with the international banks.

Alongside the response to economic crises of governments in the West and South, the other essential process was the collapse of the Stalinist model of industrial development, and the rush by the new post-Communist governments of the 1990s in Czechoslovakia, Poland, Hungary and Russia to embrace a largely laissez-faire and pre-welfare-state version of capitalist development.

These processes sped up the achievement of a 'critical mass' of the four developments discussed above. Significantly, this happened during a period of working-class setbacks, when the ruling classes had regained the initiative after the big working-class struggles of the late 1960s and the early 1970s. In some countries there were big set-piece defeats for the working class – such as the British miners' strike of 1984–1985; in other countries, there was simply a petering out of the struggles of the 1970s in disarray and disillusionment, which was further accelerated by the collapse of the Berlin Wall in 1989. All this has shaped a lot of the detail of how 'globalisation' has proceeded since the 1980s. A push towards inequality, destruction of social provision, ecological damage and increased pauperisation has been exacerbated by the ascendancy of neo-liberal ideas and policies and a corresponding decline in working-class political confidence and organisation. Although almost all capitalist countries are now complexly integrated into the world market, that is by no means true of all the world's population, as vast numbers of people – including one billion urban-dwellers radically and permanently disconnected from the formal world economy – have become a disposable or 'surplus humanity' (Davis 2006a; UN 2003; Bales 2000).

Capitalist globalisation is capital enlarged, capital expanding across the world. It is not a number of other things that it is said to be. It is not capitalism turned financial. Financial markets have expanded enormously, but the essential developments referred to here had been in train before that expansion of the financial markets. It is not capitalism turned stateless. It is not a capitalism where the nation state is withering away and where markets or transnational corporations decide everything. Globalisation is a process largely carried out or facilitated by capitalist states. It is not capitalism turned American. It is not a world where instead of the old European empires there is semi-colonial rule by the United States. The US continues to be the biggest capitalist power, but the long-term trend, operating since 1945, for its relative dominance to decline – as seen first by the rise of Germany, Japan and the European Union, and more recently by China – has not been fundamentally reversed.

Making the market 'natural'

One of the distinguishing features of this enlarged capitalism is the restructuring of how and where goods and services are produced, and accompanying that is the increased flows of human labour both within and across national borders.

We are witness to many stark examples of people and nations being drawn into the new social relations established by the market's reach into all corners of the globe. In the West the market has established itself in areas where it was previously excluded. Public utilities such as electricity, water and telecommunications are privatised, while public goods such as education, healthcare, old-age care and childcare are commodified. Despite predictions that knowledge work would become the norm in the West, with workers requiring ever-higher qualification levels in order to exercise greater autonomy, problem-solving skills and initiative, work for the majority remains mundane and repetitive and does not make use of the skills workers have already attained. The experience of work for many, however, is not captured by reference to statistics even though they provide important data on the terrain of the changing labour market. They are inadequate in presenting the lived experience of millions of workers on the wrong side of a major power imbalance, subject to the vagaries of the market, low pay and insecure tenure. For the past decade or more, however, there has been a popular ethnographic literature that has exposed the deterioration of work, working conditions, access to education and training, and power at work within the fastest-growing areas of employment (see, for example, Sennet 1998; Ehrenreich 2001, 2005; Schlosser 2002; Yates 2003; Frank 2004).[1]

The labour market remains highly variegated. Firstly, many jobs have become 'professionalised', reflecting growing sophistication in service delivery. This can be seen in the work of nurses, accountants, human resource professionals and library technicians, among others. Secondly, productivity gains associated with technological improvement has meant the disappearance of many jobs, particularly in agriculture, mining and sections of manufacturing. Thirdly, general productivity gains have generated new jobs, which are best seen as the product of affluence, including financial advisers, massage therapists, fitness instructors, travel agents, cleaners and waiters. The fastest-growing jobs in many Western economies have been in hospitality, personal services and tourism. In this category, the limitations on unions' rights to organise, combined with the removal of legal restraints on hours of work, casualisation, overtime payments and so on, have stimulated the increasing proportion of low-paid contingent workers in the workforce.

Finally, the advanced economies also rely increasingly on the influx of migrant labour from the countries of the South. Over 12 million undocumented workers are estimated to be in the US – growing food; working as nannies, housemaids, janitors, construction workers, taxi and truck drivers; or employed in fast-food restaurants and assembly-line manufacturing. And this situation is not confined to the US, the UK, France, Germany and Australia. The sharpest examples of how national economies have been integrated into the global market economy can be found, on the one hand, in the countries of eastern Europe and Russia and, on the other, in countries such as India, Indonesia, Thailand and China. The impact of integration extends beyond national statistics as huge numbers of people within those countries are pulled into the market's orbit.

As occurred 200 years ago in Britain, today the rural populations of Asia are forced from their lands as they migrate to the cities to sell their labour power. There have been large-scale migrations of people within countries such as India and its neighbours Pakistan, Bangladesh and Afghanistan, and in parts of Indochina. The mass cross-border movement of workers, often without rights or protections and accompanied by the risk of persecution and easy removal, is also a feature of the Middle East, eastern Europe and Central America. But nowhere is this more graphically demonstrated than in China, where it is estimated that over the past decade 150 million workers have migrated from poorer rural areas into the cities, and where enough new high-rise apartments will have to be built to house the 19 million new urban migrants needed to sustain the economic boom.[2]

The new working class enters into an entirely new set of social relations. The market mediates material life and social reproduction, so that all individuals must in one way or another enter into new social relations in order to gain access to the means of life. The dictates of the market – competition, accumulation, profit maximisation and increasing labour productivity – regulate not only economic transactions but also social relations in general. And it is this, the spread of the social relations of capital, which is of significance and importance (Brown 1999). Conversely those countries and regions that are unable to be part of the global market, notably in sub-Saharan Africa and the Pacific Island states, are excluded from the benefits of closer integration, the consequences of which are too often to be rendered 'failed states'.

Another critical feature of the international rearrangement of production and work is the impact on those vast numbers of people left on the periphery of development in the industrialising countries. As Mike Davis (2006b) points out, today's mega-slums – on the Cape Flats, in Rio de Janeiro's *favelas*, in cities such as Lima and Manila, and in war-torn Sadr City – are different from earlier urban concentrations of poor workers. Urbanisation has been disconnected from industrialisation and economic growth, leading to the creation of a peripheral population that is not part of the formal economy or workforce. The social role that these large concentrations of people might play is open. In some cases that informal population has been organised or kept together by remnants of the organised labour movement. But all too often, 'the informal economy creates a Darwinian competition that leads to the division of the poor and the control of the slum by bosses, gangsters and ethnic supremacists' (Davis 2006b).

In contrast, Davis presents the example of El Alto, the Quechua-speaking slum sister of La Paz, where former miners often take the lead in mobilisations, and where the result may be the reinvention of the left. A different example is that of Bombay/Mumbai. When the textile industry was operating a quarter century ago, the city was celebrated for its powerful leftist and trade union movements:

> Sectarian differences – Hindu versus Muslim or Maratha versus Tamil – were largely subordinated to trade-union solidarity. But after the closure of the mills, the slums were colonised by sectarian politics – in particular, by the extreme Maratha and Hindu party, the Shiv Sena. The result was riots, carnage and seemingly irreparable division. (Davis 2006b)

In a book of collected stories of work in the twenty-first century, Paul Mason (2007) combines vivid contemporary accounts of labour organising with historical accounts through the history of the organised workers' movement. In so doing, he argues that today's factory workers in Shenzhen, weavers in Varanasi, metalworkers in Nigeria, immigrant cleaners in London, street sellers in Bolivia, and so on, share more in common with their forebears doing the same work in Manchester, Paris, Chicago or Broken Hill a century or more ago than they might realise. Their situations and their struggles for decent conditions, respect and the right to organise and combine have much in common. In effect, Mason poses a simple key question: will the workers in the newly industrialising economies, including the new powerhouses of the world economy, take the same step of establishing independent labour organisations and political parties that enabled earlier workers to shape politics and working conditions? This is a fork in the road, for without creating organisations to pursue collectively their own interests they will move down a different path that risks solidifying the weakened industrial, economic and political positions they occupy today.

Uniting struggles, building cross-border solidarity

It has become commonplace in the labour movement to declare that global responses are needed if unions are to rebuild and reassert influence in workplaces, industries, the economy and the wider society.

When Andy Stern, president of the Service Employees International Union (SEIU), opened the SEIU convention in Puerto Rico in May 2008, the first time the union's largest meeting had been held outside the US, he told delegates in words that recalled the early labour movement's commitment to internationalism and solidarity that

> the theme of our convention is 'Justice for All'. It's a recognition that the words 'Workers of the World Unite' can no longer just be a slogan, but it's the way that workers win in a global economy. The gap between the rich and the rest of the world population is growing so wide and so fast all over the world that at this time of a global economy with multinational employers unions must go international as well.[3]

Union strategy therefore needs to evolve, to develop new strategies and tactics to keep up with changes in the national and international economy, with employers' corporate structure and with governments' legislative frameworks, or be left behind and incapable of exercising the strength to pursue workers' interests (Juravich 2007). Before and throughout the twentieth century, unions developed international links. Left-wing unions, connected as they so often were with left-wing political parties, treated international links as part of their essential political work. Right-wing unions also pursued international collaboration, often as a means of countering socialist and communist ideas within the broader labour movement. With the end of the Cold War, the demise of many far-left political parties and the rapid decline in union membership, especially in the advanced economies, the focus of many unions has shifted to the need to respond to powerful companies that operate across national borders.

Three types of initiatives are being pursued in response to the concentration and spread of corporate power. They range from structural changes that are resulting in larger, global union organisations; new comprehensive campaigns to support targeted global organising and bargaining; and legal efforts that include legal actions using international and treaty law (Youngdahl 2008: 71).

As a structural response, unions are paying increased attention to creating umbrella organisations of national unions, or global union federations (GUFs). In the past the GUFs exhibited some of the worst tendencies of big, cumbersome, bureaucratic organisations accountable to a layer of national officials and disconnected from their membership base. However, there are signs of change following the creation of the International Trade Union Confederation (ITUC) in November 2006, and the merger of a number of smaller federations and individual unions in the service and technical sector from 140 countries to form the Union Network International (UNI). An ongoing challenge in the establishment of these super-organisations is whether they can establish a genuine relevance to the workers who fund them. Ron Oswald, general secretary of a GUF, the International Union of Foodworkers, commented that he was not sure whether many workers even know that there is a global union: 'It's a brand, not a reality. International companies are clearly a reality. International unions are yet to become so.'[4]

A second trend is the consideration by some national unions of international mergers. The United Steelworkers of America (USW) announced plans to merge with Unite the Union in the UK to form the world's first global union, Workers Uniting, covering 3 million workers. The USW also signed a strategic alliance with the Australian Workers Union (AWU) in 2005 aimed at building cooperation on issues involving common employers. Unite the Union is itself the result of a series of mergers that in 2007 brought together Amicus and the Transport and General Workers' Union (TGWU), and then commenced discussions with Germany's IG-Metall about the possibility of closer organisational and structural ties.[5]

Alongside these mega-unions is another focus of developing comprehensive cross-border strategic campaigns focused on particular companies. Cross-national collective solidarity has occurred in the union movement for many decades, notably in industries such as shipping and warehousing, with the 1996 Maritime Union dispute in Australia being a prime recent example. However, campaigns targeting organising at strategic global companies, which also link with other non-union groups, provide newer, different examples of this more comprehensive campaigning and are becoming more numerous (Bronfenbrenner 2007). Also on the increase are applications of this approach in more localised settings, with the aim of organising among low-wage workers in growth industries who are recent arrivals and who may have had little contact with the labour movement (Waldinger et al. 1998; Bronfenbrenner et al. 1998, Bronfenbrenner 2007; Lopez 2004; Wills 2005; LHMU 2006; Cohen 2006; Tattersall 2007; Brown in press; Sawchuk forthcoming).

The SEIU provides some examples through its work with the UK's TGWU Driving Up Standards campaign, as well as in its campaign to organise security workers at G4S, which employs half a million workers in over a hundred countries. Within UNI the SEIU is attempting to coordinate global framework agreements with multinational cleaning companies, and through its own Global Partnerships Unit it has lent its support to the Australian Liquor, Hospitality and Miscellaneous Union (LHMU) and the New Zealand Service and Food Workers Union (SFWU) in their Clean Start campaign aimed at negotiating contracts for cleaners in high-rise buildings and international hotel chains (LHMU 2006; Tattersall 2007).

Other examples of cross-border campaigning include the No-Sweat campaigns in the UK, US, Europe, Canada and Australia, and the Clean Clothes campaign, which aims to highlight labour injustices and to support organising, focusing on the Beijing Olympics. Drawing on the human rights movement's strategy of naming, blaming and shaming, concerns over human rights, industrial rights and the environment are being merged to bring improvements in the international clothing industry. Ginny Coughlin of UNITE HERE describes these new efforts as moving from 'global solidarity to global strategy'.[6]

The greatest challenge, however, will be to organise those workers who are currently either outside of the formal economy or in areas such as the free-trade zones of China, and parts of Asia and Central America, where unions are all but prohibited and regimes of intimidation and brutality dominate.

Funari and De La Torre's film *Maquilapolis: City of Factories*, set in the Tijuana region of Mexico on the US border, shows how strategic aid and support from North American groups can help advance the work of indigenous women organisers.[7] The *maquiladoras*[8] of Tijuana attract a diverse and relatively inexpensive workforce for those international companies that establish extensive industrial parks composed of assembly plants. Companies that have set up *maquiladoras* in Tijuana include Sony, Toyota, Samsung, Kodak, Matsushita/Panasonic, Nabisco, Philips, Pioneer, Plantronics, Pall Medical, Tara and Sanyo. The film shows a group of women who had not received any entitlements once their jobs were threatened by company decisions to move to even lower-waged countries such as Indonesia. There were no unions to call on, so they became popular educators and advocates, or *promontoras*. They organised young women coming into the factories from rural Mexico, educating them about their rights, about gender issues and about the impact of the companies on their communities, the environment and so on, and eventually won their entitlements.

These examples of new organising show a glimpse of a possible future. Yet developing the necessary new strategies and tactics is made much harder in a national and international context of union decline. The challenge of developing strategies of how to respond and to imagine alternatives is difficult when the rules have changed, the environment is different, the old certainties no longer apply, and where there are new, often inexperienced organisers and workers who have little foundation in or knowledge of union history, tradition and culture. This is why the educational dimension is a critical component of the new organising for linking workers within and across national borders in order to rebuild membership and power.

Conclusions

Despite the hints of a better future, there is often a more pessimistic view widespread within the labour movement, which is that capital, especially when referred to as globalisation, is omnipotent. As US journalist Alexander Cockburn puts it, 'leftists deem capitalism invincible and fearfully lob copious documentation at each other detailing the efficient devilry of the executives of the system. The internet serves to amplify this pervasive funk into a catastrophist mindset.'[9]

Echoes of this can be found even within the important book bringing together the papers from the landmark Global Unions Conference held in New York in 2006. In her introduction to *Global Unions,* Kate Bronfenbrenner writes:

> Now the challenges are greater. Where before transnational corporations seemed at least somewhat bounded by loyalty to product, firm, industry, or country, today the largest of these firms increasingly supersede most government authority and are constrained only by the interests of their biggest investors, lenders and shareholders. (Bronfenbrenner 2007: 4)

One of the challenges for the 'new anti-capitalist movement' that came to prominence after Seattle, as well as for the labour movement inspired by the Korean and Indonesian unions, the US Justice for Janitors campaign, the Maritime Union workers of Australia, and the emerging cross-border alliances being developed, is to learn about and devise ways of facing an enemy that is in some ways more intangible. How do we move beyond demonstration after demonstration against one after another symbolic organisation – the World Trade Organization, the International Monetary Fund, the World Bank and so on? Alasdair MacIntyre posed the challenge this way: 'Actors can only answer the question "what am I to do?" once they can answer the prior question of what story or stories do I find myself a part' (MacIntyre 1985: 216). And this means making choices.

There are advantages in the expanded size and scope of the world's working class, but the challenge is to try to recompose an organised movement of global working-class solidarity out of the one-off actions now emerging across the world. This will involve some rediscovery of ideas such as internationalism and consistent democracy, but these will need to be redeveloped as new ideas to match the new developments of capital worldwide. For the ideologists of the market, nothing is easier than to believe that the existing social relations 'are themselves natural laws independent of the influence of time…eternal laws, which must always govern society' (Marx 1847/1966: 105).

The market implies offering and choice. The language of the market implies not compulsion but freedom. Yet to operate outside or contrary to the market leads to a discipline or corrective being imposed, encapsulated by phrases that include the word 'market', such as 'free market', 'market forces' and 'market discipline' (Wood 1994).

Reuniting workers with control over the means of production is therefore about more than workers' control at the level of the firm; it also requires democratic control of the economic reproduction of society. Otherwise the means of production will continue to be subject to the market-driven imperative to accumulate. Overcoming the separation of workers from the means of production involves reuniting the 'collective worker' – the whole working class – with society's means of production. It requires reconceptualising the notion of democracy. Democracy as it is presented under capitalism maintains a separation between the political and the economic spheres of life. While there has been a progressive extension of democratic rights over the political and juridical spheres, the economic domain remains governed by the notion of private property rights giving authority and power only to those who own economic resources. It is for this reason that establishing democratic control of the whole process of economic regulation of society is critical to a broader conception of democracy, one that involves a struggle for the reconstruction of the economic system on radically new principles.

Neo-liberalism's victory was to push social democracy, and sections of the left, into accepting the market as the most efficient allocator of social goods. Allocating the social product between consumption and investment, however, reflects social choices about present and future needs. Capitalism resolves this according to the criterion of profitability; democratic public discussion is largely irrelevant. These are 'private' decisions, which belong to capital by virtue of its property rights, however much they might affect the welfare of the majority. To socialise macroeconomic decisions by subjecting them to genuine democratic control is to push back the frontiers of the market, and affirm the right of the majority to regulate the processes that govern their lives (McNally 1993: 203).

The climate created by the dominance of free-market ideas within governments, and more broadly in the media and political discourse, feeds a trend of political self-censorship. Labour and social-democratic politicians and trade unionists uncomfortable with these views remain silent about other possibilities because they cannot imagine any real alternative to the market in a practical, attainable sense. Within the union movement, long-held notions of class consciousness and conflict were replaced by the ideas of tripartite consensus; international solidarity with international competitiveness; and opposition to the primacy of the market with a limited acceptance of market operations. New managerial terms such as 'benchmarking' and 'best practice' have become common.

Yet the acceptance of the market by the labour movement comes at a time when the market's excesses are particularly evident and dangerous. The end of the twentieth century can be described as a time of disillusionment. The prevailing 'anti-utopianism' stands in stark contrast with the once widespread view held by both liberal and social democracy that scientific and technological progress would raise levels of literacy, education, self-awareness, freedom and democracy – that the general level of society would rise. The paradox is that the collective abandonment of hope for anything more than individual 'prosperity' is twinned with dazzling scientific and technological realities and possibilities. Advances in biological sciences and medicine are greater than the old social optimists could have imagined. The revolution in communications and information makes possible the transformation of political democracy. Technological innovation and social productivity enable us now to casually do things that even a few decades ago were conceivable only as supernatural intervention.

Yet these scientific wonders are taken for granted and as settled as the present social relations and structures of capitalist society. No breakthrough into a society that is qualitatively better is expected because we suffer a general paralysis of imagination and vision. That may be the lesson of the twentieth century – the future is seen as a continuing, intensifying *now*, and the negative features in society will probably continue and even worsen. The crises of the late twentieth and early twenty-first century make it more important to reject such a future by reconceiving alternative ways of organising society. Without such visions it is impossible to advocate reform of work or education that is democratic and liberatory. Reviving the critique of the market and asserting the view that working people can emancipate themselves, end their alienation from the means of production and establish collective and democratic control of economic life is critical to that task.

Notes

1   See also Horwitz T, 9 to nowhere – blues in the chicken line, *Wall Street Journal*, 1 December 1994; Horwitz T, Mr. Eden's profits from watching his workers' every move, *Wall Street Journal*, 1 December 1994; and Mahler J, Commute to nowhere, *New York Times Magazine*, 13 April 2003.

2   Templer B, Defective toys and worker exploitation in the PRC, *MR Webzine*, 22 August 2007 (accessed 6 April 2009, http://mrzine.monthlyreview.org/templer220807.html); and Garnaut J, The big steel, *Sydney Morning Herald*, 6–7 October 2007.

3   Cunningham D, SEIU convention opens in Puerto Rico as teachers protest, *Workers Independent News*, 2 June 2008. Accessed 6 April 2009, http://www.4ibew.com/2008/06/01/seiu-convention-opens-in-puerto-rico-as-teachers-protest-060208/. See also the SEIU 2008 Convention website at http://www.seiu2008.org (accessed 6 April 2009).

4   Quoted in Moberg D, Solidarity without borders, *In These Times*, 7 February 2007. Accessed 6 April 2009, http://www.inthesetimes.com/article/3021/solidarity_without_borders/.

5   May J, Unions unite to challenge the multinationals, *Sydney Morning Herald*, 5 January 2007. Accessed 5 January 2007, http://www.smh.com.au/text/articles/2007/01/05/1167777277252.html.

6   Quoted in Moberg D, Solidarity without borders, *In These Times*, 7 February 2007. Accessed 6 April 2009, http://www.inthesetimes.com/article/3021/solidarity_without_borders/.

7   Funari V and De La Torre S, *Maquilapolis: City of factories* (ITVS, a CineMamás film). Produced and directed in collaboration with the women of Grupo Factor X, Colectivo Chilpancingo, Promotoras por los Derechos de las Mujeres. Vallejo, CA: California Newsreel, 2006.

8   *Macquiladoras* are the free-trade economic zones established at the border between the US and Mexico.

9   Cockburn A, On Naomi Klein's *The shock doctrine. CounterPunch* 22/23 September 2007. Accessed 6 April 2009, http://www.counterpunch.org/cockburn09222007.html.

References

Bales K (2000) *Disposable people: New slavery in the global economy.* Berkeley: University of California Press

Bronfenbrenner K (ed.) (2007) *Global unions: Challenging transnational capital through cross-border campaigns.* Ithaca, NY: Cornell University Press

Bronfenbrenner K, Friedman S, Hurd R, Oswald R & Seeber R (1998) *Organising to win: New research on union strategies.* Ithaca, NY: ILR Press

Brown T (1999) Challenging globalisation as discourse and phenomenon. *International Journal of Lifelong Education* 18(1): 3–17

Brown T (2009) As easy as ABC? Learning to organise private childcare workers. *Labour Studies Journal* 34(2): 235–251

Cohen N (2006) Hotel workers rising. *Labour* (May/June): 18–19

Davis M (2006a) *Planet of slums.* London: Verso

Davis M (2006b) *Planet of slums* interview. *Znet online magazine*, 9 May. Accessed 6 April 2009, http://www.zmag.org/znet/viewArticle/3913

Ehrenreich B (2001) *Nickel and dimed: On (not) getting by in America.* New York: Owl Books

Ehrenreich B (2005) *Bait and switch: The futile pursuit of the American dream.* New York: Owl Books

Frank T (2004) *What's the matter with Kansas? How conservatives won the heart of America.* New York: Metropolitan Books

Juravich T (2007) Beating global capital: A framework and method for union strategic corporate research and campaigns. In K Bronfenbrenner (ed.) *Global unions: Challenging transnational capital through cross-border campaigns.* Ithaca, NY: Cornell University Press

LHMU (Liquor, Hospitality and Miscellaneous Union) (2006) *Cleaners and community: United for justice.* Haymarket, Sydney: LHMU. Accessed 6 April 2009, http://lhmu.org.au/lhmu/campaigns/clean-start

Lopez S (2004) *Reorganising the Rust Belt: An inside study of the American labour movement.* Berkeley: University of California Press

MacIntyre A (1985) *After virtue: A study in moral theory.* London: Duckworth

McNally D (1993) *Against the market: Political economy, market socialism and the Marxist critique.* London: Verso

Marx K (1847/1966) In *The poverty of philosophy.* Moscow: Progress Publishers

Mason P (2007) *Live working or die fighting: How the working class went global.* London: Harvill Secker

Sawchuk P (forthcoming) Anti-colonialism, labour and the pedagogies of community unionism: The case of hotel workers in Canada. In A Kempf (ed.) *Breaching the colonial contract: Anti-colonialism in the US and Canada.* London: Peter Lange

Schlosser E (2002) *Fast-food nation: What the all-American meal is doing to the world.* London: Penguin

Sennet R (1998) *The corrosion of character: The personal consequences of work in the new capitalism.* New York: WW Norton and Company

Tattersall A (2007) Labour–community coalitions, global union alliances, and the potential of SEIU's global partnerships. In K Bronfenbrenner (ed.) *Global unions: Challenging transnational capital through cross-border campaigns.* Ithaca, NY: Cornell University Press

UN (United Nations) (2003) *The challenge of slums: Global report on human settlements.* Nairobi: United Nations Human Settlements Programme

Waldinger R, Erickson C, Milkman R, Mitchell D, Valenzuela A, Wong K & Zeitlin M (1998) Helots no more: A case study of the Justice for Janitors campaign in Los Angeles. In K Bronfenbrenner, S Friedman, R Hurd, R Oswald & R Seeber (eds) *Organising to win: New research on union strategies.* Ithaca, NY: ILR Press

Wills J (2005) The geography of union organising in low-paid service industries in the UK: Lessons from the T&G's campaign to unionise the Dorchester Hotel, London. *Antipode:* 139–159

Wood EM (1994) From opportunity to imperative: The history of the market. *Monthly Review* 46(3): 14–40

Yates M (2003) *Naming the system: Inequality and work in the global economy.* New York: Monthly Review Press

Youngdahl J (2008) Mapping the future: Cross-border unionizing strategies. *New Labor Forum* 17(2): 70–81

20 A new perspective on the 'learning organisation': A case study of a South African trade union[1]

Linda Cooper

Introduction

The critical literature on globalisation has pointed to its exacerbating effects on social and economic inequality, and its creation of new 'insiders' and 'outsiders'. Some of the discourses associated with the impact of globalisation on workplace knowledge and learning – discourses of the 'knowledge society' and the 'learning organisation' in particular – have also been critically interrogated. Fenwick (2003: 48) believes that the literature on the learning organisation is 'unapologetically rooted in the belief that learning should advance the organisational goals of competition'. While the learning organisation literature claims to meet the needs not only of employers but also those of workers, Jackson and Jordan (2000) and Mojab and Gorman (2003) argue that the learning organisation benefits only a small, elite part of the workforce; the majority of workers gain little benefit and are given little opportunity to contribute their knowledge. Perhaps the most serious critique is based on the literature's bias towards idealistic normative outcomes. Garrick (1999: 129) argues that 'the glossy "empowerment" promises that accompany many high-tech solutions for organisations to be learning enterprises tend to be like politicians' promises – unlikely ever to be delivered in full, if at all'. Gee et al. (1996: 24) describe much of the literature on the learning organisation as 'fast capitalist texts', produced mainly by business managers and consultants seeking to 'attend as textual midwives at the birth of the new work order' by creating a paper version of the new work order that they are trying hard to enact in the world.

Against the backdrop of these critiques, it is perhaps ironic that a South African trade union – one which would align itself with the poor, the excluded, and those whose work and knowledge is not often recognised – has claimed:

> An important aspect of any democratic union is that it should be
> a 'learning organisation'. That a union as an organ of struggle and
> democratic expression should always be striving to empower its
> members. That its meetings and activities, and militant actions, are
> all an environment which teaches lessons. (SAMWU 1996: 14)

How are we to make sense of this claim, coming as it does from an organisation that seeks to challenge capitalism's economic logic and power relations, rather than seeking to compete successfully within the global economy? Along with other chapters in this book, this chapter suggests that global discourses – such as that of the 'learning organisation' – are not simply reproduced at the local level, but may be reconfigured, disrupted or even subverted.

The chapter takes as a case study the Cape Town branch of the South African Municipal Workers' Union (SAMWU), a local government affiliate of the Congress of South African Trade Unions (COSATU). It invites readers to consider the trade union as a workplace, even though it is a place where people – in collaboration – labour not for profit maximisation, but for a social purpose. It explores two different contexts of informal learning within the union: organisational activity and mass action. Drawing on the conceptual tools of 'situated learning theory' and post-Vygotskian 'activity theory', it considers the range of factors that facilitate learning in these contexts. In doing this, it suggests that the notion of the learning organisation may best be realised not in the globally competitive workplace, but rather in organisations where ordinary people come together, participate and work towards a more collective social purpose.

Background to the case study

The trade union movement, with its several million members, can be seen as one of the most significant 'adult learning institutions' in South Africa, historically and currently. Over time, trade unions have invested considerable resources in organised education programmes for their members (see Vally 1994; Andrews 2003). However, arguably the most pervasive and significant processes of learning within the union movement are those associated with workers' broader involvement in their organisation, where, through their experiences of organising, meeting, taking collective decisions and engaging in collective action, knowledge is shared and new understandings are sought and produced.

There has been a self-conscious awareness within the South African labour movement that trade unions do not only promote adult education but also facilitate organisational learning. As early as 1986, soon after COSATU was formed, its first education officer captured this view in a speech to a union education conference:

> Firstly, education cannot and must not be separated from organisation...
> Secondly, education can take place anywhere, at any time and involves
> people of all ages...Any meeting, any strike, any wage negotiation, and
> any lunch break can be used as places where education takes place.
> (Quoted in Baskin 1991: 244)

Worker education has long been seen as taking place not only in trade union seminars, workshops and planned education programmes, but also in a variety of events such as meetings and rallies as well as through the day-to-day actions of workers.

Trade unions have been described as 'laboratories for democracy' (Friedman 1987: 499), which points to their role not only as sites of learning, but also as sites of knowledge production. In the early years of the labour movement, new understandings and ways of practising worker democracy and control emerged through workers' day-to-day experiences of organising and running meetings. In the process of running increasingly large and complex organisations, elected worker leaders – often with very little formal education – experimented with new forms of collective leadership. Over time, the labour movement's principles and practices of workers' control and participatory democracy became embodied in the physical and symbolic environment and day-to-day rituals of the trade union as an activity system. It is therefore possible to view the historical experience of black workers in South Africa as 'intelligence sedimented in organisation' (Scribner 1997: 313). As workers participate in trade union organisational activities today, they learn from and appropriate the knowledge of previous generations of workers.

SAMWU remains one of COSATU's largest affiliates, despite a decline in its membership in recent years as a result of post-apartheid restructuring of local government and policies of privatisation. The continued militancy among its members has expressed itself in two national strikes and a large number of more local protest actions in the period between 1993 and 2003 (SAMWU n.d.). The larger research project on which this chapter is based was aimed at documenting, analysing and theorising the ways in which knowledge is produced and disseminated within this trade union, as experienced by the workers who constitute the trade union's membership. Data were gathered through ethnographic observation of union activities and events spread over a two-year period (2001 to 2003), and this was complemented by data from in-depth individual and focus group interviews. In the course of analysing the data, three discrete data sets emerged, each linked to a specific organisational setting and bearing distinct pedagogic features: the union's organised but non-certificated education programmes; sites of everyday organisational involvement (including meetings, organising and negotiating with management); and the context of workers' mass action (see Cooper 2005).

SAMWU's organised education programmes – aimed at transferring skills as well as building collective identity and trade union consciousness – are relatively substantial in scale. However, this chapter, concerned as it is with informal or incidental learning in organisations, will not focus on these programmes, but will concentrate on the pedagogic and learning dimensions of workers' routine forms of participation in the organisation, and their experiences of learning during the course of a major national strike of the union.

Learning through organisational participation

Situated learning theory (Lave & Wenger 1991) enables a range of activities within the union to be viewed through a 'learning lens' and allows the question to be posed, what forms of social activity engaged in by members of this community of practice have learning as a significant outcome?

The most common form of organisational activity engaged in by union members is meetings. There are a range of forums in SAMWU in which workers participate and take collective decisions, ranging from general meetings of union members in their municipal work depots, to meetings of shop stewards who represent workers of a particular sector (such as electricity, water or waste management), to meetings of shop stewards who represent their constituencies at the branch or regional level of the union. Worker representatives also participate in meetings with management and in bargaining forums with employer groupings.

Meetings represent sites where learning 'is not reified as an extraneous goal' (Wenger 1998: 76). Their primary purpose is to take collective decisions rather than to educate, while meetings with management usually have a strategic purpose. Nevertheless, meetings are educational in at least two ways: union meetings facilitate information sharing and help to develop common perspectives among members, while meetings with management contribute to the renewal of leadership capacity at a time when worker leaders are constantly being siphoned off into positions of greater responsibility within the union or, increasingly, into management or government.

In meetings with management, learning frequently happens through worker representatives simply being 'thrown in at the deep end' (sometimes deliberately). For example, one worker spoke of how one of the more experienced shop stewards used to take her and her co-worker along with him to meetings with management:

> [X] was one of my mentors. What [he] used to do was…he used to take us along to meetings. We don't know a thing about the issue that we're going to discuss!…He would open the meeting, he would…put SAMWU's position there, and then [X] would excuse himself [leave the meeting]. And we were sitting there, like, we're supposed to speak now! What are we supposed to say? And we were forced in that way…and to me that was the biggest school. I mean…you were forced to do it, you see, you were left completely on your own…*ja*, that was the way that I learned. Not through the formal…through the training workshops.

In the union's own meetings, learning may be seen as taking place through 'participation in a community of practice' (Lave & Wenger 1991). This participation may take the form of simply being present, listening and observing, with 'old-timers' modelling the roles and values that 'newcomers' are expected to acquire. For example, one shop steward recalled in an interview how, when he first joined the union, he learned from observing the general secretary in meetings:

> [He] never taught me…but I used to watch him very closely, you know… His style, and the manner in which he speaks, and the manner in which he treats people, and all of those things…

Participation also takes more active forms. A shop steward who had been involved in the union's Women's Forum emphasised the value of what she learned from participating in meetings of this structure:

> We really learned a lot there. And we did a lot of things…The women in the Women's Forum developed to the extent that they could open up their

mouths and challenge the men…For me, in terms of not getting formal training within the union, a lot of my training I got through the Forum.

When asked what she had learned from her involvement in meetings of this structure, she described how it taught her not only practical skills, but also general analytical skills as well as broader dispositions:

> Public speaking…The ability to read and analyse documents…The ability to be able to develop policy…Debate, develop positions…Chairing meetings…Also the practical skills, listening skills, learning to listen to others…It taught me that you've got to do your research, you've got to prepare, then you'll be able to speak to people at whatever level…or whatever qualification you have…and then the ability to guide others and give direction. So quite a lot of things…

While much learning takes place invisibly or unconsciously through observation or participation, there are also forms of pedagogy going on in the day-to-day life of the union – more specifically, peer mentoring or 'guided participation' (Rogoff 1984: 147). As noted above, some shop stewards have union leaders acting as their mentors (deliberately or unconsciously), but often it is ordinary workers and shop stewards who play reciprocal peer-mentoring roles for one another. For example, one shop steward (a qualified librarian) recalled:

> I as a shop steward…didn't go for formal training for a long time. But the minute I was elected I was told: all right, you're going to learn on the job. And I was taught by the cleaner – the shop steward…I had to do cases, and he was there with me. He had to give me information and I would wonder: how does he know what I want? But he used to come with exactly what I wanted. Every time I picked up the phone…he'd come with exactly what I wanted.

In meetings, experiences are shared and compared through a cycle of learning that is thoroughly collective rather than individual in nature. One key dimension of this experiential learning cycle is the recontextualisation of 'local' experiences within a broader context, enabling workers to gain a better understanding of how different elements of their experience fit into the 'bigger picture'. The brief extract below, taken from a dialogue in a shop steward council meeting, illustrates how more experienced shop stewards assist newer, less-experienced shop stewards to interrogate, analyse, contextualise and conceptualise their experiences. The meeting participants had been discussing a report from the branch's health and safety committee, and the issue of privatisation was mentioned. One shop steward could not see the connection:

> Shop steward 1: What is the link between privatisation and Health, Safety and Environment?

> Shop steward 2 (Health and safety representative): They are using every excuse to get rid of our people – so where a shop steward has an injury – suddenly documents disappear, next thing he's retrenched…

Shop steward 3 (Chairperson): Members who've been injured on duty are first to lose their jobs with privatisation…

Some worker representatives play a key pedagogic role in this process of recontextualisation because of their role as 'boundary workers'. Older workers bring valuable experiences from other periods in history, while other workers bring much-needed information from outside structures and forums in which they sit as union representatives. One shop steward who played a leading role in the branch had an unusually rich set of involvements in multiple forums: he represented his branch in higher (provincial and national) structures of the union, had attended a course in adult education at a local university, and was involved in local community organisations and activist forums. He was a plumber, and the union's representative on a national tripartite policy body engaged in developing a new water policy for South Africa. He had attended local and international conferences where he had met environmental activists from around the world and engaged in international advocacy around water issues.

Often, those who promote understanding of wider and wider layers of context are fully aware of their recontextualising role and the importance of helping others to 'grasp the full picture'. For example, a shop steward in one meeting continually stressed 'the need to put things into perspective'. In another meeting the chairperson emphasised the importance of drawing interconnections between workplace restructuring and workplace education and training issues, and asked: 'How in SAMWU do we make workers understand and see the linkages?'

The trade union may therefore be seen as a community of practice (see Ball 2003) where the process of participation in routine union activities, supported by forms of mentoring and modelling, induct workers into their trade unionist roles and identities. Collective spaces offered by the union provide workers with opportunities to share and compare experiences and develop new understandings; in this context, boundary workers play a key recontextualising role by helping fellow workers to locate their local experiences within a broader context.

Learning through mass action

'Collective doing' also plays a significant role in mediating learning in the context of mass action. In July 2002, SAMWU embarked on a three-week national strike that was to become the largest strike in the country since the democratic elections of 1994. Strikers' actions included marches, 'trashing' (emptying garbage bins onto the streets), burning tyres in the city streets, occupations of municipal offices and picketing.

In the union, it is a truism that while members learn from strikes, these strikes also help to expose organisational weaknesses. For example, in the union's shop steward training manual produced after the 2002 strike (SAMWU 2003: 26), one of the workshop activities asks shop stewards to 'reflect on, and learn lessons from the strike that will help you to build strong workers' action in the future', and to 'identify the strengths and weaknesses of the union that the strike has thrown up'.

SAMWU's 2002 strike was experienced by workers as an intense and condensed learning experience. According to one full-time shop steward, 'Whatever else the strike was – it was a massive learning experience...' Learning was largely tacit and took place through participation in the special community of practice that emerged during the strike. Here, the situated learning theorists' notions of 'learning as doing' and 'knowing in action' are most clearly illustrated. For example, on my visits to the union office I observed activity that was quite frenzied – apparently unconscious, unaware, unreflective. Union activists were grappling with a large number of multifaceted complex issues, and were having to deal with them literally 'on the run'. Lessons were being learned and skills acquired which might only be reflected upon or acknowledged later.

This tacit learning was complemented by moments of self-conscious, critical reflection on experience in the midst of the strike. For example, at the union's offices on the third day of the strike I observed a meeting in which worker leaders and organisers engaged in a heated debate about how to account for the uneven support for the strike, and the 'lack of discipline' among some shop stewards. There was a lengthy process of sharing experiences, drawing lessons and debating new courses of action. This was accompanied by an explicit awareness of the importance of learning from the experience of the strike, as illustrated in such comments as: 'We need to learn from these things – we need to tighten up, spell out everyone's role, say exactly what's expected of each and every one. That's what this morning taught me...' and 'We need to learn from what has taken place here, not just for tomorrow but for the future.'

Participants not only learned practical and strategic lessons but also gained a deeper understanding of a more general kind. They learned something about how economic power functions, as well as how political power operates to protect those with economic power. For example, in a group interview after the strike, two workers discussed the role of the police during the workers' march on the first day of the strike:

> Worker 1: ...they try to protect them [management] and let us get hurt... they've got bullets, guns, batons...And our strikers go there with bare hands.
>
> Worker 2: ...With bare hands. And empty stomach.

The strike also raised broader questions that awakened in workers a desire to understand more about politics, history and how society functions. For example, in another focus group interview following the strike, one worker argued: 'We need to start giving our members political education...[Yes!][2] People don't understand how the politics work...'

The strike played a pedagogic role in a further, less obvious way: it acted as a significant evaluative moment of the union's organised education programmes. It functioned to indicate whether or not the building of collective identity and trade union consciousness – the core aims of the union's planned education programme – had been successfully achieved. It became clear in SAMWU's 2002 strike that these aims were unevenly achieved. In central Cape Town, for example, many workers did not support the strike; these included shop stewards who failed to exercise the roles, skills and political leadership capacity they were expected to have acquired through their shop steward training and on-the-job mentoring. The strike revealed different ideological and identity positions among the union's members that did not seem to have been successfully resolved by the union's planned education programmes, by the pedagogic processes happening in meetings or by the solidarity of the strike itself.

Factors facilitating learning in the union

Engeström (2002) argues that an activity system has the potential for 'breakthrough into learning activity' if it allows multiple voices and contested viewpoints to be heard, and if it is prepared to tolerate instability, internal tensions, struggles and contradictions. The 'multi-voicedness' (Bakhtin 1965/1994) of an activity system is therefore the source of productive tensions and contradictions which can, in turn, be a source of new learning and knowledge.

It has been shown above how the 'rules of practice' of the trade union as an activity system promote learning by prioritising social interaction and solidarity between social equals, thus creating the potential for widespread participation and multi-voiced interaction. In addition to this, there are two other significant features of the trade union's organisational culture that promote inclusion and participation, and thus possibilities for learning: firstly, the widely distributed nature of the educator role, and the part played by ordinary workers as educators; and secondly, the role of culturally embedded, symbolic tools of mediation, and oral performativity in particular.

Shared and reciprocal educator roles

A key feature of union pedagogy is the weak division of labour between educators and learners. In the union's organised education programmes, the educator role is relatively specialised: the educator role is clearly identified, although a range of union staff, worker leaders or outside 'experts' may step into this role. In union meetings, however, the role of educator is far more widely distributed and fluid, clearly illustrating Lave and Wenger's notion of the educator role being assumed by a 'richly diverse field of essential actors' (1991: 93) who engage in various and reciprocal forms of guided participation, modelling and peer mentoring. Boundary workers who traverse different communities of practice bring important information, which helps workers to recontextualise and understand the significance of their experiences, while ordinary workers also share experiences and work collaboratively to construct common understandings.

During the 2002 strike, the boundaries between educators and learners became even more diffuse as workers assumed the role of 'collective educator', using mass action to communicate their experiences, their identity, their worldview and their power to the world at large. This weak specialisation of the educator role and interchangeability of educator and learner roles (weak division of labour) allows ordinary workers to add their 'voice' to the union's rules of practice and contribute to the shared 'knowledge pool' of the organisation.

Culturally embedded tools of mediation

One of Vygotsky's key conceptual tools is the notion of tools of mediation, used to describe the role of people, artefacts and symbolic forms such as language, that assist the learner to appropriate the cultural tools developed through social history (Daniels 2001). In the South African trade union context, a range of symbolic tools of mediation play a key role in facilitating learning. Together, these assume the form of 'oral performativity' – a mode of communication embedded in the historical and cultural experiences of black people in South Africa (Gunner 1999), and rooted in the history of the trade union movement more specifically (Sitas 1990).

Despite the presence of large amounts of written text, oral communication dominates in union meetings, often assuming the form of a distinctive speech genre involving code-switching between different languages. Union members frequently use English when dealing with more formal knowledge such as labour law, but switch to Afrikaans or isiXhosa (the two dominant languages in the Western Cape) when expressing their strong feelings on an issue. Code-switching is a widespread phenomenon in South Africa, originating in the attempts to circumvent or transcend the institutionalised ethnic barriers of apartheid (Slabbert & Finlayson 2002). As Slabbert and Finlayson suggest, it is seen as a form of accommodation, and as symbolising the values of democracy, equality, mutual understanding and respect. In the union context, it signals the importance with which equality and respect among workers is regarded, and helps to build an inclusive, working-class identity. Storytelling is also an integral part of information-sharing and comparing of experiences in meetings, and its pedagogic mediating role is illustrated by the numerous occasions when control over 'stories' is exerted by the chair to stop shop stewards from relating experiences that do not seem relevant to the item under discussion. Meetings are often lively and boisterous and have a distinct 'carnivalesque' quality to them. The use of 'folk humour' (Bakhtin 1965/1994: 194) allows workers to celebrate their collective identity, functions to parody 'the bosses' (a subversive function), and also has a sardonic, self-mockery (critical self-reflective) function.

Emotion and the dramatic use of the body are also key tools of mediation. Debates and discussions in meetings are often highly emotional and accompanied by strong body language. For example, in one meeting a debate around privatisation was concluded with calls to 'take to the streets', 'we must do something drastic', 'they're trying to destroy the union' and 'this is a matter of life and death!' Participation in the union is not simply a responsibility or task but an act of 'passion' and commitment.

In the strike, there was an overall mode-switch (Kress 2000) from the languaged discourse of union workshops and meetings to one of visual display. This was evident in workers' public demonstrations in their symbolic use of the body; in their toyi-toying,[3] marching and dancing; as well as in their use of visual artefacts such as banners, placards, T-shirts, political symbols and the symbolic use of colour.

The forms of oral performativity that characterise many of SAMWU's meetings and strike activities are specific local reinvents of a long-standing cultural tradition within the South African labour movement, and are deeply embedded in the history and culture of black South Africans more generally. The rich performative culture drawn upon in the union context is indicative of 'grassroots creativity' and 'grassroots energy' (Sitas 1990), signalling a space for ordinary people to use familiar historical cultural resources to mediate knowledge and meaning, and give voice to their experience and knowledge. It allows for the 'dispersed educator role' referred to above, and enhances the multi-voicedness of this activity system.

Conclusion

The research presented in this chapter shows that rich examples of 'innovative learning' and 'working knowledge' may be found in organisations that have primarily a social purpose, and that seek to challenge rather than reproduce dominant social relations. The material from the case study suggests that learning may best be promoted in organisations that value collectivity and social solidarity, where a thirst for new knowledge is born out of the real experiences and needs of its members, where multiple voices are able to meet and contest, where the educative role of ordinary grassroots members of the organisation is valued and nurtured, and where the symbolic and communicative culture of the organisation is an expression from below of the cultural history of its members. Those interested in exploring the contextual conditions that make possible the enactment of a learning organisation therefore have something to learn from organisations that are oriented to social action and social change.

A cautionary note is required, however. Situated learning theories have been criticised for their neglect of power relations and, in particular, for failing to account for how broader historical and structural relations of power at a societal level might reverberate within the dynamics of any community of practice (Fenwick 2003). The research in this union suggests that broader unequal power relations within the society are echoed and reproduced, even in a relatively democratic organisation such as SAMWU. There are constraints on participation in the organisation arising from historical inequalities between workers based on language, 'race', different levels of (formal) education, gender, the urban–rural divide and the hierarchical division of labour in the workplace. All these factors promote greater participation by some, and more limited participation or exclusion of others.

Furthermore, the conditions of collectivity that historically have made possible the widely dispersed educator role within the union have been undermined over the last few years by a new and increasingly aggressive ideology of competitive upward mobility (Grossman 1999). There has been growing pressure on trade unions for greater knowledge specialisation to enable unionists to deal with a complex range of policy issues; this has been accompanied by the increased foregrounding of those with specialised expertise, and pressure from union members for formally accredited courses. There has also been a shift in the nature of the dominant tools of mediation that facilitate learning with the organisation. Over the last 15 years, there has been a process of increased 'textualisation' of union practice: a move away from more dialogical, oral forms of communication to a greater reliance on forms of written text – particularly policy and legal texts – which are more 'authoritative' and therefore more 'univocal' in form (Bakhtin 1965/1994: 78).

The contextual conditions that have promoted organisational learning within the South African trade union movement are not a given but are subject to history and to shifting power relations both within and outside of these organisations. The 'learning organisation' does not simply emerge from rational and carefully planned pedagogic and organisational interventions (as suggested by some of the management and organisational development literature). Its achievement is the result of contestation and struggle, embedded in particular social and historical contexts.

Notes

1   This chapter is a significantly revised version of the article 'The trade union as a "learning organisation"? A case study of informal learning in a collective, social-action organisational context', which was published in 2006 in the *Journal of Education* 39: 27–46.

2   A collective response by other workers taking part in the focus group interview.

3   A form of chanting-marching-dancing performed in a militant mood.

References

Andrews SD (2003) Cosatu's policy on worker education, 1985–1992: Changes and continuities. MEd dissertation, University of Cape Town, South Africa

Bakhtin M (1965/1994) Rabelais and his world. In P Morris (ed.) *The Bakhtin reader: Selected writings of Bakhtin, Mdvedev and Volshinov.* London, New York, Sydney and Auckland: Arnold Publishers

Ball MJ (2003) Considering trade union education as a community of practice. *International Journal of Lifelong Education* (May–June): 297–310

Baskin J (1991) *Striking back: A history of Cosatu.* Johannesburg: Ravan Press

Cooper L (2005) Towards a theory of pedagogy, learning and knowledge in an 'everyday' context: A case study of a South African trade union. PhD thesis, University of Cape Town, South Africa

Daniels H (2001) *Vygotsky and pedagogy.* London and New York: Routledge Falmer

Engeström Y (2002) *Learning by expanding: An activity-theoretical approach to developmental research.* Accessed 27 August 2008, http://lchc.ucsd.edu/MCA/Paper/Engestrom/expanding

Fenwick TJ (2003) *Learning through experience: Troubling orthodoxies and intersecting questions.* Malabar, FL: Krieger Publishing Company

Friedman S (1987) *Building tomorrow, today: African workers in trade unions.* Johannesburg: Ravan Press

Garrick J (1999) The dominant discourses of learning at work. In D Boud & J Garrick (eds) *Understanding learning at work.* London and New York: Routledge

Gee J, Hull G & Lankshear C (1996) *The new work order: Behind the language of the new capitalism.* Sydney: Allen and Unwin

Grossman J (1999) Workers and knowledge. Paper presented at the 1st International Conference on Researching Work and Learning, Leeds University, Leeds (September)

Gunner L (1999) Remaking the warrior? The role of orality in the liberation struggle and in post-apartheid South Africa. In D Brown (ed.) *Oral literature and performance in southern Africa*. Oxford: James Currey

Jackson N & Jordan S (2000) Learning for work: Contested terrain? *Studies in the Education of Adults* 32(2): 195–211

Kress G (2000) Multimodality. In C Cope & M Kalantzis (eds) *Multiliteracies: Literacy learning and the design of social futures*. London: Routledge

Lave J & Wenger E (1991) *Situated learning: Legitimate peripheral participation*. Cambridge: Cambridge University Press

Mojab S & Gorman R (2003) Women and consciousness in the 'learning organisation': Emancipation or exploitation? *Adult Education Quarterly* 53(4): 228–241

Rogoff B (1984) Observing sociocultural activity on three planes: Participatory appropriation, guided participation, and apprenticeship. In B Rogoff & J Lave (eds) *Everyday cognition: Its development in social context*. Cambridge, MA: Harvard University Press

SAMWU (South African Municipal Workers' Union) (n.d.) Draft history of the first ten years of SAMWU. Document made available to the author

SAMWU (1996) Towards consolidating SAMWU's education project. 2nd draft of a discussion document. Document made available to the author

SAMWU (2003) SAMWU foundation shop steward training: Workshop resource package: Modules 1–3. Document made available to the author

Scribner S (1997) *Mind and social practice: Selected writings of Sylvia Scribner* (ed. E Tobach, LMW Martin, RJ Falmagne, MB Parlee & AS Kapelman). Cambridge: Cambridge University Press

Sitas A (1990) The voice and gesture in South Africa's revolution: A study of worker gatherings and performance genres in Natal. Paper presented at Wits History Workshop, University of Witwatersrand, Johannesburg (6–10 February)

Slabbert S & Finlayson R (2002) Code-switching in South African townships. In R Mesthrie (ed.) *Language in South Africa*. Cambridge: Cambridge University Press

Vally S (1994) Worker education in South Africa: Form and context, 1973–1993. Master's dissertation, University of Witwatersrand, Johannesburg, South Africa

Wenger E (1998) *Communities of practice: Learning, meaning, and identity*. Cambridge: Cambridge University Press

21 Learning at work and in the union

Bruce Spencer

Introduction

Workers have always learned at work; learning at work is not a new phenomenon. What workers have learned has always been diverse – for example, it ranges from learning about the job and how to do the work; to how to relate to fellow workers, supervisors and bosses (the social relations of work); to gaining understandings about the nature of work itself and how work impacts on society. Some of what workers learn is useful to their employers, some is useful to themselves, some is useful to their union organisations, and some may be useful both to their employers and to themselves. Some of what they learn may have little to do with work itself. It cannot be assumed that all learning at work is translatable into 'organisational learning' and is a 'win-win' for workers and employers alike. Nor can it be argued this learning always results in 'empowerment' for workers; in some circumstances it may result in greater job control for workers, but in others it may result in the reverse. There is a tendency in the literature to slip from discussing workplace learning to empowerment to industrial democracy as if they are all one and the same process and, for example, to assume that a statement that a company is 'empowering' its workforce means that it is actually happening. Such claims always need to be tested against worker as well as employer experience and situated in a more critical understanding of the 'new workplace' and the 'knowledge economy'.

In this chapter, I explore these issues and the context of corporate workplace learning more fully, beginning with a discussion of organisational culture before moving on to examine the claimed shift from 'Taylorism' to 'teams' and the 'learning organisation'. Recognising the importance of unions as a force for democratising the workplace, I then shift the focus to an outline of often-neglected labour education provision as a way of providing genuine empowering 'workplace-related learning' for workers – learning opportunities that are not employer determined but are extensive and diverse and yet largely ignored in the workplace learning literature.

Workplace learning literature is generally focused on the 'informal' – including incidental – learning associated with work activities. It is less concerned with 'non-formal' employer and industry training, courses and programmes. Many of these training initiatives are useful to employees and result in workers learning new skills and knowledge, but some can also be criticised for being narrowly employer focused, perhaps more concerned with tying employees to a particular employer than with giving workers generic and portable skills. In critiquing the context, concepts and claims of corporate workplace learning, this chapter shares the general focus of the workplace learning literature in that it largely ignores training issues.

Learning organisational culture

It is important to note that, generally speaking, workers try to make meaning out of their work experience. It is difficult for someone to spend eight hours a day, five days a week doing something in a totally detached way, and even more difficult if a person hates every minute of it. Read any account of workers describing their work and this becomes clear. Also, workers generally want to do a good job, even if that job is menial and the conditions are appalling. The new emphasis on workplace learning should not mask this pre-existing situation. Workers everywhere would also like to have some control over what they do and how they do it. This is evidenced in a recent survey of six primarily English-speaking countries, where it was reported that workers in all countries want to have a greater say in company decision-making and participatory processes (Freeman et al. 2007). And we can guess that the same is true for workers globally.

However, workers are encouraged to learn about what is useful for the employer. It is clear that some of their learning may contribute to a 'culture of silence' (Freire 1970) and to an acceptance of the way things are. Workers may learn to accept the dominant ideology that supports management rights – for example, the idea that we are all part of a global economy and must strive to out-compete others in order to survive. This is the corporate mantra: 'there is no alternative'.[1]

To ignore power and authority at work is to ignore the realities of what it is to be an employee. Organisational culture is determined by management, and learning about that culture is learning to accept it. This perspective is evident in Senge's claim that management should create a 'sense of shared ownership' and control of the enterprise (1990: 13). As Eric Newell, former chairman and CEO of Syncrude Canada Ltd and chancellor of the University of Alberta, comments: 'Really, what we are trying to do is engage people to get them thinking like owners of the business' (quoted in Schwind et al. 2007: 471). All this may appear innocent, but the 'sense of ownership' is not the same thing as workers actually owning and controlling; it is also indoctrination.

John Storey, a leading business school professor in the UK, has commented that the 'management of culture' has become a distinguishing feature of human resource management (HRM), and dates the 'remarkable trend' away from 'personnel procedures and rules' to the 'management of culture', to the early to mid 1990s. He notes that 'managing cultural change and moving towards HRM can often appear to coincide and become one and the same project'. Corporate cultural management is 'perceived to offer the key to the unlocking of consensus, flexibility and commitment' (Storey 2001: 8).

As Storey continues, the idea behind this shift in managerial strategies is clear: consensus would displace conflict and collective bargaining; flexibility, a 'substitute term for greater management control', would increase productivity; and commitment would lift labour performance higher as 'committed employees would go the extra mile in pursuit of customer service and organisational goals' (2001: 8). To achieve all this means changing a whole set of workers' behaviours, attitudes and values. A culture that was 'pluralist' and quasi-democratic, with unions challenging management decisions in collective bargaining, would be displaced by a 'unitarist' and pretend democratic culture, with claims of 'empowerment' and 'teams'. Workplace learning therefore needs to be understood as a new HRM control strategy, not a value-free activity.

I have noted previously (Spencer 2002) the importance of Keith Forrester's observation that the increased pressure on management to improve the quality and quantity of the labour input can result in 'new forms of oppression and control in the workplace' rather than empowerment or increased worker control (1999: 88). Forrester's observation is supported by a study of workplace skills training policies in Australia and Aotearoa/New Zealand, which suggests that 'the resulting reforms have had a remarkably unilateral effect – they move control over and benefits from skill training away from individuals and unions and into the hands of private capital' (Jackson & Jordan 2000: 195). Evidence from the UK would also suggest that strong union organisation is needed to take advantage of more expansive workplace learning opportunities, and even the new legislated union learning representatives (ULRs) are in danger of becoming 'corporate' or 'state' rather than 'worker' conduits for learning (Shelley & Calveley 2007).

Few of those who write about workplace learning deal adequately with the criticism that they largely ignore these issues of power and control. For example, David Boud and John Garrick, in their introduction to *Understanding Learning at Work*, discuss some of the negative impact of workplace learning's 'market driven emphasis' but also argue for the close connection between 'productivity and the operation of contemporary enterprises' without viewing this as a core contradiction (1999: 5). A classic example of this attitude is found in Victoria Marsick and Karen Watkins chapter in the same book, where they spend 13 pages 'envisioning new organisations for learning' and then turn to a number of key criticisms. They do their best to undermine these in a couple of pages without dealing with the key issues raised by the critics, and then conclude with the desire to create a learning system 'tailored to the needs of the industry, the organisation, the division, and the individuals who work in this organisational culture' (1999: 214), as if these fundamental criticisms had never been raised!

Corporate allegiance to the primacy of shareholder and CEO interests, bolstered by the legal framework,[2] and to the central purpose of increasing profit margins, bolstered by dubious economic theory, relegates the concerns and needs of other so-called stakeholders to minority roles. The fundamental contradiction of private enterprise remains: large corporations create hierarchies of control and power and are driven by the profit motive. These relations of control, power and profit create the social relations within work and society – those of employer and employee, boss and worker. Society's social classes result from these dominant work relations. It can be argued that with the shrinkage of well-paid manual and office jobs – described as the 'middle class' in North America – even in developed economies, society is polarising into a large working class and relatively small elite. A veil may be drawn over these contradictions at times with the rhetoric of managers as 'leaders' and 'coaches' and workers as 'associates' or 'partners', but unless ownership and control change and become genuinely more equitably distributed, nothing fundamentally will have changed.

Changes at work are often exaggerated to suggest the move from Taylorism to teams, and that employee empowerment is more advanced than it actually is. More astute researchers have argued that Taylorist measurement and control at work remain or have been expanded.[3] Taylorism may have changed in form but its essential purpose has not. As Tony Brown comments:

> Most descriptions contrast team production to the 'scientific management' principles of Taylor. In fact the tendency is in the other direction – to specify every move that a worker makes in much greater detail than before. Management chooses the processes, basic production layout and technologies to be used. Speeding up the pace of work is an intended consequence of standardising production, services or software. (Brown 1999: 15)

All of this is made possible by applying new technology into the 'new workplace'. Many jobs can be described as white collar and as linked to new technology; some are being dispersed into the home (teleworkers) and are not required to be completed at a particular 'time' or in a specifically designated employer-owned 'space' – described as 'postmodern' and 'post-industrial' employment. The appearance of worker control over when and how much work is undertaken is illusionary, however, as the new computer-based work comes with constant monitoring and feedback to the employer – far exceeding what Taylor was able to do with his stopwatch and clipboard. What we have today could perhaps be described as a more 'differentiated' or 'postmodern' Taylorism.

It has also been argued that the knowledge required to successfully engage at work has changed from simple know-how to 'work process knowledge'. This is knowledge that 'links know-how to theory', a kind of knowledge that was not available in the traditional Taylorist workplace (Boreham et al. 2002). It is unconvincing to argue that workers did not previously possess something akin to work process knowledge – that is, an understanding of the production process beyond a particular worker's own job – although it might be the case that few of them ever got to apply it. But is the real purpose of 'work process knowledge' to turn workers away from understandings of ownership, authority and control, and towards accepting managerial objectives and employer ownership of value added in the production process?

We live in a 'global society' in which the gap between the richest and the poorest, between those who live full lives in the economically developed countries and those who live 'half lives at best' in the less-developed countries, is growing (Honderich 2002: 6). Many workers, even in economically developed countries, have experienced a decline in the value of real wages and must struggle to stay abreast of inflation even at low inflation rates, while the incomes of the rich continue to climb. The following quote from *Macleans* magazine is instructive:

> 'From 1970 to 1999, the average annual salary in the US rose roughly 10 per cent to US$35,864', says Paul Krugman, a professor at Princeton University. At the same time, the average pay package of *Fortune* magazine's top 100 CEOs was up an astonishing 2,785 per cent, to US$37.5 million. 'There is no rationale but avarice and greed', says [John] Crispo. 'I believe in the pursuit of self-interest, but look at what they do: they rob us blind.' (2002: 1)[4]

How important is this inequality? In his book *Greed and Good* Sam Pizzigati argues, with reference to the US, that it is 'the root of what ails us as a nation, a social cancer that coarsens our culture, endangers our economy, distorts our democracy, even limits our lifespans' (2004: vii). He adds:

> [CEOs] have never (in practice) really accepted the notion that empowering employees makes enterprises effective. Empowering workers, after all, requires that power be shared, and the powerful, in business as elsewhere, seldom enjoy sharing their power. The powerful enjoy sharing rewards even less. Corporate leaders have never accepted, either in theory or practice, the notion that enterprise effectiveness demands some sort of meaningful reward sharing. (2004: 167)

Learning organisations

With all the rhetoric surrounding new workplace organisation, the knowledge economy and the claim that we live in a post-industrial, even post-capitalist, global economy, it is easy to forget that the basic structure and purpose of large corporations have not changed – unless, as Perkins suggests, you want to argue that the modern 'corporatocracy that exploits desperate people and is executing history's most brutal, selfish, and ultimately self-destructive resource-grab' is a new post-1970s phenomenon (2006: 255). Once we acknowledge that there are different interpretations of workplace learning, and that organisations are not unitary but pluralist in nature, we can begin to examine different interests and outcomes.

Laurie Field, a proponent of organisational learning for 10 years, has rethought his commitment to the idea. He considers that the weakness in the conception of organisational learning stems, first, from a confusion about and an ambiguous use of the terms 'organisation' and 'learning'; second, from the focus on 'learning associated with technical and economic interests'; and, third, from the assumption that organisations are unitary (2004: 204–205). He concludes that 'whole organisations rarely learn. A great deal of what has been referred to in the literature as "organisational learning" is actually learning by shared-interest groups within organisations' (2004: 216).

Others have gone further. For example, Mike Welton, a one-time advocate of the value of workplace learning as 'development work' (1991), has since commented that 'harnessed to the money-code the business organisation is actually learning disabled. It is intensely pressurised to learn along a single trajectory: to enhance shareholder profits and interests' (2005: 100). If Welton's judgement appears harsh, see Perkins (2006) for an insightful insider view of global corporate behaviour.

Another problem in the mainstream work and learning literature is the tendency to treat all organisations the same. This partly reflects the imposition of business rhetoric on non-business organisations such as public services, universities, hospitals, and non-profit and non-governmental organisations. All are seen as dealing with 'clients' or 'customers' within the context of a 'business plan' and having to apply business principles to the 'bottom line'. Scant regard is paid to the notion of the 'public good' or the quasi-democratic structures that govern these organisations and distinguish them from corporate capital. Given nurturing circumstances and organisational structures, these organisations may well be capable of more democratic, less hierarchical control involving citizens, workers, their unions and managers. Nor is the workplace 'democracy' claimed for corporate learning organisations compared to the non-profit sector including worker-owned cooperatives with workers participating in major decisions, including appointing the CEO and holding him/her accountable to the worker-owners (Salamon: 2003).

It must also be noted that being a worker in a 'learning organisation' carries no guarantee of job security. It may be true that the company's competitive position depends on a more effective and intelligent use of its human resources, but this does not mean that a corporate decision about location or product development will benefit a particular work group, or that the rewards from the collective effort will be equitably distributed among the workforce. Even in those cases where employees are given a small stake in the company, they can lose. In the Enron case, employee shareholdings were locked in and became worthless, while some of the senior executives bailed, taking their inflated funds with them. The decision to close a worksite, for example, may have absolutely nothing to do with how that particular workforce has performed, or how committed they were to the 'learning organisation'.

Although some writers acknowledge different interests, they still reduce workplace learning to a list of knowledge issues to be resolved. In the process, they treat it as a reified, value-free activity independent of the profit motive, with the hope that 'perhaps somewhere can be struck a balance between employees' and employers' interests in creating the goals of workplace learning' (Fenwick 2006: 195). While this may be an honourable objective and possibly applicable to the non-profit and voluntary economic sectors, it is difficult to see exactly where workers', citizens' or Third World's interests figure in the corporate conception of the 'goals of workplace learning'.

Unions and the learning rhetoric

The current rhetoric around 'workplace learning', 'teamwork' and 'the learning organisation' in the context of the 'knowledge economy' and 'the learning society' has had an impact on labour unions. These new descriptors of corporate and state activity in the context of globalisation of production are often cited to marginalise the significance of unions. We need to remember that workplace learning is essentially about learning to become a more efficient and compliant 'human resource'. While the enthusiasm for teamwork may have some advantages for some workers, it has to be understood within the context of 'human capital theory' and new HRM strategies that seek to bypass the kind of workplace democracy that independent unionism can provide. In some cases, teamwork has also gone hand in hand with downsizing and cuts in wages and conditions. This new rhetoric emphasises unitary perspectives of workplace activity and workplace culture. Workers are described as 'stakeholders', and they are all asked to 'share the vision'. Gone is the grudging acceptance by employers of pluralism, of the recognition that from time to time workers do have legitimate differences with employers that can be settled through the more democratic procedures of negotiation and agreement. Today the independent voice of labour is to be silenced, while the sole authority of the employer is masked by the description of workers as 'partners' or 'associates'. For example, in the UK freely negotiated recognition agreements are being displaced by 'partnership agreements' that emphasise employer rights, including, in some cases, denying the rights of work groups to democratically determine their own union steward (Wray 2001).

Some employers are also hoping to turn workers away from unionisation and to bind workers to company objectives.[5] However, many workers find that unionisation remains a more satisfactory way of attempting to democratise the workplace, and to ensure their voice is heard and their rights protected (Robertson et al. 1989). It has been argued by some authors that the new HRM policies work best with strong labour unions representing workers' interests; that strong unionism and the new workplace learning policies are therefore complementary, not opposite, ways of organising the workplace; and that unions are not damaged by these new techniques. Certainly a number of unions, notably the International Steelworkers of America, have embraced participatory practices and teams, and would argue that under the right circumstances unions will not be compromised.

On the other hand, Wells (1993) argues that strong unions and new HRM policies are in opposition, and that the future of unionism is bound up with defeating the encroachment of these policies. His argument is based on the recognition that there is an imbalance of power between employer and employee, and that employees can only equal employer power through collective representation. According to this view, labour unions are a force for democracy – an independent voice for workers. They provide a platform for participation in workplace decisions on the basis of challenges to management authority through independent collective representation, not through compromising collaborative and individualised arrangements.

While some of the evidence flowing from union involvement in workplace learning may be contradictory, there has been a growing recognition of the problematic nature of union workplace learning initiatives that may only lead towards greater management control over workers and their unions (Wells 1993; Forrester 1999; Brown 1999). Never was it more important for unions to establish their legitimacy and their own distinctive 'workplace learning' programmes. With this in mind, in the remainder of this chapter I focus on the possibilities for a more progressive 'workplace-related learning' – labour education – in response to managerially determined learning organisations. In this discussion I accept the contradictory nature of unionism as a force both for opposition and for accommodation, and its tendencies towards incorporation into managerial goals, bureaucratisation, oligarchic structures and so on. But I also contend that independent active unionism may provide the best chance to democratise the corporate workplace. As Hugh Clegg (1978) suggested, collective bargaining is industrial democracy.

Labour education

Labour education refers to education and training offered by labour unions[6] to their members and representatives. The extent to which this education is provided directly by unions or by another agency or educational institution for unions varies from country to country and union to union. A main purpose of labour education is to prepare and train union lay members to play an active role in the union. It is social more than individual learning.[7]

In some cases, unions have developed a comprehensive and integrated education and training programme, such as Britain's UNISON Open College,[8] which includes labour education, basic skills, recognition of prior learning and vocational training opportunities for all union members. In Brazil, 'Programa Integrar' offers union-sponsored labour education, vocational training and educational opportunities for the employed and the unemployed, as discussed below. It is difficult to gauge how many union members benefit from core labour education programmes, but the available statistical information suggests that some 3 per cent of union members per year undergo some labour education in most developed and developing economies. The participation rate may have been double two to three decades earlier, when the economy was more buoyant and release time was more generously legislated (for example, in the UK, Australia and New Zealand), or where it was easier to negotiate (as in Canada and the US). Although unions have been weakened and union density[9] has fallen through the 1990s and the beginnings of the twenty-first century in most countries (Scandinavia excepted), unions are continuing to give education a high priority. Unions in places as far apart as South Africa and Scandinavia may be reaching 6–10 per cent of all union members if all forms of labour education are considered, and those union representatives benefiting are working directly with their own membership, which results in a much greater impact from labour education programmes – perhaps benefiting 60 per cent of union membership in any one year.

The extent of labour education also varies over time, in some cases reflecting economic circumstances, in other cases economic and legal changes. The move to neo-liberal economic policies and globalisation was accompanied in many countries by attacks on the legal rights to paid educational leave for union representatives and on union bargaining rights. The loss of educational rights happened particularly in Europe and Australia/New Zealand, where they had been most extensive, and instead became increasingly narrowly defined as rights to training for industrial relations purposes. They also became more limited in the amount of time allowed, and state funding to support this activity was either cut or abolished altogether.

New developments in labour education

'Core' labour education is changing and is being targeted at local union representatives, with different examples evident in countries where unions are active. In one country there may be more emphasis on peer tutoring, while in another country there may be significant content changes. There are also examples of new forms of representative training, such as that for European Works Council representatives in Europe, and examples of union representative training in difficult circumstances, such as those in South Africa, where unions are coming to terms with recognition and bargaining after years of opposition under apartheid. We also have reports on more sophisticated educational provision for full-time officers, which has been an under-reported area of representative training.[10]

Training recruiters is another new development within core labour education. The educational components of the Australian Organising Works programme, the US Organizing Institute and the UK's Organising Academy are important labour education responses to the decline of union influence and to shifting employment patterns. The work undertaken in organising immigrant workers in Los Angeles is a particular example that has been successful in linking union activity to community groups and community-based organising, with labour education playing a key role. The Justice for Janitors campaigns have been most impressive and have relied on educational support to bolster activity, recruitment and contract negotiation. The region around Los Angeles has bucked the trend in the US, providing a leading example of union growth. Some of this educational and organising work involves existing union representatives, and some of it is targeted at new members and would-be union representatives. It is also interesting to note that if US workers were allowed to freely join unions, without employer hostility, more would do so, which would more than double US union density (Freeman et al. 2007).

Unions are directly involved in a number of membership education programmes, some of which have a 'basic skills' or vocational purpose. The importance of this work for union building has been established in Scandinavia, Britain, Australia, South America and South Africa, and is now being emulated elsewhere. Other initiatives around union-provided basic literacy courses or vocational training courses can give organised labour a lever to improve the quality and general applicability of such programmes, in contrast to the often workplace-specific emphasis of many employer-sponsored courses. Union-negotiated 'employee development schemes' such as those at Ford's UK and US plants and in the public sector in the UK and elsewhere are also contributing to broader educational opportunities for union members.

A number of unions and union centrals organise educational programmes for specific categories of members. For example, there are women-only courses aimed at providing a learning environment where women feel more comfortable about expressing opinions and are perhaps more likely to participate than they would be in traditional male-dominated union schools. Unions are also providing family and community educational events. For example, the Saskatchewan Federation of Labour (Canada) organises a 'Summer Camp for Kids', for young people aged 13 to 16. This week-long residential camp introduces the teenaged sons and daughters of union members to trade unionism and social justice issues in the morning, and offers recreational activities that emphasise cooperation as well as fun in the afternoons and evenings.

Britain's UNISON Open College definitely represents a way forward for labour education. This programme connects with members' immediate needs and in time feeds into strengthening union activity and presence in society. It can also provide critical approaches to current issues, something that is lacking from more homogenised adult education and training. What UNISON has done is to recognise the failure of much basic adult education and workplace learning for low-paid workers and stepped in with a Return to Learn (R2L) programme that provides opportunities for workers to become better educated and to move up through their Open College to other programmes and even full degrees. It takes the 'learning society' rhetoric seriously, accessing employer and state funding and claiming time off work for their members. The courses are based on UNISON-developed educational material. Its link with the Workers' Educational Association for tutoring of R2L assures an adult education focus with materials utilising collective understandings. Unfortunately, this example of independent union learning opportunities, together with some of the more imaginative employee development schemes, is under threat from the newly legislated ULRs and Union Learning Fund in the UK. While pregnant with progressive possibilities, this programme is in danger of turning unions into narrow corporate and state conduits for vocational training.[11]

Similarly the negotiated[12] paid educational leave (PEL) programmes in Canada offer another important example of membership education, one focused on developing critical political understandings. The Canadian Auto Workers (CAW) led the way and now the Canadian Union of Postal Workers (CUPW) has followed with a similar programme. Other unions in other countries need to examine the possibilities of this approach. The main features of this programme include a negotiated, employer-paid levy to a union-controlled trust. The union uses the fund to pay for lost wages and expenses of its members who attend the four-week residential PEL course. By targeting these courses at members rather than at representatives, the unions hope to engage their members' imaginations and draw them into greater union understandings and activity. The core four-week programme has been supplemented by other courses also funded from the levy.

In Brazil, Programa Integrar has started to offer relevant vocational training and educational opportunities for the unemployed and the employed that help to strengthen the union presence. The programme illustrates that even in a hostile climate union education can succeed. It provides an example to other countries of how to build community links and to argue for alternative worker cooperative employment for union members in opposition to global corporate power. This example links with others in South America, where union members are taking back closed factories and building local economic networks. This example is particularly important as it speaks to the contradictory nature of unionism and the possibilities for a social unionism capable of displacing capitalist structures.

Although research circles[13] have been around for some time, it is clear from Swedish experience that this approach has a bright future in terms of strengthening union activity within the union as well as externally. It represents an important alternative for union members wishing to conduct independent 'workplace learning' projects.

Courses on new global management techniques have developed, with colourful titles such as 'Union Judo' – the idea being to use the 'weight' and 'momentum' of the employer to union advantage. Nor have unions ignored the issues of free trade and globalisation. These topics are by their nature difficult for single-country-based unions to handle, but additional emphasis has been given to international union activity in the last 10 years. Over and above providing courses for union representatives from works councils of transnational companies, there has also been increasing union presence on United Nations (UN) bodies. Unions have become active on international bodies discussing environmental, conservation and sustainable development issues, and these initiatives have an educational component. Unions have responded to calls for international worker solidarity, with some courses not only dedicated to garnering a greater understanding of the issues but also involving study visits and exchanges. In other examples, union educators have built units on solidarity work into basic steward courses and into membership courses. Unions have also responded to educational challenges posed by widespread computer use and the internet and are using online education for union members. An obvious use for labour online learning is to build education across national boundaries. For example, the International Labour Organization (ILO) is now working on an international labour studies programme (Belanger 2006).

The movement of production to less economically developed countries by some transnational corporations does provide a threat to unionism, but the response of international union federations and some individual unions, which are sometimes aided by NGOs, to seek 'framework agreements' may result in new opportunities for unionisation in those countries. These agreements reached with corporation head offices push them to do business only with suppliers who recognise workers' rights and independent unions. It is difficult to predict whether or not these measures will be successful in accelerating union development in countries such as Indonesia, the Philippines, Thailand and China, but union education initiatives are already under way to promote this possibility. The existence of these framework agreements and labour education initiatives means the future is more promising than might be predicted otherwise.

Conclusion

Many of the labour education initiatives outlined above have elements of both accommodation and resistance to current corporate globalisation trends. Some courses and programmes can be seen as proactive, others as adaptive, while much of labour education remains reactive. Overall, unions remain an important and positive social organisation for working people. It is the absence of strong independent unions that remains a problem for the majority of the world's workers. Some of the skills-training programmes offered through unions may appear to be little different from employer-provided schemes, but unions generally advocate portable generic skills. While the thrust of mainstream labour education is towards social purpose and social action, it is aimed at equipping workers with the analytical and organisational knowledge needed to participate democratically in the workplace and society.

Discussions of workplace learning need to acknowledge the real issues of power, authority, control, inequality and ownership and promote independent workers' learning opportunities for more real empowerment and a more genuine workplace democracy. Whereas 'workplace learning' is aimed at incorporating workers into management culture, labour education allows workers to challenge it.

Notes

1 An extreme example of this workplace learning is provided in the Michael Moore film *Sicko*, when Moore interviews a couple of former US insurance/HMO (health maintenance organisation) executives who explain how they learned to undermine the claims of clients. As one interviewee explained: the more they learned and the more successful they became, the more they were rewarded with higher salaries.

2 See Bakan (2004) for a damning critique of corporate behaviour rooted in corporate law and structures.

3 For example, Hennessy and Sawchuk (2003) discuss the deskilling and 'industrialising' of front-line social service workers following the introduction of new technology into their jobs.

4 Crooks in the boardroom, *Macleans*, 30 December 2002. *Macleans* is Canada's oldest current affairs publication and a proponent of free enterprise. John Crispo is a retired University of Toronto business professor and an outspoken champion of corporate freedom and free trade.

5 Wal-Mart and McDonald's exemplify this approach.

6 Or trade unions.

7 See Spencer (2002: 17–24) for a fuller discussion of labour education and Spencer (2006: 9–10) for a distinction between informal and non-formal learning/education.

8 UNISON is a large, essentially public sector/service union representing both blue- and white-collar workers.

9 Union density refers to the percentage of the workforce that is unionised.

10 For references and a fuller discussion of these international examples and others quoted below, please see the relevant chapters in Spencer (2002).

11 See Shelley and Calveley (2007) for an early optimistic yet cautious account of UK developments.

12 As opposed to state- or employer-provided PEL.

13 Workers conducting their own research into workplace or sector problems.

References

Bakan J (2004) *The corporation: The pathological pursuit of profit and power.* Toronto: Penguin

Belanger M (2006) A case study of online collaborative learning for union staff in developing countries. PhD thesis, Simon Fraser University, Vancouver

Boreham N, Samurcay R & Fisher M (eds) (2002) *Work process knowledge.* London: Routledge

Boud D & Garrick J (eds) (1999) *Understanding learning at work.* London: Routledge

Brown T (1999) *Restructuring the workplace: Case studies of informal economic learning.* Sydney: Centre for Popular Education, University of Technology

Clegg H (1978) *Trade unions under collective bargaining.* Oxford: Basil Blackwell

Fenwick T (2006) Work, learning and adult education in Canada. In T Fenwick, T Nesbit & B Spencer (eds) *Contexts of adult education: Canadian perspectives.* Toronto: Thompson Educational Publishing

Field L (2004) Rethinking organisational learning. In G Foley (ed.) *Dimensions of adult learning: Adult education and training in a global era.* Crows Nest, New South Wales: Allen and Unwin

Forrester K (1999) Work-related learning and the struggle for subjectivity. *Proceedings of the 1st International Conference on Researching Work and Learning.* Leeds: School of Continuing Education, Leeds University

Freeman R, Boxall P & Haynes P (eds) (2007) *What workers say: Employee voice in the Anglo-American workplace.* Ithaca, NY: Cornell University Press

Freire P (1970) *Pedagogy of the oppressed.* New York: Continuum

Hennessy T & Sawchuk P (2003) Technological change in the Canadian public sector: Worker learning responses and openings for labour-centric technological development. *Proceedings of the 3rd International Conference on Researching Work and Learning.* Tampere, Finland: University of Tampere

Honderich T (2002) *After the terror.* Edinburgh: Edinburgh University Press

Jackson N & Jordan S (2000) Learning for work: Contested terrain? *Studies in the Education of Adults* 32(2): 195–211

Marsick V & Watkins K (1999) Envisioning new organisations for learning. In D Boud & J Garrick (eds) *Understanding learning at work.* London: Routledge

Perkins J (2006) *Confessions of an economic hit man.* New York: Plume Books

Pizzigati S (2004) *Greed and good: Understanding and overcoming the inequality that limits our lives.* New York: Apex Press

Robertson D, Rinehart J & Huxley C (1989) Team concept and kaizen: Japanese production management in a unionised Canadian auto plant. *Studies in Political Economy* 39(Autumn): 77–107

Salamon L (2003) *The resilient sector: The state of nonprofit America.* Washington, DC: Brookings Institution

Schwind H, Das H & Wagar T (2007) *Canadian human resource management: A strategic approach.* Whitby, ON: McGraw-Hill Ryerson

Senge P (1990) The leader's new work: Building learning organisations. *Sloan Management Review* (Fall): 7–23

Shelley S & Calveley M (eds) (2007) *Learning with trade unions: A contemporary agenda in employment relations.* Aldershot: Ashgate

Spencer B (ed.) (2002) *Unions and learning in a global economy: International and comparative perspectives.* Toronto: Thompson Educational Publishing

Spencer B (2006) *The purposes of adult education: A short introduction.* Toronto: Thompson Educational Publishing

Storey J (2001) *Human resource management: A critical text* (2nd edition). London: Thomson Learning

Wells D (1993) Are strong unions compatible with the new model of human resource management? *Relations Industrielles/Industrial Relations* 48(1): 56–84

Welton M (1991) *Toward development work: The workplace as a learning environment.* Geelong, Australia: Deakin University Press

Welton M (2005) *Designing the just learning society: A critical inquiry.* Leicester: NIACE

Wray D (2001) What price partnership? Paper presented at the Work Employment and Society Conference, University of Nottingham, Nottingham (11–13 September)

22 Learning, practice and democracy: Exploring union learning

Keith Forrester and Hsun-Chih Li

Introduction

It appears that worker organisations are in disarray everywhere. International membership figures, together with country and regional studies such as those undertaken through the International Labour Organization (Jose 2002), indicate with few exceptions the extent and depth of this disarray. The reasons for and the solutions to the problems are complex and are shaped by different and contradictory combinations of historical, political and socio-economic contexts. The vital societal contribution of workers' organisations in the creation of labour market and social institutions that have worked towards social cohesion, access to civil and political liberties as well as the political space for democratic institutions appears to be of little concern today. It's the 'old social movement' concerned with yesterday's agenda!

Instead, politicians 'North' and 'South' embrace uncritically the claims and promised economic rewards of 'flexible specialisation', 'employee empowerment' and 'human resource development'. The militant response by labour organisations in developing economies to the submission by their political elites to neo-liberal forces, however, is often met with repression, although in other instances, such as in Chile, Korea and parts of Africa, it has led to sustained and successful campaigns for multi-party democracy. In these situations, skill development and labour market inequalities are an essential part of a wider labour societal strategy that includes enhanced human rights and wider political alliances for social change. In late capitalist economies, by contrast, employee skills and knowledge are situated more narrowly within a human resource perspective. Employee involvement, high-commitment managerial regimes and employee empowerment are the new rhetorical buzzwords within capital-accumulation strategies.

This chapter is situated within the economic circumstances primarily characterising advanced capitalist neo-liberal economies today. In it we suggest that much of the research on workplace learning and knowledge has ignored the issue of learning and unions with the result that 'worker knowing' is portrayed as either absent or lacking. We argue that situating worker learning within Bourdieu's understanding of 'practices' helps address these omissions. Our argument is informed by research data drawn from a qualitative study of workplace union learning representative (ULRs) from a major British trade union. Using our research data, we argue that particular conceptions of 'learning' by labour not only confront and contest dominant employer discourses informed by human capital theory, but also raise wider agitational issues of workplace control, design and democracy.

In the first section, we set out our critique of mainstream union policy. This is followed by an overview of the case study, where we explore differing accounts of union learning among ULRs. Instead of a descriptive outline of this recent and important initiative, we focus on uncovering the distinctiveness of the *union* nature of this example of workplace learning. We contend that despite the evidence that ULRs 'are making an enormous contribution to changing the workplace for the better', as the general secretary of the Trades Union Congress (TUC) in Britain suggests (Unionlearn 2006: 1; see also Unionlearn 2007 and TUC 2004), a number of important issues relating to the particular *union* nature of this 'enormous contribution' remain unexplored and underdeveloped in the early emerging research evidence. In the third section, we expand on the organisational concerns and analytical limitations that are raised by the case study. Using the formulations and insights developed by French sociologist Pierre Bourdieu, we argue that an expanded conceptual understanding of union learning recognises pathways of worker and union learning in addition to those identified and prioritised by British trade unions. Although politically and academically unfashionable, our claim is that a focus on union learning raises questions of democratisation within a wider societal agenda that could contribute towards a potentially radical and emancipatory perspective to 'workplace learning'. In the final section of the chapter, we suggest a number of union campaigning issues that extend beyond the current preoccupations and which result from a greater conceptual clarity about the nature of union learning.[1]

Mainstream union policy on union learning: A critique

Historically, trade unions have always been concerned with the renewal and development of their membership, and especially their lay workplace leadership. However, it is argued that, from the 1980s onwards, the current neo-liberal policy discourse on employee knowledge and skills has provided a fresh terrain for union engagement around key policy concerns and formulations that question the nature and restructuring of what is commonly understood as 'work'. An examination via case-study evidence of union learning, it is suggested, implicitly involves a critical discussion of 'learning' and the particular contexts within which this learning occurs. Many of these studies fail to recognise, explain or illustrate sufficiently strongly the differentiated and differentiating nature of knowing, in and out of the workplace. As a result there is a tendency to use overgeneralised understandings of learning or to accept uncritically the employer's 'colonisation of employee subjectivity'. By contrast, in this chapter, worker and union 'knowing' is seen to happen within particular social, cultural and political structures and relationships that are characterised by exploitation, domination and inequity. It is within such particular neo-liberal circumstances that our discussion of worker and union 'knowing' is situated, as is evidenced in the case study described in the following section.

Case study: Union learning representatives in Britain

Today most labour organisations in many parts of the world have developed an interest and often an expertise in vocational training and aspects of workplace learning. The discourse of 'skills', 'lifelong learning', 'knowledge' and 'employee knowing' potentially provides unions with the opportunity and legitimacy within which to examine and explore fresh organisational and recruitment initiatives, demonstrate the effectiveness of representation and retention for members, as well as develop alternative agendas. While labour will always be on the defensive within a capitalist economy, involvement in 'the learning society' and 'the knowledge economy' could form an important aspect of the bargaining and renewal agenda.

This is seen to be the case in Britain. Against the Thatcher onslaught of the 1980s and 1990s, British trade unions have invested substantial organisational effort and political credibility in the endorsement and promotion of workplace learning. Union involvement in vocational training and education at both policy and workplace level provided the unions with perceived solutions to their marginalisation at the bargaining table and their expulsion into the political wilderness under Conservative governments (Forrester & Payne 1999). The return of the Labour government in 1997 rewarded this turn to a 'modernised' union agenda. Funded by the Labour government (through the Union Learning Fund [ULF]) via the TUC and granted statutory recognition, some 15 000 workplace ULRs have been trained; and it is predicted that 22 000 ULRs will be in office by 2010 (Healey & Engel 2003).

Heralded as 'the quiet revolution' by the TUC general secretary, the training and networking of ULRs is seen as addressing a number of union organisational issues that include learning agreements with employers, involvement of young people and women in the union, and the creation of workplace learning centres (Unionlearn 2006, 2007; Warhurst et al. 2007; Wallis et al. 2005; Lloyd & Payne 2006; Alexandrou et al. 2005). As the TUC general secretary noted: 'Union learning reps are making an enormous contribution to changing the workplace for the better' (Unionlearn 2006: 1). Survey evidence can be seen as supporting this claim. As the evaluation of the Scottish Learning Fund reports, workplace learning delivers 'additionality' (supporting employee training where this exists), meeting a 'so far unappreciated demand for workplace learning' and acting as a 'catalyst for learning culture change amongst employees' (Warhurst et al. 2007). The creation of a national infrastructure in 2006 – Unionlearn – with regional offices and officers, extensive support literature and a much-visited dedicated website, has been accompanied by a plethora of imaginative workplace learning projects (Unionlearn 2007). As a recent research paper concludes: 'Clearly the ULF and ULRs are a breakthrough for trade union involvement in the workplace' (Calveley et al. 2003: 20).

Thus, British union involvement in issues of vocational training and skills over the last two decades appears vindicated. Involvement at the various policy 'top tables', bargaining leverage with employers and a rediscovered legitimacy and attractiveness to employees are at least partly seen to flow from sustained union activity around workplace learning. Yet, despite the seemingly good news from the survey and anecdotal evidence, there are a number of conceptual and policy issues and questions that remain underdeveloped and unexplored in this emerging evidence of ULR activity and workplace learning activity. For example, to what extent or in what ways is the British ULR initiative a distinctive *union* experience and how is the notion of *learning* to be understood and used? How does the emerging ULR experience of the last five years interrelate and, more importantly, engage with the dominant policy and ideological agendas driven by a preoccupation with employee knowledge, skills and attitude from a human capital perspective?

As indicated above, the existing survey evidence and early research studies on ULRs do not seek to address such questions. Instead, the analytical and methodological focus in general tends towards the recording of that data necessary to provide an up-to-date descriptive overview of the activities and experiences of ULRs. In most studies, the nature and extent of the union learning is equated with participation in formal courses. Given the historic disparities in access to employer-sponsored training, encouraging employee participation in any provision is an important contribution of ULRs. However, as is argued below, such a conception of learning is both very narrow and partial. Similarly, most studies investigate the distinctiveness of the union contribution to workplace learning by analytically suggesting that there is an independent union learning agenda within a partnership relationship with the employer that focuses primarily on employees' needs (Wallis et al. 2005). A rare exception to this dominant industrial relations formulation is the study by Calveley et al. (2003), where the nature of union learning is explicitly linked to debates about deskilling and job control and to issues of union renewal. This broader socio-political perspective allows the research to be seen as exploring 'the role of the ULF and ULRs in the controlling or emancipatory nature of learning' (2003: 3). In general, however, the understanding of the learning and the distinctiveness of the union dimension in workplace learning remains conceptually and politically unexplored and undeveloped.

There are a number of dangers and implications that might result from such a research design and framework that situates 'union learning' as unproblematic. Firstly, equating participation in an educational or training course with learning, for example, could lead to an overemphasis on a performance-driven focus. An unproblematic linear relationship such as this minimises or ignores the pedagogical and political tensions inherent within the employment relationship. Abstracting the learning – participation in courses – from these relationships reduces the significance of power and context in the learning. Secondly, the emphasis on formal learning reduces the extent and richness of other types and sources of worker learning and implicitly accepts the dominant deficit model informing employer and policy positions. This learning is grounded in and shaped by specific social, cultural, economic and political relationships. Rather than thinking of them as learning less or being deficient, it is possible to conceive of trade unionists as learning *differently*. However, unless understandings and formulations of learning are conceptually examined and situated theoretically, such alternative and radical perspectives remain hidden. Thirdly, perceiving union learning as unproblematic risks reifying the nature of this learning – that is, obscuring the processes that constitute the learning while at the same time suggesting an objective, external, physical quality, as in the notion of 'skill'. Fourthly, we argue that the perspective of 'employability', largely or wholly informing the framework and activities of union learning, is uncritical, ideologically driven, adaptive and limited (Forrester 2004, 2005). It accepts the neo-liberal shift of responsibility for skills and employment opportunities from the labour market to the individual and ignores the classed and racialised construction of these skills (Brown et al. 2003).

We argue that, in contrast to these limitations, an alternative conception of union learning provides an understanding of practice that begins to incorporate a distinctively *union* character (Forrester 2007).

Methodology

Given that learning is viewed in our research as social participation embedded in participants' everyday activities and life histories, it was decided to employ a qualitative case-study approach as the most appropriate methodological strategy for exploring understandings and experiences of union learning. Thirteen ULRs from one British trade union were interviewed: they were based in four regions and were chosen to reflect a variety of criteria that included occupational sector, union experience, employment experience, formal education, gender and participation in union training courses. This sample was considered adequate for the overall research aims of exploring conceptual development related to understanding the learning inherent in ULR practices. The 13 ULRs were interviewed again some six months later. This second round of interviews investigated in greater depth the practice of ULRs, explored changes in participants' contexts and viewpoints, and clarified any ambiguities from the first set of interviews.

Given the complex contextual nature of ULR learning, 3 national educational officers were also interviewed, together with 3 (out of 10) union regional officials responsible for the recruitment, training and support of work-based representatives. These officer interviews provided an insight into union aspirations, policy and structure within which ULR practice was situated. In total, 35 semi-structured interviews were conducted in 2003. These interviews mainly occurred within the participants' workplaces; all were recorded and transcribed.

In addition to the interviews, observations were made at each of the union's three-stage training courses for ULRs. Each training course is a residential-based, three-day course. Diary notes and observations were recorded. Finally, documentary and archival materials were collected. These included government policy documentation, training materials from the ULR courses, and union documentation and correspondence.

Exploring the 'union' nature of learning

Becoming a ULR is a complex process fraught with potential difficulties, including competing demands from employers and members, lack of union experience, lack of personal confidence, possible indifference from members and hostility from employers. Not surprisingly, the attrition rate for ULRs is high, although rarely documented. The performativity characterising understandings of ULR activity by both unions and government-funding streams – enrolment in courses, providing advice and guidance, accessing funds to support learning – adds further pressure to the job of a ULR as well as providing a tightly bounded framework for understanding what ULRs 'do'.

Underpinning these quantitative measures, however, are a number of broader interrelated issues that focus on the employment relationship, employer strategies and the contested understandings of employee knowledge and skills. Although there is a focus on 'the union agenda' (Wallis et al. 2005), in the research to date there is a general absence of a focus on the distinctive *union* nature of learning. A research focus on learning informed by participation rather than acquisition helps to address this absence. 'Knowing' and 'knowledge' are seen not only as socially and contextually bounded and defined but also as shaping individual and collective practice, which, in turn, shapes the context.

Within participative approaches to learning, a number of perspectives can be identified. For example, situated learning theory (Lave & Wenger 1991), with its notion of 'community of practices', has been used extensively, especially by British educationalists in work-based learning studies (Ball 2003). However, as Hodkinson and Hodkinson (2004) have argued, there remain a number of conceptual ambiguities with the 'community of practice' formulation, as well as insufficient attention and weight given to issues of conflict and power within the process of 'belonging'. In contrast, Engeström's (2001) activity theory of learning sees radical and discontinuous change – contradictions – as a central feature of development within activity systems, which forces or encourages new learning from the resolution of the contradictions characterising activity systems. The emphasis on activity has been used suggestively in the research of workplace learning and, in particular, of worker or union learning (Engeström et al. 1999; Sawchuk et al. 2006; Livingstone & Sawchuk 2005).

Our research of union learning, too, is focused on the notion of 'practices', but instead draws heavily from the thinking of Bourdieu (1998). The use of Bourdieu's formulations in the study results in part from our greater familiarity with his ideas than with, say, those of activity theorists, but we also believe that Bourdieu offers a variety of suggestive ways of conceptualising union learning that overcomes some of the ambiguities within a community-of-practice approach (Hodkinson & Hodkinson 2003). His theory can be seen as a philosophy of action condensed in a small number of interrelated key concepts such as field, position, capital, and habitus or dispositions (Bourdieu 1998). Basically, a field is a social context where people are situated and practise, and it is comprised of positions occupied by people. A field may represent a particular workplace or a non-workplace setting; it may also represent a context within a workplace or it may be broader than a workplace. A person can therefore be involved in many overlapping fields in daily life. Positions within any field are related to various capitals (Hodkinson & Hodkinson 2004). When people undertake activities in a field or in fields, the forms of capital related to their positions unavoidably interact through power relations, which in turn influence human practice. Since learning is highly practice based, fields, positions and capitals influence learning. Using formulations from Bourdieu, how do our empirical data illustrate the nature of this participation?

ULR practices: Interpreting the data

The job of a ULR is complex given that it includes both a union and an occupational responsibility. At least three contexts can be identified: the union context, the occupational context and the overlapping context between these two. For Roy,[2] who had a supervisory position within a large engineering company, there was no difference between the contexts (or fields). He reported:

> [If learning] doesn't meet the business needs…I find it quite difficult. We as training coordinators or learning reps have to stick to [company] rules and the fact that 'yes, we will develop you but we will develop you in the part of the organisation that you are working in' because at the end of the day the company is paying you to do an activity.

In contrast to Roy, Tom was a full-time union steward in an insurance company and saw ULR activity as raising 'people's consciousness about how society works and how society's resources are distributed, in most ways, in an unfair way'. While ULR everyday activities focus on the overlapping context between the union context and the occupational context, the 'workplace' conveys different understandings. Bourdieu's notion of 'fields' or contexts explicitly recognises that people are always situated in often overlapping social structures and contexts in their daily lives. Their positions and varied resources ('capitals') resulting from these positions contribute towards an analysis of the ULR fields and, therefore, of what is possible and not possible. For example, Rose worked in a university training department and had no union experience before her appointment as a ULR. Her employment field provided her with opportunities and resources (capitals) for ULR activities but limited her effectiveness as a union representative. 'It's ridiculous, 'cos I'm not a manager,' she said. Hugh, from a voluntary-sector organisation, and Howard, a university technician, both mentioned the potentially contradictory nature of occupying a training job with the role of a ULR, but due to the union-friendly and vocational nature of the training, the roles were seen as consistent and not contradictory. The occupational positions of 11 out of the 13 ULRs facilitated learning rep activities but also contributed to their differing understandings of being a ULR. Gary, from a large steel company, recognised the importance of participation, but stressed the union field when he discussed the importance of the 'experience I gained over the years as a trade union rep. And it's not a skill you learn overnight just because you have been on a learning rep course.'

Benefiting from the considerable resources available through the wider union requires participating in union activities, which was not the experience of all ULRs. 'Learning as participation' also implies less learning if there is a lack of participation. All of the four inactive or less-active ULRs wanted further training courses to compensate for their lack of activity. Failing to learn to become a ULR does not indicate that they learned nothing; rather, they learned something different. Examining participation, then, can usefully be illuminated with the support of Bourdieu's notions of field, position and capital; explanations begin to emerge of opportunities or affordances as well as constraints. As Billet (2002: 62) remarks:

> [H]ow the workplace affords these opportunities is key to the quality of learning through participation. Workplace factors structure and distribute opportunities for participation and hence, the prospects for learning.

The level of 'affordances' or 'invitational quality of the workplace' was not the same for the 13 ULRs and this contributed to their different understandings and practices. Wendy, who worked as a hospital technician, experienced severe time constraints on her role as a ULR, was inactive and began to consider resigning her role and moving into the management training department. If successful, 'all my union roles would go. I wouldn't do any of it,' she said. Her position occupationally was increasingly in conflict with her union responsibilities (field), and resolution of the conflict might entail resigning from her union positions. Affordances thus point in the direction of workplace structures, management attitudes and authority relations and were identified as decisive in shaping ULR activity in our study.

Being in similar fields, however, did not necessarily result in similar ULR activities. Tom, from an insurance-sector company, had greater opportunities for his ULR activities than Gary (from a large steel company), but he resigned from the role while Gary did not. Fields, positions and capitals appeared insufficient to fully explain current and future projected activities. Accounting for such differences were other internal subjective factors such as individual perception, values, beliefs and attitudes – 'dispositions', according to Bourdieu. In other words, the interplay between agency and structure can be explored through an analysis of individual dispositions (or life histories) and workplace affordances. Differences in dispositions partially contributed towards explaining the different trajectories of Tom and Gary. Gary's strong union disposition, for example, was influenced by his family background. 'I'll always be a trade unionist,' he remarked. 'It was something I think my grandfather was, my father was, so I grew up in a household that had trade union badges and I've never moved away from it.' Similarly Tracy, from a food manufacturing company, was a strong advocate for equity issues and women's rights in the workplace; she came from a large family in which the boys were encouraged to continue their education and the girls to leave for employment as soon as possible. 'I left school with no qualifications,' Tracy mentioned in her second interview. Both Tracy and Tony (from the engineering firm) were new to the union and enjoyed positions and capitals from their job as trainers. Tony was considering moving into a 'human resource role…into more a management role'. Tracy, by contrast, saw her position and union role as incompatible and wanted to become a full-time union officer, as this route offered more opportunities for advancing 'people's rights and working for women's rights'.

For Bourdieu, dispositions are an important feature of 'habitus'. Although not too dissimilar to social class, habitus is a 'relatively durable' system of dispositions shaped in fields (Bourdieu & Wacquant 1992: 133). Tracy's situation illustrates well this notion of habitus in making sense of her 'knowing'.

Overall, then, the research data begin to indicate that 'coming to know' for the ULRs in their various workplaces is a complex and contradictory process. Despite all being labelled as 'union' learning representatives, they differed on their understanding of 'learning' and their responsibilities and tasks attached to the role. For those ULRs who understood and experienced workplace learning as 'meeting the business needs' (as mentioned by Roy), their lack of union experience or occupational position contributed strongly towards masking or marginalising the contested nature of this workplace knowing and in accepting the dominant employer model. However, even in these instances, the challenges to and cracks in this powerful hegemonic perspective are apparent. 'It's ridiculous, 'cos I'm not a manager,' protests Rose in response to union members' views. Meeting business needs or legitimating workplace learning within union–employer partnerships depoliticises and therefore renders 'normal' relations of domination and authority. Learning safely is reduced to a cognitive task, or 'head job', instead of a practice structured by issues such as position, field, gender and social class. A conception of trade unionism that fails to be rooted and legitimated within the material inequalities of the workplace (such as power, reward, discretion, control) is likely instead to stress the personal development and professional qualities of the ULR role. Important as these qualities are for any union position, too great an emphasis points towards a human resource perspective rather than that of trade unionism. Disagreement and contestation (as in Gary's case) is replaced by consensus and inactivity (as in Tony's case).

Bourdieu's theory of practice tells us that action is more than ULRs having conceptions of and thinking meaningfully about their job and the social world, as McDonough illustrates in her study of public service workers (McDonough 2006). Becoming a ULR also involves adaptation to the constraints of social, economic and political arrangements within the workplace and within the wider societal context. However, as the above discussion of ULRs in our sample suggests, many ULRs (and workers in general) do not uncritically accept managerial perspectives or restructuring strategies. Instead they struggle to create, appropriate and transform such efforts when they are perceived as hostile to their own interests.

In summary, Bourdieu's formulation of practice helps, firstly, to develop an understanding and appreciation of the complex and contradictory nature of union learning within and outside of work. Secondly, Bourdieu's notion of practice directs analytical and empirical attention to the material and cultural circumstances that shape and are shaped by ULR activity in learning to become a ULR. Both these points entail implications for British trade unions that extend beyond present concerns, as discussed in the next section.

Learning for democratisation and against subjectification

We have suggested that participatory, informed perspectives of learning provide a fruitful framework for situating workplace, worker and union learning. A number of strategic issues emerge from such a perspective that begin to contribute to an alternative agenda that engages with the dominant human capital concerns and that progresses beyond the simplistic identification of union autonomy within an employer partnership. There is, for example, a possible emergent agenda of workplace democratisation that is driven by union understandings, union priorities and union actions. Situating union knowing within particular employment structures and relations encourages a focus on wider issues of control, cooperation and opposition within the labour process. As Casey (2003: 632) argues:

> Reconceptualising the learning worker is vital for both the articulation of a moral ideal, and for the imagination of learning organisations and learning economies beyond the currently truncated conceptions.

Similarly, Fuller and Unwin's (2003) notion of an 'expansive' and 'restrictive' learning environments continuum is located in their desire to situate learning within wider participative concerns and move beyond 'the currently truncated conceptions'. As they report, 'we have been increasingly concerned to understand the interaction between institutional context, workplace learning environment and individual learning' (2003: 412). Their emphasis on 'institutional context', however, moves the analysis towards a more organisational rather than sociological focus. Olssen (2006) also develops this preoccupation with learning and democracy when he warns against understandings of learning that 'run the distinct possibility of merely facilitating the ongoing reproduction of established economic and political relations' (2006: 225). Flecker and Hofbauer (1998: 114) make a similar point to those of Casey and of Fuller and Unwin, but focus instead on the 'mismatch between the formation of the self in contemporary society and organisational strategies of capitalising on the subjective factor'. They argue that this mismatch between organisational design and individual aspirations is resulting in a 'superfluous subjectivity'. The case for democratic engagement results from recognising that worker 'aspirations and expectations… necessarily exceed what working life can deliver for the vast majority of people' (1998: 114). Rather than accepting the dominant human-capital-inspired view of deficit worker knowing, the 'turn to learning' provides unions with an agenda and a variety of measures that address the 'superfluous subjectivity' together with worker capacities and aspirations that 'far exceed those required by production' (1998: 114).

Conclusions

The chapter has used the formulations of Bourdieu to illustrate the complex and contradictory but rich possibilities for union learning within the workplace. Situating ULR within a practice framework addresses a number of issues and questions that have failed to be considered in the early emerging research evidence about what ULRs do. A number of alternative but interrelated themes have emerged from the approach and analysis adopted in our case study and which are absent from union considerations. Firstly, and in contrast to the dominant 'deficit' model of employee learning, workers are always learning. As a matter of surviving within the labour market, they *have* to learn. They might well learn different things in different ways to those promoted by the employers, but they do learn. Implicitly, employers recognise the value of this knowing by attempting to appropriate this intimate workplace knowledge.

Secondly, worker 'knowing' is shaped by the socio-economic relationships and structures of the workplace and the wider society. These relationships are of a particular historical character characterised by exploitation and conflict. As such, conceptions of learning based within such circumstances raise important labour-process issues of control, authority, opposition and 'democracy'. Understanding learning as practice and practice as learning within this distinctive *capitalist* working environment begins to provide a distinctive *union* character and direction to this learning. As such, a union-inspired workplace bargaining agenda can be envisaged which promotes learning but which is situated within a critical labour-process perspective.

Thirdly, Bourdieu's conceptions, such as dispositions and habitus, provide a vehicle for overcoming the arbitrary and mystifying boundaries and distinctions between the workplace and other aspects of worker lives (everyday learning). Learning is a class issue rather than a head job!

Fourthly, a Bourdieuian-inspired framework provides the basis for a campaigning and critical union dimension to national policy initiatives. Instead of a neo-liberal focus on human capital imperatives, there are possibilities for the construction of an emanicipatory agenda that places human development and learning at the centre of a *union*-driven agenda.

Fifthly, the nature of 'work' in 'workplace learning' needs to be an explicit aspect in understandings and practices of learning. The capitalist nature of 'work', it has been argued, shapes, constrains and characterises what is known and what it is possible to know. Engaging with the historically distinct nature of this labour provides a fundamental distinctiveness to union knowing.

Implicit, then, in the analysis and commentary of understanding union learning as more than participating in courses (whether organised by the union or by the employer) has been the suggestion of alternative union priorities, campaigning objectives and policy agendas that result from a promotion by unions of workplace learning. A failure to critically engage with human capital sentiments ('employability') that shape employer and government policy risks reproducing existing material, social and political structures of domination and exploitation. As Rogers and Streeck (1994: 142) remind us, 'capitalism's social as well as economic viability depends on the limits society manages to impose on it'. For British trade unions, membership learning and education could be an important part of contesting such limits and constraints. In doing so, union learning could address substantially the perception of crisis that has been pervasive across the union movement in recent years by visibly demonstrating a critical sense of having and shaping a future.

Notes

1 All quotations used in the discussion of the empirical data in this chapter are taken from Hsun-Chih Li (2006).

2 All names used in the case-study discussion have been changed to respect anonymity.

References

Alexandrou A, Dwyfor Davies J & Lee J (2005) Union learning representatives: A case study of the Public and Commercial Services Union. *Journal of In-service Education* 31(1): 9–26

Ball M (2003) Considering trade union education as a community of practice. *International Journal of Lifelong Education* 22(3): 297–310

Billet S (2002) Critiquing workplace learning discourses: Participation and continuity at work. *Studies in the Education of Adults* 34(1): 56–67

Bourdieu P (1998) *Practical reason: On the theory of action*. Oxford: Oxford University Press

Bourdieu P & Wacquant LJD (1992) *An invitation to reflexive sociology*. Cambridge: Polity Press

Brown P, Hesketh A & Williams S (2003) Employability in a knowledge-driven economy. *Journal of Education and Work* 16(2): 107–126

Calveley M, Healy G, Shelly S, Stirling J & Wray D (2003) *Union learning representatives: A force for renewal or 'partnership'?* Business School Working Paper No. 10, University of Hertfordshire

Casey C (2003) The learning worker, organisations and democracy. *International Journal of Lifelong Education* 22(6): 620–634

Engeström Y (2001) Expansive learning at work: Toward an activity theoretical reconceptualisation. *Journal of Education and Work* 14(1): 133–156

Engeström Y, Miettinen R & Punamaki R-L (eds) (1999) *Perspectives on activity theory*. Cambridge: Cambridge University Press

Flecker J & Hofbauer J (1998) Capitalising on subjectivity: The 'new model worker' and the importance of being useful. In P Thompson & C Warhurst (eds) *Workplaces of the future*. London: Macmillan

Forrester K (2004) 'The quiet revolution'? Trade union learning and renewal strategies. *Work, Employment and Society* 18(2): 413–420

Forrester K (2005) Learning for revival: British trade unions and workplace learning. *Studies in Continuing Education* 27(3): 257–270

Forrester K (2007) Becoming visible? Notes on work, union learning and education. In S Shelly and M Calveley (eds) *Learning with trade unions: A contemporary agenda in employment relations*. Aldershot: Ashgate

Forrester K & Payne J (1999) 'A sort of metamorphosis': The role of trade unions in widening participation in lifelong learning. *Widening Participation and Lifelong Learning* 1(2): 24–32

Fuller A & Unwin L (2003) Learning as apprentices in the contemporary UK workplace: Creating and managing expansive and restrictive participation. *Journal of Education and Work* 16(4): 407–426

Healey J & Engel N (2003) *Learning to organise*. London: Congress House

Hodkinson H & Hodkinson P (2003) Individuals, communities of practice and the policy context: School teachers' learning in their workplace. *Studies in Continuing Education* 20(1): 3–21

Hodkinson H & Hodkinson P (2004) The significance of individual's dispositions in workplace learning: A case study of two teachers. *Journal of Education and Work* 17(2): 167–182

Jose AV (ed.) (2002) *Organised labour in the 21st century*. Geneva: International Institute for Labour Studies

Lave J & Wenger E (1991) *Situated learning: Legitimate peripheral participation*. Cambridge: Cambridge University Press

Li H (2006) The ways union representatives learn. PhD thesis, University of Leeds

Livingstone DW & Sawchuk PH (2005) Hidden knowledge: Working-class capacity in the 'knowledge-based economy'. *Studies in the Education of Adults* 37(2): 110–122

Lloyd C & Payne J (2006) *British trade unions and the learning and skills agenda: An assessment*. SKOPE Issue Paper 12, Oxford and Cardiff Universities

McDonough P (2006) Habitus and the practice of public service. *Work, Employment and Society* 20(4): 629–647

Olssen M (2006) Understanding the mechanisms of neoliberal control: Lifelong learning, flexibility and knowledge capitalism. *International Journal of Lifelong Education* 25(3): 213–230

Rogers J & Streeck W (1994) Productive solidarities: Economic strategy and left politics. In D Miliband (ed.) *Reinventing the left*. London: Polity Press

Sawchuk PH, Duart N & Elhammoumi M (eds) (2006) *Critical perspectives on activity: Explorations across education, work and the everyday*. Cambridge: Cambridge University Press

TUC (Trades Union Congress) (2004) *The quiet revolution: The rise of the union learning representative*. London: Congress House

Unionlearn (2006) *Making a real difference. Union learning reps: A survey*. London: Congress House

Unionlearn (2007) *Unionlearn with the TUC: One year on*. London: Congress House

Wallis E, Stuart M & Greenwood I (2005) 'Learners of the workplace unite!' An empirical examination of the UK trade union learning representative initiative. *Work, Employment and Society* 19(2): 283–304

Warhurst C, Findlay P & Thompson P (2007) *Organising to learn and learning to organise*. Unionlearn Research Paper 2, London

Pedagogical innovations in higher education

23 Critical friends sharing socio-cultural influences on personal and professional identity

Vivienne Bozalek and Lear Matthews

Introduction

The search for innovative ways to enhance the knowledge and skills of adult learners in distinct cultural domains is a challenge familiar to educators. We contend that what is taught in the classroom is influenced by and related to economic, political and social forces in the wider societal context (Giroux 2006). Comerford (2005) stresses the importance of social work educators providing a learning context where students can engage across social, economic and cultural differences and interrogate the social structures that create their social identities. She regards this as important, as social work students do not have enough exposure to those whose identities differ from their own. In the South African higher education context, this is true not only of social work students, but also of those in other professions too because of the consequences of geographical separation due to the apartheid legacy (Bozalek et al. 2007).

The purpose of this chapter[1] is to examine the ways in which e-learning is able to provide opportunities to explore the impact of cultural and economic factors on the personal and professional identities of adult learners in two different societies: South Africa and the United States. To this purpose, as social work educators from Empire State College (ESC) in New York City, USA, and the University of the Western Cape (UWC) in Cape Town, South Africa, the authors met in 2005 at UWC to deliberate on how to incorporate an e-learning module involving social work students from both higher education institutions who could be identified as 'non-traditional learners' in these two contexts. The UWC social work learners who were identified to take part in the project were those who had entered the institution via recognition of prior learning (RPL). This meant that they had entered the institution through the development of a portfolio of evidence and where their prior experience had been assessed as equivalent to a student entering with a school-leaving qualification giving access to higher education. The ESC students had their prior learning essays evaluated for credit towards their degree.

Northedge (2003) notes that, in the context of diversity, higher education poses social and intellectual challenges to those who are not familiar with the terrain. This would apply particularly to lifelong learners in higher education who enter through alternative routes and those who have not been prepared to engage in academic discourse, such as the social work learners referred to in this chapter. To meet the diverse needs of learners, as educators we decided that we could depend neither on the banking mode of knowledge transmission nor on the laissez-faire student-centered approaches that could leave students floundering. Rather, we saw it as important to provide scaffolded, supportive, participatory environments where learners could become actively engaged in knowledge communities (Northedge 2003; Von Kotze 2003; Rose 2004). Knowledge communities can also be referred to as 'communities of practice' and seen as relational and contextual (Contu & Willmot 2003; Comerford 2005).

In this chapter, we examine the possibilities that trans-institutional and cross-continental collaborative learning between students as peers creates for them to become critical citizens and critical friends. We use the online writings and voices of students to demonstrate the depth of their communication and to give some idea of their understanding of the module, how they interacted as critical friends, the way the interaction provided spaces for reflective practice, and how the students were able to identify differences and commonalities with each other through the process. Finally, we examine some of the benefits and critiques identified by the students of this mode of learning.

Students as critical citizens

A combination of an e-learning environment with the use of innovative pedagogical practices has the potential to provide a context where relational and contextual learning can take place (Knowles 2002). Through discussion and deliberation on how we could enable these students to collaborate and engage in such knowledge communities with each other across institutional and geographical contexts of the USA and South Africa, we decided to co-present an e-learning module on advanced social work ethics. This module was designed to incorporate pedagogical practices which enable educators to understand students' backgrounds and prior learning experiences, and which enable students to gain access to and reflect on their own and others' constructions of personal and professional moral identities. Furthermore, students or learners were requested to reflect on how their personal values may affect their professional practice. We were hopeful that engaging in this task would provide opportunities for students to engage in innovative trans-institutional and cross-continental collaborative learning experiences.

Through their interactions across geographical contexts with reference to their own experiences, it was hoped that there would be a possibility of students becoming what Giroux (2006) refers to as 'critical citizens' or 'critical agents', in that they would be able to understand and critique their own social identities and structural positioning with a peer in another context. This chapter investigates the correspondence between learners performing a task in which they were asked to examine their own notions of what it means to be a morally good person; the influences of their gendered, raced and classed values and backgrounds on their professional practice; influences of religion or the 'unseen world'; and their responses to each other about these matters in order to facilitate dialogue across the boundaries of geographical location and institution.

These tasks are in line with Comerford's (2005) convictions that in order to prepare students to engage across differences, it is important to provide them with structured tasks that allow them to mutually explore their social identities. She is also of the opinion that 'the learning process must include emotional, cognitive, spiritual and behavioural dimensions' (Comerford 2005: 133). As social work educators, we were interested in investigating the extent to which these tasks, in an e-learning environment, would enable students to examine issues informing their understanding of their own subjectivities that have affected their practice as student social workers.

Students as critical friends

We envisaged this interaction between students as peers to be fulfilling a dual function – that of participatory parity in the social work pedagogical practice while simultaneously exposing students to situations of diversity and similarity across geographical locations. Attempts to work towards a degree of participatory parity (Fraser 1997, 2000) in the classroom mean that students must come to respect their own abilities as learners and co-creators of knowledge (Bozalek 2004). In e-learning it is possible for the lecturer to assume a position of facilitator of learning or to be what Salmon (2003) refers to as an e-moderator. This approach allows a shifting of epistemic authority (Sánchez-Casal & Macdonald 2002) by challenging the hegemonic teacher–learner relationship through the creation of opportunities for students to engage with each other as critical friends, with the e-moderator playing a more supportive and scaffolding role.

These shared constructions of knowledge are capable of providing richer frameworks for the cross-fertilisation of ideas than those provided only by the frame of reference of the lecturer (Longfellow et al. 2008; Rourke & Anderson 2002). Consequently, learners are able to 'cultivate a diversity of socially embedded truth claims out of which epistemic wholeness develops' (Sánchez-Casal & Macdonald 2002: 3). This e-learning experience was attempting to incorporate a contextual approach to the meaning given to human experience by lifelong learners across situations of difference. We were attempting to understand learners' experiences and their interpretations and reflections on these, as well as how they interact across borders in relation to these experiences.

During 2006, four senior undergraduate RPL social work students – two from UWC and two from ESC – engaged with each other on how their own values impact on their ethical decisions in social work practice, under the guidance of the authors of this paper, Professor Lear Matthews (ESC) and Professor Vivienne Bozalek (UWC). This was part of an ethics module for UWC social work students, which then became part of the ESC curriculum as well.

In the following section, we examine aspects of the e-learning correspondence between students who engaged with each other as critical friends, as well as some of their reflective essays after completing the module. In doing this we attempt to ascertain the value the interaction had for students who have similar life situations and prior learning needs, and demonstrate the rich communication and interaction that was made possible through the e-learning exercises. This required students to evaluate their previous experiences in social work practice and how their personal values impacted on the situations.

Students' perceptions of the module and of the notion of 'critical friend'

This is how one of the ESC students understood the tasks she was given:

> As an ESC student, I was required to complete two assessments [assignments] that consisted of multiple parts. Therefore, each assessment generated approximately five essays. In addition to writing one's own essays, we were required to read and critique our partner's essays. One assessment required that we read an article by Mattison (2000) and our country's Social Work Ethics guidelines and respond to a series of questions. All exchange of essays and discussions were to be communicated through KEWL[2] e-learning.

Another student expressed understanding of the notion of 'critical friend' as follows:

> An ESC student was matched with a UWC student. This pair was known as 'critical friends'. As critical friends we critiqued each other's work and gave constructive feedback.

The concept of 'critical friend', which was initiated by the educators in this module and which the students took on board, is one that originates in educational action research (Smith 2004). The idea of getting students to interact as critical friends through an e-learning platform across different contexts was similar to the intentions Costa and Kallick (1993) had of critical friends – that is, to critique another's experience by providing data and asking critical and provocative questions of each other's work, and by using each other's feedback to provide different lenses with which to view reality. Taylor (2000) sees a critical friend as being a colleague or fellow student who would be truthful in his or her response, willing to change attitudes and behaviours, point out inconsistencies, and be attentive to his or her partners. Thomas (2004) adds to these ideas of the role of a critical friend as that of raising questions about the notions of the situatedness of power and oppression. Cross et al. (2004), who presented a workshop for allied health professionals on linking reflective practice to evidence of competence, noted that in an individualised, isolated context it is difficult for professionals to become aware of and critique their own practice. In contrast, participating in conversations with peers as critical friends can lead to new dimensions of learning, as it enables professionals to open themselves to other interpretations and questioning of their actions. Longfellow et al. (2008) found that students as peers are better able to pass on skills to each other as they feel less intimidated and safer with each other. Further, Rourke and Anderson (2002) found that students' peers were more responsive, interesting and structured than their instructors.

The outcomes mentioned in the previous paragraph were the sort of responses that we were hoping for between the critical friends in our project. The following reflections from an ESC student indicate that our intentions and hopes in relation to this were in fact borne out:

> It was enlightening and rewarding because we were different in our views, not in a conflicting and confrontational way, but different. This actually allowed for better discussion and brought differed or varied perspectives to the dilemmas that we faced.

Examples of students being able to question each other and providing advice for how to deal with professional dilemmas are depicted in the excerpts below:

> I strongly agree with most of your thoughts and comments, and therefore must share in some of your beliefs on what is indeed a morally good person. It is, however, such a question of judgement that I know it may present as a challenge in your work at times, or in the future. I am wondering how easy will it be for you to work with those who you do not view as morally good?
>
> Again I agreed with most of the thoughts and ideals reflected in your essay. I do wonder about the part that states 'Morally good individuals would display a strong sense of character and would thus not be easily influenced to engage in practices which are not congruent with his/her beliefs'. I am not sure about this. I have knowledge of some people who were or are great advocates for human rights and equality, but who were not committed or 'good' to their immediate family (spouse and children). Some of these same advocates have very strong vices – alcohol, drug use, sex outside of committed relationships. I do believe morally good people can acknowledge their shortcomings and admit these weaknesses.

> You were very open and honest in noting your discomfort in working with this patient. It seems you have learned a very valuable lesson in working with this particular patient, in terms of not making assumptions. I would like to gently encourage you to come into new situations open and ready to learn more about the person. I encourage this because in this patient's situation you were able to find out something very useful from your supervisor, but there may be times when you or your supervisor will not have the information that you need to allow you to engage with the person. You may have to do the investigation by talking with the patient and asking questions that will help you. For example, he may not have been a person of colour, but he may have had an abusive childhood, or some other factor that made him feel like an outsider. For those clients we don't 'like' it is important to find some quality that we can like, connect to, or relate to; that quality will then hopefully become the point of engagement.

> In this particular essay, you expressed a sense of openness and respect for others and their religious/spiritual beliefs. I think this is a good baseline when working with others of various faiths/religious and spiritual beliefs. You also speak about spiritual beliefs not being used as

an excuse for discriminatory, harmful and unjust practices. I agree with this statement, but I also know it is very hard to uphold. All religious doctrine (such as the Bible) [is] interpreted and written by humans. We have already acknowledged the fact that all humans have bias. Therefore religious doctrine and teachings will most probably promote some type of bias, whether intentional or unintentional.

David Boud and Sue Knights (1996) refer to the work of Smith and Hatton (1993), which notes that critical friends or learning partnerships between students provide more successful reflection possibilities in written assignments than do interactions between students and staff. The above excerpts show the freedom that students seem to feel in reflecting on their own and their critical friend's experiences and work, similar to reports by Longfellow et al. (2008) and Rourke and Anderson (2002).

Reflection on learning

Johnstonn and Olekalnns (2002) found that deeper learning and critical thinking are more likely to occur where students reflect on their own learning, where the stimulus for learning is issues from previous experiences, and where assessment practices reward the critical analysis of material. They further emphasise the importance of providing opportunities to apply knowledge in a number of different contexts. For this reason students were given a number of different assignments that required them to engage with each other as critical friends. The following excerpt from an ESC student demonstrates the impact of the pedagogical practice on her ability to think about her own work as a social work student:

> One assessment asked very pointed questions regarding our [the students'] views and values on morality, culture, gender, class, ethnic background, spiritual and religious beliefs, and how those values impact on our social work practice. It was very interesting for me because without knowing or seeing my critical friend, yet from reading her essays, I knew her views were influenced by her experiences, background and beliefs. Her beliefs strongly stood out in her essays. I wondered if she was aware of how much her values impacted on her work. What was even more amazing during this assignment was the realisation that I had in terms of my own work. It was through reflecting on her work that I realised my views were different from hers, if not only, then mostly, because of my own experiences, background and values. I realised that my views were not only different (even if slightly) as a result of living in the US, but also as a result of living in New York City and the social environment that exists within this city.

Differences and similarities

The tasks provided students as critical friends with the possibilities of identifying commonalities and differences with each other. It was interesting to both students and educators that these critical friends found points of identification across geographical contexts, due to similar experiences of racialised and gendered othering and oppression. The following excerpts provide some examples of the sorts of reflections that students shared with one another about their racialised and gendered subjectivities:

> Because we held different views, I imagined we held different roles in our current lives. I shared my background with her beyond what the assignment required. My critical friend did the same. We discovered we were very similar. We are both women of African descent, mothers, working full-time out of our homes while pursuing our education. We therefore faced similar challenges, while facing different challenges.

> …there was something so strikingly different in our responses. Here came the better understanding of self. We sometimes believe our experiences are universal or global…they often are, but they differ. Your experience with oppression has been so vastly different from my experience with oppression. My oppressive experiences probably do not compare to those that she has faced. I do know poverty, but the poverty that we both know is different. Our desire to reach for an education may have been prompted or motivated by the same sources, oppression and poverty, but our access has been different. So with all these differences, how could we possibly have the same values, even though our skin bears similar shades of colour?

One student succinctly described her experience of gender and racial oppression, and the ways in which it influenced her interpersonal and group relations:

> My life experiences have taught me most importantly to refrain from judging people, as I have been in many circumstances where people have judged me from one aspect of my life and not by the whole entity of me. In doing this, they were usually terribly wrong. As a girl, I recall most boys in my class being astonished that I was very intelligent and that I had a wonderful grasp on math. This was something they did not expect from a female. As a good student in school, I recall many of my teachers assuming I came from a stable home. They assumed a troubled child could not function well in school. As an African American, I am always surprised, and slightly upset, when people on the other end of the telephone assume I am white. I suppose they have determined there are specific accents, tones or vocabulary that distinguishes black people from white people. As a mother, teachers and school staff never expect me to ask the questions that I do in reference to my children. In this particular situation I do not know what aspect puts them in such an unexpected situation. In any case, all of the assumptions that people have placed on me by how they have judged me has taught me that one powerful lesson, to resist and refrain from judging other people. It has also taught me to use all effort to accept people by their own definition, or at their own word.

What is generally apparent from these excerpts of students' writing is the students' awareness that the politics of everyday life – practices engaged in by themselves and their family members – are actually suffused with power when looked at through the lenses of race and gender. Furthermore, the impact of these sorts of experiences on their practice as social workers was shared openly with their critical friends as peers, albeit physically distant ones. Whether students would have felt comfortable to share their views and experiences with academic staff is not known, but we would imagine that this would not be the case.

Benefits for students of engaging in the e-learning experience

The students involved as critical friends in this cross-continental exchange expressed appreciation for taking part in the process and identified similarities even though they were from geographically disparate contexts. It would seem from the students' comments that e-learning has the potential to expose students who would otherwise not have the opportunity to traverse locations to peer experiences across geographical contexts:

> I must acknowledge the growth that I have experienced from sharing with a student from a different country. It was even more rewarding because we lived and faced similarities. I believe this project gave my critical friend and I the opportunity to experience the impact of universal issues. Many students (especially those facing oppression) do not have the opportunity to travel and experience the world. Travelling gives people a better view of local issues in comparison to universal issues. Therefore those who don't have the opportunity to travel internationally usually do not have the opportunity to have an understanding of these two varying issues and the broader view that is developed through this experience. It has been my experience that international exchange via web learning is just as valuable as, and probably more accessible than, the more traditional international exchange student learning projects. It is my hope that we will extend this opportunity to more students.

> It is through this extensive cross-cultural exchange project that I have gained a richer understanding about how this impacts on who I am and how I view the world. So while I learned about others, I also learned about 'self'. I am impressed with the 1996 South African Constitution Bill of Rights. I think that those ideas will help to create a moral society, and we in the United States have much to learn from other countries about the inherent dignity and self-worth of all human beings.

> I was pleased to be asked to take part in the cross-cultural course on social work ethics. What made the class unique and challenging was the fact that it was an exchange between students in the NYC [New York City] metropolitan area [Empire State College] and the University of the Western Cape in South Africa. This program offered students the

opportunity to share their different perspectives with one another. What I really learned was that being a social worker really forces one to hold back on judgements or one needs to work in an area in which their values are congruent with the agency's mission.

Critique of the module

Students reported that they would have liked more and better training in the learning platform used for communication. One student was also vocal about what more could have been included in the module:

> From a cross-cultural perspective I think it would have also been interesting to engage in a dialogue about major social problems/ stereotypes between the two cultures; identify fact from fiction and get some personal perspectives on social problems within the two cultures. For example, NYC may be perceived as one of the most dangerous large cities in the world, but in actuality it has one of the lowest incidents of crime as compared to other large North American cities. How do these stereotypes and perceptions also relate to major social problems and what ethical dilemmas may surround these major problems?

The students further noted that in designing the module, this innovative forum should provide the opportunity for discussing critical issues relating to social justice in the two selected societies. They suggested that this would not only enhance their knowledge base of contemporary social problems, but would also contribute to the development of intervention skills that are informed by social changes, community needs and current perspectives on the problems.

Conclusion

Examining how personal values influence one's work as a professional practitioner is important for human services workers, as they are required to be reflexive in their practice (Clegg 2004; Fook & Gardner 2007; Knowles 2002; Taylor & White 2000). The pairing of social work adult learners at the University of the Western Cape and Empire State College as 'critical friends' allowed them as peers to relate and respond to issues of identity, such as culture, gender, class and ethnicity, as they impact firstly on their own values, and then on their professional practice (Costa & Kallick 1993; Cross et al. 2004; Taylor 2000; Thomas 2004). The findings revealed that the e-learning experience unexpectedly created a forum for intimacy in its broadest sense (intellectual sharing and emotional unpacking) to develop across geographic locations – thus enhancing the participants' strengths and abilities to function effectively as professional practitioners. Similar findings are corroborated by authors such as Dysthe (2002) and Knowles (2002). The findings also demonstrate the potential for collaborative teaching and learning cross-continentally and across institutions.

The study sets the stage for re-examining the role of educators and learners in facilitating ideas about work, knowledge and learning across cultures; validating the role of peers in meaning making; and achieving learning objectives (Longfellow et al. 2008; Rourke & Anderson 2002). It can be viewed as a model for further institutional exchange, and as a vehicle for learning and teaching. Dominelli (2007: 194) notes the important role of educators 'internationalising the social work curricula (academic and practicum) and socialising practitioners to embrace emancipatory approaches to social work', which would increase comprehension of similarities and differences across cultures. Given the 'freedom' to interact online, these students utilised a 'virtual forum' to successfully identify and explore the ways in which social, economic and political factors in their respective socio-cultural contexts affect them personally and professionally.

Notes

1   This chapter is a revised version of the article 'E-learning: A cross-institutional forum for sharing socio-cultural influences on personal and professional identity' published in 2009 in *International Social Work* 52(2): 222–233. It is published here with the permission of Sage Publications.

2   The open-source learning management system used by the University of the Western Cape.

References

Boud D & Knights S (1996) Course design for reflective practice. In N Gould & M Baldwin (eds) *Social work, critical reflection, and the learning organisation.* Aldershot: Ashgate

Bozalek V (2004) Recognition, resources, responsibilities: Using students' stories of family to renew the South African social work curriculum. Accessed 9 April 2009, http://igitur-archive.library.uu.nl/disserations/2004-1203-094505/

Bozalek V, Rohleder P, Carolissen R, Leibowitz B, Nicholls L & Swartz L (2007) Students learning across differences in a multi-disciplinary virtual learning community. *South African Journal of Higher Education* 21(7): 812–825

Clegg S (2004) Critical readings: Progress files and the production of the autonomous learner. *Teaching in Higher Education* 9(3): 288–298

Comerford S (2005) Engaging through learning – learning through engaging: An alternative approach to professional learning about diversity. *Social Work Education* 24(1): 113–135

Contu A & Willmot H (2003) The importance of power relations in learning theory. *Organisation Science* 14(3): 283–296

Costa A & Kallick B (1993) Through the lens of a critical friend. *Educational Leadership* 51(2): 49–51

Cross V, Liles C, Conduit J & Price J (2004) Linking reflective practice to evidence of competence: A workshop for allied health professionals. *Reflective Practice* 5(1): 3–31

Dominelli L (2007) The future of social work education: Beyond the state of the art. *International Journal of Social Welfare* 5(3): 194–201

Dysthe O (2002) The learning potential of a web-mediated discussion in a university course. *Studies in Higher Education* 27(3): 313–414

Fook J & Gardner F (2007) Practising critical reflection: A resource handbook. Maidenhead: McGraw-Hill Open University Press

Fraser N (1997) *Justice interruptus: Critical reflections on the 'postsocialist' condition.* London: Routledge

Fraser N (2000) Rethinking recognition. *New Left Review* 3: 107–120

Giroux HA (2006) Academic freedom under fire: The case for critical pedagogy. *College Literature* 33(4): 1–43

Johnstonn C & Olekalnns N (2002) Enriching the learning experience: A CALM approach. *Studies in Higher Education* 27(1): 103–117

Knowles AJ (2002) E-learning in social work education: Emerging pedagogical and policy issues. *Currents: New Scholarship in the Human Services* 1(1): 1–17

Longfellow E, May S, Burke L & Marks-Maran D (2008) 'They had a way of helping that actually helped': A case study of a peer-assisted learning scheme. *Teaching in Higher Education* 13(1): 93–105

Northedge A (2003) Rethinking teaching in the context of diversity. *Teaching in Higher Education* 8(1): 17–32

Rose D (2004) Democratising the classroom: A literacy pedagogy for the new generation. Paper presented at Kenton Khahlamba Conference, KwaZulu-Natal (September)

Rourke L & Anderson T (2002) Using peer teams to lead online discussions. *Journal of Interactive Media in Education* 1: 1–21

Salmon G (2003) *E-moderating: The key to teaching and learning online* (2nd edition). London and New York: Routledge Falmer

Sánchez-Casal S & Macdonald CL (2002) Introduction: Feminist reflections on the pedagogical relevance of identity. In A Macdonald & S Sánchez-Casal (eds) *Twenty-first-century feminist classrooms: Pedagogies of identity and difference.* New York and Basingstoke: Palgrave Macmillan

Smith DL & Hatton N (1993) Reflection in teacher education: A study in progress. *Educational Research and Perspectives* 20(1): 13–23

Smith R (2004) A matter of trust, service users and researchers. *Qualitative Social Work* 3(3): 335–346

Taylor BJ (ed.) (2000) *Reflective practice: A guide for nurses and midwives.* Buckingham: Open University Press

Taylor C & White S (2000) *Practising reflexivity in health and welfare: Making knowledge.* Buckingham: Open University Press

Thomas J (2004) Using critical incident analysis to promote critical reflection and holistic assessment. In N Gould & M Baldwin (eds) *Social work, critical reflection, and the learning organisation.* Aldershot: Ashgate

Von Kotze A (2003) Building communities of practice in project-based learning: A prerequisite for working towards more inclusionary curricula? *Journal of Education* 29: 9–28

24 Towards effective partnerships in training community learning and development workers

John Bamber and Clara O'Shea

Introduction

The Scottish Community Learning and Development Work-Based and Part-Time Training Consortium (the Consortium) was established in 2005 to provide a more solid basis for work-based and part-time routes to professionally endorsed qualifications in the field of community learning and development (CLD). This chapter draws from the results of the Consortium's work in developing these routes (Bamber et al. 2007). The investigation focused mainly on practice while drawing selectively from relevant literary sources and research, and consisted of analysis of course documentation; an online survey of 102 current CLD students (28 per cent of the overall population); individual and group interviews with educators, learners and employers; consultative workshops with key stakeholders; and observation of teaching and learning processes.

Undergraduate work-based and part-time CLD students in professional training in Scotland are likely to be mature females, with non-standard entry qualifications and significant domestic and work commitments – circumstances that make it difficult to engage with higher education. Our focus in this chapter is on the capacity of the learning experience to equip such students with the requisite practice knowledge for a successful career in CLD. An effective experience would exploit the significant opportunities for learning in addressing live problems and issues in the workplace. The key to success is in helping learners to connect work experience, programme content and their own professional development. Much depends, however, on unlocking the potential in the respective roles and contributions of training providers, employers and learners themselves. In essence, this turns on collapsing false dichotomies between the academy and the workplace and creating effective working relationships between all stakeholders. We argue in this chapter for an integrated approach to training, which highlights the importance of three interlinking elements: 'responsive academies' attuned to the needs of work-based and part-time students, 'expansive workplaces' systematically supporting learning and development, and 'active learners' who take responsibility for their own learning.

Work-based learning in context

Worldwide political, socio-cultural and economic factors, such as massification, managerialism, bureaucratisation, marketisation and globalisation, have profound effects on training providers and learners, which are refracted in particular ways in different countries. In the UK, Gallacher and Reeve (2000) have charted the emergence of four contending discourses with regard to approaches to work-based learning in a higher education context. These discourses concern issues of partnership, relevance, flexibility and accreditation. There is an uneven pattern of development in these discourses, but all signal a potential threat to the role of universities. According to the authors:

- there is greater pressure on the universities to work more closely with employers in contributing to the processes of economic change and development;
- universities are expected to be increasingly flexible in their modes of delivery in meeting the lifelong learning agenda; and
- an increasingly wide range of organisations and agencies are expected to contribute to meeting learning needs. (Gallacher & Reeve 2000: 4)

All of these factors, they argue, imply changes in the curriculum, pedagogy and relationships associated with work-based learning. It is certainly the case that the UK government has been a major player in steering providers in the directions noted by Reeve and Gallacher. This can be seen most markedly in the *Leitch Review of Skills: Prosperity for All in the Global Economy – World-class Skills* (Leitch 2006). In accepting the government's belief in the need to outperform the world's most advanced post-industrial economies, Leitch emphasised economically valuable skills, arguing that the UK needed to raise the proportion of people with high skills across the labour force. This national effort would require 'a rebalancing of the priorities of HE [higher education] institutions to make available relevant, flexible and responsive provision that meets the high skills needs of employers and their staff' (Leitch 2006: 68).

A number of reports in Scotland, including *Life through Learning; Learning through Life* (Scottish Executive 2003), *Closing the Opportunity Gap* (Scottish Executive 2004) and *Skills for Scotland: A Lifelong Skills Strategy* (Scottish Government 2007), have also been instrumental in shaping the local context of training. Although the latter report sets skill development within a wider concern about achieving social justice objectives, such as increasing the standard of living for poorer sections of society, the danger is that the concept of lifelong learning becomes synonymous with a supply-side economic strategy, with learning seen narrowly as the acquisition of specific skills predetermined in a top-down fashion by government-supported agencies and corporate interests. This maybe an overly pessimistic view, however, not least because the environment itself is subject to change and development as learners act upon it. In fact, the *Leitch Review* specifically warns against the skills agenda being centrally planned (Leitch 2006: 4). A broader view, giving due emphasis to learning needs determined by individuals in particular work settings and workplaces, can be seen in the UK's Chartered Institute of Professional Development's definition of work-based learning as 'a self directed, work-based process leading to increased adaptive capacity. Individuals "learn to learn" and possess the capabilities that enable them to do so…to help to build and retain competitive advantage' (CIPD 2005: 50).

These policy developments have focused research and the attention of academics and other interested commentators. In their comprehensive report for the UK's Higher Education Academy, for example, Nixon et al. (2006) state that research was needed to substantiate or challenge assumptions that higher education is necessarily the best provider of work-based learning. They argue that there is a cross-sectoral interest in the development of the workforce, which requires a shift from the prevailing idea that universities provide academic content while industry concentrates on skill development.

Certainly such concerns and issues are emerging globally. For example, in a Swedish context Ekholm and Härd (2000) argue that there is a discernible shift in responsibility for education and learning from the public to the private and civil spheres. In their view, the dismantling of education monopolies requires directions to be determined and tasks allocated between different educational and learning environments. Subsystems should be designed in relation to each other. Ekholm and Härd sound a critical note in relation to formal education's ability to provide a basis for practical action in everyday life and work: 'The practical situations in which knowledge can be profitably used are often not found in organised education' (2000: 35). In Australia, Boud and Solomon (2000) encapsulate the relationship between work and learning in the following terms:

> The challenge for the work-based learning curriculum and those who support it is to ensure that the potentially mutually reinforcing nature of work-based learning is effectively utilised and that conflicts between the exigencies of work and learning are minimised. This can only happen if all the parties involved – learners/workers, workplace supervisors and academic advisers – are mindful of the potentials and the traps, and they are appropriately resourced in terms of the materials and expertise needed. (2000: 4)

Our work in Scotland represents an attempt to capitalise on the learning potential inherent in work-based learning. We have analysed and then drawn from five different types of partnership within the field of CLD (see below) to model a more integrated approach to curriculum that valorises the respective contributions of training provider, employer and learner. Any effective approach, we argue, must exploit the distinctive features of work-based learning.

Distinctive features of work-based learning

Work-based learning is a participative, active process. As Felstead et al. (2005: 362) aver, it is 'a process in which learners improve their work performance by carrying out daily work activities which entail interacting with people, tools, materials and ways of thinking as appropriate'. This is in marked contrast to the notion of 'learning as acquisition' – a 'product with a visible, identifiable outcome, often accompanied by certification or proof of attendance' – a process in which teaching and learning are viewed in the abstract and educators transmit knowledge to learners (2005: 362). 'Learning as participation' considers teaching and learning to be a social and interactive experience where knowledge is not simply received but is constructed through reflection as learners engage with real problems in a given context. Meaning making comes from the sharing of ideas, experiences and reflections on practice. Thus, collaborative and participative methods of learning draw on the rich context of actors and actions that are common in situated learning. The participative approach can be aligned closely to a social constructivist perspective in which learners form their meanings within a community of practice (Wenger 1998). In such communities, workers continually negotiate and renegotiate tacit understandings, mutual meaning and a shared repertoire of communal resources (Barab & Plucker 2002).

However, work-based learning can be problematic. As Barab and Plucker (2002) note, in work situations there may be little observable teaching and large quantities of learning. As such, learning may not be transparent or easy to quantify. This is one reason why work-based learning remains a contested area – it 'challenges the very essence of universities as the primary source of knowledge' (Nixon et al. 2006: 22). Nor can it simply be assumed that the workplace is conducive to learning. As research has shown (Fuller & Unwin 2004), some organisations are 'expansive' and others 'restrictive' in the range of opportunities given to employees for learning. In other words, some are more supportive than others. Moreover, as Barab and Plucker (2002) argue, people perform differently in different settings even when undertaking comparable work or addressing the same problems. This contextual influence challenges prevalent notions of competence and performance as a possession of the individual.

In our work for the Consortium, we have found that a common understanding of competence is essential if employers, academic institutions and learners are to collaborate effectively. As Reeve and Gallacher (2005) have argued, problems of effective partnership arise from the different cultures and different understandings of learning and knowledge. They argue that there is a lack of extensive or systematic evidence that examines just what employers may be seeking from higher education, and what evidence there is 'suggests that the demand for the kind of education and training which universities are likely to provide through Work Based Learning (WBL) degrees is in fact limited' (2005: 225). This difference in the goal of training is posited as 'achievement orientation' on the part of employers, with little interest in abstract concepts and material not clearly relevant to the current work situation. In the CLD field, it is also the case that there are contrasting conceptions of academic qualities and professional competence. These can be seen in the Scottish Credit and Qualifications Framework (SCQF 2005), which provides the framework for higher education programmes, and the Community Education Validation and Endorsement (CeVe 1995) group's formulations, which approve professional training courses in CLD. The former stresses intellectual qualities expressed in terms of the exercise of critical faculties, while the latter emphasises concrete activity where performance is ultimately a matter of skill. If taken at face value, the differences between the two frameworks appear to reflect a theory–practice split. However, as Bamber (2007) has argued, they can be considered as complementary in that both point towards the ideal of a 'critically competent practitioner'.

This conception of critical competence includes the idea that learners actively develop knowledge as they engage with the 'why' and 'how' of practice. Bringing the why and how together in support of learning requires an integrated approach to training. As Nixon et al. (2006) have shown, it is necessary to recognise the interdependence of academia and the workplace in shaping professional competence. Interdependence is enhanced when instruction is 'situated' or presented in the context of a specific topic or problem, which is always shaped by wider organisational and social influences (Barab & Plucker 2002). In CLD training this aim can be met fully as learners are required to engage with real, live problems. Operating in contexts of collaboration with other, more experienced practitioners means that work-based learners can become knowledgeable and skilful with respect to the specific practices in certain contexts. The focus on the resolution of practice problems can therefore enhance the capacity for reflection on the results of one's actions that lies at the heart of professional development. In such situations, it is the practice of the learner's community that creates the potential 'curriculum' in the broadest sense. Community can be understood concretely as a function of the interactions between the various contributors to the learning experience. In CLD training, community can be analysed in terms of the training partnerships in Scotland.

Types of training partnership in CLD

Through our work for the Consortium we have been able to map five different types of partnership in the CLD field, each with unique benefits and challenges. They evidence a spectrum of academy–workplace relations, which can be described broadly as mutual support, learning partnerships, provider-employer and agency-host, employer-provider, and brokerage:

1. *Mutual support*: Mutual support partnerships range from fairly informal to formal relationships with long-standing agendas, to one-off occurrences where the workplace supports the learner in participating in training provision.
2. *Learning partnerships*: In learning partnerships the academic institution works with an agency in the community to provide an integrated curriculum that both partners have responsibility for, with the training provider and agency involved in designing and delivering the programme. There are nuanced differences in these partnerships depending on whether the training provider is located within an academic institution or in the community alongside the agencies.
3. *Provider-employer and agency-host*: The provider-as-employer and agency-as-host arrangement can be problematic, as the training provider is also the learner's employer and the workplace acts as a host organisation for the learner in a similar manner to hosting a long-term placement. This type of relationship usually develops in relation to funding restrictions, rather than being the preferred choice of either the training provider or the workplace.

4. *Employer-provider*: The employer-as-provider is not a straightforward example of academy–workplace relationships. This is because the workplace has taken on the additional role of trainer and there may not be a second party, such as an academic institution, involved in training provision.
5. *Brokerage*: Brokerage arrangements attempt to bring together employers, learners and training providers so that they can, for example, identify and reach agreement with funding partners, develop and maintain relationships between trainees and host organisations, provide study support for trainees, and facilitate relationships between host organisation supervisors and trainees.

Brennan and Little (2006: 9) state that 'high level employer engagement in relation to teaching and learning is characterised by situations where the employer and the higher education provider have an equal and shared interest in ensuring high standards of education and training'. Not all of those involved in the partnerships described above have an equal or shared interest, however, and there are particular issues in the different types of academy–workplace relationships. For instance, a challenge arises when the training provider is also the learner's employer. In this case, the workplace becomes more like a long-term placement than a normal work experience, which can undermine the significance and the authority of the workplace. The provider-employer and brokerage types can also be susceptible to confusion for trainees regarding roles, responsibilities and the place of their project work within the host organisation. With respect to the brokerage form in particular (and in common with other work-based programmes), learners or supervisors can prioritise the work element over study.

Although there may be a mutual regard for supporting the learning, as Reeve and Gallacher (2005) note in their discussion of the problematic aspects of partnership, responsibility for the formal curriculum lies strongly with the academic provider. This tended to be the case in the partnerships we observed. Reasons for this tendency are that higher education training providers may resist the aspects of work-based learning that could be perceived to cede control of the curriculum and threaten the traditional role of the academy as the repository of knowledge. Academics may also think that the focus on skill development undermines the kinds of higher-order learning promoted in conventional degree programmes, emphasising critical thinking, analysis and the ability to synthesise ideas. While such concerns have merit, the distinctive feature of work-based learning is that it presents live opportunities for engagement in practice problems, and the necessary processes of reflection require precisely the kind of higher-order learning promoted by academe. Discerning educators know this and capitalise on the benefits in appropriate curricular and pedagogical responses. On the other hand, employers may also claim that academics cannot understand the specifics of particular work practices, and berate the academy without fully appreciating that universities prepare graduates in a general way for professions and vocational areas.

Although a major issue for employers in CLD is finding the resources necessary to engage in working in purposeful partnership with the academy, we detected a deeper, philosophical problem that also needs to be addressed. In our view, there is a need for a more holistic conception of skill that universities and employers can commit to, which is why we are in favour of the idea of 'critical competence'. This view of competence recognises that particular occupations are shaped historically by generations of practitioners and that the accumulated learning must be made available to succeeding generations. Training institutions have a central role to play in this 'passing on'. It also accepts that constant change driven by socio-economic factors means that work-related processes move on and must alter in line with the requirements of new markets or social conditions. In all of this, workers should have the capacity to develop relevant practice knowledge where existing knowledge is outdated, inappropriate or inadequate to the task. In developing such a capacity, it is instructive to remember that while guidance and learning-support roles are a crucial part of the network of learning, they are not necessarily the learner's first port of call. Boud and Middleton (2003) found that workers might choose to minimise the need for supervisor involvement and instead favour learning that occurs horizontally in interactions with peers, without resort to conventional knowledge hierarchies. As Billet notes (2001), rather than being dependent on teachers, learners can actively and continually construct their own knowledge, drawing on the role of co-workers. Our research confirms Billet's point in that respondents rated peer support as 94 per cent important and 89 per cent effective in supporting their learning. We also found that the peer group is about much more than support, because if properly utilised within the curriculum the group can be a powerful site of collective learning in which participants share ideas, experiences and reflections on practice.

It is clear from the above discussion that the different arrangements might in certain respects be strong or problematic in linking the academy and the workplace. Our work for the Consortium has led us to conclude that the key elements of successful partnerships can be elaborated in terms of three interlinking elements: 'expansive workplaces' systematically supporting learning and development in the workplace, 'responsive academies' attuned to the needs of work-based and part-time students, and 'active learners' who take responsibility for their own learning. Where these three elements interact appropriately, learners are more likely to develop the capabilities that we associate with critical competence.

Effective partnerships

The expansive workplace

Although most academy–workplace relationships are complex and multifaceted, one thing is clear: effective workplaces are proactive in their approach to learning. Recent work by Evans et al. (2006) on the 'expansive workplace' helps to identify characteristics that maximise opportunities for learning. The framework can be used to analyse the character and quality of learning environments and cultures, identify opportunities and barriers to learning, conceptualise different approaches to individual career progression and explore the lived reality of learning for workers. See Table 24.1 for an abbreviated version of the framework.

Table 24.1 *The expansive–restrictive framework*

Expansive	Restrictive
Cross-boundary groups and communication encouraged	Bounded communication
Managers as enablers/facilitators	Managers as controllers
Pursuit of formal qualifications valued/supported	Pursuit of formal qualifications not valued or supported
Expanded job design	Restricted job design
Participation in multiple communities of practice inside and outside the workplace	Restricted participation in multiple communities of practice
Planned time off the job	Virtually all on the job
Progression for career	Career static

Source: Adapted from Evans et al. 2006: 40–41. Used with permission.

In creating an expansive environment, it is essential that the workplace has an understanding of the goal of learning, the processes by which this can be achieved and the ways in which it can contribute to creating a more effective learning process. The case study in Box 24.1 is based on a real agency in Scotland (although names have been changed) and illustrates some elements of an expansive CLD workplace.

Box 24.1 *The 'Opportunities' Project*

> Lauren, a work-based, community-based learner, is a single parent who became involved in her local community when the lack of childcare became an issue. She became chair of a local parenting group and got involved in Opportunities, a local voluntary organisation. The board of trustees saw the potential for Lauren's development, and believed that offering her an opportunity to develop into a qualified CLD worker would help Lauren, her organisation and her local community. The board felt that even if Lauren moved on from her current organisation, the community would still benefit from her expertise, and that a formal qualification would be valuable to her. The organisation created a trainee position (which Lauren had to apply for), and gave her study leave and support as she undertook her study. Her employer explained that this was as much a learning experience for the workplace as it was for Lauren, as she was the first person the organisation took on as a student. Her supervisor and the organisation found they were learning from the materials, questions and ideas she was bringing back to the organisation. The organisation has since grown and now has a second work-based learner undertaking the programme, who is benefiting not just from study but also from the organisation's now more experienced approach to his learning.

A key role in the expansive workplace is that of the field-based supervisor. In CLD training programmes we found three general ways in which this role is fulfilled.

First, there are line managers who may take an interest in encouraging their worker's learning but whose primary goal is to manage. Second, there are placement supervisors who usually undertake some form of agreement or contract to ensure that the learner has an appropriate learning experience. Third, there are mentors or practice supervisors who do not have direct input into the workplace or the academy but instead facilitate the integration of learning from both environments. These non-managerial roles facilitate the integration of practice experience, programme content and professional identity across the two environments of the academy and the workplace. They draw on the learner's prior knowledge and experience and current taught learning and work practice, to stimulate processes of self-discovery and foster critical reflection. Mentoring usually involves regular one-on-one sessions with the learner.

Specific curriculum-related activities that help connect the placement to the taught component of the programme are less common, however. In cases where the taught programme and the placement are treated as separate entities, there is the potential to reinforce rather than overcome unhelpful theory-practice divides. Therefore, an expansive workplace is not by itself sufficient to fully support learners in the development of critical competence. Facilitating learners in their movement into and through the space between the academy and the workplace also requires a responsive approach from the academy.

The responsive academy

An integrated approach to training depends on an effective alignment between a learner's work experience and the goals of teaching, learning and assessment. In other words, it turns on the extent to which knowledge is not pre-packaged but develops through the use of projects, action research and daily work practice as learners critically reflect on their experiences. In a responsive academy – in other words, one that is aware of and able to tune in to the learning potential in live problems confronting learners – the taught element is 'situated' in the context of a specific topic or work problem that provides meaning to the material. Learning outcomes emphasise underpinning knowledge and understanding, applying theories and constructs in a workplace setting and developing personal and professional skills through practical experiences. The first-year course, Professional Practice 1, is an example of an attempt to bridge the divide between taught and practice elements of training. An overview of the course is given in Box 24.2.

Box 24.2 *Professional Practice 1*

Learning objectives are shaped by the completion of 8 tasks relating to all courses in the first-year taught curriculum. Four times during the 6-week block placement, for example, students have to select a reading from other first-year courses and lead a discussion with their supervisor connecting the reading to

→

issues arising in the placement. The student's progress is monitored through continuous reflective practice in relation to the 8 tasks through discussion with the supervisor during weekly supervision sessions. Practice is assessed on a pass or fail basis. Supervisors comment on the student's performance in relation to the tasks and provide an overall assessment of the student's development on placement. This is to highlight areas of achievement and indicate future learning objectives. At the end of the placement, students submit two copies of their workbook tasks (amounting to approximately 2 000 words) including a summary reflecting on how they have integrated learning from the taught and practice elements in the degree programme.

Professional Practice 1 illustrates how curriculum design can support learning by incorporating work-based learning activities, peer learning, and opportunities to test out ideas in discussion and dialogue and then in self-reflection. The process of learning is significantly assisted by appropriate assessment. Although the workplace may have little input into the grading of tasks, all key stakeholders consulted during the course of our work for the Consortium made it clear that assessment activities need to bridge the academy and the workplace to facilitate the integration of theory and practice. This was considered to be essential for professional development. Our survey respondents were asked to rate those activities that facilitated this development most highly in terms of *helpfulness* in facilitating learning and *effectiveness* in assessing learning. Learners rated individual activities such as individual projects and presentations more *effective* for assessing their learning (76 per cent in both cases) in comparison to group projects and presentations (65 per cent in both cases). Essays rated second highest among learners as both helping and assessing learning, which may relate to the use of essays in work-based learning as opportunities to examine praxis and to integrate the practice and taught learning elements.

The success of an integrated approach is, however, also dependent on the skills and knowledge of the people who guide and support the learner. A number of higher education providers have developed a 'personal tutor' role. This is usually a lecturer in the institution who will coach and guide the learner in all aspects of their development. The personal tutor will meet regularly with the learner in one-on-one sessions, although at one university we discovered that the personal tutor might also bring together a group of their tutees. The role is generally to facilitate the learner's clarification of goals, formalise learning agreements, negotiate placement opportunities and support the learner's development of their professional portfolio. Personal tutors also help learners keep records of their academic work, undertake placement visits and help learners navigate the rules and regulations of the degree programme.

It should be clear from the above that expansive workplaces and responsive academies are essential to the integrative approach. Equally important, however, in securing an effective learning experience leading to the development of critical competence is the role and contribution of the learner.

Active learners

CLD workers need to be able to analyse and reflect on learning that arises from performing workplace tasks in a dynamic context. These tasks relate to the challenging, open-ended problems of practice and often involve collaboration and cooperation between individuals with different roles and expertise. The goal is to improve the worker's practice, and beyond this to enhance organisational performance. It is often the case that new techniques and approaches are needed to meet difficult situations. Teaching and learning processes therefore need to support learners in developing the attributes of the self-directed, reflective and reflexive practitioner. Brodie and Irving (2007) have argued that assessment in work-based learning should focus on the following:

- *learning* – with students learning how they learn, as well as theories, approaches to learning and how to make the most of learning opportunities;
- *critical reflection* – reflecting on learning, applying forms and theories, establishing validity, applicability and appropriateness;
- *capability* – including self-auditing, target setting, interpersonal and transferable capability.

An innovative approach to supporting self-directed learning at one university utilises a combination of a portfolio and a practice panel. The personal development portfolio was devised to help students critically reflect upon and analyse their practice. The portfolio is a systematic means of keeping records and includes a record of significant experiences, readings, and outcomes of personal and group reflection; issues identified for discussion with peers and tutors; evidence of course activities, projects and assignments; and evidence of fieldwork competence. Twice during each academic session, students meet with an accreditation panel consisting of the student's personal tutor and a fieldworker. The panel uses a professional competence framework for discussion, and works with the student to advance his or her professional development.

From the discussion in this section, it should be clear that these three elements – the workplace, the academy and the learner – need to interact in a mutually supportive way in order to promote the development of critically competent practitioners. Considering this kind of partnership working as a 'system' (Margaryan 2006) helps to further clarify what is required in terms of the role of the learner in the workplace, the resources and people needed to develop the learner in both workplace and academic environments (such as a qualified supervisor, mentor and colleagues), the community of practice within which these interactions are set and the types of activities that are available to the student. This way of analysing work-based and part-time routes illustrates Boud and Solomon's observation that

> [i]n work-based learning, the activities of working and learning often take place in the same location at the same time. The learning involved is often multi-modal. There may be no sign that a shift from one mode to another has taken place. This can create additional tensions and an extra process for the work-based learner to manage. (2000: 5)

Having elaborated what we take to be the key elements in an effective CLD training partnership, we now present a model that accords appropriate weight to the essential and distinctive contribution of each of the three elements discussed throughout this chapter, while showing them in a fluid and dynamic relationship.

Situating the curriculum

The findings from our work for the Consortium can be expressed in a model that expresses the iterative relationship between work and learning, and the multimodal nature of learning (Figure 24.1). This learning is understood not just in physical terms, such as attending block teaching or undertaking a placement, but also in terms of the learners' awareness of themselves as a learner-worker, and the ways in which they integrate different aspects of their learning across the two environments.

The model acknowledges that training takes place within an overall socio-cultural context that heavily influences learning and learners. As indicated previously, the policy environment in Scotland is replete with the steering intentions of government, as can be seen in a succession of government-issued reports (Scottish Executive 2003, 2004; Scottish Government 2007). We have acknowledged that the danger with such policies is that lifelong learning is reduced to a supply-side economic strategy, with learning seen narrowly as the acquisition of skills. Instead, we pose an integrated approach in which 'active learners' take responsibility for their own learning in seeking to resolve defined practice problems as they move mentally and physically between the workplace and the academy.

Figure 24.1 *An integrated model of work-based learning*

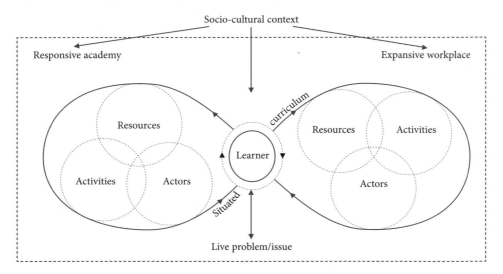

Source: Bamber et al. (2007: 18)

In addressing live issues and problems, learners become critically competent by engaging with elements in the academy, such as taking notes from a lecture and accessing a resource from the library, or with opportunities in the workplace, such as interacting with colleagues or talking things over with a supervisor. The model therefore points to the fluid and dynamic nature of a 'situated curriculum', involving attempts to address and resolve the sorts of issues and problems that characterise the field of practice. The interaction between agency and structure is mediated, on the one side, by a 'responsive academy' attuned to the needs and requirements of non-traditional, work-based learners and, on the other, by the 'expansive workplace', geared up to support professional development in a variety of ways. The bounded spaces of academy and workplace seen in Figure 24.1 are opened up through the learner's interactions and engagement with live problems as he or she moves physically and mentally through both spaces. This opened space presupposes a purposeful partnership between the academy, the workplace and the learner.

The intentions of the model can be illustrated in a concrete way with reference to the real example of a partnership involving a multifaceted and integrated approach to work-based learning in CLD in Scotland (see Box 24.3).

Box 24.3 *A Purposeful Partnership*

PP is an independent voluntary organisation with charitable status that provides a community-based, work-based degree programme validated by a local university. The programme aims to meet the needs of local communities and employers and specifically to widen access to higher education and professional qualifications for local people. The organisation works in partnership with employers in a number of ways, including learning provision and brokerage relationships that can cover a partnership approach to funding, recruiting and training local people with histories of voluntary activity in their communities. As one employer noted: 'We are coming from different backgrounds but we are trying to do the same thing in terms of supporting students, to get learning in a different way, do community learning out in the field here.'

Employers are key to an interdisciplinary and inter-agency management approach for PP. Employers are represented at the Employers' Forum, at the Workplace Supervisors' Forum and on the management board. Through these three mechanisms, employers are able to offer perspectives on the current programme and emerging demands. One employer spoke of being able to voice her concerns with the programme when they arose, adding, 'It seems to be taken on board right away...I think they enjoy an outsider looking in.' These forums are formal places to discuss the progress and support needs of individual learners, although many informal mechanisms also exist for input on such matters. As one employer stated: 'It does feel very much like a partnership that is based around an individual student.'

→

Employers involved with PP see the value in this form of collaborative relationship in terms of developing the skills and confidence of a worker; the passion, energy and commitment the learner brings to the workplace; the opportunities that a learner's learning brings for other team members to critically reflect on their own practice; the opportunity for workplace learning that arises from the new influx of ideas, materials and thinking; and the particular outcomes of learners' work.

PP learners also spoke highly of learning within such carefully structured partnership arrangements. In particular, they cited the benefits of merging theory and practice, with one learner explaining, 'This course enables me to be at work and learn at the same time, to connect the two and understand it better.' Another benefit frequently mentioned was the inter-agency links created by the students themselves as they supported each other in the development of community-based events for their work, and shared resources and ideas. The words of one survey respondent best sum up this partnership approach overall: 'If it had not been for PP, I would never have been offered this opportunity of a lifetime.'

Conclusion

Bringing together the access and emerging skills agendas will demand imaginative educational responses. In CLD training, one such response would be to adopt an integrated approach to training in which people in working and learning environments can guide, facilitate and support work-based learners. Equally important, however, are the curricular activities that encourage the integration of working and learning. Fully exploiting the educational potential in these activities requires institutional change, rethinking curriculum and embracing a different way of learning utilising live problems and issues. When students are fully engaged in addressing such problems, they can be said to have truly accessed higher education because they are developing the capacities required by CLD practitioners. Above all, the learner is the central element in securing an effective learning experience and key to any effective partnership.

References

Bamber J (2007) Towards a discursive pedagogy in the professional training of community educators. EdD thesis, Department of Higher and Community Education, University of Edinburgh

Bamber J, O'Shea C, Ball WI & Wallace G (2007) *Situating the curriculum: Developing an integrated approach to work-based and part-time training in community learning and development*. Dundee: Scottish Community Learning and Development Work-Based and Part-Time Training Consortium

Barab SA & Plucker JA (2002) Smart people or smart contexts? Cognition, ability, and talent development in an age of situated approaches to knowing and learning. *Educational Psychologist* 37(3): 165–182

Billet S (2001) *Learning in the workplace: Strategies for effective practice*. New South Wales: Allen and Unwin

Boud D & Middleton H (2003) Learning from others at work: Communities of practice and informal learning. *Journal of Workplace Learning* 15(5): 194–202

Boud D & Solomon N (2000) Work as the curriculum: Pedagogical and identity implications. Paper presented at the Working Knowledge: Productive Learning at Work Conference, University of Technology, Sydney, Australia (December)

Brennan J & Little B with Connor H, De Weert E, Delve S, Harris J, Josselyn B, Ratcliffe N & Scesa A (2006) *Towards a strategy for workplace learning: Report to HEFCE by CHERI and KPMG*. Bristol: Higher Education Funding Council for England. Accessed 30 March 2009, available at http://oro.open.ac.uk/6437/

Brodie P & Irving K (2007) Assessment in work-based learning: Investigating a pedagogical approach to enhance student learning. *Assessment and Evaluation in Higher Education* 32(1): 11–19

CeVe (Community Education Validation and Endorsement) (1995) *Guidelines for graduate and postgraduate qualifying community education training*. Edinburgh: Learning Connections

CIPD (Chartered Institute of Professional Development) (2005) *Latest trends in learning, training and development: Reflections on the 2005 training and development survey, CIPD*. London: CIPD

Ekholm M & Härd S (2000) *Lifelong learning and lifewide learning*. Stockholm: National Agency for Sweden

Evans K, Hodkinson P, Rainbird H & Unwin L (2006) *Improving workplace learning*. Abingdon: Routledge

Felstead A, Fuller A, Unwin L, Ashton D, Butler P & Lee T (2005) Surveying the scene: Learning metaphors, survey design and the workplace context. *Journal of Education and Work* 18(4): 359–383

Fuller A & Unwin L (2004) Expansive learning environments: Integrating personal and organisational development. In H Rainbird, A Fuller & A Munro (eds) *Workplace learning in context*. London: Routledge

Gallacher J & Reeve F (2000) *Work-based learning: The implications for higher education and for supporting informal learning in the workplace*. Working Chapters of the Global Colloquium on Supporting Lifelong Learning (online). Milton Keynes, UK: Open University. Accessed 26 June 2007, http://www.open.ac.uk/lifelong-learning

Leitch S (2006) *Leitch review of skills: Prosperity for all in the global economy – world-class skills*. London: HM Stationery Office

Margaryan A (2006) Learning communities and repositories: Underpinning the vision. Presentation at the Symposium 981 Would you care to share? ALT-C Conference, Edinburgh (September)

Nixon I, Smith K, Stafford R & Camm S (2006) *Work-based learning: Illuminating the higher education landscape*. York: Higher Education Academy

Reeve F & Gallacher J (2005) Employer–university 'partnerships': A key problem for work-based learning programmes? *Journal of Education and Work* 18(2): 219–233

Scottish Executive (2003) *Life through learning; learning through life.* Accessed 20 September 2007, http://www.scotland.gov.uk/Publications/2003/02/16308/17776

Scottish Executive (2004) *Closing the opportunity gap.* Accessed 20 September 2007, http://www.scotland.gov.uk/Topics/People/Social-Inclusion/17415/opportunity

Scottish Government (2007) *Skills for Scotland: A lifelong skills strategy.* Accessed 23 September 2007, http://www.scotland.gov.uk/Publications/2007/09/06091114/0

SCQF (Scottish Credit and Qualifications Framework) (2005) *Guidelines for the recognition of prior informal learning* (RPL). Accessed 20 September 2007, http://www.scqf.org.uk/downloads/rpl/SCQF%20RPL%20Guidelines-final-030805.pdf

Wenger E (1998) *Communities of practice: Learning, meaning and identity.* Cambridge: Cambridge University Press

25 Insights from an environmental education research programme in South Africa

Heila Lotz-Sisitka

Introduction

This chapter reflects critically on a 15-year environmental education research programme located at the intersection of dynamics affecting development, policy and education in South Africa (and globally), namely *workplace learning and professional development*, and *sustainable development*. These dynamics are interrelated in that sustainable development cannot occur without change-oriented workplace learning (with associated professional development), given its cross-sectoral, dynamic and multidimensional nature. The review of the research programme demonstrates that workplace learning occurs in a complex discourse context, and is interrelated with professional development provisioning as well as wider education and training system reforms towards lifelong learning. Research on professional development and workplace learning is often shared as 'findings' to be used. As Bourdieu and Wacquant (1992) have remarked, the research report is a product of the history of the symbolic struggles it is part of – and, in a very real way, the report contributes to the *creating* of the reality it is analysing. This chapter reports on some research-related symbolic struggles we have been engaged with. At the same time, the chapter also contributes to creating the reality that it is analysing – that is, improved research direction for a workplace learning research programme.

Following an overview of the complex discourse context in which the research takes place, I present a review of the first 15 years of the research programme. In this review, I outline our orientation to research, and discuss some of the significant insights gained through this research work, and the limitations experienced. I then consider the turning point in the programme, and conclude with some of the new directions that are emerging as we move into a new era of research – one that parallels the introduction of a new era of research in the wider South African National Qualifications Framework (King 2007; Parker & Harley 2007).

The wider context of reorienting education towards sustainability

As South Africa is learning from the national and global energy crisis, and from the ever-more-obvious impacts of global climate change, strengthening capacity for developing and implementing sustainable development practices in all sectors of society is no longer an item on the nation's wish-list, or a rhetorical concern, or a matter for the privileged. Sustainable development issues (such as the ubiquity and cost of fossil fuel use; degradation of ecosystems and ecosystem services; and climate changes) impact on households at every level of the social strata, and on all sectors of society. Small and large production systems are implicated and affected, as are service providers and the social sectors, including the healthcare sector. Development thinkers are beginning to state that energy issues, global climate change impacts and social inequalities are likely to be some of the most pressing development challenges of the twenty-first century. Change-oriented workplace learning processes across the sectors and knowledge fields of the National Qualifications Framework (NQF) are necessary for implementing sustainable development practices in South Africa. International policy commitments to sustainable development (such as Agenda 21 and the Johannesburg Plan of Implementation ratified at the World Summit on Sustainable Development in 2002) and the constitutional clause that enshrines the right to a healthy environment for all South African citizens and ensures that resources are to be managed wisely for current and future generations have not yet fully made their way into the education and training system. To give added impetus to the role of education and training in enabling a sustainable society, a UN Decade of Education for Sustainable Development was approved for 2005–2014 by the UN General Assembly under Resolution 57/254 (UNESCO 2005).

Ecologically oriented sustainable development practices such as energy reduction, pollution control and cleaner production, environmental impact assessments, environmental health practices, sustainable design, and so on are increasingly becoming necessary in almost every formal workplace, as they affect the competitiveness, trade and production opportunities of a wide range of sectors, and future opportunities for quality of life more widely in society. The human rights movement has long drawn attention to the need for socially sustainable practices in work and society. Slow to emerge are economic models and practices that are sustainable within a context of a finite planet with limited resources to sustain a growing population, the most promising being full cost accounting – which is not widely adopted or accepted. The environmental education research programme that I review in this chapter has, for the past 15 years, been concerned with the improvement of education and learning that enhances and strengthens these and a range of other environment and sustainability practices in workplaces. The research programme is, however, not confined by the boundaries of the formal production-centred workplace only, due to the complex discourse context in which such environmental education processes are located.

A complex discourse context

For the past 30 to 40 years at least, the environmental movement has been debating contested approaches to ensuring socio-ecological sustainability at both global and local levels. Three main (and increasingly intertwined) discourse streams have emerged within this wider new social movement (Martinez-Alier 2002; Dryzek 2005) and all three have affected learning in workplaces. The first and oldest of these discourses is a wilderness-centred conservation discourse, which is essentially protectionist and preservationist in nature. This discourse has been critiqued for being nature centred and for excluding human–nature–development relations. This discourse has mainly affected learning in those workplaces established for formal conservation purposes.

A second, more recent but increasingly powerful discourse is the sustainable development discourse. This discourse deals primarily with eco-efficiency and with achieving a proposed 'balance' between economy, society and environment. It is essentially oriented towards more benign development using ecological modernisation strategies and cleaner technologies (most favoured by Northern economies and economists), although it could also be oriented towards social justice discourses of more equitable sharing and use of resources (most favoured by Southern NGOs and social justice movements). This discourse is permeating most modern workplaces as industries and production centres around the world are called to account for the 'triple bottom line' and to show ethical allegiance to the wider concerns of a common future for all of humanity on planet earth. Pushed by more powerful governments, this discourse is prominent in contemporary global policies, which in turn influence national policies. However, sustainable development discourse has been critiqued (mainly by Southern NGO activists) for being little more than a new form of 'corporatism' and for its rapid appropriation by the market. Despite progress with ecological modernisations that have led to visible changes in production processes and impacts, not enough progress is being made in changing human development models that remain based on an essentially unsustainable trajectory of increased production and consumption. The lack of progress is revealed annually in environmental and human development reports of ever-expanding environmental degradation and continued social injustices (MEA 2005; UNEP 2007).

The third discourse that has emerged in the context of the environmental movement is an environmental justice discourse that focuses on attaining fairness in a fragile world by aiming to achieve more equitable patterns of resource distribution and use and addressing power relations associated with global and local resource flows. This discourse affects mostly those workplaces concerned with activism and ecological democracy. Because of fundamental power imbalances and the dominance of the neo-liberal growth model at a global level, it has not been able to permeate mainstream workplaces.

In a country like South Africa all three discourses are both visible and necessary. Dryzek (2005) argues that, for learning to take place, it is necessary to take account of the different discourses that arise in society, and that these competing discourses will 'stand and fall' by (a) their ability to resolve the problem of the liberal capitalist economy and (b) their capacity to facilitate and engage people in social learning towards sustainability. He explains that environmental issues feature high levels of complexity that are magnified as ecological systems interact with social, economic and political systems, which does not make provisioning of professional development for workplaces where these issues are dealt with an easy task. Scott and Gough (2004) have argued that sustainable development in itself is a change-oriented learning process that affects all levels of education systems and requires a constant engagement with open-ended education processes. Ongoing reflexivity is needed in seeking new and better ways of responding to the complexity of the sustainable development challenge – hence the need to review research related to these processes in an ongoing manner.

Starting out

In this section of the chapter I review two periods of research in the Rhodes University Environmental Education Unit[1] and the associated community of practice research programmes. These can be temporally framed: the first from 1990 to 2000/02, and the second from roughly 1998/2002 through to 2005/07. As indicated by these time allocations, there are some overlaps as some of the streams of research conducted in the first phase continued into the second phase, and are still pertinent and carried forward by some researchers today.

Phase 1: Before the NQF

This research programme was established in the early 1990s along with the Chair of Environmental Education at Rhodes University during the emergence of the South African post-apartheid educational transformation process. A critical issue identified by the Chair in the early 1990s was the lack of available professional training opportunities for environmental educators who were, at the time, working in the range of workplaces outlined above (i.e. conservation workplaces, traditional production workplaces, education and activist workplaces) (Janse van Rensburg 1993). In response, a part-time year-long semi-distance programme was set up to address this need in partnership with members of a wider community of practice whose common domain was the advancement of environmental education as a professional field in South and southern Africa. This professional development course was unique as it allowed for national participation in an 'open-entry, open-exit' programme of learning that used not levels or grades, or specific workplace contexts, but criteria of full participation and completion of a set of praxis-based assignments for completion requirements. The programme grew in popularity and gave rise to a number of applications to specific contexts, such as teacher education, industry and conservation, as well as to applications in other country contexts, such as Zanzibar, Zambia, Malawi, Swaziland, Namibia and Zimbabwe. Efforts were made to develop a set of course materials that documented best available knowledge and orientation to learning. We also focused on refining the praxis-based workplace assignments and on establishing an assessment process that was reflexive and learning oriented (Janse van Rensburg & Le Roux 1998; Lotz-Sisitka 2004). In the first few years of its existence (1990–1998), research associated with this programme was primarily oriented to investigating how the programme functioned and how it could be more effectively implemented, across a diverse range of emerging applications and discourse contexts. The interest was primarily on the orientation and quality of the educational programme and how it was being experienced by learners, as well as its perceived relevance to workplaces and professional competence.

Research questions that emerged in this phase of the research programme included how course materials could be more effectively designed and used to enhance praxis-based work assignments (Molose 1999); how language, culture and context affected learners' responses to the programme (Heylings 1999); how learners were articulating and experiencing professional development through engaging with the programme (Janse van Rensburg & Le Roux 1998); how mediation processes were taking place in the programme (Jenkin 2000); and how praxis-based assignments were working in relation to the change objectives of the course (Motsa 2004). The research also encompassed investigations into the models of process, assumptions about participation in learning, and the curriculum framework guiding the programme (Janse van Rensburg & Le Roux 1998; Lotz 1999).

Theoretical frameworks guiding this phase of the research programme were drawn from Beck's (1999) *World Risk Society*, which explores the need for reflexivity in society in response to manufactured environmental risks. We also drew on Berger and Luckman's (1966) theory of the social construction of knowledge, which allowed the various discourse contexts to co-exist in the programme, and on critical theories emphasising the empowerment of individuals (Fien 1993). Popkewitz (1991) provided insights into the genealogies of modern education systems and the political economy of educational reforms. These provided impetus for the design of critically oriented education programmes that would (it was assumed at the time) challenge some of the structural functionalist assumptions of the wider education project that emerged within modernisation (Janse van Rensburg 1993; Janse van Rensburg & Le Roux 1998).

Research designs were primarily interpretive and/or critical in orientation. Course participants were interviewed, assignments were examined, tutors were interviewed, and profiles of individual course participants and their experiences on the programme were compiled. Most research activities were confined to the tutoring–learning interactions in the course programme context. Few ethnographic or workplace-based investigations into the application or longer-term validity of the programme's intentions, objectives and outcomes were undertaken, and few extensive workplace-learning observations took place. Where these did occur (as in the studies undertaken by Jenkin [2000] and Motsa [2004]), some disjunctures between the change-oriented discourse and intentions of the course and the culturally and structurally conservative workplace environments were identified. At the time, we had not fully established the extent to which course participants could freely practise and use their 'new-found' skills and knowledge in the workplace (Jenkin 2000; Motsa 2004), as most of our research observations were confined to the teaching–learning setting (i.e. the course context itself). The studies outlined above also adopted a critical interest, in the sense that they were concerned with the empowerment of individual learners on the programme. With this emphasis on teaching and learning and the quality of the learning experience, and our interpretive studies, a number of valuable research insights into course design for workplace learning were gained in this phase of the research programme (Lotz-Sisitka 2004), although most were oriented towards the former rather than the latter.

Phase 2: Moving with the NQF

The promulgation of the South African National Qualifications Authority Act (No. 58 of 1995) signalled a new era for those concerned with the professional development and training of people in workplaces. Of critical concern to our environmental education community of practice was the way in which the successful and innovative open-entry, open-exit professional development course programme could 'align' with the outcomes-based, assessment-standards framework of the NQF, and how this programme might allow for greater access to education and training opportunities and formalised career pathing (Raven 2005; Lotz-Sisitka & Raven 2008). We were also interested in finding out whether it could provide 'credits' for portability across different qualifications in the NQF. To understand the complexity of the array of issues introduced by the NQF into our community of practice, we made the decision to participate in the building of the NQF. We wanted to ensure that adequate qualifications frameworks for environmental education would be available on the NQF, so that our courses could be legitimately accredited and that workers and employers could benefit from the redress, access, quality and portability intentions of the NQF. By this time we had realised that there were no available career paths or qualifications routes for those entering the field of environmental management or education in South Africa. We therefore contributed to standards-generation processes in the context of an emerging NQF, and helped to research competency frameworks necessary for the design of qualifications (Olvitt & Hamaamba 2006).

Parallel to this field-based development work, we undertook a range of research initiatives to understand the outcomes-based framework of the NQF and its implications for course design and assessment in the context of environment and sustainability practices. Our concern was to avoid a narrowing of the quality of the praxis-oriented and reflexive learning interactions that we had established in the first phase of the programme (Raven 2005; Wigley 2006). We sought to address in our ongoing research some of the major critiques of outcomes-based education, most notably its tendency to narrowly predetermine and instrumentally structure learning (McKernan 1993).

Some examples of research questions addressed in this phase include the identification of environmental management competences needed in different workplaces, and their implications for standard setting and workplace skills planning (Dingela 2002; Hamaamba 2005). Other, more complex research questions explored the conceptualisation and implementation of the competence framework of the NQF (Raven 2005) and how course processes should be designed and oriented towards enhancing reflexive and applied competence within the NQF. We also continued to research assessment practice and the efficacy of our course materials and their use (Raven 2005), and assumptions of participation guiding teaching and learning interactions at the course/workplace interface (Price 2007). A new emphasis on course development networking (Lupele 2007) emerged with the need to support the earlier expansion of the programme to multiple contexts and countries.

Theoretical frameworks in this phase of the research programme shifted to embrace engagements with sociological and critical realist theories of structure, agency and change (after Giddens 1984 and Archer 1995, 2007). Critical realist causal analyses (Sayer 2000) and a recognition that not everything is socially constructed brought new insights into participatory course processes, and to institutional and other constraints influencing courses in their wider context (Price 2007; Lupele 2007). We were also able to understand environment and sustainability practices as being historically, culturally and materially located, and not simply as relativist 'social constructions' (a discourse that permeated some of our earlier concepts and educational practice). Beck's (1999) *World Risk Society* thesis also came into stronger focus in the context of understanding reflexivity and uncertainty as an important epistemological issue in our teaching and learning processes. Significant for education, learning and epistemology is an understanding that knowledge is fallible, that some of what we are dealing with in the context of environmental risk is known, but much remains unknown, creating an epistemological context of uncertainty and unawareness (Beck 1999; Raven 2005). This understanding allowed Raven (2005) to critically analyse the framing of reflexive competence in the NQF, and to propose that if a course is to support the development of reflexive competence, this needs to be within an open-ended framework of reflexivity and change, which cannot always be predetermined by articulations of what reflexive competence is or ought to be. This finding was counter-intuitive to the outcomes-based NQF framework being proposed by the government at the time (Lotz-Sisitka & Raven 2008).

Research designs in this phase of the programme differed from those in the earlier phases of the research, due mainly to the mix of macro-level policy studies and micro-level course process investigations. The widening of interest away from course processes per se to institutional contexts of course development and design also required different research designs. In this phase, greater emphasis was placed on theoretical frameworks and interpretation of data in relation to these frameworks (e.g. the structure–agency–change relation), and on causal mechanism explanations that are made possible by critical realist research methods and theories such as Latour's actor-network theory (Price 2007; Lupele 2007).

As in the previous phase of the research, a number of useful research insights were gained at both macro- and micro-level. A greater understanding of the macro–micro relationship relating to policy, institutional change and course processes was gained. Few issues were resolved, however, as we seemed unable to bring the macro and micro foci together in our research programme. For example, we have still not been able to resolve the issue of how to assess learning within an outcomes-based policy context in ways that do not narrow or constrain the learning process from the outset, and which can accommodate the unawareness associated with a risk epistemology in complex discourse contexts (Raven 2005). We are also confused about whether or not the NQF has enhanced the quality of our courses, and we are still struggling to adequately locate our training programmes within the wider NQF and its structures (e.g. to obtain funding for learnerships even though our research indicates that there is a demand for learnerships in workplaces). To some extent, this might be linked to the complexities and difficulties experienced with the NQF itself. For example, the NQF has been critiqued for becoming too bureaucratic, for losing focus on the valuable role of expertise in assessment and standard setting, and for undervaluing structured and procedural knowledge in favour of 'generic' outcomes statements that are opaque and without knowledge substance. Our confusion may also be because we still have inadequate research tools and approaches to make the connection between macro- and micro-level interactions in the learning process. It may also simply be because we have been too intent on both: contributing to the NQF *and* researching our practice within this changing and unstable context. And it may also be because our orientation to the research has continued to be defined primarily by our education institution interest.

A turning point: Focusing on workplaces

By 2005, we had realised that our research was primarily education and training institution centred, although it had broadened to include the wider institutional setting of the NQF. A study by Wigley (2006) into workplace contexts and learning–structure–agency relations, and the insights into the structure–agency–learning relationship gained from the studies of Raven (2005), Price (2007) and Lupele (2007),[2] provided the impetus for us to shift our gaze towards the structure–agency–learning relationship in workplace contexts. This led to a greater emphasis on contextual analyses, and a better understanding of how workplaces and associated learning processes are influenced and shaped by culture, history and longer-term social processes and established knowledge practices (Lupele 2007; Price 2007; Wigley 2006). To open up this dimension in our research programme further than was possible in the studies reported on so far, we have literally had to turn our workplace learning research programme 'inside out' and move into the workplaces to understand learning interactions and their relation to sustainability practices in these workplaces. We have consequently started to put our (previously dominant) interest in courses, course design, NQF structures and assessment practices to one side as we attempt to gain deeper insight into workplace learning and sustainability practices in workplaces, and the learning–structure–agency relation.

To implement this 'shift' we have had to work with new theoretical frameworks, and we have made a start with Lave and Wenger's theory of communities of practice (Lave & Wenger 1991). So far we have undertaken two studies to research learning interactions in communities of practice (Downsborough 2007; Pesanayi 2008), and we have identified a wide variety of learning resources and learning interactions that exist in such communities of practice. We have focused specifically not on legitimate peripheral participation, which is the dominant concept of learning in the communities of practice theory, but rather on cultural, historical and contextual influences on learning interactions, and the diversity of learning interactions that exist in these communities of practice. These include, for example, drawing on inter-generational knowledge resources and engaging critically with tensions and contradictions that emerge within everyday practices. Most significant in relation to environment and sustainability practices have been the insights gained into the way that communities of practice attempt to resolve ambivalence and tensions associated with these practices. We have noted, too, that the training programme can be either enabling or constraining of agency in such situations (Pesanayi 2008). As can be seen from this brief discussion, the communities of practice framework and the shift to researching workplace learning interactions in communities of practice is providing new and different kinds of insight into workplace learning and education and training programmes oriented towards sustainability.

As we take this work forward we are also not entirely sure that the communities of practice framework will provide us with adequate theoretical and methodological tools for fully transforming our workplace learning research programme, but we will continue to explore the possibilities embedded in working with this theoretical framework. From where we stand at present, the communities of practice framework seems to be more oriented towards understanding some of the micro-technologies of learning. In the Pesanayi (2008) study, we found that critical realist causal analysis provides a useful under-labourer to the communities of practice framework in probing more deeply aspects of the micro-technologies of learning in relation to history and context (i.e. macro-influences). We are now beginning to design research instruments that can help us understand sustainability practices in their cultural historical contexts and in the wider activity systems of workplaces, drawing on cultural historical activity theory, communities of practice and critical realism (Engeström 1987; Sayer 2000). In this process we are also drawing on social change theory, which argues that we can only really make our way through the world by engaging reflexively with our concerns in relation to society (Archer 2007). For education, training and workplace learning, this means involving people actively in reflexive practices in workplaces, and building the learning capabilities necessary for participation in such practices. We see this as important in understanding what decisions people make in relation to sustainability practices in workplaces, and how they are influenced to make these decisions.

We are also starting to develop a deeper insight into the nature of sustainability practices. For example, we have already marked out that such practices are characterised by a complex discourse context (as outlined above), that they are often characterised by an epistemology of uncertainty or risk (after Beck 1999), and that they are contradictory and characterised by conflicts of interest (with each other and with the status quo) (Wals 2007). Bourdieu's (1980) theory of practice has also been helpful in that he explains that practices are time and space bound (i.e. there is a temporal and a spatial dimension to them); that they are 'experience laden' in the sense that much of what is practised is tacit or not made explicit but simply done; that practices are not easily interpreted from descriptions of them; and that practices are characterised by an improvisory and strategic logic. We are therefore at the point of developing research instruments that will allow us to probe the relationship between sustainability practices (and their nature) and change-oriented workplace learning processes.

Our research designs are changing (once again!), becoming more ethnographic and observation centred and reliant on a series of in-depth interviews with learners as well as with managers, trainers and others significant to the learning process in workplaces.[3] We are also finding the need to undertake more historical research, using document analysis. In some cases, we are also working with participatory methodologies to develop new mediation tools with learners in workplaces to address the ambivalences and tensions that arise. Our methodologies are more oriented towards identifying and interrogating arising tensions in workplaces as potential sources of learning, and towards reflective discussions with learners in workplaces to trace their reflexive deliberations and decision-making processes. More time will be required before we can report fully on the insights gained and the implications of transforming our research programme.

Future challenges

This shift in our research programme is not dissimilar to wider shifts in research taking place within the NQF community, and it is perhaps no small coincidence that we are now working with the South African Qualifications Authority (SAQA) in a research partnership to probe the nature of change-oriented workplace learning processes with a view to informing standards-generation processes, evaluation of standards and quality cohesion in the NQF (King 2007; Parker & Harley 2007). At a recent NQF colloquium in 2007, which deliberated the NQF as a cohesive and inclusive system, there was agreement among those participating that research in the NQF community in South Africa, with SAQA as its apex organisation, 'should move beyond policy debates and research into attitudes to the NQF's intents and basic structure, towards investigation of the *real dynamics* of implementation across sectors' (King 2007: 62; italics added). The key object of study, it was argued, should be on 'how the world of regulations, policies and guidelines interacts with *the world of daily practice and pragmatic needs*' (2007: 62; italics added). The latest phase of our research programme is oriented towards generating a deeper understanding of the world of daily practice and pragmatic needs.

This review of researching workplace learning in an environmental education community of practice in South Africa over the last 15 years has revealed some significant shifts in direction in the research programme. Our early research interests were oriented towards filling a gap in the field, and to ensuring high-quality teaching and learning practices for the professional development of learners in workplaces. Our gaze was on these teaching and learning practices, and our interests were primarily the empowerment of the individual and the individual's ability to contribute to environment and sustainability workplace activities through praxis-based assignments. With the advent of a new policy framework for education and training in South Africa in the form of an outcomes-based NQF, our research gaze shifted towards the institutional context of teaching and learning, and towards 'making sense' of new policy frameworks in relation to our earlier teaching and learning practices. Our gaze was still directed primarily from the institutional context, and from the structural functionings of the education and training policy environment. After becoming somewhat confused and frustrated with our difficulties to marry macro- and micro-levels through our research, we made another significant 'turn' in the research programme. We turned it 'inside out' and shifted our gaze almost entirely to the workplace, leaving the education and training context to one side (although we retain an interest in the interface between training interventions and workplace learning). At each turn, different methodologies and theoretical frameworks became useful to generate appropriate data and to allow for meaningful interpretations.

At this stage of the research programme, we are still heading out with our inside-out turn, but we do foresee that, through the new era of the NQF and its research agenda, we will be able to meet up with the NQF once again, but this time with our 'inside out' lenses and gaze from the workplace.

Notes

1   Rhodes University is a university in the Eastern Cape in South Africa. It has a long-standing environment and sustainability education programme located in the Faculty of Education which aims at integrating environment and sustainability into all levels and phases of the education system, and includes a focus on workplace learning and community education (see http://www.ru.ac.za/eesu). The programme works within a wider community of practice in South and southern Africa.

2   These were all PhD studies conducted within the broader research programme.

3   We currently have three PhD projects in development in this area, all of which are due to be completed in 2010/11.

References

Archer M (2007) *Making our way through the world: Human reflexivity and social mobility.* Cambridge: Cambridge University Press

Archer MS (1995) *Realist social theory.* Cambridge: Cambridge University Press

Beck U (1999) *World risk society.* London: Polity Press

Berger P & Luckman T (1966) *The social construction of reality.* Garden City, NY: Doubleday

Bourdieu P (1980) *The logic of practice.* Stanford, CA: Stanford University Press

Bourdieu P & Wacquant L (1992) *An invitation to reflexive sociology.* Chicago: University of Chicago Press

Dingela MS (2002) Towards qualification for environmental practitioners: A study of roles and competencies of entry level environmental managers. Master's thesis, Rhodes University, Grahamstown, South Africa

Downsborough L (2007) Social learning processes in a citrus farming community of practice. Master's thesis, Rhodes University, Grahamstown, South Africa

Dryzek J (2005) *The politics of the earth: Environmental discourses* (2nd edition). Oxford: Oxford University Press

Engeström Y (1987) *Learning by expanding: An activity theoretical approach to developmental research.* Helsinki, Finland: Orienta-Konsultit

Fien J (1993) *Education for the environment: Critical curriculum theorising and environmental education.* Geelong, Victoria: Deakin University Press

Giddens A (1984) *The constitution of society: Outline of the theory of structuration.* Cambridge: Polity Press

Hamaamba T (2005) Training needs for municipal employees: A case of Makana Municipality. Master's thesis, Rhodes University, Grahamstown, South Africa

Heylings P (1999) Professonal development in environmental education in Zanzibar, Tanzania: Distances encountered in a semi-distance learning course. MEd thesis, Rhodes University, Grahamstown, South Africa

Janse van Rensburg E (1993) Negotiating boundaries of space, time and theory in a distance learning course in environmental education. In C Criticos, R Deancon & C Hemson (eds) *Education: Reshaping the boundaries.* Proceedings of the 20th Kenton Conference, Scottburgh, KwaZulu-Natal (October)

Janse van Rensburg E & Le Roux K (1998) An evaluation in process: Evaluation of the Rhodes University/Gold Fields participatory course. Research report. Rhodes University, Grahamstown, South Africa

Jenkin NP (2000) Exploring the making of meaning: Environmental education and training for industry, business and local government. Master's thesis, Rhodes University, Grahamstown, South Africa

King M (2007) Going beyond the buzz into the real business: A response to the second NQF colloquium. *SAQA Bulletin* 10(2): 56–62

Lave J & Wenger E (1991) *Situated learning: Legitimate peripheral participation.* New York: Cambridge University Press

Lotz HB (1999) *Developing curriculum frameworks: A source book on environmental education amongst adult learners.* Howick, KwaZulu-Natal: SADC Regional Environmental Education Centre

Lotz-Sisitka HB (2004) Curriculum deliberation amongst adult learners in South African community contexts at Rhodes University. In P Blaze Corcoran & A Wals (eds) *Higher education and the challenge of sustainability: Problematics, promise and practice.* Dordrecht: Kluwer Academic Publishers

Lotz-Sisitka H & Raven G (2008) South Africa: Applied competence as the guiding framework for environmental and sustainability education. In J Fien, R Maclean & M-G Park (eds) *Work, learning and sustainable development: Opportunities and challenges.* Dordrecht: Springer/UNEVOC

Lupele J (2007) Investigating professional development and institutionalisation of courses in the SADC Environmental Education Course Development Network. PhD thesis, Rhodes University, Grahamstown, South Africa

Martinez-Alier J (2002) *The environmentalism of the poor: A study of ecological conflicts and valuation.* Cheltenham: Edward Elgar

McKernan J (1993) Perspectives and imperatives: Some limitations of outcomes-based education. *Journal of Curriculum and Supervision* 8(4): 343–353

MEA (Millennium Ecosystem Assessment) (2005) *Ecosystems and human well-being: A framework for assessment – summary.* Washington, DC: World Resources Institute

Molose V (1999) Use of materials development in the Rhodes University/Gold Fields environmental education participatory course. MEd thesis, Rhodes University, Grahamstown, South Africa

Motsa E (2004) Praxiological assignments in the Rhodes University/Swaziland participatory course in environmental education: A case study of one assignment. Master's thesis, Rhodes University, Grahamstown, South Africa

Olvitt L & Hamaamba T (2006) Identifying needs and opportunities for local government environmental education and training in South Africa. *Southern African Journal of Environmental Education* 23: 122–137

Parker B & Harley K (2007) The NQF as a socially inclusive and cohesive system: Communities of practice and trust. *SAQA Bulletin* 10(2): 17–37

Pesanayi T (2008) Investigating learning interactions influencing farmers' choices of cultivated food plants: A case of Nyanga and Marange communities of practice, Manicaland province in Zimbabwe. Master's thesis, Rhodes University, Grahamstown, South Africa

Popkewitz T (1991) *A political sociology of educational reform: Power/knowledge in teaching, teacher education and research.* New York: Teachers College Press

Price L (2007) A transdisciplinary explanatory critique of environmental education. PhD thesis, Rhodes University, Grahamstown, South Africa

Raven GC (2005) Enabling reflexivity and the development of reflexive competence within course processes: A case study of an environmental education professional development course. PhD thesis, Rhodes University, Grahamstown, South Africa

Sayer A (2000) *Realism and social science.* London: Sage Publications

Scott W & Gough S (eds) (2004) *Key issues in sustainable development and learning: A critical review.* London: Routledge

UNEP (United Nations Environment Programme) (2007) *Global environmental outlook report.* Nairobi: UNEP

UNESCO (2005) *International implementation scheme for the UN Decade on Education for Sustainable Development (2005–2014).* Paris: UNESCO

Wals AEJ (2007) *Social learning: Towards a sustainable world.* Wageningen, Netherlands: Wageningen University Press

Wigley JJ (2006) Understanding workplace-based learning contexts to inform curriculum development: The case of a level 5 environmental education, training and development practices qualification. Master's thesis, Rhodes University, Grahamstown, South Africa

Contributors

Dr John Bamber
Department of Higher and Community Education
Moray House School of Education
University of Edinburgh, Scotland
john.bamber@ed.ac.uk

Dr Barbara Barter
Adjunct Professor
Memorial University of Newfoundland and Labrador, Canada
bbarter@nf.sympatico.ca

Ms Anannya Bhattacharjee
International Organiser
Jobs with Justice, India
anannya@jwj.org or anannya48@gmail.com

Dr Bob Boughton
School of Education
University of New England, Australia
bob.boughton@une.edu.au

Professor Vivienne Bozalek
Director of Teaching and Learning
University of the Western Cape, South Africa
vbozalek@gmail.com

Dr Mignonne Breier
Human Sciences Research Council
Cape Town, South Africa
mignonne.breier@gmail.com

Dr Tony Brown
Faculty of Education
University of Technology
Sydney, Australia
Tony.Brown@uts.edu.au

Professor Shauna Butterwick
Department of Educational Studies
University of British Columbia, Canada
shauna.butterwick@ubc.ca

Dr Linda Cooper
Higher and Adult Education Studies Development Unit
Centre for Higher Education Development
University of Cape Town, South Africa
Linda.Cooper@uct.ac.za or comaka@iafrica.com

Ms Freda Daniels
Division for Lifelong Learning
University of the Western Cape, South Africa
fjdaniels@uwc.ac.za

Professor John Field
Centre for Research in Lifelong Learning
University of Stirling, UK
john.field@stir.ac.uk

Dr Keith Forrester
Lifelong Learning Institute
University of Leeds, UK
forresterkeith@googlemail.com

Dr Jonathan Grossman
Department of Sociology
University of Cape Town, South Africa
Jonathan.Grossman@uct.ac.za

Professor Gunilla Härnsten
Department of Education
Växjö University, Sweden
gunilla.harnsten@vxu.se

Dr Jennifer Hays
Department of Social Anthropology
University of Tromsø, Norway
Jennifer.Hays@sv.uit.no

Dr Kaela Jubas
Faculty of Education
University of Calgary, Canada
kjubas@ucalgary.ca

Mr Arlo Kempf
Ontario Institute for Studies in Education
University of Toronto, Canada
akempf@oise.utoronto.ca

Mr Moeketsi Letseka
Department of Educational Studies
College of Human Sciences
University of South Africa, South Africa
Letsem@unisa.ac.za

Dr Hsun-Chih Li
School Inspector
Department of Education
Taipei City Government, Taiwan
adamli@tpedu.tcg.gov.tw

Associate Professor Heila Lotz-Sisitka
Murray & Roberts Chair of Environmental Education & Sustainability
Rhodes University, South Africa
H.Lotz@ru.ac.za

Dr Rosemary Lugg
Senior Education Adviser
SPAN Consultants
The Hague, Netherlands
rosemarylugg@yahoo.co.uk

Dr Irene Malcolm
Institute of Education
University of Stirling, UK
i.malcolm@yorksj.ac.uk

Dr Judith Marshall
Steelworkers Humanity Fund
Toronto, Canada
jmarshall@usw.ca

Professor Lear Matthews
Community and Human Services
State University of New York
Empire State College, US
Lear.Matthews@esc.edu

Professor Shahrzad Mojab
Department of Adult Education and Counselling Psychology
OISE/University of Toronto, Canada
smojab@oise.utoronto.ca

Malika Ndlovu
New Moon Ventures
'healing through creativity'
himoon@yebo.co.za

Ms Clara O'Shea
Department of Higher and Community Education
Moray House School of Education
University of Edinburgh, Scotland
coshea@staffmail.ed.ac.uk

Professor Ulla Rosén
Department of Humanities
Växjö University, Sweden
Ulla.Rosen@vxu.se

Dr Peter H Sawchuk
Ontario Institute for Studies in Education
University of Toronto, Canada
psawchuk@oise.utoronto.ca

Professor Harry Smaller
Faculty of Education
York University, Canada
hsmaller@edu.yorku.ca

Professor Hilary Sommerlad
Centre for Research into Diversity in the Professions
Leeds Metropolitan University, UK
H.Sommerlad@leedsmet.ac.uk

Dr Bruce Spencer
Centre for Work and Community Studies
Athabasca University, Canada
bruces@athabascau.ca

Professor Paul Tarc
Faculty of Education
University of Western Ontario, Canada
ptarc2@uwo.ca

Professor Astrid von Kotze
Adult Education Practitioner
Cape Town, South Africa
astridvonkotze@gmail.com

Professor Shirley Walters
Division for Lifelong Learning
University of the Western Cape, South Africa
swalters@uwc.ac.za or ferris@iafrica.com

Index

collaborative; work-based learning, academy–workplace partnerships
community
    organisation 142–147, 148
    rural 237–239
    and rural education 241–242, 243–244
    society as 237
    struggles, South Asians in the USA 143–144
    and workplace learning 338–339
community learning and development (CLD) 335
    see also communities of practice; work-based learning; work-based learning, academy–workplace partnerships
competence 338–339
    competency-based training (CBT) 81
    critical competence 339, 341, 347
    reflexive competence 190
    and work-based learning 338–339, 341, 347
Congress of South African Trade Unions (COSATU) 45,47
constructivism 62
Consultative Forum on Curriculum 50, 51
continuing education 67–68
continuing professional development (CPD) 65, 116 see also professional development
control see social control
corporations
    and class 298
    globalisation of 252, 255–257, 272–273
    and organisational learning 300–301
    and rural communities 237, 243
    see also transnational corporations
corporatist state 46, 52, 55
COSATU see Congress of South African Trade Unions
Council on Higher Education (CHE) 49–50, 53, 54
CPD (continuing professional development) 65, 116
critical competence 339, 341, 347
critical friends see students as critical friends
culture
    culturally embedded tools of mediation 292–293
    'culture-making' 237
    intercultural learning 161
    management of 297–298
    organisational culture 291, 297–300

and qualifications 24
rural 237, 239, 243
trade union 260, 266, 279, 291, 293
see also indigenous knowledge systems (IKS); indigenous knowledge systems (IKS), San; institutional culture; language; organisational culture
curriculum
    Consultative Forum on Curriculum 50, 51
    of experience 161, 164
    formal and informal learning 36
    indigenous knowledge systems (IKS) 203
    legal profession, UK 116, 117
    outcomes-based education 184
    participatory curriculum design 22–23
    and practical wisdom 189, 191, 192
    and rural values 244
    school 51
    training partnerships 339, 340, 343–344
    work-based learning 337, 346, 346–348

D
decolonisation 82–85
deficit model of learning and training 81, 312, 319
democracy
    and capitalism 280
    democratic learning 152
    democratic transition (SA) 43–48, 63–64
    illusion of democracy (USA) 148
    and trade union solidarity 280
    workplace democratisation 318
Department of Education
    and the National Diploma in Education (NDPE)184–186
    and the National Qualifications Framework (NQF) 48, 49, 50, 52–53
    Norms and Standards for Educators 190–191
    and recognition of prior learning (RPL) 185–186
Department of Labour 48, 49, 52–53
development
    and decolonisation, Timor-Leste 82–85
    development theory 85
    and donors, Timor-Leste 76, 77, 79, 82, 85
    and education 89
    international development agencies 76–78, 80, 82–85
    and lifelong learning 64

personal 17–20
reconstruction and development 82–85
and social control 77, 78
see also under professional development; sustainable development
developmentalism and postdevelopmentalism 256–257
developmental state 51, 53, 54, 55, 256–257
discourse theory 43, 56n4, 188–190, 191
discrimination 7–9, 24, 38, 98, 108 see also class; centre/periphery; exclusion; gender; marginalisation; racism
discursive practice 43–46, 47, 48, 50, 55
dislocation 149–150
dispossession 11, 14, 61
DoE see Department of Education
DoL see Department of Labour
domestic violence/gender oppression 144–145
domestic workers and knowledge 208–209
    and academic knowledge and power 214–216
    claiming and denying knowledge 210–211
    elevated and denigrated knowledge 213–214
    and experience 208, 211, 213–215, 218–219
    feigning knowledge 211
    hierarchies of knowledge 215–216, 217–218
    knowledge and understanding 214
    utopianism 210, 213
    wisdom and denigrated compassion 211–213
donors, Timor-Leste 76, 77, 79, 82, 85 see also international development agencies
drop-out rates, higher education 91–92, 92
    academic failure and career guidance 95–96
    institutional cultures 96–97
    internationally 92–93
    and labour market pathways 98–100, 98, 99, 100
    lack of finance 93–95, 93, 94, 95
    personal and family reasons 97–98
drop-out rates, San 196

E
East Timor see Timor-Leste
ecology/environment 197, 204 see also sustainable development

Mexico
  export-processing zones
    (*maquiladoras*) 252, 257,
    278–279
  guest workers (Canada),
    lifelong learning 155,
    157–158, 162–163
  sweatshops 163, 252
  as a USA labour pool 155–156
  see also North–South worker
    exchanges (Canada/Mexico)
migration 142
  migrants in Gurgaon, India
    149–150
  and urbanisation, Asia 275
  visibility and invisibility 142,
    147–148, 150–151
  see also under guest workers
    (Canada), lifelong learning;
    immigration
military occupation and neo-
  liberalism 255–256
morality *see phronesis*
mother-tongue education 203–204

N
NAFTA 156, 252, 257–258
Namibia, Village Schools Project
  (VSP) 200–201
National Commission on Higher
  Education (NCHE) 49–50,
  51, 52
National Committee on Further
  Education 50
National Education and Training
  Forum 46, 50
National Education Coordinating
  Committee 45
National Education Crisis
  Committee 44, 45
National Education Policy
  Initiative (NEPI) 45–46,
  47, 184
National Professional Diploma
  in Education (NPDE)
  184–187, 191
National Qualifications
  Framework (NQF) 43–44,
  56n3, 64–65
  criticisms of 358
  equivalent struggles against
    apartheid 44
  implementation as hegemonic
    expansion 50–52
  and indigenous knowledge
    systems (IKS) 202
  and national unity 48–50
  ruptures within 52–54
  and skills development 49, 50,
    51, 53
  standardisation and
    differentiation 64
  and the state 54–55
  and sufficient consensus 46–47

see also South African
  Qualifications Authority
  (SAQA)
National Skills Development
  Strategy (NSDS) 65
National Standards Bodies (NSBs)
  50–51, 66–67, 66–67
National Student Financial Aid
  Scheme (NSFAS) 95, *95*
National Training Board (NTB)
  44, 45, 46, 47, 49
National Union of Metalworkers
  of South Africa (NUMSA)
  45
NCHE 49–50, 51, 52
neo-liberalism 8, 13, 52
  Chile 258
  and citizenship 256
  control over universities
    230–231
  effects on teacher training
    124–125
  and globalisation 13, 255–256,
    273
  and the human rights
    movement 256
  market fundamentalism
    255–256, 280
  and military occupation
    255–256
  and the state 255–256
  and trade unions 254, 257–259
  see also capitalism;
    globalisation
NEPI 45–46, 47, 184
new economy 64
  and emotional labour 169,
    170–173, 179
  informal learning 126
non-government organisations
  (NGOs) 77, 81, 145, 200,
  202–203
*Norms and Standards for
  Educators.* Department of
  Education 190–191
North American Free Trade
  Agreement (NAFTA) 156,
  252, 257–258
North–South labour dynamics
  151–153, 155 *see also*
  North–South worker
  exchanges
North–South worker exchanges
  (Canada/Mexico) 252, 261
  and colonialism 253–254
  Northern privilege 254, 259
  paternalistic attitudes 264–265
  perceptions of South 253–254,
    257, 259–260
  and racism 253–254
  'Thinking North–South'
    education 258–260
  and trade unions 252,
    254–256, 257

see also North–South worker
  exchanges (Canada/other
  countries); trade unions,
  international solidarity;
  United Steelworkers Union
  (Canada)
North–South worker exchanges
  (Canada/other countries)
  Gerdau Workers World
    Council 262–267
  international solidarity
    254–256, 257, 258–261,
    262–267
  new knowledge 261–266
  new skills 266–267
  trade union comparisons
    261–262
  see also North–South worker
    exchanges (Canada/
    Mexico); trade unions,
    international solidarity
NPDE 184–187, 191
NQF *see* National Qualifications
  Framework
NQF, Timor-Leste 80–81, 85
NSBs *see* National Standards
  Bodies
NTB 44, 45, 46, 47, 49
NUMSA 45

O
organisational culture 291,
  297–300 *see also*
  institutional culture
organisational learning 285, 294,
  296, 300
othering 253–254
outcomes-based education (OBE)
  51, 184
outcomes-based education and
  training (OBET) 62

P
participatory learning 286–289,
  315–316, 338
participatory society 12–13
pastoral work 190–191 *see also*
  phronesis
patriarchy 11
  and domestic workers 209
  South Asians in US 145–146
  and women's labour 13, 24–25,
    34
  see also gender
People's Education 44, 45
personal development 17–20,
  317, 345
phronesis 182
  different forms of 188–191
  and experience 182, 190
  love, compassion, care 189,
    190, 191
  and recognition of prior
    learning 182